Palgrave Studies in European Union Politics

Edited by: **Michelle Egan**, American University USA, **Neill Nugent**, Manchester Metropolitan University, UK, **William Paterson**, University of Birmingham, UK

Editorial Board: **Christopher Hill**, Cambridge, UK, **Simon Hix**, London School of Economics, UK, **Mark Pollack**, Temple University, USA, **Kalypso Nicolaïdis**, Oxford UK, **Morten Egeberg**, University of Oslo, Norway, **Amy Verdun**, University of Victoria, Canada

Palgrave Macmillan is delighted to announce the launch of a new book series on the European Union. Following on the sustained success of the acclaimed *European Union Series*, which essentially publishes research-based textbooks, *Palgrave Studies in European Union Politics* will publish research-driven monographs.

The remit of the series is broadly defined, both in terms of subject and academic discipline. All topics of significance concerning the nature and operation of the European Union potentially fall within the scope of the series. The series is multidisciplinary to reflect the growing importance of the EU as a political and social phenomenon. We will welcome submissions from the areas of political studies, international relations, political economy, public and social policy and sociology

Lauren M. McLaren
IDENTITY, INTERESTS AND ATTITUDES TO EUROPEAN INTEGRATION

Justus Schönlau
DRAFTING THE EU CHARTER
Rights, Legitimacy and Process

Palgrave Studies in European Union Politics
Series Standing Order ISBN 1–4039–9511–7 (hardback) and ISBN 1–4039–9512–5 (paperback)

You can receive future titles in this series as they are published by placing a standing order. Please contact your bookseller or, in case of difficulty, write to us at the address below with your name and address, the title of the series and one of the ISBNs quoted above.

Customer Services Department, Macmillan Distribution Ltd, Houndmills, Basingstoke, Hampshire RG21 6XS, England

The Europeanization of British Politics

Edited by

Ian Bache
Senior Lecturer in Politics
University of Sheffield, UK

and

Andrew Jordan
Reader in Environmental Politics
University of East Anglia, UK

First published 2006 by
PALGRAVE MACMILLAN
Houndmills, Basingstoke, Hampshire RG21 6XS and
175 Fifth Avenue, New York, N.Y. 10010
Companies and representatives throughout the world

PALGRAVE MACMILLAN is the global academic imprint of the Palgrave
Macmillan division of St. Martin's Press, LLC and of Palgrave Macmillan Ltd.
Macmillan® is a registered trademark in the United States, United Kingdom
and other countries. Palgrave is a registered trademark in the European
Union and other countries.

ISBN-13: 978–1–4039–9519–3 hardback
ISBN-10: 1–4039–9519–2 hardback

This book is printed on paper suitable for recycling and made from fully
managed and sustained forest sources.

A catalogue record for this book is available from the British Library.

Library of Congress Cataloging-in-Publication Data
The Europeanization of British politics/edited by Ian Bache and
    Andrew Jordan.—New ed.
        p.   cm.—(Palgrave studies in European Union politics)
    Includes bibliographical references and index.
    Contents: Polity—Politics—Policies—Comparative conclusions.
    ISBN 1–4039–9519–2
    1. Great Britain—Politics and government—1945–   2. Great Britain—
    Foreign relations—European Union countries.   3. European Union
    countries—Foreign relations—Great Britain.   4. European Union—
    Influence.   I. Bache, Ian.   II. Jordan, Andrew, 1968–   III. Series.
    JN238.E87 2006
    320.941—dc22   2006045363

10   9   8   7   6   5   4   3   2   1
15   14   13   12   11   10   09   08   07   06
Transferred to Digital Printing in 2007

To our children: Thomas and Anna; Lauren and Ben

Contents

Part III Politics

Part IV Policies

Part V Comparative Conclusions

List of Tables and Figures

Tables

Figures

Foreword

The question of how the processes of 'Europeanization' work has triggered a lively debate among those who study European integration. This volume is a valuable contribution to this debate, and it has a sharply defined focus on the experiences of the United Kingdom over the years, across policy domains, and across levels and venues of governance and politics. The editors and authors follow a carefully specified road map in addressing their subject. On the one hand, they offer well-grounded empirical analyses of particular experiences of British adaptation to membership of the European Union. On the other hand, they seek to reformulate these adaptations within the broader theoretical frame of the literature on Europeanization, a theme laid out by the editors in more detail in Chapter 2. The volume is the fruit of a collective project supported by both the Economic and Social Research Council (ESRC) and the University Association for Contemporary European Studies (UACES), which joined forces to convene a group of scholars from across the United Kingdom to work together on this shared endeavour. Systematic efforts have been made at all stages of the project through to this final publication to fit the pieces of the jigsaw puzzle together into a coherent overall picture. The coverage of the volume understandably reflects the research interests of the participants in the project. Thus, five policy case studies are included from a much larger potential range, and some political dimensions are included and others are not, the obvious absentee being British parliamentary processes. Plenty of opportunity is, therefore, left for other scholars to add to this compendium of empirical and analytical material complementary studies of other aspects of the Europeanization of the United Kingdom.

Does the volume lay to rest all the wider debates about Europeanization? Of course, not! This volume falls within the mainstream of those studies of Europeanization that are mainly focused on the impacts of the European Union on the politics and policies of its member states and on the variety of observable adaptive reactions. This pattern of 'EU-ization' is both important and interesting but it may not be the whole story. In further analyses of the United Kingdom and its European environment, there will surely be scope for adding to this volume further research on other dimensions of Europeanization that may relate to broader political, social and economic developments across the wider European continent. Just to take one obvious example, the United Kingdom has, over recent years, radically altered its human rights legislation, partly to incorporate the European Convention on

Human Rights and partly faced with 'events'. It is indeed an interesting question as to what part the European Union and its jurisprudence have played in this still evolving process. This volume, thus, should be an incentive to others to tease out some of these other issues in further refining the story of the United Kingdom and 'Europe'.

Helen Wallace
European University Institute
May 2006

Acknowledgements

This book has been in gestation for some time, during which we have accumulated a number of debts of gratitude both individually and as co-editors.

Ian Bache   As Convenor of the UACES Study Group and ESRC Seminar Series on The Europeanization of British Politics (2003–2005), I would like to thank both organizations for their financial support, and Stephen George for his key role in these activities before his retirement in 2003. Over the period, six group/seminar meetings took place in the Department of Politics at the University of Sheffield, as well as a concluding conference at Sheffield Town Hall. For their help in organizing the meetings, my thanks go to Sarah Cooke, Sylvia McColm and Katie Middleton. In organizing the conference, my co-editor Andrew Jordan provided invaluable advice and support, which I am very grateful for.

In addition to those individuals featuring in this volume, thanks go to the other seminar participants – Alex Balch, Paul Byrne, Adrian Cashman, Philip Catney, Anne Corbett, Roger Duclaud-Williams, Mark Flear, Matthew Flinders, Robert Geyer, Emily Gray, Kerry Howell, Oliver Kiessler, Jane O'Mahony, Jill Preston, Tim Richardson, Martin Smith and Nigel Waddington – and the conference speakers Nick Clegg, Andrew Gamble, Robert Ladrech, Dennis MacShane MP (Minister for Europe), Linda McAvan MEP and Claudio Radaelli. I would also like to thank Nick for his many astute comments on the group's papers during his time as co-tutor on my L3 module on Europeanization, at Sheffield in 2004, and also the students on that module (2003–2005).

Andrew Jordan   My participation in this book project was facilitated by the financial support I received from the ESRC (via its Programme on Environmental Decision-Making, Award No.: M535255117) and the Leverhulme Trust (which awarded me a Philip Leverhulme Prize fellowship in 2004). The National Europe Centre at the Australian National University in Canberra kindly provided me with a visiting fellowship in 2005, which allowed me to complete my contribution to the final drafts of Chapters 1, 2 and 17.

Together as editors, we would like to thank all the contributors to this volume for remaining keen and committed throughout the demanding process of putting it together. As authors, we are very grateful to Andrew Gamble and Andrew Geddes for comments on Chapters 1, 2 and 17, to Stephen George and Simon Bulmer for their comments on the concluding chapter, and to Michael Blomfield for his valuable editorial work. Our gratitude also goes to the series editors, Michelle Egan, Willie Paterson and Neill Nugent, and to Alison Howson from Palgrave Macmillan, for the unstinting support and encouragement they have given during the editing process. Of course, any remaining errors and omissions are entirely our own responsibility.

Ian Bache, Sheffield
Andrew Jordan, Norwich

Notes on Contributors (IB/AJ)

David Allen is Professor of European and International Politics and Head of the Department of Politics, International Relations and European Studies at Loughborough University. His most recent publications include the chapter on Britain in *The Member States of the EU* (Bulmer and Lesquesne eds 2005) and the chapter on Cohesion and the Structural Funds in the 5th edition of *Policy-Making in the European Union* (Wallace, Wallace and Pollack eds 2005)

Ian Bache is Senior Lecturer in Politics at the University of Sheffield. He was Convenor of the UACES Study Group and the ESRC Seminar Series on 'The Europeanization of British Politics and Policy-Making' (2003–2005). He is currently completing a book on *Europeanization and Multi-level Governance*.

Jim Buller is Lecturer in Politics at the University of York. He has written a number of books and articles on British Politics and the European Union and has recently co-edited a special issue of *Public Policy and Administration* entitled, *Understanding the Europeanization of Public Policy* (Vol. 17, No. 2, 2002).

Simon Bulmer is Jean Monnet Professor of European Politics at the University of Manchester. He has recently completed ESRC-funded projects on policy transfer in the EU and on devolution and European policy making in the UK. His most recent books are on EU-member state relations, devolution and EU policy making and the role of Germany in Europe.

Martin Burch is Professor of Government at the University of Manchester. He has recently completed an ESRC-funded project on devolution and EU policy making in the UK (http://les1.man.ac.uk/devolution/) and is author of books on policy making cabinet government and devolution.

Rachael Chapman is a Research Fellow at the Local Governance Research Unit (LGRU), De Montfort University. Her principal research interests include: Europeanization, multi-level governance, legitimacy, the third sector, public participation and regeneration. She completed her doctoral thesis at Sheffield University on third sector participation in the South Yorkshire Objective 1 Structural Fund Programme in 2005.

Michelle Cini is Reader in Politics in the Department of Politics, University of Bristol. She has published in the field of European Competition and State Aid Policy and the Politics of the European Commission and more recently on EU-Malta relations.

Thomas Conzelmann is Assistant Professor of International Relations at Darmstadt University of Technology and team leader of an international research group on 'Soft Modes of Governance and the Private Sector' within the EU-funded Network of Excellence 'CONNEX'. He has published on various aspects of EU policy and politics, and is co-author of a standard coursebook on the EU.

Jenny Fairbrass is Lecturer in Strategic Management at the University of Bradford and the Director of Studies for the International Business and Management Programme. She is also an Honorary Research Fellow at the ESRC Centre for Social and Economic Research on the Global Environment at the University of East Anglia.

Andrew Geddes is a Professor of Politics at the University of Sheffield. He specializes in the politics of migration and British relations with the EU. Recent publications include *The Politics of Migration and Immigration in Europe* (2003) and *The EU and British Politics* (2004).

Ricardo Gomez is an Honorary Research Fellow in Government at the University of Manchester. He was a member of the ESRC project team on devolution and EU policy making. He has published books and articles on the English regions, UK devolution and European Union foreign policy.

Andrew Jordan is Reader and Philip Leverhulme Prize Fellow at the School of Environmental Sciences, University of East Anglia, Norwich. He is a Research Director of the £2.6 million ESRC Programme on Environmental Decision-making (PEDM) in the Centre for Social and Economic Research on the Global Environment (CSERGE).

Adam Marshall is a Research Fellow at the Centre for Cities, a unit of the Institute for Public Policy Research (IPPR). He is also affiliated with the Centre for International Studies at the University of Cambridge, where he completed his doctoral thesis in 2003.

Tim Oliver is currently completing a PhD in the Department of International Relations, London School of Economics. His thesis explores the changing nature of British foreign policy making. His principal research interests also include: British foreign policy, UK–EU relations, Whitehall and European foreign and defence policy.

James Smith is Lecturer in Politics at the School of Law and Social Sciences, Glasgow Caledonian University. His principal research interests include: Europeanization, multi-level governance, territorial politics, Scottish government and politics. He has published various articles on the impact of Europeanization on the Scottish Office and the Scottish Executive.

Erin van der Maas is currently completing his PhD research at the Department of Industrial Relations, London School of Economics. He is also a visiting supervisor in Industrial Relations at the Department of Engineering, University of Cambridge and visiting lecturer in Human Resource Management at the Business School, Greenwich University.

Abbreviations and Acronyms

(E)DOP	Cabinet Sub-Committee on European Issues
ABI	Association of British Insurers
AEEU	Amalgamated Engineering and Electrical Union
AEP	Association of Electricity Producers
ASLEF	Associated Society of Locomotive Engineers and Firemen
BAT	Best Available Technology
CAP	Common Agricultural Policy
CBI	Confederation of British Industry
CCAT	Competition Commission Appeals Tribunal
CED	Community Economic Development
CFP	Common Fisheries Policy
CLA	Countryside Land and Business Association
COES	Cabinet Office (the European Secretariat)
CPRS	Central Policy Review Staff
CSF	Community Support Framework
CWU	Communication Workers' Union
DEFRA	Department for the Environment, Food and Rural Affairs
DGFT	Director General for Fair Trading
DGs	Directorates-General
DoE	Department of the Environment
DTI	Department of Trade and Industry
EAD	External Affairs Division (Scottish Executive)
EC	European Community
ECB	European Central Bank
ECHR	European Convention on Human Rights
ECJ	European Court of Justice
ECSU	European Central Support Unit (Scottish Office)
EEAS	European External Action Service
EEC	European Economic Community
EFD	European Funds Division (Scottish Office)
EFTA	European Free Trade Association
EIA	Environmental Impact Assessment
EIVG	European and International Vision Group (South West region)
EMAS	Eco-Management and Audit Scheme
EMS	European Monetary System
EMU	Economic and Monetary Union
EPP	European People's Party
ERDF	European Regional Development Fund

ERM	Exchange Rate Mechanism
ERT	European Round Table of Industrialists
ESF	European Social Fund
ESG	European Strategy Group (North West region)
ETUC	European Trade Union Confederation
EUD	European Union Division
EUS	Ministerial Committee on European Union Strategy
FCO	Foreign and Commonwealth Office
FEI	Federation of Electronics Insurers
GLA	Greater London Authority
GMB	Britain's General Union
GOs	Government Offices for the regions
GPMU	Graphical Paper and Media Union
ILO	International Labour Organisation
LGIB	Local Government International Bureau
LIFE	Financial Instrument for the Environment
MAFF	Ministry of Agriculture, Fisheries and Food
MEP	Member of the European Parliament
MINECOR	Ministerial Group for European Co-ordination
MPC	Monetary Policy Committee
MSA	Maastricht Social Agreement
MTFS	Medium Term Financial Strategy
NCVO	National Council for Voluntary Organisations
NECP	Network Europe Contact Points
NFU	National Farmers' Union
NGO	Non-Governmental Organization
OECD	Organisation for Economic Co-operation and Development
OFT	Office of Fair Trading
OMC	Open Method of Communication
OPD(E)	Ministerial Sub-Committee on European Questions
PMCs	Programme Monitoring Committees
PMO	Prime Minister's Office
PMPU	Prime Minister's Policy Unit
QMV	Qualified Majority Voting
Quango	Quasi-autonomous non-governmental organization
RA	Regional Assembly
RDA	Regional Development Agency
Rechar	EC structural fund programme for the regeneration of coalfield areas
REGLEG	Group of Regions with Legislative Powers
RSPB	Royal Society for the Protection of Birds
SEA	Single European Act
SGP	Stability and Growth Pact

SPD	Single Programming Document
T&G	Transport and General Workers' Union
TUC	Trades Union Congress
TUFE	Trade Unionists for Europe
TUPE	Transfer of Undertakings and Protection of Employment legislation
UKIP	United Kingdom Independence Party
UKRep	United Kingdom Permanent Representation to the EU
UN	United Nations
WEEE	Waste Electrical and Electronic Equipment
WMIE	West Midlands in Europe
WWF	World Wide Fund for Nature

Part I
Introduction

1
Britain in Europe and Europe in Britain

Ian Bache and Andrew Jordan

The reason why the issue of Europe has been so persistent and so divisive is that there is a lot at stake. For the future of British politics there is no more important issue, involving as it does a reassessment of British identity, security and political economy, and a judgement about the relative priority to be given to Europe as opposed to other relationships, particularly those with America. Such choices occur rather rarely but when they do they often trigger political realignments which can constitute major turning points in the life of parties and states. (Gamble, 2003: 114)

Introduction

The relationship between the European Union (EU)[1] and its member states has long been central to the study of European integration. Classic debates involving federalists, intergovernmentalists and neofunctionalists have revolved around both normative and analytical concerns relating to the power and autonomy of the state[2]. Nowhere have these debates had greater resonance than in Britain. So much so that the EU has become central to the practice and academic study of contemporary British politics.

Even a cursory glance at the domestic political developments in the period since Britain joined the EU in 1973 would amply confirm this view. The EU is implicated in such landmark events as Labour's long period in opposition from 1979, the fall of both Margaret Thatcher and John Major and the ensuing crisis in the Conservative party, and the origins and core political project of 'new' Labour. The political effects of Britain in the EU, or, more properly, of EU membership on Britain, have been profound. The European issue is emotive, politically charged and highly sensitive. Yet, for those seeking political power it is an issue that must be confronted.

Despite this, there is a curious imbalance in the academic literature on the subject of 'Britain and Europe'. While there is an extensive literature

3

on Britain's relationship with the EU (*inter alia,* Baker and Seawright, 1998; Buller, 2000; Daddow, 2004; Geddes, 2004; George, 1992 and 1998; North-cott, 1995; Young, 1998), there are relatively few detailed studies of the domestic impact of membership. The last significant contribution of this type (Bulmer *et al.,* 1992) has now been overtaken by events. Instead, there have been numerous studies of specific issues and sectors that, until now, have remained isolated from each other.

Moreover, the study of British politics more generally continues to margin-alize the European dimension. While an increasing number of academics reject a focus on the traditional organizing perspective of the Westmin-ster Model (Bache and Flinders 2004; Gamble, 2000; Hay, 2002; Pierre and Stoker, 2000; Rhodes, 1997; Richards and Smith, 2002; Wilson, 2003) for its narrow conceptualizations of power (for example prime ministerial vs. cabinet), its obsession with the machinations of Whitehall and West-minster and its neglect of the international context of British politics, the integration of the international dimension into the study of British politics has lagged behind other advances, such as the alternative lens of the 'governance' approach. The EU, in particular, continues to be often treated as an optional extra on British politics courses, both reflecting and reflected by its treatment in most textbooks as a stand-alone chapter somewhere near the end of the volume, following discussion of the 'key' issues. There are some exceptions to this treatment, which should be acknowledged. In particular, Gamble's (2003) book, from where the epigraph of this book is taken, puts analysis of Britain's relationship with Europe at the centre of the debate on the future of British politics. This is where we believe it belongs.

In this volume we bring together both established academics and a new generation of scholars all of whom are actively involved in researching the domestic impact of EU membership. Moreover, these scholars are collectively neither 'Europeanists' nor British politics specialists. While some authors are predominantly associated with one field or the other, many are active in the study of both the EU and British politics, while others approach their subject thematically. This mix hopefully ensures that we do not privilege either the domestic or EU dimension in our approach and analysis. On this, of course, the reader will ultimately decide.

Britain in Europe

Britain's relationship with the EU has generally been variously described as 'awkward', 'reluctant' or 'semi-detached'. Prominent among these descrip-tions is George's (1990, 1994) notion of Britain as an 'awkward partner', built on Britain's early abstention from membership and subsequent behaviour as a member. This characterization has resonance with the British public's deep scepticism towards the European integration process. This mood of alienation has not been helped by the failure of British political elites to promote the advantages of integration. Instead, a largely hostile press has been given free rein to highlight the weaknesses of EU membership and in so doing deepen the sense of scepticism. Divisions within and between parties on the EU have stymied the development of a more sophisticated and informed debate on the merits (or otherwise) of integration. This domestic dynamic has shaped a distinctive British approach to Europe, which needs to be understood when attaching the epithet 'awkward'.

There has certainly been a relatively consistent line taken by successive British governments in terms of the key elements of European integration. At its core, the British position has been consistently in favour of an enlarged and mostly intergovernmental EU, led by independent states. One of the alternative visions – federalism – is such a dirty word in British politics that no ambitious mainstream politician uses it in public. Equally consistent has been successive governments' desire to remain closely engaged with the United States. Churchill's words to de Gaulle, as the Second World War came to a close, are striking:

The Americans have immense resources. They do not always use them to the best advantage. I am trying to enlighten them, without forgetting, of course, to benefit my country. (cited in Bogdanor, 2005: 689)

Similar words might so easily have been uttered by many subsequent prime ministers, not least Tony Blair in the context of the post-9/11 decision to support the US invasion of Iraq. Others, notably Thatcher, may have been less pragmatic and more ideologically motivated in their support for the United States. The consequences, though, are essentially the same: at key moments Britain's relations with the United States and the EU respectively have created tensions, which have generally been resolved to the detriment of its pro-European credentials.

Alongside the classic view of Britain as an awkward partner is a similarly orthodox view that late membership has been to Britain's great cost. Because Britain joined the European club late, so the argument runs, the rules had already been set in favour of the founding member states. These were not merely technical constraints, but 'reflect the fact that the constitutional attitudes and political practices of the founding fathers were very different from those to which the United Kingdom was accustomed' (Bogdanor, 2005: 695). The constitutional foundations of the EU are based on the separation of institutional powers and political coalitions rather than the British traditions of a centralized state, informal constitution and an adversarial 'winner-take-all' style of party politics. Moreover, by 1973 policies across a range of crucial sectors had already been developed that – as this volume demonstrates – diverged from settled British practices.

Britain's initial reluctance to join the EU is explained partly by its 'special relationship' with the United States, but also by its commitment to the remnants of its Empire and the evolving commonwealth of independent states. Together with Europe, these were seen as three 'spheres of influence' through which British foreign policy could most effectively be organized in the post-Second World War period. To commit to Europe at this early stage would, it was thought, reduce Britain's influence over the other two spheres of influence. Only as the realities of British post-war influence became clear, in particular through growing awareness of relative economic decline and the shortcomings demonstrated at Suez in 1956 (see Oliver and Allen, Chapter 12), did Britain apply for EU membership. However, its applications in 1961 and 1965 were vetoed by de Gaulle because he perceived British entry as a 'Trojan Horse' for US interests in Europe. The third application, lodged in 1970 following the resignation of de Gaulle the previous year, finally led to British accession in January 1973 (along with Denmark and Ireland).

These three applications spanned both Conservative (1961) and Labour (1965 and 1969) governments, with accession taking place under the Tory leadership of Edward Heath. It was Heath who recognized the need to do a political deal with Paris, and in particular to reassure the French that Britain would not act as the US representative within the EU: something the Heath government, if not its successors, faithfully carried out. It was the change of government in 1974 (from Conservative to Labour) that signalled the first significant challenge post-membership. Wilson's Labour party was divided on membership and, as a compromise, had campaigned for a renegotiation of the terms of entry. In the end, a cross-party alliance of political elites ensured a positive vote in favour of continued membership.

If the 1975 referendum was an illustration of British discomfort, the post-1979 Thatcher governments demonstrated greater awkwardness. Yet, even this was really a case of selective rather than complete awkwardness. On the question of securing a rebate on British contributions, Thatcher was relentless. She was undoubtedly 'awkward' in demanding reform of the Common Agricultural Policy (CAP) and in her opposition to the development of effective redistributive (social and regional) policies, believing these to be an insidious form of 'socialism through the backdoor'. But on market reform generally and the single market programme specifically, Thatcher was a leading advocate and Britain a willing implementer of EU measures. In short, Thatcher's approach to Europe was not simply pragmatic – like her embrace of the Reagan Administration in the United States – but had a distinct ideological component.

While Thatcher's approach to Europe cemented her reputation as an 'iron lady', it was also instrumental in demonstrating her ultimate fallibility. Her inability to compromise on European issues both with other EU leaders and within her own party, along with misjudgements in areas of domestic policy, was central to her downfall. As Bulmer (1992: 1–2) notes, Thatcher managed to lose four cabinet ministers over European issues in the last four years of her period as prime minister.

Yet, we should not be too quick to see this as just a failing of Thatcher's leadership. It is true that her leadership style and the centralizing thrust of her governments could not have contrasted more with the political and institutional patterns in Brussels. It is also true that after over a decade as prime minister, Thatcher had begun to believe in her own 'iron lady' image and appeared unaware of her increasing political vulnerability. However, the issues raised by European integration went to the core of the Conservatives' conception of sovereignty, political identity and particular brand of market economics (see Geddes, Chapter 8).

Her successor, John Major, fared little better and, with a much smaller parliamentary majority than Thatcher following the 1992 election, limped his way to defeat in 1997 following a succession of wounds inflicted by internal critics over Europe. This was despite Major winning a leadership election mid-term that he had called to silence these critics. Major's European problems were not simply inherited from Thatcher, because he in turn developed his own style of 'awkwardness' in the form of the Maastricht opts-out on Stage 3 of monetary union (the euro) and the social chapter. Under his leadership, awkwardness metamorphosed into pure obstructionism following the 'mad cow' disease in 1996, when the government threatened to veto all non-essential EU business unless concessions were made on the ban on the export of British beef.

The defeat of Major in 1997 was followed by successive Conservative general election defeats in 2001 and 2005. The party remains divided, and while the big issues for British politics of Euro membership and the draft Constitutional Treaty have dropped down the political agenda, Europe is still the issue that most divides the Conservatives. All the indications are that unless the 'Europe issue' is resolved – or in some way or another finessed – the Conservative party may find it difficult to again persuade the electorate of its suitability for government. In 2005, the new leader David Cameron made a symbolic gesture to the Euro-sceptics in the party by withdrawing the British Conservative MEPs from the European People's Party (EPP) grouping in the European Parliament. That this may have damaged the party's relations with key players in the EU, was not Cameron's immediate concern: securing internal support was. Temporarily at least, Cameron had managed to 'finesse' the issue within the party: how long this would last once the 'big issues' of Europe re-emerged remained to be seen.

New Labour, New Europe?

Despite continuing reluctance in some areas, Labour's position on Europe was transformed in opposition. The advocacy of withdrawal, along with its anti-nuclear position, was central to the biggest electoral defeat in the party's history in 1983. From that moment on, Labour began its long haul back to office with a succession of internal reforms and policy changes, complemented and driven by progressively moderate leaderships. The overwhelming vote in favour of Blair's leadership election in 1994 was illustrative of the scale of transformation that had taken place within the party. The years of powerlessness in opposition, while radical Conservative govern-ments led Britain further away from Labour's values both domestically and internationally, forged a pragmatism that was ultimately celebrated by the majority of the party and driven with gusto by Blair under the doctrine of the 'third way'. Large parts of the labour movement, trade unionists and local councillors in particular, had slowly turned to Brussels in the 1980s and 1990s. The Conservatives had closed the door firmly in their face when they sought more effective social and redistributive policies through national channels. In the 'new' Labour party headed by Blair, the EU was a friend, not a foe. Britain's interests were best served by working with and not against the key players. Of course, this new position did not eliminate the Atlanticism of the past. Rather, the third way involved transcending such dilemmas; that is, under Blair's leadership, Britain would be a bridge between the Europe and the United States.

The election of the Blair government in May 1997 was widely celebrated in Brussels. In opposition, Labour had spoken of the damage done to British interests by the Conservatives in Europe and promised a 'step-change' in Britain's approach to dealing with the rest of the EU. For Europhiles in the party, however, Gordon Brown's subsequent announcement just a few months later that Britain was not ready to join the single currency, did very little to put this promise into action. However, New Labour's decision to sign and implement the social chapter rejected by the Tories was an important symbol of positive intent.

But, New Labour's ability to 'bridge' the USA and the EU was tested to breaking point following 9/11. After widespread European support for the US invasion of Afghanistan, New Labour's decision to support the US inva-sion of Iraq soured its relations with key EU partners, particularly France. However, in an enlarging Europe, New Labour had more allies than in an EU of 15. Thus, while Iraq exposed old fissures in the old EU, it highlighted the prospect of a different balance of power between what the US Defense Secretary Donald Rumsfeld infamously termed 'old' and 'new' Europe.

Yet, New Labour's scope for influence in the EU is not connected exclus-ively to its Atlanticism. New Labour's ideas, and particularly its relatively successful record of managing the economy, have become increasingly attractive to other EU states as they have come to face the economic pres-sures and attendant policy dilemmas that Britain had largely addressed in the 1980s. Moreover, some European partners acknowledged that Britain had moved from an Anglo-American model of capitalism under the Tories to an Anglo-Social model under Blair. The latter, with a strong emphasis on social protection illustrated by policies like the guaranteed minimum wage and working family tax credits, is more palatable to those member states seeking to restructure their economies in less Thatcherite ways.

But, this alternative model is still either misunderstood or rejected in some quarters. A key issue in the French rejection of the Constitutional Treaty in

May 2005 was the perceived British influence over its content that threatened social and welfare policies. Ironically, the vote in France (and subsequently the Netherlands) may have strengthened the British position within the EU and enhanced the prospect for a new European model shaped by New Labour. Not only did the vote damage the French, but it also allowed Britain to postpone indefinitely a vote on the Constitution that the government seemed certain to lose. In so doing, Britain was once again crowned Europe's 'awkward partner', although for once, there were many other candidates.

Still awkward?

For four years, the Blair government tried to take Britain closer to the 'heart of Europe'. Things changed after 9/11, but British influence within Europe was not eviscerated and, if anything, experienced a slight upsurge following the French referendum. Constructive relations between Britain and member states hostile to the Iraq invasion had been rebuilt.

However, the prospects for British leadership remained constrained by its non-participation in the euro. On this issue, the outlook remained uncertain. The five economic tests set by Gordon Brown were in some respects a camouflage to disguise the real test: whether the government could win the promised referendum on entry. However, there was a further complication relating to both Brown and his department, the Treasury. Brown long coveted the New Labour leadership and so sought to create maximum autonomy to make an impact as chancellor. This political dimension was compounded by the Treasury's long-standing reputation as one of the least Europeanized Whitehall departments (see Bulmer and Burch, Chapter 3). Should Brown succeed in taking over the New Labour leadership and become prime minister, at least the political dimension would be neutralized. This would, of course, leave the considerable problems of confronting Treasury interests and mobilizing popular support for entry.

So how did the balance sheet stand on British awkwardness in 2005? Most observers would accept that the Blair government was the most pro-European since Heath's in the 1970s. Yet, fault lines persisted within the Labour party and British politics more broadly that kept Britain one step removed from the heart of Europe. While New Labour had high-profile 'red lines' written around the social security and tax harmonization parts of the draft Constitution, abstention from the euro remained the single most important issue. If this made Britain an awkward partner, it was no more or less awkward than Sweden and Denmark, who were also outside the Eurozone. Moreover, the relative Europeanism of the Blair government on issues such as defence and social policy served to expose how much British obstruction in the past allowed other states to hide their opposition to integrationist measures. Allen (2005: 129) illustrated this in relation to France and Germany, which vetoed the extension of qualified majority voting in a number of areas supported by the Blair government in 1997. If we add to this the French and Dutch votes against the constitution, we should perhaps conclude that Britain should no longer be considered *the* 'awkward partner'. At most perhaps it might be considered a member of an 'awkward squad' in the EU whose composition fluctuates according to the issue and its relation to perceived national interests. In the concluding chapter, we return to consider notions of awkwardness in the light of the contributions to this volume. More specifically, we address the contrasting themes of continuity and change in the British approach to Europe, not least since 1997.

Europe in Britain

As noted above, most of the scholarship on Britain–EU relations has focused on Britain's behaviour in the EU, to the relative neglect of the intrinsically related issue of how EU membership has affected Britain. The reasons for this neglect are to be found partly in the academic division of labour between Europeanists, who focus on the EU system, and comparativists, who focus on the study of individual member states. Of particular importance has been the dominant position of the 'Westminster Model' in the study of British politics, which celebrates the longevity and supremacy of national institutions (see also Chapter 2). But it also reflects a widely held belief, perpetuated by politicians eager to dispel fears about power being 'lost' to Brussels, that changes to British practice would be and have been insignificant. Wallace (1973: 91), for example, noted the feeling of quiet confidence in Whitehall before accession that Britain would 'not have much difficulty in coming to terms with the requirements of Community membership'. Earlier, Heath had fought hard to portray the EU to the British public as an organization which posed little serious threat to sovereignty and whose practices accorded with those of Britain's (Young, 1998: pp. 214–256).

In the first major empirical study of domestic adaptation to EU membership, which was undertaken almost twenty years after membership (George, 1992), Britain was characterized as a 'semi-detached' member of the EU, playing a full role in some areas but not in others. In the study, Bulmer (1992: 16) summarized the key features of Britain's semi-detachment as:

> the reluctance or aversion to relinquishing national sovereignty despite the realities of economic interdependence; the slowness of British political forces in adapting to EC membership; and the unwillingness to confine foreign and foreign economic policies to the European arena.

Yet, alongside these features of awkwardness or reluctance were found examples of cooperation. Here, Britain's record on faithfully implementing the single-market programme was a key example. Moreover, the argument was made that Britain's assiduous approach to implementation contributed to its perceived awkwardness in EU negotiations: 'the principle of not agreeing to any proposal unless it can be implemented, which may seem obstructive in Britain's European partners, is a product of the UK administration's legalistic attitude to enforcement' (Butt Philip and Baron, 1988: 639).

More generally, the study identified the different rates of adaptation amongst key actors and institutions: central government, local government, the political parties and pressure groups. Much of the adaptation had taken place on a 'technical level' as 'civil servants and interests groups learned how to operate in the EC process, rather than resulting from or leading to a political conversion among political actors in favour of the EC' (George, 1992: 203). The study concluded that Britain's political institutions had been particularly ill-suited to adapting to EU membership for reasons touched on above, namely: an aversion to ceding national sovereignty; an attachment to the United States; a pattern of economic activity that distanced Britain from other European states, particularly in the sense of having more global commercial links; and an impatience with visions of an 'ever closer union' to which other member states were attached.

On issues of coordination, the study found that European policy was in the hands of the European Secretariat in the Cabinet Office and, although the Foreign Office view sometimes prevailed, at other times the Treasury view was more influential. This was particularly the case under Margaret Thatcher, whose view 'more frequently coincided with that of the Treasury than with that of the Foreign Office, which she suspected of being too pro-EC' (George, 1992: 205). Both the Ministry of Agriculture Fisheries and Food (MAFF) and the Department of Trade and Industry (DTI) were found to be influential on issues that directly affected them. The study concluded that the appearance of semi-detachment given by British policy might in part be the consequence of this institutional pluralism within the central state, given the tight mandates given by British negotiators. Despite this pluralism, the study found that 'a sustained attempt had been made by successive Governments of different political persuasions to play a "gatekeeper" role, preventing the process of European integration from dissolving their control' (George, 1992: 205).

While there was a 'steady' rate of adaptation at the technical level, the process of adaptation was found to be uneven across the administrative and political spectrum, as well as across different policy areas. On the latter dimension, it was found that 'the less high-profile and politically sensitive the sector, the more smoothly has British policy adapted to working in a "normal" Community manner' (George, 1992: 5). However, the study was concerned primarily with understanding the importance of domestic politics for Britain's European policy, what in the Europeanization discourse would be considered 'uploading' (see Chapter 2). As such, it did not explore adaptation in great detail and had no case studies of different policy sectors, save for an introductory overview.

With the relative exception of the Liberal Democrats, the political parties have spectacularly failed to try to persuade the public of the benefits of EU membership. As George (1994: 255) noted, 'not even the Heath Government made any real effort to convert the British people to Europeanism'. The fault lines within the major parties have been discussed above, but the biggest fault line in British politics over the EU is the one between political elites and the public. While there is scepticism over Europe at the far ends of the political spectrum, which overlaps the outer reaches of the Labour and Conservative parties, the political elite as a whole is far less cynical of European integration than the general public.

In this context, even relatively pro-European governments are heavily constrained in how they engage with the EU. As Allen (2005: 130) said of the Blair government 'a Europeanized government has been forced to cut its cloth to suit a non-Europeanized polity'. One consequence is that in order to get things done, pro-European politicians end up speaking in one tone in Brussels and in another at home, thereby compounding the sense of public cynicism still further. The role of the press here is pivotal, most of which is largely hostile to the EU and prone to sensationalism in its coverage. In short, nowhere is the public debate over European integration and its effects more emotive, politically charged and, above all, plainly distorted than in Britain.

The George study adopted the 'domestic politics approach' developed by Simon Bulmer (1983). This approach emphasized the importance of political process and not just rational calculation in shaping EU-member state relations. It argued in essence that 'Britain's economic and political relationship with the world system is mediated by its national political system . . . *British politics matters.* Different economic structures, political traditions, institutional forms all culminate in different national patterns of European policy' (Bulmer, 1992: 2, 25). In applying this approach to the study of Britain, the conclusion was that British semi-detachment was not a 'policy dreamt up in Whitehall', but rather one that had a 'strong institutional logic permeating the political system, economic markets, and public administration' (Bulmer, 1992: 29). This institutional emphasis remained prominent in the debates on Europeanization (Chapter 2).

Europeanization: a new analytical departure

While the main aim of this volume is to document and better understand the domestic impact of EU membership, we do so in a way that seeks to add to our theoretical understanding of Europeanization more generally. As noted in Chapter 2, Europeanization has emerged as a central theme in the study of European integration because it raises new and important questions about the nature of the integration process and its effects on member states. Moreover, it emphasizes the interactions between the two: in short, scholars cannot fully understand either the nature of the integration process or its relationship to the politics of member states unless they understand both.

Featherstone (2003: 5–6) illustrated the growth of interest in the concept through the increasing number of academic articles focusing on 'European-ization' and, through an analysis of these articles, argued that 'the increasing usage of "Europeanization" appears to reflect a shift in the research agenda, as well as of fashion'. Bulmer and Radaelli (2005: 339) also noted the tend-ency of some scholars to use the term to 'rebrand' existing research themes. However, they identified in addition a number of 'real world' developments that have shifted the research agenda in the direction of Europeanization. These included: the institutionalization of the internal market, involving many new regulations for domestic actors to contend with; the advent of economic and monetary union (EMU), creating not only a single currency and an interest rate regime for the participating states, but also greater inter-dependency in a range of related policy areas; the increase in regulatory competition between states resulting through increased marketization; and, finally, the process of enlargement, which has necessitated a 'colossal exer-cise in policy transfer' (Bulmer and Radaelli, 2005: 339).

By the early 2000s, the field had started to consolidate around a set of distinctive perspectives, each of which has a particular understanding and definition of Europeanization. These perspectives, which are summarized in Chapter 2, have been tested in a range of empirical contexts. For example, scholars have recently looked at Europeanization in different sectors within one country (for example Germany – see Dyson and Goetz, 2003; Italy – see Franchino and Radaelli, 2004; and the new member states from Eastern Europe – see Schimmelfennig and Sedelmeier, 2005). Attempts have been made to explore Europeanization in a range of states within one sector (for example for environmental policy, see Jordan and Liefferink, 2004) or across a mix of sectors and countries (Featherstone and Radaelli, 2003). Much of this work is summarized in a number of books and chapters that seek to map out the state of the art in Europeanization analysis (for example, see the chapters in Bulmer and Lesquesne 2005a; Featherstone and Radaelli, 2003; as well as Lenschow, 2006 and Radaelli, 2004).

The Europeanization literature is, as Chapter 2 explains, still relatively underdeveloped, and predominantly institutionalist in its orientation. The 'political' dimension, which we highlight in Chapter 2, is one that – given our discussion above – we expect to have some significance for at least some of our cases. We address the findings on this in our concluding chapter. To date though, the Europeanization literature has identified three headline findings, which are widely agreed upon.

Simplifying greatly, the first finding is that some aspects of member state structures and activities appear to have been more deeply affected (that is, 'Europeanized') by the EU than others. In particular, existing scholar-ship suggests that polities (that is, national administrative structures such as departments, parliaments and implementing agencies) and politics are relatively resilient in the face of Europeanizing pressures, whereas national policies have been much more deeply transformed (Anderson, 2002; Jordan, 2003; Radaelli, 2004: 22). The second is that Europeanization is not the same as convergence. Some elements of national systems are said to be converging, whereas others seem to be resilient to centripetal forces, thus producing a highly differentiated pattern – what Cowles *et al.* (2001: 1) refer to as 'domestic adaptation with national colors', and Börzel (2005: 61) terms 'clustered convergence'. The third main finding which is generally agreed on by scholars is that, despite the focus on the downward impact of the EU on member states, Europeanization is, in some respect or another, also a two-way process in which states also seek to upload their preferences to the EU level. Bulmer and Radaelli (2005: 339) suggest, 'the challenge is to model the impact of European integration on domestic policy, knowing that at the same time domestic politics is a major factor at work in EU political change'. In Chapter 2, we show that scholars remain divided on precisely how to handle this in their definitions and models of Europeanization.

Finding explanations for the first of these two core findings continues to challenge Europeanization scholars. Olsen (2002) argues that they are in turn related to the flow of influence coming down from the EU as well as the pre-existing structure of member states. Olsen argues that EU pressures are more likely to have an impact in the domestic arena under the following circumstances: 'the more precise their legal foundation; when they are based on hard law rather than soft law; when the affected parties (constituent units) have been involved in developing the arrangement; the greater the independence of their secretariat; if the secretariat is single-headed rather than multiple-headed; and the greater the financial autonomy of the institution or regime' (Olsen, 2002: 933). These have in turn been related back to variations in the nature of the EU initiative or decision (the EU tends to disseminate policies as opposed to administrative systems), the malleability of different features of national practices (policies generally being seen as more adjustable than machinery of government issues) and the degree of fit between EU and domestic preferences and practices. The second explanation points to different characteristics at the national level, which mediate the pressures coming down from the EU. Because of these, the overall response at national level is highly differential, because:

> the most standard institutional response to novelty is to find a routine in the existing repertoire of routines that can be used. External changes are interpreted and responded to through existing institutional frameworks, including existing causal and normative beliefs about legitimate institutions and the appropriate distribution, exercise and control of power. (Olsen, 2002: 932)

Our own approach to dealing with the third empirical finding – the potential for two-way causality – is summarized in Chapter 2.

The purpose and structure of the book

Despite the 'Europeanization turn' in EU scholarship, there are surprisingly few studies of single member states across a range of sectors and institutions (the main exception is Dyson and Goetz (2003)), that systematically analyse and compare developments across a range of domains.

The contributors to this volume consider Europeanization in relation to the three dimensions of polity, politics and policy. This is not only a useful subdivision of the broad category of 'politics' that allows us to draw comparisons across the three domains, but also mirrors the approach taken in the comparable study of Germany. This study (Dyson and Goetz, 2003: 386) found that 'the overall pattern of Europeanization is characterized by the contrast between progressively Europeanized public policies, a semi-Europeanized polity, and a largely non-Europeanized politics'. Moreover, it identified an 'at best' loose linkage between effects in the three domains. More generally, Dyson and Goetz found that while Germany continued to engage intensively in all aspects of integration, its power to influence (or 'upload' to) the EU level appeared to be in decline. Consequently, the pattern of Germany's relationship with the EU was shifting 'from co-existence and co-evolution to co-evolution and contestation' (Dyson and Goetz, 2003: 367). We return to this study in our concluding chapter, where we draw comparisons with the British experience.

The contributors to this volume are experts in their respective fields who have actively been engaged in empirical research on Europeanization. While they have been asked to provide an overview of developments in their field, their contributions are original and research-led and thus go beyond the standard textbook approach of summarizing the existing literature. To ensure a common approach, they all agreed to work with a shared definition of Europeanization and a common set of questions. These are summarized in Chapter 2. We hope that this editorial guidance, along with the participation of all of the contributors in the activities of a three-year study group supported by the University Association for Contemporary European Studies (UACES) and a related Economic and Social Research Council (ESRC) seminar series, gives this volume added coherence.

Our main audience is those involved in all aspects of teaching and learning connected to the EU and British politics, but we hope that it will also better inform the public debate about the effects of EU membership. The issue of 'Europe' in British politics has never been higher on the agenda, yet the debate still remains surprisingly ill-informed, refracted as it is through the distorted lenses of party politics and the mass media.

In the next chapter we discuss the concept of Europeanization and set out our conceptual framework in more detail. In Part II of the book, we present our first set of case studies on the Europeanization of the British polity, with chapters covering central government (that is, Whitehall), the

Foreign and Commonwealth Office, government in Scotland, the English regions and local governance. Part III moves on to consider the Europeanization of the politics dimension, with contributions covering political parties, organized interests, trade unions and the third sector. Part IV presents a cross section of policy studies, namely, foreign affairs, monetary, competition, environmental protection and regional policies. In the final part of the book we present our comparative conclusions and reflect specifically on the themes and issues raised in this and the next chapter.

Notes

1. While noting that the EU has developed from bodies previously described as the 'EEC' and 'EC', for sake of convenience and consistency we use EU throughout the volume except for where citing material that uses these other descriptions.
2. 'Britain' here is used as shorthand to refer to the United Kingdom of England, Scotland, Wales and Northern Ireland. For an informed discussion of the development of the United Kingdom, see Gamble (2003: 42).

2
Europeanization and Domestic Change

Ian Bache and Andrew Jordan

Introduction

'Europeanization' is not a new term, but the growing interest in the domestic consequences of European integration has raised its profile enormously in recent years making it something of a 'hot topic' (Bulmer and Radaelli, 2005: 632). In turn, this scholarly attention has generated a need for new theories, analytical frameworks and conceptual tools (Buller and Gamble, 2002; Hix and Goetz, 2000). The term 'Europeanization' broadly relates to the *impact* of the EU on its member states. Judging by the recent proliferation of books and articles bearing the word 'Europeanization' in their title (for empirical evidence, see Featherstone, 2003 and Mair, 2004), it is undoubtedly now one of *the* key themes in EU scholarship.

However, as is often the case with emerging concepts, the meaning of Europeanization is contested. After almost a decade of detailed scrutiny, there is still no single theory of Europeanization (Bulmer and Lesquesne, 2005b: 11; Radaelli, 2004: 25), and according to two well-known exponents the prospect of ever finding one seems 'improbable' (Bulmer and Radaelli, 2005: 356). We give a flavour of this debate below. However, this plurality in the use of different approaches and methods leaves the field looking somewhat disorderly; it also casts doubt on the extent to which the term has genuinely added value to better-established approaches to understanding the construction and operation of the EU. For example, some scholars refer to Europeanization as an exclusively EU-related phenomenon, while others see it as a phenomenon that is associated with, but by no means exclusively connected to, the EU. Beyond this very basic distinction, conflicts over sub-themes and more technical usages of the term 'Europeanization' abound. In a recent review, one important contributor noted the 'considerable confusion and disagreement about both the content and the scope of the concept' (Lenschow, 2006). Even sympathetic critics warn that in the wrong hands, terms like 'Europeanization' and 'globalization' can easily become 'catch-all, default *explananda* for almost everything that cannot be explained at the domestic level' (Mair, 2004: 339).

These problems notwithstanding, it would be foolish to dispense with the term entirely. The EU mostly certainly does 'matter' in daily political life at the national level, and understanding why, how and when it matters is an important research challenge. While the field of research around the term 'Europeanization' has still not reached a mature stage, it has already provided important and puzzling insights into the changing nature of relations between the EU and its member (and accession) states. Part of the problem can be put down to youthful exuberance, that is, that theory development and definitional contestation in this field has run too far ahead of detailed empirical testing (which in turn has tended to be a rather incremental and ad hoc affair). One of the purposes of this volume is to offer a detailed comparative empirical test of different interpretations of Europeanization in one large member state – namely Britain.

The rest of this chapter has five parts. In part two, we describe the development of the field since its origins in the 1970s. In part three, we outline the different interpretations and definitions of the term 'Europeanization', and the research programmes that flow from each one. Part four discusses the main analytical challenges that remain to be tackled, while in part five we present our own analytical framework that guides the rest of this volume. The final part draws together the threads of our argument and looks forward to the rest of the volume.

The development of the field

Intellectual origins

The Europeanization literature might be traced back to Peter Gourevitch's seminal article on the international sources of domestic politics (Gourevitch 1978). Its roots, though, are rather more disparate than one scholarly contribution. More than anything else, it arose from a growing awareness among scholars of the EU's growing importance in the politics of its member states. European integration theories were simply not up to the job of explaining these domestic effects, so scholars set out to find something that would. This awareness developed soonest among scholars studying the implementation of EU law and policy. Indeed, some of the first Europeanization studies were conducted by lawyers and consultancy-type bodies, but they did not use the term 'Europeanization' (Jordan and Liefferink, 2004: 4). One particularly influential line of analysis argues that implementation problems arise when the EU asks states to do what they cannot, or do not want to, do. In other words, they emerge when EU requirements 'misfit' with national practices (Börzel, 1999; Héritier, 2002; Héritier *et al.*, 1996, 2001; Knill, 1998; Knill and Lenschow, 1998). The misfit concept is an integral aspect of more top-down accounts of Europeanization (see below).

One of the earliest and most cited uses of the term comes from Robert Ladrech (1994: 69), who defined Europeanization as 'an incremental process reorienting the direction and shape of politics to the degree that EC political and economic dynamics become part of the organizational logic of national politics and policy making'. He argued that because domestic politics was being changed by the response of domestic organizations to the changing context brought about by EU membership, 'organizations respond to changes in the perceptions of interest and value that occur in the principles, norms and institutional design of the regime in which they are embedded' (Ladrech, 1994: 71–72). Although Ladrech observed certain Europeanization effects in France, he did not suggest that the effects of the EU would be the same across all member states. Thus, fears of harmonization or homogenization were unfounded. Instead, domestic factors played an important role in shaping the nature of the Europeanization effects in France, and so, he surmised, would do so elsewhere. Ladrech's arguments about the importance of domestic mediating factors were borne out in subsequent studies.

Thus, in an early study explicitly applying the Europeanization concept to the study of the effects of EU membership on the machinery of British central government, Bulmer and Burch (1998: 603) argued that 'while change has been substantial, it has been more or less wholly in keeping with British traditions'. At key junctures, the administrative response had been shaped by the way in which key political actors had perceived the integration process. Consequently, 'the construction of the issue of integration interacts with the prevailing characteristics of national governmental machinery to explain the different starting points for national adaptation' (Bulmer and Burch, 1998: 606). Smith's (2001a: 160) study of the Scottish Office came to strikingly similar conclusions.

Conceptual refinement

While early studies focused on the downward flow of pressures from the EU to the national level, later ones increasingly highlighted the interactive two-way relationship between member states and the EU. As well as being 'downloaded' by the member states from the EU level, ideas and practices are also 'uploaded' from member states to the EU level (Börzel, 2002). The argument here is that if states can get their existing policy-preferences accepted as the preferences of the EU, they will have less trouble adapting to the EU policy when it comes into force. As Meny *et al.* (1996: 5) noted:

> [o]ften, the most effective results are achieved through controlling the initial stages of the development of a policy...The advantages accrue to those leading countries which succeed in convincing the Community institutions and public opinion that their options or solutions are the best.

A comparative study of environmental policy by Börzel (2002) emphasized how national executives tried to minimize the domestic implementation costs of EU environmental initiatives by seeking to upload their own preferred policy models to the EU level. Different state executives had different uploading strategies, according to both their policy preferences and their capacity to participate at the EU level. The key distinction made was between the 'pace-setting' strategies of those state executives actively seeking to promote their preferences at EU level and the 'foot-dragging' strategies of those seeking to delay or block EU action to avoid heavy implementation costs. A third strategy of 'fence-sitting' described those states that did not seek to advance or block policies, but worked opportunistically with both pace-setters and foot-draggers to trade their support on environmental policy for reciprocal support in other policy areas.

While this interactive dynamic of Europeanization was widely recognized, much empirical research continued its focus on downward pressures. Of particular note was a multi-state study by Cowles *et al.* (2001), which focused on the EU effects on 'domestic structures'. The study focused on two particular categories of domestic structure: policy structures, defined broadly to mean the content of policies through to changes in political, legal and administrative arrangements; and system-wide domestic structures relating to changes in the nation state, its society and economy. The findings of this study echoed those of Ladrech (1994), in that they highlighted the importance of national factors in shaping outcomes. In particular, they emphasized the importance of the degree of 'fit' between EU-level changes and existing domestic structures, policies and practices. Poor fit implies strong pressure to adapt; good fit implies weak pressure. The extent to which adaptive pressure leads to domestic change depends on five intervening factors: multiple veto points in the domestic structure, facilitating institutions, domestic organizational and policy making cultures, the differential empowerment of domestic actors and learning (Cowles *et al.*, 2001: 2). Since around 2000, a great deal of energy has been invested in trying to identify and understand the most obvious intervening variables (Börzel, 2005; Jordan and Liefferink, 2004: 9–10).

Defining Europeanization

In these debates over the meaning of Europeanization, several core approaches have emerged. In this section, we highlight six main uses of the term 'Europeanization'. Some of these overlap, others do not. The six categories are as follows:

1. A top-down process of domestic change deriving from the EU.
2. The creation of new powers at EU level.
3. The creation of a new, European lodestar of domestic politics.

4. The horizontal transfer or 'crossloading' of concepts and policies between states.
5. An increasingly dense, two-way interaction between states and the EU.
6. A discursively constructed external constraint on national autonomy.

These uses are only the most popular ones. Helen Wallace (2000) among others has argued that the EU is itself a product of Europeanization which she feels has a much longer history and geographical span than simply the EU. As such, she believes that there is a need to distinguish between Europeanization and 'EU-ization'. In a similar vein Olsen (2002) has argued that Europeanization could also be used to describe the territorial expansion of the EU (for example the process of enlarging the EU to incorporate new members), or the process through which European forms of governance spread out to other parts of the world. Although this contribution was meant to prevent academics from getting too locked into particular frames of reference, defining Europeanization this broadly risks 'stretching' (Radaelli, 2000) it to breaking point.

Before running through these six in more detail, it is worth noting a number of core differences. For example, Category 2 takes the EU as the main focus of change (that is, the dependent variable), whereas the rest – to a greater or lesser extent – take the EU as the direct or indirect origin of developments at member state level (that is, the independent variable). This is seen most clearly in the top-down Category (1), where the EU is very much the key independent variable. We now look more closely at these main categories.

1. Europeanization as the top-down impact of the EU on its member states. This is the oldest and the most widely adopted usage of Europeanization and the one with most relevance to this study. Héritier *et al.* (2001: 3) defined Europeanization in this sense as 'the process of influence deriving from European decisions and impacting member states' policies and political and administrative structures'. In this mode, the EU acts in a very top-down fashion through legal and other policy acts. Buller and Gamble (2002: 17) referred to Europeanization as 'a situation where distinct modes of European governance have transformed aspects of domestic politics'. More recently, Bulmer and Radaelli (2004: 4) suggested that Europeanization consists of 'processes of a) construction b) diffusion and c) institutionalization of formal and informal rules, procedures, policy paradigms, styles, "ways of doing things" and shared beliefs and norms which are first defined and consolidated in the EU policy process and then incorporated in the logic of domestic (national and subnational) discourse, political structures and public policies'. In all these interpretations, the process of domestic change originates in the EU and travels down to the member states.

2. Europeanization as the accumulation of policy competences at EU level. Cowles *et al.* (2001: 2–3) equated Europeanization with 'the emergence and development at the European level of distinct structures of governance'. In this mode, Europeanization is synonymous with European integration – that is, the development of the EU itself. Consequently, it is generally eschewed as a working interpretation of Europeanization, as it appears not to add much to traditional theories of European integration.

3. Europeanization as the growing importance of the EU as a reference point for national and sub-national actors (for example Hanf and Soetendorp, 1998: 1). In this mode, the EU is akin to a lodestar that is difficult, if not impossible, to ignore. As the EU's powers have grown, national actors have adjusted their expectations and activities, for example lobbying directly in Brussels and Strasbourg rather than through their national governments.

4. Europeanization as the horizontal transfer of concepts and policies between member states. Significantly, these transfers may involve the EU (in the sense that states are members of it), without being directly caused by it. As such, the EU simply provides an arena for inter-state communication and/or competition (Jordan *et al.*, 2003). Bomberg and Peterson (2000) related Europeanization to the similarly popular term 'policy transfer', while Burch and Gomez (2003: 2) and Howell (2003) have argued that it encompasses examples of 'crossloading' through which states share ideas and practices. In this mode, the EU is at best a facilitator of inter-state transfer, through mechanisms of learning and borrowing, for example the open method of coordination (OMC).

5. Europeanization as the two-way interaction between states and the EU. This definition arose inductively from empirical observations that states routinely pre-empt domestic adjustment by shaping an emergent EU policy in their own image (Bomberg and Peterson, 2000: 8; Kassim, 2005: 287) (see above). In other words, they seek proactively to 'domesticate' the EU by uploading national models to the EU. On this view, Europeanization is 'circular rather than unidirectional, and cyclical rather than one off' (Goetz, 2002: 4). Laffan and Stubb (2003: 70) similarly describe Europeanization as 'the process whereby national systems (institutions, policies, governments) adapt to EU policies and integration more generally, while also themselves shaping the European Union'.

6. Europeanization as a discursive frame of reference for national actors. According to this view, the pressure for change 'coming down' from the EU is not treated as an objectively defined reality. On the contrary, it may well offer a discursively constructed constraint behind which domestic actors can hide their real intentions. For example, Hay and Rosamond (2002) argued that national politicians and policy makers routinely invoke 'Europe' to legitimize financially costly and politically controversial measures such as labour market reform, anti-competitive measures or environmental protection (see, Buller, 2000; Buller and Gamble, 2002; Dyson and Featherstone,

1999; Radaelli, 2004). This is done through the use of language ('parliamentary sovereignty', 'Brussels bureaucrats') and symbols like the Queen's head (Rosamond, 2003: 52–55).

In order to give this book a clear analytical focus, we provide our own definition of Europeanization for the contributors to engage with. But before we do this, we first summarize some of the key analytical issues that the Europeanization literature continues to grapple with. Throughout, we try to concentrate on the implications they have for our own definition.

Key analytical challenges

The mechanisms of change

Those offering a top-down view of Europeanization have made the most progress in explaining the causal process through which EU-level processes lead to domestic change. According to this view, Europeanization requires some adaptation pressure to exist between the EU and its member states. Without it, Europeanization cannot logically occur. In other words, a basic 'misfit' (Börzel, 2002) (or 'mismatch' – Héritier, 2002) is seen as a necessary condition for Europeanization. However, those advocating a top-down view concede that the presence of a misfit is not a sufficient condition for Europeanization (Börzel, 2005: 52). This observation has triggered a lively debate about the role of different intervening variables (for reviews, see Börzel, 2005; Haverland, 2000, 2003; Jordan and Liefferink, 2004: 9–11; Radaelli, 2003). For Radaelli (2004: 12), the problem goes well beyond finding the 'right' intervening variables; he suggests that top-down approaches are '[e]xcessively structural . . . there is not enough room for agency'. Other writers, as we shall show below, also feel that they simplify too much of what goes on in the 'black box' of the state – namely, party political contestation, discursive interpretation, pressure group politics and so on.

That said, the misfit concept does appear to work quite well (although not perfectly – see below) in areas where the EU actively disseminates clear obligations in the form of rules, regulations or other, less binding statements of intent such as white papers or action programmes (Jordan and Liefferink, 2004). But in other policy areas, in which the EU's competence is weaker and/or more contested (for example social and home affairs policy), or has co-evolved with national policy (for example telecommunications policy) (Thatcher, 2004), other interpretations of Europeanization seem to fare rather better (Bulmer and Radaelli, 2005). This appears to broadly confirm the point about the nature of the EU's activities made by Olsen (2002).

This lack of correspondence between the predictions of the top-down approaches and the findings of empirical analysis has prompted scholars (starting with Knill and Lehmkuhl, 1999, 2002) to look for associations between the *mode* of EU action and different patterns of Europeanization that emerge at the national level. Again, there is a similarity here with the work of Olsen (2002) (see above), and also Knill and Lehmkuhl (1999, 2002). For example, Bulmer and Radaelli (2005: 341–346) usefully distinguish between the following: *governance by negotiation* at EU level, *governance by hierarchy* and *facilitated coordination*. *Governance by negotiation* essentially relates to the process of agreeing the rules at EU level (that is, our Category 2), although this definition seeks to emphasize the fact that states will often try to shape this process by uploading their preferred ideas to the EU (that is, our Category 5). *Governance by hierarchy* is characterized by a high degree of power delegated to supranational institutions and the use of 'command and control' mechanisms in putting EU policies into place. In areas where there is a clearly defined policy model (so-called positive integration – for example 'market correcting' activities such as regional or environmental policy) flowing down from Brussels, Europeanization is relatively coercive in nature. By contrast, in areas of so-called negative integration, the EU simply pushes for the removal of existing barriers to free trade (that is, market-correcting policies such as competition, monetary or taxation policy). Then, Europeanization tends to take on a much more horizontal form (that is, our Category 4) as political opportunity structures at domestic-level (and EU-level) change 'in the light of the redistribution of power and resources between domestic actors' (Knill and Lehmkuhl, 1999: 14). Finally, *facilitated coordination* refers to areas of policy where national governments are the key actors. Here, EU law is not prominent: there is often unanimity voting in place; or the EU is mainly an arena in which ideas are exchanged bilaterally, for example via the OMC (De la Porte, 2002). In this setting, Europeanization tends to adopt a less hierarchical and coercive form (for example horizontal cross loading – our Category 4). That is, it occurs as actors develop new, shared understandings of policy problems in areas where the EU's competence is weaker, such as foreign or immigration policy. We discuss our own typology of the various processes in Table 2.1.

Table 2.1 Different types of Europeanization

	Voluntary	**Coercive**
Direct	intended impact of an EU initiative unopposed by dominant member state actors	intended impact of an EU initiative opposed by dominant member state actors
Indirect	unintended or inadvertent impact of an EU initiative on the member state unopposed by dominant member state actors	spillover consequences of coercive-direct Europeanization in one area to another

Source: Adapted from Bache (2003).

In summary, Bulmer and Radaelli (2005) hypothesize that governance by hierarchy (that is, where a clear EU 'model' descends downwards from Brussels) generates greater pressures for domestic change (albeit in different ways according to different policy areas), than under the two modes. Their emphasis is very much on describing the different processes through which Europeanization can occur, rather than explaining the pattern of Europeanization that appears in particular member state. In a way, they are simply saying that some interpretations of Europeanization are likely to work better in some circumstances than others, thus contextualizing the much more technical debate about the precise importance of misfits and/or different mediating variables. However, the problem with their approach is that not all EU policies can be categorized in this neat and clear-cut way – often, hierarchical and less-hierarchical elements are bundled together (Lenschow, 2006; Vink, 2003: 66).

What is being impacted?

Another issue that is strongly contested is the nature of the dependent variable. Or, to put it in less positivistic terms, what precisely is being impacted by the EU? In this respect, Dyson and Goetz (2002) helpfully distinguished between first-generation and second-generation Europeanization studies. They argued that the former emphasize the more formal, observable consequences of EU membership, whereas the latter focus on less formal and less observable changes.

An example of a 'first generation' approach is Jordan and Liefferink's (2004) study of national environmental policy. In order to improve the comparability between cases, it concentrated on the Europeanization of national policy: to wit, the structures, style and content of policy. In the view of second-generation studies, Europeanization is not limited to changes in political-administrative structures and the formal content of national policy because, 'European values and policy paradigms are also to some (varying) degree internalized at the domestic level, shaping discourses and identities' (Olsen, 2002: 935). Similarly, Cowles *et al.* (2001) referred to the Europeanization of national structures at large, which they take to include policy structures (political, legal and administrative arrangements) and 'system-wide' structures (for example legal systems, sub-national government, business–industry relations, citizenship norms and even public understandings of the legitimate role of the nation state).

Anderson (2002: 9) captured the broader concerns of second-generation analyses by distinguishing between three different categories of domestic impact, namely changes in interests, changes in institutions and changes in ideas. While these categories are separated for analytical purposes, in reality they are not independent. Actor interests are shaped both by the institutional framework, which constrains the range of possibilities, and by the value structure through which individual actors perceive their interests.

Moreover, while these categories are identified for analytical purpose as domestic categories, in reality they are not sealed off from the external environment. So, 'membership in the EC/EU "matters", in that it automatically entails multi-layered interactions of interests, institutions, and ideas at and across the national and supranational levels' (Anderson, 2002: 10).

This volume considers the impact of the EU on its member states, that is, some comparable aspect of a member state's form or function. But which one? Clearly, there is a balance to be struck here between breadth and depth, and simplicity and complexity. A useful point of departure here is Radaelli's (2003: 55) taxonomic distinction between different 'domains' of Europeanization (see Table 2.2), because it is broad enough to encompass some of the

Table 2.2 Domains of Europeanization and change

Domains of Europeanization	Extent and direction of Europeanization
Domestic structures 1. Political structures (a) Institutions (cabinet–assembly relations)	
(b) Public administration (c) Inter-governmental relations (d) Legal structure	**Direction of policy change (see Table 2.3)** Retrenchment Inertia Absorption Accommodation Transformation ← – → – 0 + ++
2. Structures of representation and cleavages (a) Political parties (b) Pressure groups (c) Societal-cleavage structures	
Public policy (a) Actors (b) Policy problems (c) Style (d) Instruments (e) Resources	Ditto
Cognitive and normative structures (a) Discourse (b) Norms and values (c) Political legitimacy (d) Identities (e) State-traditions – understanding of governance (f) Policy paradigms, frames and narratives	Ditto

Source: Adapted from Radaelli (2003: 35).

'softer' impacts while also specific enough to permit a structured dialogue to occur between those contributors to an edited volume such as this. It is noteworthy that this table mixes different elements of polity, politics and policy covered in the empirical chapters of this book.

The process of impact

In investigating the process of impact, Bache (2003) made a distinction between the intended impact of an EU initiative (*direct Europeanization*) and inadvertent impacts (*indirect Europeanization*). This distinction draws attention to the one made in our definition of Europeanization below, between the EU's impact on 'politics in the domestic arena' rather than on 'domestic politics'. The latter suggests an emphasis on the inadvertent impact of the EU on areas of domestic jurisdiction only, while the former incorporates both these and the formally intended impact of EU initiatives.

In seeking to highlight partisan politics and ideological values in the domestic response to EU initiatives and decisions, Bache (2003) made a further distinction between *voluntary Europeanization* (that is, those EU initiatives embraced by key domestic actors) and *coercive Europeanization* (that is, those EU initiatives opposed by key domestic actors). These are typologies at either end of a continuum, with the reality of most domestic reactions likely to be somewhere in between the two extremes, with most EU initiatives provoking a range of responses within the domestic arena and the eventual impacts shaped by processes of negotiation and bargaining between both domestic and supranational actors.

Again, herein lies a distinction between direct and indirect impacts. Thus, voluntary-direct Europeanization is the willing adoption of EU decisions in a given area (for example, compliance with EU regional policy regulations), while voluntary-indirect Europeanization refers to the adoption of EU preferences, practices or policies in another area (for example adopting EU approaches to regional policy in domestic regional policy). Similarly, coercive-direct Europeanization refers to the forced acceptance of European preferences, practices or policies in a given area, while coercive-indirect Europeanization refers to spillover consequences of coercive-direct Europeanization in one area to another. These dimensions, which are summarized in Table 2.1, emphasize the interactive dynamics between the EU and member states levels, highlighting the possibility of different routes towards and responses to Europeanization.

There are obvious overlaps here with the typology developed by Bulmer and Radaelli (2005) and described above. For example, instances of governance by hierarchy (our Category 1) would fit more neatly into the top right hand cell of Table 2.1, whereas instances of facilitated coordination (that is, our Category 4) are more likely to appear in the top and bottom left hand cells.

Measuring the domestic impact

Börzel and Risse (2000, 2003) and Börzel (2005) have categorized different degrees of domestic change through EU membership (see Table 2.3). *Absorption* arises when the misfit between EU requirements and prevailing domestic characteristics is low. Therefore EU requirements are simply absorbed without substantially modifying national policies. *Accommodation* occurs when states adjust their pre-existing policies while leaving their core features intact. As the misfit is small the amount of domestic adaptation will be low. *Transformation* relates to a situation in which states can only implement EU requirements by fundamentally altering their existing protection systems.

The final two points on the scale refer to more specific circumstances. *Inertia* arises when states deliberately block EU requirements by either not implementing policies or engaging in partial compliance. Regardless of whether the misfit is large or small, the amount of domestic change will be limited, at least until sufficient political pressure has built up to deliver the necessary national adaptations. *Retrenchment* occurs when states do not simply block EU requirements at the implementation stage, but consciously develop new national policies that diverge from EU requirements. Consequently, national policy becomes more, not less, national.

Table 2.3   Degrees of domestic policy change

	Difference between EU and national policy (the 'misfit')	Level of domestic change
Inertia	varies	small: states resist change (but this often increases adaptive pressure and leads to change in the longer term)
Retrenchment	varies	negative: states actively resist adaptive pressure by stressing their unique features ('nationalization')
Absorption	small	small: states incorporate/domesticate EU requirements without substantially modifying national policy
Accommodation	medium	medium: states accommodate/mediate EU requirement adapting existing policy while leaving its core features intact
Transformation	High	high: domestication fails; states forced to substantially alter or replace existing policy

Source: Adapted from Börzel and Risse (2000, 2003) and Börzel (2005).

Although this framework is widely advocated, very few scholars have sought to employ it in empirical research. Jordan and Liefferink (2004) employed it in their study of ten member state environmental sectors and found surprisingly very few cases of transformation. While not explicitly employing the whole framework, Burch and Gomez (see Chapter 6) and Bulmer and Burch (1998) have noted several instances of what might be termed 'incremental transformation' in Britain. In this book, we have asked the contributors to see whether the framework is a useful device to assess the degree of change in their case. We report back on their findings in the final chapter.

Disentangling causes

Another serious analytical issue is how to disentangle the impact of the EU from other drivers of domestic change, not least the effects of globalization and important national political and policy developments. Unless these rival explanations are fully considered and steps taken to control them, Europeanization risks being 'a cause in search of an effect' (Goetz, 2001: 211). Research suggests that when the three are compared, some instances of 'Europeanization' may not be as clear-cut as first thought (Radaelli, 2004: 24). For example, Jordan and Liefferink (2004) studied the environmental policies of ten states. They focused on this sector expecting to find evidence of strong top-down impacts. To their surprise, they discovered that:

> Europeanization has probably only been a weak and indirect cause of ... policy convergence ... [It] has removed the most obvious outliers ... and brought the environmental systems of the economically peripheral states ... up to the same level as the states in the more industrialised north

But as Radaelli (2003: 48–49) very honestly points out, stressing the need for multi-causal analysis is one thing, but actually doing it is another entirely. In order, therefore, to disentangle the EU's effects, we asked the chapter authors to do try and disentangle the causes of domestic change. There are at least four ways that this can be done, namely through:

1. careful historical analysis (that is, is there an obvious change after EU membership, or does it pre-date membership?) (see Jordan and Liefferink, 2004);
2. employing a bottom-up, inductive approach (that is, starting with domestic changes and tracing back causal chains to identify the underlying triggers) (Radaelli, 2003: 50–52). Exemplars of this approach is Franchino and Radaelli (2004) and Ugland (2003);

3. actively exploring the counterfactual; that is, what would have happened without the EU? (Anderson, 2003: 47–48; Radaelli, 2004: 8; Schmitter, 1999);
4. comparing states within and outside the EU (see Jordan and Liefferink, 2004).

We comment on how our chapter authors handled the issue of causality in the concluding chapter.

Political dynamics

Finally, there is a need to respond to the criticism made by Mair (2004), among others, that existing Europeanization research has focused on institutional dynamics to the relative neglect of political dynamics (see Category 6 above, for example). The point being made here is that there is a danger in viewing Europeanization as an external pressure that is imposed on states from the outside. For scholars of British politics, it is equally important to know how the EU is 'used' by domestic actors. As Mair (2004: 344) puts it: 'there seems little room for political or partisan contestation in Europeanization – whether we speak of the actors involved, who usually tend to favour de-politicization in any case, or of the analysts and scholars, who tend to see politics as being irrelevant to the issues at stake'. This would require research to focus more on issues of domestic political legitimacy and political contestation. Europeanization scholars do not have to look particularly hard to find good examples of either of these in Britain (see Chapter 1). In the concluding chapter we assess the importance of the political dynamics in relation to our empirical studies.

Our analytical framework

In this book, the term 'Europeanization' is used to frame an analysis of the impact of European integration on British politics. Drawing on the state of the art discussed in the sections above, we assume that the phenomenon is complex, that disentangling key variables is likely to be difficult, and that care is needed in ascribing causality to Europeanization rather than globalization or domestic changes. Our focus here is on the domestic effects of EU membership, whatever the dynamics and processes. As such, we offer a relatively straightforward definition of Europeanization as:

> *the reorientation or reshaping of politics in the domestic arena in ways that reflect policies, practices and preferences advanced through the EU system of governance.*

In developing our interpretation and definition, we have tried to address as many of the analytical concerns summarized above, that we can. For example, while our definition might appear to sit most easily with a top-down approach, it works also with the notion of Europeanization as a two-way interaction, which we assume will be important for some of our cases – not least in the absence of 'a clear, vertical chain of command, in which EU policy descends from Brussels into the member states' (Bulmer and Radaelli, 2004: 641). Furthermore, we are alive to the possibility that state preferences can be uploaded and transmitted through the EU system of governance. We have specifically asked the contributors to this volume to engage critically with the possibility that Europeanization might have occurred through a variety of mechanisms but are traceable to the EU. However, we are clear that for Europeanization to have occurred there must be evidence of some reorientation or reshaping domestically that can be traced back to the EU processes, whatever the origin of these policies, practices or preferences.

Throughout, we have been careful not to straightjacket the contributors by insisting that they consider only our definition to their respective sector, actor or institution. Indeed, one of the aims of this book is to assess how far other interpretations of Europeanization might be relevant to Britain. Where relevant, our contributors have employed contrasting interpretations of Europeanization alongside our preferred definition. However, to ensure coherence and consistency without at the same time entirely foreclosing debate, each contributor was asked to respond to a common set of questions. These were:

- What has been Europeanized and to what extent?
- When has Europeanization occurred and in what sequence?
- How and why has Europeanization occurred, and via what EU-level mechanism?
- Were there winners and losers through Europeanization?
- What factors explain the domestic response to Europeanization pressures and how should the process be characterized?
- Has Europeanization had any other important long-term effects?

We have modelled these on a very similar set of questions that were first published by Featherstone and Radaelli (2003) and subsequently adapted by Dyson and Goetz (2003: 34–35) to a study of the Europeanization of Germany. By operating in this way, we hope to strengthen considerably the contribution made by this volume both to conceptual debates on Europeanization as well as to the empirical stock of knowledge about the domestic effects of EU membership in Britain. This approach also facilitates comparison with the findings of these other studies.

Conclusions

Clear definitions remain elusive and there is still a great deal of animated debate between scholars of Europeanization about background concepts and analytical methods. Ten years of academic effort has still not managed to fashion Europeanization into an agreed theory of how the EU affects its member states (and how they, in turn, affect it). For the most part, Europeanization scholars have managed to identify causal factors, but are still way short of measuring their relative importance or defining the conditions under which they may or may not operate (Lenschow, 2006). In this sense, it is probably fair to admit that it has metamorphosed from being 'a loose background concept' to a more systematically applied term (Bulmer and Lesquesne, 2005b: 11). Therefore, it certainly *does* deserve to be included in the analytical 'tool box' of EU scholarship. We do not share the view that Europeanization is simply a 'faddish' term (Featherstone, 2003: 1), or that it has limited utility as an organizing concept (Kassim, 2000: 238). On the contrary, it is now being used to shed light on the dynamics of the EU enlargement process (Schimmelfennig and Sedelmeier, 2005), both in terms of the acceptance and assimilation of the formal *acquis communautaire* by accession states, and in terms of the pressures on accession states to conform to less formal, but nonetheless important, norms of democratic behaviour – that is, acceptance of both the 'regulatory pillar' and the 'normative pillar' (Bulmer and Radaelli 2004: 2). Indeed, recent work does seem to suggest that some of the first generation of Europeanization scholars (those who – to quote Radaelli (2004: 44) – performed 'impact studies' in a narrowly defined area of national political life) greatly underestimated the potential for significant domestic change to emerge via less hierarchical and coercive processes (see the discussion of Europeanization via facilitated coordination above). In the final chapter, we explore this question in relation to the continuing Europeanization of British politics.

Part of the problem for Europeanization scholars is the complexity of the phenomena they are seeking to understand. Traditionally, political scientists studying international (or, in our case, European) politics have sat at a different 'table' (Almond, 1990: 19) to the comparativists studying individual member states. With few exceptions, scholars have tended to work within one tradition or the other, departing only insofar as it is useful to their broader purpose (which for international relations scholars is understanding international dynamics and for comparativists is describing and explaining domestic structures and processes). While the phrase 'intellectual apartheid' may exaggerate the extent of the division between the two (Bulmer, 1994: 355), until relatively recently the attempts made to work across this divide have been few and far between. This is why Europeanization research is both so exciting and also so problematic, because it forces analysts to work across the age-old divide in the discipline of Political Studies (or Political Science – to raise yet another problem). But the effort made is, we believe, very much worthwhile. According to Mair (2004: 346) 'some of the very best and most innovative and challenging work in political science is now being carried out by scholars working in the field of European integration and Europeanization'. One of the declared purposes of this book is to add something to the lively debate about Europeanization. At the same time, however, we would also like to demonstrate empirically that 'a full understanding of British politics is impossible without a comprehension of the [EU] and Britain's place therein' (Rosamond, 2003: 39).

Part II
Polity

3
Central Government

Simon Bulmer and Martin Burch

Introduction

The UK central government's adaptation to European integration has been a long-term process. It can be traced back to the 1961 application by the Macmillan administration to join the European Communities (EC). The process developed in earnest after the UK's accession in 1973. However, accession was not, at least so far as the machinery and operation of government is concerned, a 'big-bang' event, since adjustment had begun before accession, and the EU of today has developed massively compared to the EC of 1973. The effect of this widening integration upon UK government was slow and accretive and took place in a relatively unseen manner. The cumulative effect of the changes, however, amounted to a substantial and significant alteration in the pattern of UK government and policy making. Thus, over time a transformation of UK government took place that could be regarded as a quiet revolution. The election of the Blair government in 1997, and its re-election with a second landslide majority in 2001, gave the process of adapting to Europe a considerable shift in pace and direction as the government sought to bring about a 'step-change' in the UK's relationship with its EU partners.

This gradual and quickening Europeanization of UK central government over the period since 1973 is the subject of this chapter. In the following pages we review what has taken place and seek to ascertain how big a shift has been involved. We explore the changes in central government from the perspective of Europeanization. We begin, however, with some remarks about how we understand that concept and how we organize the empirical part of the chapter. Our approach to Europeanization, in keeping with the discussion in Chapter 2, is concerned with both the top-down impact of the EU upon the member state and the explicitly two-way nature of Europeanization. We recognize that there is an iterative process under way, not least because the adaptation of the UK governmental system is designed in part to ensure effective input into EU policy making in Brussels. Thus, we see adjustment to the EU as a process of aligning two institutional logics: that of the

EU and that of UK governance. This adjustment process entails two separate steps. One is that domestic institutions must find suitable ways of processing EU business. The lowest adjustment cost is incurred by incorporating EU business into the pre-existing domestic logic of governance through some switching mechanism. However, domestic institutions must also adapt their procedures so as to be able to make an effective contribution to those EU dynamics.

We term these two components of institutional response to Europeanization 'reception' and 'projection' (Bulmer and Burch, 2000a, 2002). They have some similarity with the notions of downloading and uploading highlighted in Chapter 2, but they are more focused on the task of policy handling and the capacities and skills required to effectively fulfil that task, rather than on the content of policy *per se*. Reception involves a much larger part of UK government than projection because so much of British policy has a European dimension. To take a concrete example, the Department for the Environment, Food and Rural Affairs (DEFRA) is subject to a wide range of EU policy: on the environment, food standards, agriculture and fisheries. But whilst a large part of the ministry's organization and officials work within guidelines set by the EU, a rather smaller subset is engaged in the projection side, that is, formulating UK input into proposed legislation or other decisions. Thus, we argue that reception is only one response to Europeanization. A separate step is the projection response. Projection refers to the development of machinery for securing an effective voice in the formulation of policy in Brussels. It means learning the rules of the EU game, and that they may be different from those in the domestic political system.

A further response to Europeanization is to regard it as an opportunity structure for resolving domestic policy problems that are perceived not to be properly resolved within a national context, for example because their scale goes beyond that of the nation state. This response involves making systematic use of projection in order to make an imprint on the activities of the EU and to help determine the shape of policy initiatives that are later downloaded from EU level back to the initiating nation state.

In what follows, we examine how UK central government has adapted to pressures emanating from European integration in the period up to 1997. We then explore the record of adaptation under the Blair government. This historical approach enables us to provide a sense of the sequence of Europe-related developments at the centre of the state. In both phases we pay particular attention to the extent of Europeanization as reflected in changes in three aspects of central government.

- changes in formal authority and established institutional structures
- changes in opportunities for action
- changes in the political and organizational values underlying the operation of UK central governance.

We argue that up until 1997 the reception side of central government's response was well developed, but the systematic use of projection was less evident. The Blair government has attempted to re-set the balance and to exploit more effectively the projection side of the relationship with the EU.

Adaptation before 1997

The UK government commenced its adaptation ahead of accession in 1973. Indeed, the broad framework of adaptation emerged at the time of the negotiations for entry in 1961. This involved establishing a cabinet committee system to handle EC matters at both ministerial and official levels; the creation of a co-ordinating mechanism across Whitehall (initially run from the Treasury, and, from 1966, the Cabinet Office); and the drawing together of legal expertise on community treaties, regulations and directives (Bulmer and Burch, 1998: 608–09; Wallace and Wallace, 1973). All this was well established prior to UK entry in 1973 and was wholly in keeping with traditional ways of working in Whitehall. Thus, by the time of accession, most of the broad features of UK central government's approach to handling EC matters were already in place. They comprised: delegating detailed consideration of substantive policy to the relevant UK ministry; identifying the important legal dimension to integration, and placing it under the authority of the Treasury Solicitor's Office; ensuring that policy was co-ordinated effectively within Whitehall through reliance on traditional cabinet mechanisms; and the emergence of a set of core ministries at the heart of European business, with an outer circle having more intermittent involvement. At the time of accession the core ministries affected by substantive EC involvement were the Ministry of Agriculture, Fisheries and Food (MAFF), the Treasury, the Department of Trade and Industry (DTI), the Foreign and Commonwealth Office (FCO), and Customs and Excise.

The co-ordination of European policy making – that is, the projection of UK policy into Brussels – as well as a measure of general oversight was achieved through a small central secretariat in the Cabinet Office (the European Secretariat) (COES). Its three or four top personnel plus legal advisers, along with key players in the Prime Minister's Office (PMO), the FCO and the UK's Permanent Representative to the European Communities, formed the hub of the government's European policy making network. These personnel, both ministerial and official, plus one or two others from the Treasury and the two departments most consistently and substantially involved in European matters (namely agriculture and trade and industry), formed the inner core of the European policy making network. Formally speaking, co-ordination was achieved through the system of cabinet committees at both ministerial and official levels. Co-ordination of negotiating positions has been assisted through the regular Friday meeting, which takes place in the Cabinet Office under the chair of the Head of the European

Secretariat, with the UK's Permanent Representative in attendance along with senior officials from the FCO and the Treasury and officials from the departments whose business is being discussed. The Friday meeting reviews business coming up in the EU in the weeks ahead and the UK line to be pursued. This co-ordinating net stretched out into Brussels through the United Kingdom Permanent Representation to the EU (UKRep), and engaged, as the need arose, personnel in other domestic departments. At first, other than those departments already mentioned, few others were involved.

This structure and approach to handling European business was adapted over the period from 1973 largely to take into account the development of EC/EU competences and the consequent growth of business and the spread of the network to include all central government departments. The basic principles did not change despite the considerable expansion in EC/EU-related activity. It was simply that new European policies, such as on the environment (see Jordan, 2002, 2003), necessitated the involvement of a widening group of Whitehall officials and ministers in putting into effect, and shaping, European policy. The 1992 Maastricht Treaty, with its creation of a 'third pillar' to co-ordinate policy on Justice and Home Affairs, had a similar effect with the Home Office joining the group of key players. New recruits to 'the core' were a function of the development of new policy activities at EU level. Perhaps the most significant of these recruits was the prime minister, who was drawn more regularly into European business following the inauguration of regular summit meetings (the European Council) in 1975. Key players at ministerial level are thus the Prime Minister and Foreign Secretary, the latter having the lead on EU institutional matters and the chair of the cabinet's ministerial committee on European issues.

Departments outside the core group mentioned above have been involved in EU business in a less intensive manner. Departments responsible for policy areas such as employment, education, social security and the like have been affected by EU policy, to be sure. However, whilst they may have quite important duties to adhere to in respect of EU legislation, they are outliers in terms of projecting policy into the Brussels arena. Their participation in the EU policy making machinery is very much on an 'as needed' basis. The so-called territorial departments, which provided central government's presence in Scotland, Wales and Northern Ireland, were each also gradually drawn into the European policy making network. Their ability to play a significant role was very limited because they were too small in resource terms, too far from the centre, and sometimes neglected. However, they became increasingly active and more assertive in this area of policy from the early 1990s: the Scottish Office in particular (see Smith, Chapter 5). The government offices in the English regions, set up under the Major government, also became drawn into EU policy, especially as it affected economic regeneration through the application of the structural funds (see Burch and Gomez, 2002 and Chapter 6).

The resilience of established institutional structures goes a long way to explaining the very limited adaptation at domestic level. The UK's centralized system of government, majoritarian rule, parliamentary sovereignty, cabinet system, different constitutional traditions and so on, all represented fundamental and well-established aspects of the political system. The United Kingdom was not formally required by the EU to alter these established ways of operating, nor did it choose to do so. Indeed, for quite separate domestic reasons, some of these established features were arguably reinforced. For example, the Thatcher government abolished the metropolitan counties in England and created a more centralized system of territorial power than beforehand (Marshall, Chapter 7). However, the predominant picture is not one of exacerbating adaptation to the EU, but of small adjustments, designed to 'translate' EU needs into compatibility with the existing traditions of UK central government. Thus, the handling of EU policy conforms to the basic tenets of the UK state system: centralized, cabinet and cabinet committee-based, and yet with considerable authority left to departments in cases where prime ministerial and core executive power[1] is not asserted.

In addition to institutional resilience, a further factor that has limited the development of European policy has been party politics. Indeed, a central feature in the development of UK European policy is that a relatively efficient, well co-ordinated and smoothly run state machine has throughout been constrained in the actual development and delivery of policy by problems thrown up in the party political sphere. Both before and throughout membership, European issues have been a source of division in and between the parties (Young, 2000) (see also Geddes, Chapter 8). This aspect has greatly constrained the activities of ministers especially when the governing party had a small parliamentary majority, as in the case of the second Major administration (1992–97).

Limited institutional change was paralleled by limited exploitation of the opportunities arising from EU involvement. One important possibility was for the prime minister to avail himself or herself of the opportunities afforded by the European Council, to advocate a European policy solution to a domestic problem. In fact, this channel was initially used in a negative sense: to demand re-negotiated terms of membership or budgetary and agricultural reform. One clear projection opportunity came in the mid-1980s, when Mrs Thatcher was able to get the single market programme approved by the member states as part of a wider reform package.

What of changes in political and organizational values? Here, also, the EU effect was limited. The UK approach to handling European business remained imbued with principles derived from the political and organizational cultures of central government. Significant amongst these are: the notion of departmental lead on policy, and light monitoring and co-ordination from the centre; an organizational culture of reciprocity and trust; and the practice of sharing information and of informing the centre (that is, in the case of Europe, the COES) of matters that are likely to concern it. These practices combine central oversight with involvement of necessary participants on a 'need-to-know' basis. They are backed up by norms of collective decision-making, expressed through conventions such as that of collective responsibility. The pattern, therefore, has been one of adapting existing ways of doing things rather than one of major change.

In summary, the adaptation of UK central government to European integration over the period up to 1997 was principally one of absorbing EU business into the practices established domestically over the last decades. The UK constitution, unwritten though it may be, served as a constraint on any adjustment pressures emanating from Brussels. The deadweight of history was supported by an institutional culture that was satisfied with the Whitehall/Westminster machinery. The fragile political support for deeper integration meant that the new opportunities that were afforded by engagement in integration were utilized in a very limited manner. In short, institutional adjustment was limited. But it was widespread. By 1997, every department had been obliged to invest resources into the monitoring of EU activity. All had EU divisions or offices of some form. It was through these many impacts that the business of UK central government may be seen to have undergone a quiet revolution as a result of the EU's effect. But the domestic response was primarily reception rather than projection. The utilization of the opportunities created by the EU for pursuing UK policy goals was only attempted infrequently, notably in respect of the single market programme.

Adaptation after 1997

The Blair government not only has built on established trends in UK/EU policy making, but has also set up new structures and processes, which potentially shift the field on which European policy is played out at the domestic level. In general, there has been an enhancement of the projection capabilities of UK government and an attempt to get away from a passive and reactive approach to the EU. This represents a shift from the previous accretive and evolutionary pattern of adaptation. More staff and resources, especially at the core, have been devoted to European policy making. In addition there has been an attempt to change the attitude towards the benefits and potentials of the EU project, and to 'mainstream' Europe in the activities of all departments. There have also been important changes in the structure of the state, which have required adjustment to the ways in which European policy is made and implemented. In making these changes, the Labour government has benefited from a more benign attitude towards Europe on the part of its parliamentary party compared to its predecessors. Indeed, Labour came to terms with Europe while in opposition, thus permitting the development of a more upfront, strategic and positive approach (Bulmer, 2000).

So far as formal authority and established institutional structures are concerned, there has been a significant centralizing of EU policy handling at the heart of the UK/EU policy process. More resources and powers of direction have been given to the very 'centre' of government. In effect, there has been a streamlining of effort at the top through integrating more closely the work of the COES and No 10. The secretariat has, as from August 2000, been substantially augmented. Its personnel increased from 9 senior officials to 16 – with 4 senior staff and 12 desk officers. Its status was raised through the appointment of Sir Stephen Wall, succeeded in 2004 by Kim Darroch, as head of the secretariat, with the position of Permanent Secretary, and the title of Prime Minister's Adviser on Europe and an office in No 10. This step was complemented by closer connections between the secretariat and members of the Prime Minister's Policy Unit (PMPU). The effect of this enhancement of the core has been to give a more executive thrust to policy making and to open up the opportunity for a more directive approach to European policy making at the very top.

This change in part reflects the style of the Blair administration, but it also reflects a longer-term trend of centralization which can be traced back to the Callaghan administration (Burch and Holliday, 1996: 22–24, 2004: 17–21). In addition, there is a direct EU effect at work here in that there has been increasing requirement for more involvement by heads of government in EU policy making. What the Blair government has done is to significantly extend established trends, whilst aligning UK practice with an institutional logic emanating from the regular European Council meetings and bilateral summits.

Overall, European policy making is more focused on the core executive and directed from it. Yet, there are areas where the remit of the 'centre' is not so tight. A particular feature of the organization of central government since 1997 is the way that executive authority is split between the Prime Minister and his staff, on the one hand, and the Chancellor of the Exchequer and the Treasury, on the other. This fault line had consequences for the economic aspects of European policy. The Treasury still has a somewhat negative effect on European issues through expenditure concerns (see Bulmer and Burch, 1998: 618--19). But it is in relation to monetary issues that the Treasury has most influenced the adaptation of the UK to EU pressures through the development and evaluation of the five economic tests required before the government would recommend joining the euro zone (see Buller, Chapter 13). As under the Major government, the Treasury has kept charge of the development of policy in relation to the European currency. This factor reflects an important division of authority within UK government. It serves as a continuing limitation on the pace and content of policy development, and reflects a stance that has arguably grown more restrictive in the period since 1997.

Turning to changes in the way opportunities have been exploited, a characteristic feature of the Blair government's approach has been a much more significant effort to realize the potential for affecting the inter-governmental forces and interests which shape EU policies and initiatives. The aim has been to condition the climate of debate surrounding the run-up to key EU decisions through greater contact and liaison at member state level, leading to exchanges of information, alliances on policy initiatives and long-term coalition building. This approach was enshrined in the so-called 'step change programme' from which much else has followed.

The step change programme grew out of a review, requested by the prime minister after the UK Presidency in the first half of 1998, of both the substance of UK positions on various policies and the general approach to Europe and how these might be improved. It concentrated on isolating the issues on which the UK could take the lead and the strategy and tactics to be employed. The review recognized the need for the UK to be more positive and pro-active, and thus more able to shape EU agenda setting at an early stage. Closer engagement on European issues with other member states and EU personnel was seen as critical to doing this. The step change project envisaged a ten-year programme for shifting the UK's position on Europe and other member states' perception of it. This networking offensive had two main foci for relationship building. The first is between the UK ministers and officials and their counterparts in member states. Recognizing that formal relations between Germany and France had, since the 1963 Elysee Treaty, been the cornerstone of the development of EC/EU, it was felt that the UK needed similarly to court closer ties with partners. The second focus of attention was the relationships between ministers and their party contacts on the centre left in Europe. These initiatives were complemented by a project to try to help shape UK public opinion by encouraging more dissemination of information on the EU, counteracting misinformation and publicly campaigning on EU issues.

Of these initiatives, the contacts with member state personnel were seen as the most important avenue for development. The more Euro-focused line departments (MAFF, Department of Environment and DTI) were already well engaged in such contacts, but in other departments, both officials and ministers, were less practised at the tasks of networking and shaping initiatives. To assist in this activity, the Bilateral Department of the European Union Division in the FCO was created and this took over responsibility for all the member state embassies and diplomatic posts from the West European Department. Thus, for the first time all things EU were brought within the same command structure. This basic structure was maintained and augmented in reorganizations in 2002 and 2004 as the FCO moved over from a command structure, to a more fluid system based on directorates organized more around themes or tasks than geographic areas. Under these changes, the Bilateral Department ceased to exist and its activities were distributed across the relevant units of the EU Directorate. The aim of this was to create closer integration between the various EU activities in the FCO (see Allen and Oliver, Chapter 4).

The objective of changing public attitudes involved giving a higher profile and larger campaigning role to the position of Minister of State for Europe and the creation of a public diplomacy function largely located in its EU (Internal) Department. This unit was also given the task of monitoring the bilateral contacts programme. The whole effort was overseen by an inter-departmental committee, the Ministerial Group for European Co-ordination (MINECOR), chaired by the Minister of State for Europe, which drew together all the departmental ministers responsible for Europe, plus the Europe ministers from the devolved administrations. The committee initially met about once every six weeks and, amongst other matters, examined the progress of the bilateral contacts programme. By 2004, MINECOR was deemed to have served its purpose and ceased meeting.

The step change programme did not itself address the issue of how best to ensure a strategic approach to Europe. Unlike its predecessors, the Blair administration was not deeply divided over Europe, so overall European strategy questions could be drawn together at the ministerial level. Initially, this seems to have been largely handled through ad hoc meetings involving the prime minister and their EU advisers and the Foreign Secretary and other relevant ministers. It was not significantly developed in the Cabinet's European Policy Committee chaired by the Foreign Secretary. However, the need to prepare for an eventual decision and possible actions on UK member-ship of the euro led to the creation, in June 2003, of a cabinet committee on European Strategy, the Ministerial Committee on European Union Strategy (EUS). This is chaired by the Prime Minister and serviced by the Economic and Domestic Affairs Secretariat. However, EUS has only met very infre-quently (ca. annually).

Clearly, these changes in exploitation of the opportunities created by membership of the EU reflected the internal dynamics and political prefer-ences of the government. But there was a significant Europeanizing dimen-sion, namely the recognition that the UK was failing to fully exploit the opportunities available to it to shape EU policy at an early stage. This direct Europeanizing effect has been characterized by institutional changes designed to improve the projection side of the UK's approach to Europe. However, it is notable once again that these changes have been achieved by improving the 'switching mechanisms', that is, greater alignment between the two institutional systems is achieved within existing structures and trends of UK governance. In particular, the reinforcement of resources around the PM reflects wider enhancement of the core executive and espe-cially of the PMO and the Treasury (Burch and Holliday, 2004).

Labour's more directive, strategic and proactive approach reflected changes in political and organizational values. The most important political change was in the attitudes and values of the governing party, and its leadership group. Labour was more at ease with the concept of European integration than any government since Heath's in the early 1970s. Blair's own perception of the UK in Europe over the last thirty years was one of missed opportunities, lack of understanding, a tendency to follow rather than lead, and a cautious and laggardly response to initiatives (Blair, 2000, 2002). In order to redress this legacy, during the 1990s Labour decided to take a much more active and pro-European approach, especially on those issues which it was deemed in the national interest to pursue.

Organizationally, diplomats and home civil servants had become very accustomed to dealing with EU business. However, the principle of civil service neutrality meant that the consequent organizational and cultural changes in individual departments had not been capitalized on. Strategic thinking about the EU had been politically divisive under John Major, and hence for officials it was consequently taboo. With a different set of policies, officials could play their part in projecting UK initiatives in the EU. By aligning the new political line – a more positive, 'can-do' approach to Europe – with latent organizational resource, the Blair government had the will and wherewithal to make contributions to the EU agenda.

This shift in approach has not been uniform because the political and organizational circumstances have not been uniform. Nor, characteristically, has Tony Blair wanted to move too far ahead of public opinion, which has remained amongst the least supportive of integration in the EU. Emblematic of the lack of uniformity has been the position of the Treasury. Chancellor Gordon Brown has been notably less warm on European policy than Blair. Organizationally, the Treasury has itself embraced European integration less than other key departments have. Outside a small group of European specialists, it still tends not to 'think European', or engage very much in Europe. This situation is partly a matter of Brown's political preferences (Buller, Chapter 13), partly an organizational matter, and partly a prioritization given to global economic institutions within the department.

These attempts to re-position the UK government on Europe have led to changes in the constellation of key actors at the core of UK European policy making. As we have seen, the office of Prime Minister and the role of his advisers on Europe have been enhanced. The increase in the size of the COES, the raising of the status of its leading officials and its focus on No. 10, have extended the prime minister's ability to act on EU-related matters. Also, Blair's more executive, almost presidential, style has meant that the secretariat has been able to speak with more authority to other departments – except the Treasury. These developments provided additional clout to the already established position of prime minister as lead player in relation to European policy making, brought about by the creation of the European Council in 1975. The bilateral aspect of the step change initiative has encouraged cabinet ministers to undertake more regular and purposeful interaction with their European counterparts.

Given the changes in position, how have these actors responded by exploiting the opportunities available to them? A number of initiatives have been launched by the UK government at EU level, notably on such policies as labour market reform, economic competitiveness, defence and asylum. In terms of bilateral ministerial visits, they were initially skewed towards France and Germany with 70 and 88 ministerial visits respectively in the year 1999–2000 (FCO, 1999, 2000, 2001). In the following year, more was done to exploit contacts with Spain and Belgium (who held the EU Presidency). The 'step change', bilateral programme also contained some innovative features which adapt established European ways of working with an emphasis on networking and coalition building. Notably, the least active core department in terms of ministerial contacts was the Treasury. So, the overall picture of the actual exploitation of the opportunities envisaged in the step change programme has been uneven. Generally though, significant new opportunities for actors have been created and extra resources put in place. However, it is noteworthy that, by 2004, explicit references to the step change programme were no longer evident in government documents (FCO, 2004). The performance of the programme is no longer evaluated because it is deemed to have successfully raised the government's European diplomacy to a new level.

Beyond the inner core of UK European policy makers, the key changes have affected both organizational values and the distribution of formal authority. In relation to the former, all departments and government agencies have been asked by the prime minister to heighten awareness of European issues across all levels and sections. This is a continuation of previous initiatives aimed at mainstreaming EU business across central government. There is much variation across departments, but overall the degree of European awareness increased over the period. This is in part a product of the slow 'socializing' effect that extended involvement with the EU has brought into play over three decades of membership. In part it is also a product of the deliberate post-1997 effort by the Blair government to inculcate across the board more awareness of matters European. Amongst departments that have significantly enhanced their engagement has been the Home Office, which has been increasingly drawn in on matters concerning immigration, asylum and combating organized crime.

The key change in formal authority affecting the outer circle of UK EU policy makers has been a change in responsibility for nearly all domestic policies that have a significant EU content. Policy development in these areas has, since July 1999, had to accommodate the input of the new political authorities established in the devolved territories, especially Wales and Scotland (see also Smith, Chapter 5). Although relations with the EU are reserved to the UK as the member state government, responsibility for implementation of EU requirements falls upon the devolved administrations within their territories. This arrangement has been interpreted as requiring that the devolveds should be involved in the formulation as well as the implementation of policy. In effect, the basic structure of the state has been changed creating a potentially more varied interpretation of 'national' European interests and objectives (Bache and Jordan, Chapter 1; Bulmer *et al.*, 2002; Burch *et al.*, 2005; Fairbrass, Chapter 9). As a result, the European policy making process in the UK has become less self-contained within the central state. And though the sources of change have been domestic, a greater alignment has emerged in regard to the pattern of governance in other EU states.

Conclusion

In this chapter we have argued that the period prior to 1997 was one of gradual adaptation of UK central government to EU membership. The process of change was incremental, in response to EU developments and consistent with normal patterns of business in Whitehall. However, the pervasive nature of EU business meant that, by the time of John Major's government, all ministries had established European offices and the work of a substantial set of civil servants was affected by EU business. We believe that this process brought with it a quiet revolution. It was quiet because the political context was more often than not divided on European integration. And when it was not divided, for instance during the Thatcher era, the general policy towards European integration was one of reluctance. Thus, governments had no inclination to draw attention to the changes that had occurred and were pretty reluctant to embrace new opportunities.

However, the widening of the impact of EU policy across the breadth of central government had quietly transformed the pattern of governance in the UK (Bulmer and Burch, 2000a). The FCO no longer monopolizes international diplomacy. Important parts of British policy, notably agriculture and trade, had to fit in with EU commitments. A varying proportion of developments in many policy areas were subject to an agenda that could not be controlled by British government departments or the Cabinet. Almost all ministers and a sizeable proportion of officials were engaged in EU negotiations, with the resultant need to travel or otherwise communicate with their counterparts in partner governments and the EU institutions. Developments such as these amounted to a transformation in the conduct of UK central government and policy making. This process of Europeanization happened gradually and cumulatively, yet the sum of the small steps and adjustments involved has amounted, over time, to a significant change in central government. A notable feature of the UK approach was that it was much more geared to the task of reception than projection.

Post 1997, the gradual, cumulative pattern of Europeanization has been accelerated and encouraged by a steady push from the top. Beyond the amplification of past trends, we argue that there has been a significant change in the handling and approach to European policy making during the Blair government, in that Labour has been able, at ministerial level and throughout government, to take a more directive and strategic approach

to Europe. This has been possible because, compared with previous administrations, there have been fewer deep divisions within the party leadership over Europe. Consequently, strategic considerations concerning Europe
have been developed at ministerial level across government without deep
discord. The significant qualification to this observation is that the Chancellor and the Treasury are a kind of *domaine réservé* in this process. Nevertheless, the Blair government has improved the UK's projection capacity,
notably through the step change programme. The result is a better balance
between the two responses and a more proactive agenda shaping approach
to the EU.

As noted in Chapter 2, one of the difficulties with Europeanization is
isolating the flow of causation. A key problem is the fact that the 'object' –
in this case UK central government – has not been static. Indeed, over the
period of nearly half a century that we are concerned with in this chapter,
there have been many changes that have been quite unrelated to Europe.
Individual governments have reconstructed Whitehall ministries, direct rule
was introduced in Northern Ireland, new public management techniques
and executive agencies have been introduced and so on.

This problem of disentangling cause and effect becomes particularly acute
under the Blair government. On the one hand, it has sought to increase
its engagement in the EU while at the same time the pace of reform and
change within the EU has accelerated: so far, two sets of treaty reform,
another seeking endorsement, plus the largest enlargement in the history
of integration. On the other hand, domestically the UK constitution has
been subject to multiple reforms including: devolution and decentralization, independence for the Bank of England, electoral reform (notably in
devolved authorities and for the European Parliament), incorporation of the
European Convention on Human Rights (ECHR), reform of the House of
Lords, modernization of the House of Commons, and the introduction of a
Freedom of Information Act.

Clearly in these latter instances, there are a number of primary and direct
causes, but European considerations are either a significant background
factor or one of a number of direct influences helping to shape them. We
have also noted that the pattern of Europeanization in the UK central government involves adapting the requirements of EU participation to Whitehall's
ways of doing things. Here, the Europeanizing effect is direct, but is trans-
lated into member state practices (a feature that has been noted in the
case of many other member states (Olsen, 2002)). The slogan seems to be:
'Europeanization yes, but on our terms'.

We have also seen a kind of secondary form of Europeanization as, for
example, through the constitutional reform agenda noted above. Of these,
devolution resonates with the emergence of multi-level governance in the
EU; the member states have been enjoined to introduce a common electoral
system for European elections; Bank of England independence fulfilled a

requirement for a later step to joining the euro; and the ECHR is a European construct, even if it falls under the Council of Europe in Strasbourg rather than being part of the EU itself. In all these instances, changes with a direct domestic origin have nevertheless brought the UK closer to European patterns, while European influences have played a part in the development of proposals, but, as it were, at second remove. We suggest that any attempt to understand Europeanization has to take into account these indirect, second-order and background effects.

Our use of reception and projection has also raised matters concerning top-down approaches to Europeanization (Chapter 2). Clearly there is a closely integrated two-way process at work. Moreover, the 'bilateralism' that is part of the step change programme indicates an important horizontal dimension to Europeanization as a top-down process from the EU level to member states. The stress on bi-lateralism – that is, negotiation between member states – for purposes of managing and shaping policy initiatives is generally recognized as an important aspect of a successful member state's contribution to EU policy making. Thus, from the vantage point of the member state, the EU level needs to be understood in two senses: as covering the universes of activities encompassed in (a) inter-governmental relations outside the formal institutions of the EU and (b) the EU institutions themselves. It seems to us that Europeanizing effects might be understood more broadly as those that may emanate from member states collectively, or from a group of them, as well as from the supranational structures and processes of the EU.

Finally, if the potential for projecting the UK in Europe is presently greater than ever before – Whitehall personnel are more aware and more engaged, and there is leadership and a strategic vision of the UK's place in Europe – has it led to more effective policy outcomes? This is a question posed in the introduction to this book and, in the case of UK European policy making, it is a tricky question to answer. The step change programme was presented as a ten-year project, and thus, at the time of writing, it is still early to judge. In any case, measuring the effects of diplomacy and enhanced networking is notoriously difficult. Certainly the impact on British public attitudes to Europe seems to have been marginal. These still remain a significant drag on any efforts to pursue an innovative and leading approach in Brussels. The impact of the UK position on the Iraq war on alliances and contacts with other EU member states, along with the euro retreat of June 2003 (see Buller, Chapter 13), has tended to confirm the traditional perception of the UK as a reluctant partner. Nevertheless, a number of initiatives have been successfully launched by UK government at EU level, notably on labour market reform, economic competitiveness, defence, and agricultural and rural policy. There is now more of a UK fingerprint on EU initiatives in these policy areas than was previously the case. In sum, the Blair government has certainly brought about a change in activity and purpose, and this has contributed to some notable policy successes. However, the great contribution of the Blair government to the development of UK European policy making has been to highlight and augment the skills of effective projection as one of the keys to successfully making an impact in the EU.

Notes

From 1996 to 2005 we conducted over 100 interviews with serving and retired UK officials and ministers. Our initial research (1996–98) was under the ESRC's Whitehall Programme, award no. L 124251001. We are grateful to the ESRC, our interviewees, and to members of the UACES study group and ESRC seminar on the Europeanization of British politics for their comments on earlier drafts. This chapter draws on part of the empirical material used in an article which applies a specific causal model of Europeanization to UK central government (see Bulmer and Burch, 2005).

1. The core executive comprises, in institutional terms, '... cabinet, cabinet committees, Cabinet Office, Prime Minister's Office, parts of the Treasury, the major government law offices and parts of the machinery which manages the executive's immediate support base, the governing party in Parliament' (Burch and Holliday, 1996: 1–2). It is best regarded as constituting the hub of a number of task networks. These extend out into other parts of central government as appropriate. The EU network is one of these. For an examination of the operation of the core executive in terms of the networks centred on it see Burch and Holliday (1996).

4
The Foreign and Commonwealth Office

David Allen and Tim Oliver

Introduction

The Foreign and Commonwealth Office (FCO) has been dealing with European integration for over fifty years and has, like the British government in general, demonstrated a mix of enthusiasm and suspicion regarding its evolution. Such a long and close involvement has inevitably had an impact upon the way the FCO operates, the way it sees the world, and how others perceive and work with it. This chapter will concentrate on the impact of European Union (EU) membership on the FCO and on its role in the making and implementation of British foreign policy. Specifically, we assess the extent to which these activities have been Europeanized.

When applying the definition of Europeanization adopted in this volume to the FCO, we need to consider the impact of domestic, societal and constitutional changes, as well as transformations in the international and European system such as Britain's relative decline as a world power since 1945. It is also important to recall that the FCO is not a department confined to London or indeed the UK, but that it is also a complex system of overseas posts and diplomatic networks.

We will begin by examining the history of the FCO by focusing upon its interactions with European integration, recognizing that this has been only one of a number of key challenges for the FCO in recent years. We will examine the organization of the FCO and compare the situation today with the period when Britain first joined the EU in 1973. The current structure of the FCO reflects a cumulative adjustment to change over a considerable period of time, although the pace of this change has quickened over the period of membership. As we will see, the FCO's position within British central government has been both enhanced and challenged by European integration.

In the remainder of this chapter, we will explore several arguments. First, that the FCO has experienced a relative decline in control over Britain's policy making towards the EU. Second, that the patterns of adaptation shown by the FCO have been in line with the wider patterns of adaptation shown throughout Whitehall that is, major change has been kept to a minimum with an emphasis on adaptation of existing procedures (see Bulmer and Burch, Chapter 3). Third, that the FCO has been subject to a wide variety of pressures for change, of which Europeanization is only one. Fourth, that the development of European Political Cooperation (EPC) and now the Common Foreign and Security Policy (CFSP) has given the FCO a particular area of competence over which it alone has expertise, and that this has compensated to some extent for the loss of influence over general domestic and European issues. The FCO has had to face the challenge of sharing its previously exclusive control of Britain's external relations with subnational authorities and domestic departments, as well as supranational organizations such as the EU – a change which reflects the continuing 'blurring of the boundaries' between the domestic and the foreign (see Hocking 1999; Hocking and Spence 2005).

History, development and structure of the FCO

The history and role of the FCO in the making and implementation of British foreign policy has been told in a number of places and warrants only a brief reprise here (see Wallace 1975; Clarke 1992; Dickie 1992, 2004). The Foreign Service can be traced back to 1479 and the Foreign Office to 1782. Until the mid-1960s, the UK chose to handle its imperial and post-imperial relationships separately from its dealings with the rest of the world. The Colonial Office, the India Office, the Dominions Office and the Commonwealth Relations Office all slowly merged over time to form the Commonwealth Office and, in 1968, the Foreign and Commonwealth offices themselves merged to form the present FCO. The present Diplomatic Service was established in 1965, amalgamating the Foreign Service, the Commonwealth Service and the Trade Commission Service (Clarke 1992: 77).

While this chapter does not specifically examine international development policy, it is worth noting that the administration of British aid has a complex history of semi-detachment from the FCO. Overseas aid was traditionally administered by the Foreign Office, but in 1964 the Labour Government created a separate Ministry of Overseas Development headed by a cabinet minister. Since then Conservative governments have chosen to handle aid through an Overseas Development Administration under the overall control of the FCO whilst Labour governments preferred a separate ministry. In 1997, the incoming Labour government maintained this pattern by establishing the Department for International Development (DFID) headed by Claire Short, whose post was granted a full seat in the Cabinet.

The Foreign Office and now the FCO have always held a central role in the management of Britain's external policies. This role has been challenged by the relative decline of Britain's position in the international system and by the changing nature of international relations which has seen a shifting agenda, the growth of interdependence and multilateral attempts to manage that interdependence. Despite these trends the FCO has managed to retain a central role in the shaping and management of Britain's external relations. The most significant example today of Britain's involvement in multilateralism is, of course, its membership of the EU. Faced with the contradictory pressures of rising demands and diminishing resources, the FCO has firmly resisted 'external' attempts to reform it, whilst demonstrating an effective willingness and ability to make the necessary internal adaptations. It is a measure of the FCO's adaptive ability that the Diplomatic Service has successfully retained its separate and unique status within the structure of British government and that successive Foreign Secretaries have preserved their senior position within the British Cabinet hierarchy. The position of Foreign Secretary remains one of the most important posts in the British government, although the particular importance of the relationship between Prime Minister and Foreign Secretary has been modified in recent years by the growing power of the Prime Minister's office in Downing Street which is itself partly a consequence of Britain's involvement with the EU (see Owen 2003).

The general expansion in the number of states in the international system has been a particular challenge to the FCO's determination to preserve Britain's international status through retention of a global representation. The FCO managed this in response to the proliferation of states from decolonization in the 1960s and 1970s; the new challenges posed by the emergence of new states in the post-Soviet world of the 1990s has proved more testing and the FCO has struggled to keep up with its major European rivals. In 2003, Britain maintained 233 posts of which 153 are embassies (compared with just 136 countries in 1968), whilst Germany maintained 208 posts and France 279 posts (see FCO 2003a). In April 1999, the FCO had a total of 5635 UK-based staff, of whom 2295 were serving overseas (whilst Germany had 3361 and France had 5669 staff); although these figures partly reflect a continuing British tradition of, and preference for, employing quite high numbers of local staff in its missions abroad (see FCO 1999). Demands on overseas posts have grown whilst the increased ease and speed of both travel and communications has raised contradictory doubts about the purpose of, and need for, the current structure of overseas posts (Riordan 2003).

As a result of such changes the FCO has been the subject of a number of formal inquiries and reviews. The Plowden (1964), Duncan (1969) and Berrill (1977) reports all made recommendations that the FCO initially resisted but eventually accepted to a degree. More recently, the 1992 Structural Review, the 1995 Fundamental Expenditure Review, the 1996 Senior Management

Review and the work that led to the recently published FCO Strategy Document (FCO 2003b) were all conducted 'in house', albeit with the participation of outside consultants, and produced recommendations that the FCO has seemed more inclined to adopt. The latter reviews were partly occasioned by a self-perceived need to rethink certain aspects of the FCO's work (its staffing policies in the face of such demands as racial and sexual equality of opportunity, better career development, family issues and security) partly by the need to find further financial savings and partly by the general trend of governmental reform.

The FCO continues to be led by a Permanent Under-Secretary (PUS), who is responsible both for the administration of the FCO and the work of overseas posts through a Board of Management and for strategic policy advice to ministers through a Policy Advisory Board. In recent years, the work of the PUS has become increasingly focused on the management of the FCO and its diplomatic offices around the world. The post of Political Director, which was initially created so that Britain could play its part in the EU's system of EPC, is now effectively the top policy advisory post. Whereas twenty years ago the PUS would accompany the Foreign Secretary or Prime Minister on their travels overseas, it is now usually the Political Director who clocks up the air miles whilst the PUS stays in London. The specific position of Political Director can be explained in terms of Europeanization in that the FCO willingly adapted its management structure so as to effectively participate in the EPC. This adaptation has led to spillover whereby the Political Director now plays a larger role than perhaps originally intended. However, the different roles played by the PUS and Political Director are the result of both EU membership and other factors, especially the need for improved management within the FCO.

The basic FCO unit remains the geographical desk within a geographical Department and Command. This has come under pressure due to the considerable growth in functional departments in response to the 'internationalization' and 'Europeanization' of a number of traditional domestic issues and to the growth of multilateral fora. Despite this, the FCO has resisted suggestions that, as a multi-functional organization, it should reorganize itself around its functions, although in the case of EU membership this is now changing. The Fundamental Expenditure Review of 1995 argued for the preservation of a structure based on regional and multilateral organization partly because of the high estimated cost of restructuring the FCO and partly because of the continuing logic of geographical specialization. The FCO believes that its knowledge of specific countries and its development of bilateral relationships that span across a number of specific functions adds significant value to the advancement and coordination of British interests. If the FCO were to be reorganized along functional lines then the fear would be that a number of functions could then be 'hived off' to domestic ministries along the lines suggested by the 1977 Central Policy Review Staff (CPRS) Report. Peter Hain

(2001), when a Foreign Office Minister, published a pamphlet in which he advocated the scrapping of departments based on geographical divisions in favour of 'issues' departments dealing with subjects such as human rights, the environment and conflict prevention. To the extent that the 'desks' for other EU member states have recently been removed from a geographical command and placed within functional (EU) departments then Hain's proposals seem to be gaining acceptance, at least as far as the management of European multilateral and bilateral policies are concerned.

Within the FCO, the problems raised by the proliferation of functional and multilateral commands cutting across the geographical divisions is best illustrated by reference to arrangements for dealing with the countries of Western Europe and the EU. Across Whitehall, the coordination of British foreign policy is no longer exclusively controlled by the FCO. Long gone are the days when all contacts with the outside world were handled by the FCO acting as some form of 'gatekeeper'. Today, just as the FCO has sprouted a number of functional departments that in many ways 'shadow' the work of Home Departments, so, in turn, most Home Departments have developed their own international and European sections (see Bulmer and Burch, Chapter 3). The FCO continues to play a major role in the coordination of all these different aspects of Britain's external policy but the system also recognizes that, with reference to a number of cross-cutting issues, the FCO is not the unchallenged sole determinant of the overall British interest but merely an 'interested' department amongst many others. In these cases, the Cabinet system and the work of the Cabinet Office provide consistency and coherence. At the very top of the decision-making process, the British Cabinet is meant to be collegial and the doctrine of collective responsibility pertains, although this idea has been regularly challenged (Owen 2003). In practice many decisions are delegated down to Cabinet Committees of which the Committee on Defence and Overseas Policy (DOP) and the Committee on the Intelligence Services both chaired by the prime minister and the Sub-Committee on European Questions ((E) DOP), chaired by the Foreign Secretary, are the most important in relation to foreign policy (see Blair 2001).

As well as re-emphasizing, reinforcing and, where appropriate in Europe and South Asia, reorganizing, its geographic Commands, the FCO has also sought to implement a policy of devolving both financial and management responsibility down through Commands to departments and to overseas posts in line with similar developments elsewhere in the government service. Attempts have been made to improve the role of policy planning in the FCO (partly in association with other EU foreign ministries), to better associate the work of the research analysts with their customer departments and to reorganize the management structure so that those responsible for policy planning and advice and those responsible for the management of resources are more closely associated with each others work. This latter objective has been partly achieved by devolution and partly by unifying the Policy Advisory Board and the Board of Management and strengthening their links with the Commands as well as their 'visibility' to the rest of the FCO. A number of these reforms can be tracked around the Foreign Ministries of the other EU member states but whether this can be described as Europeanization is a debatable point.

The FCO has also been forced to take into account the growing interest of the wider public in foreign policy both in the UK and abroad. The FCO has been criticized for being slow to react to public opinion especially with regard to EU issues. Similarly the FCO has been heavily criticized for attempts to cut the budget and restrict the activities of both the BBC World Service and the British Council at a time when the importance of this type of 'public diplomacy' was becoming more rather than less significant. However, the FCO now appears to be paying more attention to Parliament, the wider British public and the public opinions of those countries that Britain seeks to influence. The Fundamental Expenditure Review devoted a whole section to the growing importance of public diplomacy and to the need for the FCO to develop a public diplomacy strategy statement as well as individual country strategies. Indeed, the FCO now has a Public Diplomacy Department and, in EUD (I), (European Union Division) a Public Diplomacy Section. At a recent seminar of all the UK's present and former ambassadors to the EU, the present incumbent and his immediate predecessor both commented on their changing roles, with much less time being spent in the Council of Ministers and much more time being spent on more traditional ambassadorial work with interest groups and members of the European Parliament (Menon 2004).

It is easy to forget that overseas diplomatic missions also cater to the needs of national citizens residing or visiting overseas, a situation that with the growing number of tourists and ease of working abroad (especially within the EU) has placed considerable pressures on the FCO and its overseas missions. Such pressures have already led some EU member states, including the UK, to share diplomatic assets and support. However, for the UK and the FCO, the experience of handling the crisis of the 9/11 terrorists attacks was almost entirely British in outlook and learning. This mainly stemmed from New York being the one city in the world where every state has at least some form of diplomatic representation and therefore some means of dealing with its nationals in that city when an emergency occurred. The experiences of the British Consulate in New York essentially helped to write the guidelines on how to deal with any future such atrocities. Dealing with incidents such as Bali and Istanbul bomb blasts, the 2004 Indian Ocean tsunami and Hurricane Katrina have brought into the equation the opportunities for help and assistance from the EU and member states. But in each case the UK response has been essentially British rather than collectively European.

Some of the changes noted above are the result of Thatcherite management reforms. Indeed, during Mrs Thatcher's period in office, the FCO was subjected to a continuous level of criticism by a dominant prime minister who became increasingly interested, as all long-serving prime ministers tend to, in playing a major role in foreign affairs (Hill 1996: 71–77; Craddock 1997). Supported by Charles Powell, her Private Secretary for Overseas Affairs and former FCO career official, Mrs Thatcher's problems with Europe, which she associated with the pro-European leanings of the FCO, led her to contemplate, but in fact never to seriously implement, the possibility of building up Downing Street's foreign policy capabilities as a counter to the central role played by the FCO. This would, especially from the FCO's viewpoint, create something akin to a US-style National Security Council.

John Major showed no real inclination to side-step either the Foreign Secretary or the FCO in the handling of foreign policy in general or in relation to the EU specifically. In April 1998, Mr Blair rejected proposals put forward by some of his colleagues for creating a powerful Prime Minister's Department based upon a reconstructed Cabinet Office (Preston and Parker 1998). However, there was a small controversy over the revelation that the Prime Minister had appointed several overseas personal envoys (Lords Levy, Paul and Ahmed). Press comment saw these appointments as indicative of 'an American style of foreign policy' (Watt 2000) and noted the fact that these envoys were unaccountable to Parliament and could be seen to be part of a process that by-passed the FCO. When Mr Blair was returned to office in 2001, however, he did take significant steps to enhance the role of Downing Street over both EU policy and foreign policy towards the rest of the world. He chose to move two of the Cabinet Office Secretariats (dealing with Overseas and Security policy and with the EU) into Downing Street under the control of his two foreign policy advisors – Sir Stephen Wall (ex head of UKRep) and Sir David Manning (ex head of the UK Delegation to Nato).

The movement of the European and Overseas and Defence Secretariats from the Cabinet Office to Downing Street has ratcheted up the role played by the prime minister. This in part reflects the interest shown by the current prime minister in foreign affairs and his 'presidential style'. At the same time it also stems from much longer-term patterns such as the growing number and importance of EU summits in giving direction to the Union, the growing political links between European political parties, and the need to address European issues at a national and party level. For the FCO, this has brought mixed results. There have been repeated complaints about the FCO being sidelined from policy making on issues such as the Iraq war, the EU Constitution, relations with Washington and the general overall strategy and justifications behind British foreign policy (see Kampfner 2003; Owen 2003). The perceived need for overall strategy from Downing Street has provided an impetus to give direction but has usually failed to provide follow up with the necessary detail. This has led to complaints from departments, including the FCO, that are required to implement often poorly thought-out strategies. A letter to the *Financial Times* on 26 April 2004 from 52 retired British diplomats attacking the prime minister's position in the Middle East was one of the most visible signs of such unease amongst the diplomatic service.

The FCO and the challenge of Europe

The previous sections demonstrate that the FCO has been under continual pressure to adapt to external changes. The extent to which the influence of the EU can be disentangled from the other pressures requires careful analysis. In this section we map in more detail some of the areas where the EU has had the most profound effect upon the FCO.

As noted above, participation in the EU has focused attention on the blurring of the boundaries between the domestic and the foreign. A considerable amount of EU business is conducted by officials from the home civil service working in domestic ministries such as the Department of Trade and Industry (DTI) and the Department for the Environment, Food and Agriculture (DEFRA) (see Bulmer and Burch, Chapters 3; Jordan, Chapter 15), and also others such as the Home Office and the Treasury (see Buller, Chapter 13). Where most dealings with European and foreign governments were once conducted through the FCO and Britain's embassies, now there are direct dealings between domestic ministries and their opposite numbers in the other EU member states (Smith 1999: 234–35). This has highlighted a number of issues of both coordination and control that have challenged the FCO's dominant role in the identification and pursuit of British interests overseas, or at least within the EU (Bender 1991; Spence 1993; Blair 1998).

This growing domestic–European interface and the challenges it poses to the FCO are best understood by recalling that proposals have been regularly put forward for a separate European Ministry. The FCO has always resisted such proposals. Indeed, successive Foreign Secretaries have shown little enthusiasm for suggestions that the present Minister of State for Europe be elevated to cabinet rank. The FCO has argued that a Foreign Secretary stripped of his or her EU responsibilities and prerogatives would suffer an enormous loss of political stature on the world stage. Furthermore, removing the EU from the UK department of state responsible for external affairs would also represent a major political and symbolic change that would touch the nerve of national sovereignty and the Westminster model of British central government. Nevertheless, the idea has been raised several times (Macintyre 1999) and was also discussed within the Convention on the Future of Europe, with the suggestion that senior cabinet ministers reporting directly to prime ministers might be permanently based in Brussels and charged with sustaining the authority of the European Council. Proposals to transfer the management (as opposed to the coordination and strategic consideration) of EU business to the Cabinet Office or to Downing Street produce a similarly negative response from the FCO.

While such developments have challenged the FCO, it has also gained a little from the centralizing tendencies that EU membership has encouraged: namely the rise of 'an informal, yet powerful elite comprising Number 10, the FCO, the Cabinet Office and the UK permanent representation (UKRep)' (Smith 1999: 233). However, the British system of coordination, whilst giving the FCO a major role, is also designed to ensure that where necessary the FCO is treated as just another interested department and not as the sole determinant of the UK national interest (see Bulmer and Burch, Chapter 3). The role of the European Secretariat, which arranges, chairs and records the results of interdepartmental discussions at all levels (Blair 1998: 161–67), ensures that the FCO cannot claim sole ownership or authorship of EU policy. The Cabinet Office is also responsible for the process whereby Parliament is informed and consulted about EU legislation. The FCO is usually represented in the European Secretariat, but only with one official in a team of about seven – the rest coming from the home civil service.

However, one has to be careful about making too much of the restraints on the FCO's role in EU policy making and coordination. The European Secretariat remains quite small, although large by Cabinet Office standards, and it relies to some extent on FCO support. Similarly whilst UKRep is indeed an unusual embassy, with more than 50 per cent of its staff being drawn from the home civil service, the head of UKRep, the Permanent Representative, has always been an ambassador from the FCO and the FCO retains the right to oversee its instructions. The position of Permanent Representative is an extremely powerful one with the incumbent responsible for the day-to-day management of EU business in Brussels as well as usually playing a pivotal role in Treaty negotiations within the Intergovernmental Conference framework (Menon 2004). The very style of EU negotiations and policy making places the Permanent Representative and UKRep at the heart of an intensive and ever changing dialogue with London. The Permanent Representative additionally gets to return to London each Friday to participate in EU policy making meetings within both the FCO and the Cabinet Office – an opportunity resented by some home-based officials and envied by some other ambassadors.

Thus, despite the constraints mentioned above and elsewhere in this chapter, the FCO has succeeded in retaining a significant role within the UK's system for managing relations with the EU. Because of its competent handling of EU business, the FCO has earned the respect of, and worked smoothly with, other government departments. It has been quite relaxed about allowing other departments to get on with EU business that clearly sit within their exclusive competence. The FCO has considered and rejected the idea of charging other departments for the work that its overseas posts carry out for them; it has instructed those departments, such as European Union

Department (Internal) who 'face' domestic ministries, to consult with them about their requirements vis-à-vis FCO posts overseas and it has sought to maintain its position, if not of supremacy, then at least of *primus inter pares* in the overall direction of British foreign policy. Although Smith (1999: 234) argues that 'as EU business increases, the FCO and the Cabinet Office are losing control and departments are increasingly conducting business with the Commission and other member states directly' on important EU matters, the FCO retains a significant degree of influence.

The recent reorganizations detailed above have seen EU matters and bilateral relations with individual EU member states pioneer a movement away from a geographical structure to one where they are handled within the same Command – the EU Command. In 2005 it had three departments (External, Internal and Eastern Adriatic) that report to the FCO Director for 'Mediterranean Europe, Bilateral, Resources' and in turn to the Director General European Union. CFSP currently comes under the EU External department, but still provides a secretariat for the FCO Political Director, who has chief operational responsibility for the UK's input into the CFSP process. The European Command brings together all the departments and desks dealing with Europe, EU member states and non-members. As a result, most elements of European policy have now been brought within the same arrangements inside the FCO: a change reflected more widely across the FCO's structure.

Another significant change has been the increasing number of FCO staff working or having some contact with EU issues as a result of the impact of CFSP, the growing scale of European coordination at overseas diplomatic missions and the increased scope of European policy. In particular, the European Fast Stream programme within Whitehall has provided the FCO with a constant supply of diplomats with an excellent working knowledge of the EU. This has not, however, been confined to just the FCO: a large number of civil servants in other departments have also gained valuable European experience through this route. Such is the scale of the 'Europeanists' in the FCO that they have been seen to supplant the 'Arabists', traditionally seen as holding the dominant position in the FCO. This has created something, as one UKRep diplomat noted, of a 'creative tension' within the FCO, and has not gone unnoticed by those who regard the FCO as too pro-European.

However, it is not just Euro-sceptics who voice their concerns about the growing imbalance within the FCO towards the EU. Some diplomats from posts outside the EU point to the continuing high number of resources allocated to European posts in comparison to those allocated to missions outside the EU. This in part reflects the growth of 'mini-Whitehall' style British diplomatic postings in EU member states where domestic, European and international affairs merge more so than beyond the EU and require a larger allocation of resources. This is not to say that overseas missions beyond the EU have been immune from such a process or indeed from Europeanization. The continuing development of the CFSP has resulted in overseas posts holding regular coordination meetings with the representations of other member states. However, there exist differing levels of enthusiasm for such meetings, with one senior British diplomat arguing that they were akin to a social gathering of most Western allies that was only notable because of the absence of the Americans. Some also question the value of holding such EU coordination meetings (over 2000 a year between diplomats of the EU Missions at the United Nations) when this time could be better spent lobbying and completing other essential diplomatic work. Others argue that the real work is completed by the larger member states such as the UK, France and Germany, and cannot be considered as truly representing the whole EU given the limited representations of many smaller EU Members combined with the circumscribed role of the European Commission's external offices. However, the momentum within the FCO and other member states' diplomatic services towards a coherent EU diplomatic effort is aimed at inculcating a natural reflex to work with one another and the EU representations. The challenge for the FCO lies in ensuring that this does not result in pressure to merge representations. In particular, ideas to create an EU Permanent Seat on the UN Security Council have been fiercely resisted by the UK and the FCO. The FCO was also not too distressed to see the demise of the Constitutional Treaty, which proposed a European External Action Service (EEAS).

Europeanization might therefore be seen as having catalysed a situation in which the changing nature of foreign policy combined with budgetary and management changes to force the FCO to adopt a more functional structure rather than one based on geography. At the same time, the FCO has sought to retain some aspects of its geographical structure, and in turn ward off other government departments attempting to coordinate these functional areas, by preserving the pivotal role of the ambassador in overseas posts. Thus, in the name of coherence and consistency, the FCO has successfully defended some form of 'gatekeeper' role both at home and abroad, even though the participants in the foreign policy process are increasingly drawn from a number of non-FCO sources. Again, this is most clearly seen in the key roles that UKRep plays in the overall management of British policy towards the EU (Clarke 1992: 102–104; Dickie 2004: 122–24).

The aforementioned FCO 'Strategy Report' (FCO 2003b) was an attempt to better deploy the FCO's resources. On the one hand it demonstrated how the UK has shown due significance to the role of the EU by committing key resources to it, and on the other hand it showed how the UK has sought to retain the capability to operate as an independent actor in the wider international system. The strategy document suggests that whilst the FCO may well have experienced Europeanization, it is not necessarily either integrating or converging with the foreign ministries of the other EU member states. The same might also be said of the relationship with Washington, to which the document also attaches great significance. At the same time, the Strategy Report – while discussing the operation of the FCO – does explore the main foreign policy concerns of the UK, and in this the document shares many similarities with the European Union's own strategy document, 'A Secure Europe in a Better World: The European Security Strategy' (European Council 2003). Both emphasize the importance of effective multilateralism for tackling problems ranging from international terrorism and the spread of weapons of mass destruction (WMD) through to environmental crises and human rights abuses. The two documents share a great many similarities and while they share some areas in common with the National Security Strategy of the United States (White House 2002) the UK and EU documents seem to have more in common. This in part stems from the strong British input to the EU document and again returns us to the idea of Europeanization being a circular process. Indeed, the very emergence of the FCO's Strategy Document at about the same time as the EU's Security Strategy report might indicate a move away from the pragmatism that has been seen to characterize UK foreign policy making to a more strategic approach.

Indeed, one area of possible adaptation, which previous governments have resisted, concerns developments in the EU and the institutional consequences of pursuing CFSP. The British government, despite finding it increasingly difficult to devote the necessary resources to its foreign policy machine, has not been tempted by the European option of pooling resources – particularly those overseas – although Britain and France (outside the EU framework) announced plans in 1999 to work more closely together in Africa (Peel 1999). Proposals to establish joint EU embassies and eventually to establish a full-blown European diplomatic service (Allen 2004) have been viewed with suspicion by Britain. In March 1999, the Foreign Secretary proposed the establishment of a permanent committee of deputy political directors in Brussels to steer and reinforce the CFSP. The idea of this committee was clearly to keep control of the CFSP firmly in the hands of national foreign ministries by boosting the Council of Ministers and the Council Secretariat rather than enhancing the Commission's external powers. This British proposal led in time to the creation of the Political and Security Committee (COPS), which is a good example of what has been described as the 'Brusselsization' of the CFSP process (Allen 1998). This is also a good example of the circular nature of Europeanization as, having advocated the establishment in Brussels of something like the COPS, the FCO now has to adjust to its existence!

Conclusions

The key problem when examining the Europeanization of the FCO is that it operates simultaneously at the national, European and international levels. It is not easy to discern the process of Europeanization against such a background. That said, there are areas where Europeanization is manifest. These include: the structure of the FCO in terms of both the Political Director and the PUS; the management of desks for EU member states and the growing importance of the European command; the growth in the role of UKRep and other 'mini-Whitehalls' in Brussels; the increased prominence of 'Europeanists' in the FCO; the EU coordination work in overseas posts; the more prominent role played by the PM and Downing Street; and the FCO's involvement in the development of the CFSP.

Such developments have not occurred overnight but rather over decades. Indeed, it is essential to recall that the FCO has played a central role in how the UK has approached European integration since before the signing of the Treaty of Rome. The FCO has generally developed responses that resemble 'fine-tuning' rather than radical reform. In turn, these have enabled the FCO to retain a central position in the making and implementation of British foreign policy. Indeed it has been argued that EU membership has provided opportunities for the FCO, along with the DTI and MAFF/DEFRA to 'increase their role and autonomy' (Smith 1999: 235).

The FCO has in turn responded reasonably well to change, regardless of whether the stimulus has come from within the UK, from Europe or from the wider international system. As we noted above, its basic tactic has been to strongly resist all attempts to impose reform from outside, whilst quietly making some fairly radical adjustments to the way that it organizes itself and carries out its work. The changes in the substance of foreign policy and the blurring of boundaries between foreign and domestic policy have forced the FCO to work much more closely with other government departments, within both Britain and abroad, and to organize itself for the demands of multilateral (of which the EU is the most significant) as well as bilateral diplomacy and negotiation. In this sense, Europeanization has been the most obvious sign that the FCO cannot play a traditional role of gatekeeper through which all contact with the outside world must flow; in turn undermining also the idea that the FCO is the only institution that understands the outside world. Such roles are now impossible. Indeed the FCO (and the rest of Whitehall) now accepts that such a role is no longer plausible. However, the FCO remains the central department for monitoring, managing and, with Downing Street and the Cabinet Office, coordinating the direction of British foreign, and to a lesser extent European, policy. In this sense, the EU has redefined the role of the FCO as a 'gatekeeper'.

All in all, the FCO has been neither a winner nor a loser from Europeanization. For the FCO has been given a greater field in which to engage while at the same time facing burgeoning pressures in terms of financial limits, global problems and domestic shifts, which are in part also fed by European pressures. Europeanization has both strengthened and weakened the foreign policy of the UK (see also Oliver and Allen, Chapter 12), and at the same time strengthened and weakened the role played by the FCO. If there is an element of decline in the role of the FCO in relations with EU member states then this should be understood as a relative decline given the emergence of the intensive multilateralism, bilateralism and transnationalism that is part and parcel of the politics of the EU and increasingly international relations in general.

As if to reflect the diverse levels at which the FCO operates and its wide variety of offices and outlooks, there is no single process by which Europeanization has occurred. Top-down Europeanization can apply to the position of the Political Director or the demand that Member States overseas diplomatic representations increase coordination. Indeed, the proposal in the currently defunct European Constitution to create a European Foreign Minister could bring considerable top-down pressures for greater co-operation. At the same time, the UK and the FCO have been involved in EPC and now CFSP from their inception (unlike Britain's relationship with the EU more generally) and have succeeded in uploading British concerns at the EU level. That the recent EU Security Strategy Document reflected British concerns is in part a result of it being written by a British diplomat (and former advisor to the PM) Robert Cooper – someone who could well be described as a Europeanized British diplomat. Indeed, British attempts to shape EU external relations have been a key element of British membership and of transatlantic relations. Here, though, we again see the limits to Europeanization as we must also account for the role of Nato and the United States. Indeed, the role of the United States (easily overlooked as a major military, economic and political power in Europe) has been central to British – and in turn FCO – approaches to CFSP and the EU; this has diminished the extent to which Europeanization of the FCO has been 'voluntary'.

There is one final impact of Europeanization that deserves mention. This chapter has raised some questions about the ability and willingness of the FCO to adjust to the general challenge of a transformed world and the specific challenge of EU membership. Our conclusion is that whilst the FCO has undoubtedly proved itself to be a foreign ministry capable of both responsiveness and flexibility (although Peter Hain, when an FCO Minister, talked of his 'frustration that the FCO machine is geared to responding to new circumstances mostly by incremental shifts in emphasis' (Watt 2001)), it has yet to be fully tested by, or called upon to serve, a government willing to adopt a consistently proactive EU policy. This in itself brings us to face one of the key questions about Europeanization: that it only takes place when the issues are not sufficiently important. If the Labour administration were to actively pursue the objectives as laid out in Robin Cook's 1997 mission statement of 'exercising leadership in the European Union, protecting the world's environment, countering the menace of drugs, terrorism and crime, spreading the values of human rights, civil liberties and democracy and using its status at the UN to secure more effective international action to keep the peace of the world and to combat poverty', then for some the FCO might find its organization and working practices more fundamentally tested than it has to date, with Europeanization being much more evident.

The FCO is often described as being akin to a 'Rolls Royce' of government machinery. Indeed, it remains a traditional, debonair and highly effective instrument and symbol of the British state and of British power. In part, this stems from European cooperation and the changes the FCO has adopted in part as a response to the EU. Indeed, like Rolls Royce, now owned by the German producer BMW, the FCO looks set to rely heavily for future success on a continuing investment in European cooperation.

5
Government in Scotland

James Smith

Introduction

The UK has traditionally been viewed as a centralized state in the sense that all forms of government below the national level are essentially creations of the centre. In this respect, the powers, status and nature of sub-national levels of government have been determined (and frequently modified) by the Westminster parliament. From 1885 until the late 1990s, the Scottish Office represented the key manifestation of sub-national government in Scotland. Although part of the Whitehall hierarchy, this was an unusual government department in the sense that it possessed a multi-functional policy remit and multi-departmental infrastructure, and had the ability to exercise limited degrees of territorial autonomy by way of 'tailoring' UK policies to accommodate Scottish concerns and circumstances (a similar model was later applied in both Wales and Northern Ireland). In 1999, this arrangement was superseded by a more fully developed form of political devolution, with the powers and responsibilities of the Scottish Office expanded and transferred to a new Scottish Executive operating within the framework of a directly elected Scottish Parliament.

This chapter examines how Europeanization came to impact upon the institutional basis of territorial government in Scotland across a thirty-year period. The focus is first upon the long-term impact of the EU on the Scottish Office (1973–1999) and then secondly the Scottish Executive (1999–). The aim throughout is to examine the trajectory and relative depth of Europeanization experienced in this particular case, and assess the extent to which Europeanization has in fact been influenced by not only the broader structural and procedural context of the UK administrative system as a whole, but also the territorial dimension that is, factors specific to Scotland. In so doing, it should also be possible to ascertain where this case-study sits in terms of broader theoretical definitions and conceptualizations of Europeanization set out in Chapter 2.

The Europeanization of government bureaucracy

According to the interpretations set out by Bache and Jordan in Chapter 2, the experiences of the Scottish Office and Scottish Executive can be most easily measured against a 'top-down' conceptualization of Europeanization, which sees downward pressures for change stemming from membership of the EU as the national (and sub-national) levels adapt to governing actors, processes and institutions framed at the European level.

A common thread running through existing analyses of the impact of Europeanization on government bureaucracy is one key observation: while membership of the EU has wrought immense changes across a range of policy competences within member states and has affected how that policy is formulated, discernible patterns of change and adaptation within departments and the procedural machinery of national government systems has been much more limited (Page and Wouters 1995; Bulmer and Burch 2001: 75; Jordan 2001b: 6; Olsen 2003: 524–525). Within this context, studies of Europeanization have found historical institutionalism to be a useful benchmark or, at the very least, a good analytical starting point (for example, Cowles *et al.* 2001; Knill 2001). Indeed, Bulmer and Burch (2001: 75) highlighted the attractions of such an approach, arguing that the lack of a deepseated modification to national government bureaucracy in the face of EU influences can be partly explained using historical institutional interpretations. These argue that national administrative structures and procedures are robust in the face of EU pressures. The Europeanization of bureaucracies might thus be seen to fit into the 'coercive-indirect' mould as any pressures for administrative change are resisted and any resulting change kept to the bare minimum necessary in order to accommodate European business.

However, this line of argument assumes that such Europeanizing pressures exist in the bureaucratic domain in the first place. In this respect, it may well be that the 'top-down' model of Europeanization is less persuasive when applied to the Europeanization of bureaucracy than to the Europeanization of policy. Indeed, it is entirely possible that the Europeanization of bureaucracy is more dynamic, variable and subject to inter- and intra-member state interaction than a wholly 'top-down' interpretation would otherwise suggest.

Either way, it seems important to consider a mixture of factors and variables in seeking a fuller understanding of how Europeanization has impacted upon domestic government bureaucracy. In effect, there seems much to support Jordan (2001b: 6) and his argument that the culture, values, history and role of individual actors within particular departments (what he terms the 'software' of policy making) may be just as important in shaping Europeanization outcomes as the formal rules, procedures and administrative structures (the 'hardware' of policy making). For Jordan (2003), the fact that the 'softer' factors have not been sufficiently taken into account would help to explain why those approaching Europeanization, particularly from historical institutionalist perspectives, have been able to suggest that changes to bureaucratic infrastructure have been limited by comparison with the impact on policy. Tellingly, however, even those deploying historical institutionalism are careful to qualify their approach and emphasize the need to accommodate cultural factors and the role of individual actors within a broader historical institutional framework (for example, see Bulmer and Burch 2001: 74; Knill 2001: 25–27).

This chapter seeks to assess the true nature and extent of bureaucratic and administrative forms of Europeanization. More specifically, the analysis will begin by offering a brief account of the most readily identifiable forms of bureaucratic Europeanization to have affected Scottish administration, that is, the impact in terms of 'hard' variables such as departmental structures and processes. The *extent* of this impact upon hard variables plus the nature and extent of any impact upon 'softer', more abstract variables such as a department's history and tradition, broader cultural factors and the attitudes and behaviour of individual actors within the department will then be assessed against two predictions. First, those interpretations and models that suggest that change has been limited or otherwise ring-fenced (for example, Page and Wouters 1995). Second, those that suggest more far-reaching changes are taking place to national administrative systems as a result of the EU's influence (for example Wessels and Rometsch 1996a). Following on from this, an attempt will then be made to ascertain what implications, if any, the territorial features of the Scottish Office (and Scottish Executive) had upon its subsequent Europeanization. Finally, it seeks to explore the appropriateness and utility of 'top-down' conceptualizations of Europeanization in the bureaucratic realm.

The Scottish context: mediating factors

The forms of Europeanization that have most affected Scottish governance have arguably been dependent upon three key sets of factors. The first concerns wider patterns of bureaucratic Europeanization that are in evidence across other member states (for example Ladrech 1994; Page and Wouters 1995; Wessels and Rometsch 1996b; Mittag and Wessels 2003). The second relates to the significant impact which national administrative traditions have upon the more specific forms taken by structural change within a given member state (for example Wessels and Rometsch 1996b: 329–330; Kassim 2003: 102–104). The third and final set of factors revolves around the fact that even within one member state, the nature of bureaucratic Europeanization need not be consistent and homogeneous. In this respect, the traits and characteristics of single departments are afforded the opportunity to have an effect on the specifics of structural change (for example Edwards 1992: 81–83; Wallace 1996: 68; Bulmer and Burch 1998: 603).

In general, this serves to reinforce the point made earlier that care has to be exercised when seeking to apply an overtly 'top-down' definition of Europeanization to the bureaucratic domain. Thus, whilst national administrations and departments are responding to downward adaptation and accommodation pressures, they also input to and shape the very processes of European integration that are generating Europeanization at the national level. Therefore, there would appear to be an element of dynamic, variable interaction both within the parameters of national administrative systems themselves and between these systems and any 'top-down' Europeanizing pressures.

At one level, elements of the Scottish experience clearly illustrate how the specifics of change could manifest themselves in practice. Thus, the creation of dedicated European co-ordination units in the European Funds Division (EFD) and a European Central Support Unit (ECSU) were tangible examples of structural accommodation within the Scottish Office, as were the establishment of the Executive Secretariat (External) and later the External Affairs Division (EAD) within the Scottish Executive. In terms of ministers and civil servants executing their day-to-day business, the influence of Europeanization has become even more evident in a number of ways. For example, ministers could be confronted by European business in full Cabinet or Cabinet Committee (particularly OPD(E) – the Ministerial Sub-Committee on European Questions; later renamed (E)DOP – Cabinet Sub-Committee on European Issues). More significantly, for senior officials from Edinburgh, participation in the Cabinet Office's European Secretariat's network of committees could form a substantial proportion of their Europeanized activity. Many parts of the Scottish Office and Scottish Executive have also been involved in more or less continuous bilateral discussions and co-ordination with other Whitehall departments on EU-related issues, particularly in relation to agriculture, fisheries and the structural funds. In Brussels itself, ministers and civil servants have also found themselves embroiled in various forms of interaction with the UK Permanent Representation to the EU (UKRep) and EU institutions during the course of European policy making processes. Finally, for certain parts of the Scottish Office and Scottish Executive (particularly the agriculture and fisheries, environment divisions and EFD), Europeanization entailed a substantial role in terms of implementing EU policy obligations. For more details on the above, see Smith (2001a,b, 2003), Sloat (2002) and Bulmer *et al.* (2002).

In summary, there seems little doubt that the Scottish Office and Scottish Executive have undertaken a number of practical and readily identifiable adaptations to EU pressures, which have been far from negligible or peripheral in their overall impact. However, the more intriguing question addressed in the remainder of this chapter concerns the long-term depth and extent of these changes in Scotland. In effect, was the Scottish experience closer to Page and Wouters' (1995) suggested scenario, whereby Europeanization greatly affects policies but not governmental infrastructures, or has it more in common with alternative scenarios characterized by deeper-seated administrative changes?

By digging deeper so as to take more account of the 'software' (Jordan 2001b: 6) of policy making (history, culture and the role of actors within individual departments), this alternative approach looks for evidence of the 'incremental-transformative change' identified by Bulmer and Burch (2001: 81) among others (for example Jordan 2003). This approach is consistent with an historical institutionalist perspective, which suggests that limited bureaucratic Europeanization can coexist with more extensive policy Europeanization.

The next section takes the first of these scenarios and measures it against the Scottish experience. The section after that performs a similar analysis using the latter scenario.

Limitations to Europeanization in Scotland

Current scholarship suggests that existing administrative conventions and traditions in Scotland played a significant role in determining the final shape of adaptation processes within the Scottish Office. In one sense, this need not have led to a more limited form of Europeanization. Indeed, it may even have strengthened the accommodation of the European dimension in certain ways. For example, with regard to the implementation of policy, the Scottish Office experience, like that of other UK departments, encompassed a strive for efficiency and thoroughness in ensuring that every single piece of EU legislation was faithfully put into effect. These factors perhaps contributed to a degree of Europeanization more robust than that which prevailed in some other member states; indeed, it could be regarded as an instance of 'voluntary-direct' adaptation in Bache and Jordan's typology. In other senses, however, the predominance of established traditions may have served to limit (or ring-fence) the depth of Europeanizing outcomes.

Empirical findings on cultural change within Scotland appear to support the latter argument. For example, the impact of European training programmes and secondments was, in many ways, relatively limited. Their key purpose was to facilitate a narrower form of adaptation, that is, to give Scottish Office officials a practical grasp of EU structures and procedures, and to highlight different ways of using them to pursue Scottish interests. The development of a European – or *'communautaire'* – spirit was very much a secondary goal. In these respects, the extent of cultural change was strictly limited. The style of administrative operations did not change, and any shift in emphasis which did take place did not really extend beyond responding more quickly to the possible implications and effects wrought by a growing 'foreign' dimension to the department's existing work and remit (Fraser 1998; Hamilton 1998). In terms of Bache and

Jordan's typology, the limited nature of cultural change could thus be classified as 'voluntary-indirect' in the sense that while civil servants willingly embraced training and secondment experience for practical purposes (to facilitate handling of European matters), any cultural change was limited and certainly unintended as far as the actors involved were concerned.

Additionally, apart from a few pockets of resistance to change during the early years following accession, Europeanization did not take on the more political forms that arguably appeared in some other member states. For example, Goetz (1996) has suggested that the German bureaucracy became politicized in the sense that it came to act as an institutional motor, seeking to drive forward the European integration process. In this respect, Scottish Office civil servants did not outwardly adapt explicit views on the merits or otherwise of European integration and/or allow these to permeate their work:

> It was a fact of life that we were in Europe. We had a job to do and had to get on with it; we were there to serve ministers, not to have opinions on the politics of the matter. (Cormack 1998)

This finding mirrors the situation in other Whitehall departments (Edwards 1992: 66–67; Armstrong and Bulmer 1996: 256). Traditions of neutrality and apoliticism continued to prevail, prohibiting any deeper, politicized form of change. Finally, the Europeanizing influence of secondments could be seen to have been even more limited. Rather than officials 'going native' or seeking to import European styles and working methods, those returning from placements tended to reinforce existing national culture, largely as a result of sceptical encounters with a more politicized bureaucratic infrastructure in Brussels. In particular, some secondees from the Scottish Office found it difficult to come to terms with the degree of politicization across the directorates-general (DGs) of the Commission. In such respects, any 'contagion' effect (Page and Wouters 1995: 197) was clearly absent. If identifiable forms of Europeanization outcomes had actually transpired in these respects, these would have fallen into the 'coercive' category. However, the fact that tangible change did *not* take place again lends weight to the argument that, given the dynamics and variable cultural factors involved, not all aspects of bureaucratic Europeanization fit neatly into the typology. Indeed, in this particular instance, it is debatable whether Europeanization has actually occurred at all.

From a broader perspective, the limits to Europeanization can be discerned in several other ways. For example, it was clear that forms of structural accommodation within the Scottish Office tended to follow an accretive route (see Smith 2003). In this respect, apart from EFD and ECSU (and later the EAD within the Scottish Executive), there was no great restructuring of departments and divisions or creation of a large number of posts devoted solely to EU matters. European business tended to be accommodated within the confines of existing infrastructure and was handled by staff who continued to be engaged in other, non-EU-related tasks. Indeed, along with the cultural dimension of change, adaptation processes within the Scottish Office seemed to be broadly characterized by accretion and incrementalism that, at face value, may have lessened the overall impact of Europeanization.

The general approach of civil servants was to initiate practical measures, as and when necessary, to meet immediate practical objectives. In this sense, there was arguably little in the way of a deep-seated re-alignment of structure or culture. In short, these findings correlate with Page and Wouters' (1995) *conclusion* that the Europeanization effects have been limited (because deep-seated change has not taken place) though not with their *explanation* for this outcome (that is, that there is, as yet, no common European administrative style or model for national bodies to copy or subsume).

Deep-seated Europeanization?

What evidence is there to support the alternative scenario of deep and profound changes? Following accession, an elite-level decision was taken within the Scottish Office not to use large-scale European units or divisions (Fraser 1998). In one respect it was simply deemed more practical for relevant responsibilities to be dispersed and handled by existing units. In addition, however, a secondary consequence of this approach was that it arguably engendered, in the long term, a more deep-seated form of Europeanization. This stems from the fact that existing units and divisions were more likely to be exposed to front-line EU tasks and responsibilities. A less thorough form of adaptation may have resulted if divisions had been able to delegate or transfer European commitments to a potentially cumbersome, all-embracing European unit. It was also arguably true that the thoroughness of Europeanization was further advanced by the calibre and enthusiasm exhibited by many of those officials assigned to European tasks. As noted earlier, officials maintained an apolitical stance, although this did not prohibit an 'apolitical enthusiasm' from developing. The fact that different departments across Whitehall have been able to adopt varying degrees of effort and outlook in adapting to the European dimension whilst simultaneously maintaining an apolitical stance on the merits or otherwise of European integration *per se*, has already been noted in the existing literature (Edwards 1992: 81–83; Wallace 1996: 68; Buller and Smith 1998: 166). In the case of the Scottish Office, ministers were quick to note how their officials remained apolitical but at the same time grasped the European nettle in firm, confident and non-reluctant fashion (Brown 1998; Younger 1998).

A number of explanations for this 'enthusiasm' can be put forward. First, it would appear to rest with the attitudes and approaches exhibited by officials themselves, namely the 'we had a job to do and had to get on with it' philosophy alluded to earlier. Secondly, there can be little doubt that the territorial lobbying element was highly significant. In this respect, Scottish ministers and officials have always drawn attention to the priority of 'getting the Edinburgh line across' (whether in London or Brussels), in seeking to secure the best possible policy outcomes for Scotland. With this in mind, it is hardly surprising that the Scottish Office (and later the Scottish Executive) would pursue their contributions to discussions on, say, the European Regional Development Fund (ERDF) or the Common Fisheries Policy (CFP) in an 'enthusiastic' manner.

Of perhaps greatest significance, however, in indicating the existence of deeper forms of Europeanization were the patterns of practical experience that prevailed. A key example centres on the Scottish Office being able to use its 'Euro-enthusiasm' and nurturing of Euro-expertise to good effect in the course of interdepartmental discussions in Whitehall. According to George Younger (1998), a former Secretary of State for Scotland, this represented the department making use of 'extra muscle' (in seeking to forward territorial inputs successfully at the Whitehall level) that stemmed from its broader, proactive approaches to Europeanization processes. This 'muscle' could manifest itself in various ways. For example, a former Head of the European Secretariat within the Cabinet Office in London recalls the Scottish Office making notable inputs to committee discussions on the ERDF (Hadley 1998). Moreover, the dedication exhibited by those Scottish Office officials dealing with European matters markedly reduced the extent to which the department relied on the Cabinet Office's European Secretariat. For example, Younger (1998) was certainly of the belief that in seeking out information on particular issues, 'you got a better answer, much quicker, if you dealt direct with UKRep and the EC institutions'.

By implication, therefore, it would seem that the Scottish Office was one of those departments identified by Spence (1993: 56–57) which, due to having built up their own expertise, did not have to over-rely on the European Secretariat's advice and support functions. From the perspective of the Scottish Office, the fact that lower grade officials had developed direct EU-level contacts over time meant that there was less need to depend upon Whitehall channels for information provision (Hamilton 1998; Younger 1998). Similarly, the establishment of a permanent office in Brussels is perhaps of relevance in that, while this development is clearly linked to political as well as administrative changes stemming from devolution, it does not mark discontinuity with what went before. In other words, it could be argued that the approaches adopted by some officials – which might be termed proactive as opposed to reactive – resulted in a more thorough and intense form of Europeanization, than would otherwise have prevailed. Indeed, it could be argued that this goes beyond even the 'voluntary-direct' type of Europeanization described in Chapter 2. In effect, 'top-down' pressures were not merely 'unopposed' or 'accepted', but the actors concerned seemed to have wanted to go further via a form of 'bottom-up' engagement.

Other aspects of the Scottish experience seem to reinforce these points. As with other departments (Bulmer and Burch 1998: 621; Hadley 1998), the Scottish Office was aware that the elaborate and fast moving nature of developments within the Commission made it imperative for Edinburgh to nurture its own direct links with individual DGs, as well as rely on the efficient but often over-stretched services provided by UKRep. In effect, this could be seen as going beyond the bare minimum of Europeanization, that is, it represented a deeper form of immersion, driven by the perceived need to exert influence in Europe. This state of affairs holds distinct echoes of the deeper form of Europeanization predicted by Wessels and Rometsch (1996a,b), namely where intense change results from an increasing 'fusion' between national and EU administrative systems. It also chimes with Bulmer and Burch's (2001: 93–94) argument that bureaucratic Europeanization has impacted deeply upon the institutions of government. They accept that this change has been limited in the sense that it has not entailed radical overhaul or restructuring. However, they also argue that by taking into account the more abstract factors such as culture, attitudes and the role played by individuals (that is, 'software') alongside the purely structural determinants of institutional change, a fuller picture of domestic change emerges. Thus, while the broad pattern may seem limited (that is, slow, incremental change), the cumulative impact runs deeper.

The influence of territorial factors

As noted above, many aspects of Europeanization within the Scottish Office mirrored broader patterns or trends evident in other Whitehall departments. Key examples included incremental and accretive approaches to structural change and the maintenance of apoliticism within the ranks of the civil service. From the outset, however, it was suggested that while Europeanization processes might display certain common features as they affected the UK administrative system generally, it was also likely that the intensity and *specific* impact of adaptation would vary between departments.

A number of key, long-standing features of territorial governance in pre-devolutionary Scotland can be highlighted – ones that may have shaped the processes and outcomes of Europeanization. These included: the parallel existence of variable but generally limited measures of territorial policy autonomy alongside traditionally high levels of centralized control in London; the multi-functional remit of the Scottish Office itself and its multi-departmental infrastructure; and questions relating to the 'dual role' (that is, the department not only representing Scottish interests in London but also representing UK government in Scotland) and the political legitimacy of work carried out by its ministers (given that they were elected in UK general elections and could thus exercise power on the basis of minority support in Scotland).

The roots of departmental distinctiveness

In certain respects, where traditional departmental characteristics did have an impact on what might broadly be termed 'territorial Europeanization', the overall effect tended to be limited. For example, in terms of structural accommodation, a tendency towards accretive change in the Scottish Office mirrored developments across Whitehall. Within this context, however, interviews revealed how some civil servants felt that the Scottish Office's status as a territorial department, one step removed from the heart of Whitehall, made it easier to adapt to a new and more 'remote' centre of power in Brussels. Similarly, like many Whitehall departments, the Scottish Office recognized the general benefits to be gained from secondments to EU institutions and UKRep. Again, however, a territorial dimension was present insofar as there was a perception in Edinburgh that such representation was an essential means of ensuring that Scotland's voice was heard directly. It was also true that the multi-functional background of Scottish Office officials often made them attractive targets for UKRep (see Smith 2001a). These and other examples serve to indicate the more or less ring-fenced nature of distinctive territorial outcomes within a broader UK setting.

Notwithstanding the above, there were nevertheless instances where Europeanization in Scotland assumed more distinctive forms. For example, it is clear that adaptation processes had variable effects across different parts of the Scottish Office (see Scottish Office 1995, 1997). These variable outcomes indicated the impact of the department's multi-functional remit and its existence as a conglomeration of mini-departments. For example, within the Scottish Office the mini-department dealing with education policy was much less affected by Europeanization than its counterpart dealing with agriculture and fisheries. While this variability was not unique to the Scottish Office, it can be argued that the structure and multi-functionalism of the latter made it a more exaggerated and protracted feature than was the case in other territorial departments. In fact, in this instance the Scottish Office was a microcosm of general patterns of change in Whitehall.

Similarly, approaches to change adopted by many of the Scottish Office officials involved were not as personally hostile to European integration as their counterparts, for example, in the Treasury (Edwards 1992: 81–83; Buller and Smith 1998) and, during the 1970s and 1980s, the Department of the Environment (Jordan 2002: 43). Indeed, by contrast, a non-politicized form of proactive enthusiasm could be perceived. To some extent, this sprang from the basic fact that workload pressures across a range of policy areas left Scottish Office officials with little option but to press ahead with the immediate task in hand. In other respects, the enthusiasm could be attributed to the post-accession lead set by a number of individuals within the upper ranks of the civil service hierarchy in Edinburgh. A key motivation here was the desire to secure favourable outcome for Scotland from the ERDF and the CFP. While it is true that all this took place elsewhere in the UK, it nonetheless adopted a distinctive form in Scotland.

Following on from the above, the more co-ordinated strategic reforms initiated within the Scottish Office from the early 1990s also stand out (Scottish Office 1991a and see Smith 2003). Any distinctiveness in this respect could be partly attributed to traditional territorial characteristics. With particular reference to the 'legitimacy gap', it may be that a changing political climate in the late 1980s, with the opposition Scottish National Party and Labour parties taking increasingly proactive positions on the European issue, forced a reappraisal of tactics in the then Conservative-led Scottish Office (Mitchell 1996: 275). Equally, the reforms of the 1990s were rooted in factors such as the long-term attitudes and approaches exhibited by officials towards adaptation processes, as mentioned above, and the personal initiatives set in motion by Ian Lang, the then Secretary of State for Scotland (Lang 1991).

However, any distinctiveness was yet again ring-fenced by broader developments. Thus, a heightened awareness and focus on EU issues within the Scottish Office from the early 1990s ran concurrent to similar, if uneven, developments across Whitehall. In particular, during this period several 'quantum jumps in integration' referred to by Bulmer and Burch (1998: 613–614) imposed heavier Europeanizing pressures upon the whole of Whitehall. Furthermore, such distinctiveness as did exist was not pushed forward solely by traditional territorial factors. Instead, it stemmed from a broader Whitehall environment that allowed for a measure of flexibility in the way that departments handled their adaptation processes. In this sense, Scottish Office flexibility (and any consequent distinctiveness) was, as with other Whitehall departments, afforded from without rather than stemming from within. However, it might be argued that the sensitivity of territorial politics allowed the Scottish Office greater room for manoeuvre in relative terms.

Territorial factors post-devolution

The change of the Scottish Office into the Scottish Executive might have been expected to change how the European dimension was accommodated at the territorial level. Probably the most obvious change is that, on the surface at least, there is arguably now a greater degree of transparency, accountability and legitimacy in terms of how EU matters are framed and handled within the Scottish context. Of key significance in this respect is, of course, the fact that the Scottish Executive is directly accountable to a territorially elected body, the Scottish Parliament. The very existence of the Parliament has arguably subjected EU-related matters in Scotland to much greater public scrutiny. The activities of the Parliament in this respect (and in particular its European and External Committee, which meets at 2–3 week intervals and produced 30 major reports between November 1999 and June 2004) far outstrip the more limited scrutiny of the Scottish Office's

EU activities. These were generally restricted to parliamentary questions at Westminster and the occasional EU-related report of the House of Commons Scottish Affairs Committee.

It could be argued that these activities have served to enhance transparency (in terms of accessing information), accountability (in terms of holding the Scottish Executive to account) and legitimacy (in terms of the territorial-based electoral mandate underpinning the Executive's actions). However, it could be argued that fundamental change in all three respects has been limited and that as far as EU-related matters are concerned, the devolved infrastructure is in many ways just a 'democratised Scottish Office' (Sloat 2002: 73). Much of this stems from the apparent lines of continuity between the pre- and post-devolutionary regimes as regards territorial *executive* (as distinct from *parliamentary*) involvement in European business.

Although the Scottish Parliament and Executive have been devolved much responsibility for the implementation of EU policy in Scotland, in overall terms the EU dimension is considered to be a non-devolved matter (the final say on all issues has been reserved by London). As such, the scope for territorial factors to influence Europeanization processes in Scotland is, in many ways, much as it was before devolution. Of particular relevance here is the fact that Scottish involvement in EU policy processes continues to be constrained within the parameters of overall UK activity in this field. Moreover, that territorial input is channelled through the interdepartmental co-ordination mechanisms in Whitehall and Brussels. In this respect, the concordats (which set out the formal arrangements for territorial inputs to EU-related matters) between the devolved administrations and White-hall departments are based heavily on pre-devolutionary practice. Indeed, they could be regarded as merely 'codifying prevailing practices which were widely understood and unproblematic' (Bulmer *et al.* 2002: 67–68).

This is not to suggest that continuity between the pre- and post-devolutionary regimes has been absolute, because clearly it has not. As illustrated above, the scrutiny and transparency of EU policy making in Scotland has changed markedly with the arrival of the Scottish Parliament. Equally, the Scottish Executive has been able to Europeanize itself in ways that the old Scottish Office would have been unable and frankly unwilling to do (for example opening a permanent office in Brussels). In fact, it has even been suggested that the Executive has taken 'a step too far' on occasions. For example, in 2001 the Foreign and Commonwealth Office apparently clamped down on what it regarded as over-zealous attempts by Scottish ministers to assert the extent of their regional autonomy at both European and international levels (Wright 2002: 216–217).

Despite such developments, however, continuity appears to be the order of the day. Although devolution in the UK may have run parallel to a wider growth in regionalism across Europe during the 1990s, the weight of evid-ence points to UK devolution being primarily a domestically driven project, with little EU influence (Bulmer *et al.* 2002: 171; Sloat 2002: 20–21). This serves to downplay the significance of any 'top-down' Europeanizing pressures. In relative terms, however, devolution is still in its formative stages. The trajectory of Europeanization may well become more volatile if, as Bulmer *et al.* (2002: 171–172) have suggested, different political parties hold the reins of power in Edinburgh and London. Then, we may begin to see Europeanization assuming more distinctive territorial paths as the devolved administrations flex their sub-national muscle within an EU setting. As a signatory to the 'Salzburg Declaration' in 2003, the Scottish Executive has certainly made it clear that it wishes to see 'an enhanced role for the legislative regions within the EU' (Group of Regions with Legislative Powers (REGLEG) 2003; Scottish Executive 2004: 2).

These sources of departmental flexibility (pre- or post-devolution) notwithstanding, the significance of the above for the study of bureaucratic Europeanization is quite clear. In short, the evidence presented here clearly adds fuel to Jordan's (2001b and 2003) argument that an understanding of the true nature and extent of departmental adaptation to Europe depends as much upon the analysis of 'softer' cultural and actor-centred factors as it does on the study of institutional hardware. Crucially, however, the influence of these various factors must be viewed collectively if their true impact is to be realized. For example, out of the 'softer' factors there is no doubt that individual actors can play an instrumental role. Thus, Kerremans and Beyers (1998: 17) cited instances in the Belgian system where departmental adaptation to the EU was stimulated by the appointment of senior civil servants with a keen interest in European affairs. Equally, within the UK, John Gummer exerted a discernible influence on the Europeanization of the Department of the Environment during his tenure as Secretary of State for the Environment (Jordan 2001b: 30). At the same time, however, the true measure of Gummer's proactive influence could only be ascertained when taking into account other 'softer' factors, in particular, the reactive, hesitant and sometimes hostile approaches to Europeanization which had been evident in that department prior to Gummer's arrival (Jordan 2001b: 9). By the same token, whilst there is evidence to suggest that Ian Lang had a very direct impact on the course of Europeanizing developments within the Scottish Office in terms of his personal, proactive influence (Scottish Office 1991b: 1; Stewart 1998), the nature of Europeanization continued to be influenced by the same 'apolitical enthusiasm' of civil servants that had influenced patterns of EU adaptation in Edinburgh since the early 1970s.

Conclusion

On the basis of the above arguments, the nature of bureaucratic Europeanization processes, as illustrated by the Scottish case, become a little clearer. In short, Page and Wouters' (1995) conclusions are justified to some extent in that Europeanization has not involved the wholesale importation of a common European model or style of administration that serves, in effect, to supplant national bureaucratic forms. Where they are wrong, however, is in their argument that while policies and policy processes have been substantially Europeanized, governing institutions within member states have remained largely untouched. In one sense, the Scottish experience does confirm that national administrative traditions and culture affect the course of development in a given case. Within the UK, for example, paths of change within the Scottish Office and Scottish Executive were influenced by broader factors relating to, amongst other things, a culture of administrative efficiency and political neutrality.

However, it would be wrong to assume that this state of affairs led to a more limited or restricted form of Europeanization in Scotland. In this sense, the deeper forms of change witnessed in the Scottish case justify the need to place Europeanization in a wider context (Ladrech 1994; Meny *et al.* 1996), whereby changes in bureaucratic method and style become inextricably linked with changes in policy and policy processes. In sum, therefore, the evidence relating to the department in question shares much in common with the distinction offered by Wessels and Rometsch (1996a,b), namely that broader processes of Europeanization entail institutional *fusion*, whereby changes stem from increased interaction between national and supranational levels of administration, but do not lead to full institutional *convergence*, whereby a common, homogenous system of European administration emerges.

Another finding of this case study relates to the interpretations of Europeanization described in Chapter 2. As far as bureaucratic Europeanization is concerned, this definition of change has general utility in seeking to explain how and why domestic government departments undergo processes of change in seeking to accommodate and adapt to EU membership. However, whilst various aspects of the Scottish experience could be seen to fit relatively neatly into the direct/indirect and voluntary/coercive typology described in Chapter 2, other aspects did not appear to be quite so compatible. In particular, the 'apolitical enthusiasm' within the ranks of Scottish officials seemed to push beyond even the 'voluntary-direct' variant of Europeanization and towards something more akin perhaps to a 'bottom-up' classification in the sense that responses to Europeanizing pressures could be proactive as well as merely willingly (or voluntarily) reactive.

The Scottish case also re-emphasizes the importance of incorporating 'softer', cultural factors within a historical institutional understanding of bureaucratic Europeanization (Bulmer and Burch 2001: 74; Knill 2001: 25–27). In this respect, the advantages of looking at longer-term trends and historical factors inherent to a particular department and its position within the broader context of a national administrative setting offer a more detailed and nuanced picture of Europeanization. However, even when taking these 'softer' factors into account, the Scottish experience mirrors that of other Whitehall departments, in that the relative extent and depth of Europeanization is not as easy to pinpoint as historical institutionalist scholars sometimes imply. On the one hand, there are aspects of bureaucratic change that suggest that the impact has been generally limited. The accretive and incremental nature of structural modifications and general absence of large-scale restructuring of departmental infrastructure are both significant in this respect. Equally, the scope of cultural change could be regarded as minimal to non-existent in the sense that there has been little or no evidence of the Scottish bureaucracy directly importing European styles or methods of administration into Scotland, or of large numbers of civil servants 'going native' in Brussels.

On the other hand, the Scottish experience does suggest the existence of deeper change, which is commensurate with Wessels and Rometsch's (1996a,b) notion of 'institutional fusion'. In particular, it is clear from the Scottish case that the territorial dimension (in terms of policy remit and sub-national autonomy) has been instrumental in shaping the precise forms of bureaucratic Europeanization, albeit with such territorial influence being ring-fenced by broader developments in Whitehall. In this respect, the very existence of a 'bottom-up', 'apolitical enthusiasm' in terms of accommodating EU-related business may have been partly rooted in a desire on the part of the Scottish Office and the Scottish Executive to secure the best possible outcomes for Scotland. However, such a strategy, coupled with other long-standing characteristics of Scottish administration, may have served to intensify the Europeanization processes experienced in this particular case.

6
The English Regions

Martin Burch and Ricardo Gomez

Introduction

The English regions in their present guise began to emerge as distinct entities from the late 1980s. Their involvement in European policy making has always been restricted, as indeed has been the role of the English regions more generally. However, since then the regional tier has developed significantly, as the English regions have played an increasingly important part in economic regeneration policies and initiatives. Many of these initiatives have been funded through EU schemes. Thus, ostensibly the EU has been a significant driver in the development of this increasingly important tier of governance in England. In this chapter we consider the extent of Europeanization at this regional level in England. Following Bache and Jordan (Chapter 2), the way we have approached this concept and its definition is to regard it as fundamentally concerned with the study of domestic change which is evident through what might be termed 'the EU effect'. That is, change that would not have happened or would not have happened in the way it has if it were not for the existence of arrangements and relationships consequent upon the establishment and development of the EU. So, a starting point for our analysis is that Europeanization concerns the nature of and the processes whereby this EU effect is manifested. We then draw in the concept of Europeanization used in this volume as a working definition to be applied and considered in the light of the evidence we present.

We recognize, as discussed in Chapter 2, that an approach to Europeanization needs to give some attention to the challenging research design issues of: (a) isolating the Europeanizing effect from other effects; and (b) determining the degree of Europeanization that is taking place. Responding to (a) is quite tricky and it is a point we come back to in the conclusion to this chapter, where we note that our definition of an 'EU effect' offers a way of beginning to address this issue. Dealing with the *degree* of Europeanization (b) requires establishing and applying criteria for evaluating the scale of the effect. We do this by using concepts we have developed in a larger project, which we draw on to provide the empirical material in this chapter (Bulmer and Burch, 1998, 2000a, 2002; Bulmer *et al.* 2002). More pertinently, as far as this exercise is concerned, they offer general categories within which one can plot and across which one can evaluate the extent of Europeanization. So our analysis involves examination of the Europeanization of institutions. We see institutions as having four dimensions along which Europeanization can be evaluated. Thus, we look at the EU effect on:

- the *systemic dimension,* affecting the constitutional rules and the basic structure of the state and government;
- the *organizational dimension,* affecting the formal set-up of offices and key positions, and including the distribution of formal authority and resources of money and staff;
- the *process dimension,* affecting the processes whereby business is handled, information distributed and policy decisions determined, and including the networks established to fulfil these tasks;
- the *regulative dimension,* affecting rules, guidelines and operating codes as well as the capacity for strategic guidance (that is, the means to ensure that tasks are fulfilled and that forward thinking is undertaken).

In determining the degree of Europeanization we adopt Radaelli's categorization of four possible outcomes – inertia, absorption, transformation and retrenchment (see Bache and Jordan, Chapter 2). In the light of our evidence, we add a further category of transformation through evolutionary change. Here, change appears to involve absorption, but when looked at over a significant period of time the cumulative and persistent nature of what has taken place actually amounts to a transformation in how things are done or how tasks are carried out. In the following pages, we examine Europeanization in the English regions in two phases. In Phase 1 (1990–97), European forces, notably EU funding schemes, are at the very centre of change. In the second phase, following the election of the Labour government in 1997, the picture is more complex. Having examined developments at the regional level in both these phases, in our concluding remarks we return to the wider conceptual questions about cause and effect and how to understand the extent of Europeanization.

The EU and the emergence of the new English regionalism: 1990–97

At the end of the 1980s a wellspring of change had begun to rise in certain English regions. Dissatisfaction among local elites, especially those in the North East, North West and Yorkshire and the Humber, about inter-regional economic disparities and the failure of national policy to address them, eventually prompted these actors to seek alternative routes to dealing with regeneration and attracting financial support. This 'new English regionalism' had practical and pragmatic roots and began to emerge from the bottom-up. With the exception of the North East, it lacked popular foundations (Burch and Rhodes 1993: 3–4; Burch and Gomez 2002: 769). But it did represent the start of a tentative process of growing regional awareness and activity.

It is important to acknowledge the direct Europeanizing effect of EU regeneration funds and the impact they had on the emergence of this new type of regional governance in England. In particular, the requirements for formulating and implementing European Regional Development Fund (ERDF) and European Social Fund (ESF) spending programmes had a significant administrative impact and a more modest impact on the development of regional structures and processes. Two principles introduced in the 1988 reforms to the ERDF – partnership and programming – had a lasting effect on the handling of European business in the English regions (on local effects, see Marshall, Chapter 7). The partnership concept, incorporated in the 1988 Framework Regulation governing the structural funds, codified a Commission commitment to the inclusion of subnational actors that had existed since the foundation of EU regional policy in the 1970s. It required tripartite consultation between the Commission, member states and designated subnational authorities in the formulation of development plans, the implementation of programmes and the monitoring and evaluation process. The move to programming saw the introduction of multi-annual development plans and strategies, and an obligation on national governments to consult with subnational implementing authorities. One consequence of these changes was an increased scope for regional actor involvement. From 1990 onwards many began to be drawn into the ambit of the new funding mechanisms.

In effect, in the early 1990s, two trends came together: a bottom-up regional awareness and concern, coupled with a more regionally focused EU funding policy. This was the critical moment from which the new pattern of English regionalism began to emerge. The pattern of change thereafter is spasmodic but persistent and it is manifested across all institutional dimensions. The requirements of European funding initiatives are at the very heart of these changes, though the degree of change varies significantly across the English regions.

The EU and overall system changes

Changes in the structure of the state affecting the English regions were minimal before 1997. Regionalism was not encouraged by successive Conservative governments, which had gradually reduced the powers of local authorities while simultaneously enhancing the authority of the centre and Quangos (Stoker 1996). EU policy making was tightly controlled by Whitehall (see Bulmer and Burch, Chapter 3). Even where developments in the structural funds regulations stipulated that subnational players should participate in decision-making and delivery processes, the centre maintained a powerful role as gatekeeper (Bache 1999). Thus, the potential Europeanizing effect of EU regional policy was mediated through central government institutions and they proved adept at absorbing the impact of European integration on their own terms (Bulmer and Burch 2000b: 9).

Despite the dominance of central government in the UK system, one change in the structure of the state during the 1990s that stands out in retrospect was the creation of nine Integrated Regional Offices, later to become Government Offices for the Regions (GOs), in April 1994. This initiative was part of the Major government's manifesto pledge to strengthen the coordination of policies at regional and urban levels (Mawson and Spencer 1995: 14). On the face of it, the GOs bolstered central government's presence on the ground at regional level. The evidence is that the interests of the regions remained secondary to those of the centre. Yet, the establishment of the GOs unintentionally aided the development of regionalism in at least three ways. First, it linked the notions of integrated policy and regional delivery in the minds of Whitehall decision-makers. Second, it encouraged the development of regionally focused interest networks. And third, it gave a push to regional identities by finally establishing what were to become accepted as the standard boundaries for the English regions. These effects were marginal in impact to begin with, but they constituted a shift in the principles underlying state organization at the subnational level. Although there is a Europeanizing element in this, in essence these changes reflect domestic factors.

The EU and organizational changes

During the 1990–97 period, the impact of the EU on the English regions was more discernible in terms of organizational change than system-wide change. It principally manifested itself in the adaptation of the emerging regional tier to involvement in structural funds programmes. Much of the formal authority for the administration of the structural funds remained with Whitehall, but the regions were more systematically drawn into the formulation and implementation of individual programmes. There were also early signs of the potential transformative impact of the EU as regional players adapted to the decision-making processes and methods of working required by the Structural Funds regulations.

It was, however, the operation of the GOs that provided the principal organizational innovation up to 1997. This mainly revolved around their role in the structural funds programmes. Consequently, GOs in those regions that received larger amounts of funds were initially the most engaged in relation to European issues. They played a key role in coordinating the regional input into and in drawing up the Single Programming Documents (SPDs) for the 1994–99 period, which set out each region's strategic development framework and indicated the level of funding that would be required. The GOs were also designated as the managing authority for ERDF programmes

(Wells 1995: 11). Despite the involvement of regional actors in the formulation of the SPDs, the final product tended to reflect the preferences of the centre more than those of regional actors (Wells 1995: 12; Bache 1998: 99). However, there is also evidence that indicates a change in the balance of power between the centre and the regions resulting from the creation of GOs. In the North West and Yorkshire and Humber, for instance, the GOs acquired a reputation for helping to pull together sub-regional interests. In more general terms, the day-to-day relationships between GO officials and other regional players, together with personnel secondments between organizations within regions, promoted a process of learning with and about each other that was focused on a regional perspective. So, while the centre continued to hold sway over policy, a subtle shift in emphasis towards the regional tier had begun.

A related set of organizational changes was also evident in the civil society aspect of the emerging regional polity. Specifically, this period saw the formation of regionally based groupings drawing together the voluntary and private sectors and others from the public sector. Again, the structural funds were significant here. For the European Commission, the formulation and delivery of ERDF development strategies was heavily dependent on information exchange with subnational actors. To fulfil this demand, subnational bodies had to develop more of a regional focus and began to concentrate more lobbying and information-gathering capacities at that level (Burch and Gomez 2002: 772). A further indicator of the increase in subnational lobbying activity was the opening of 17 subnational offices in Brussels during the early 1990s (John 1994a: 739). Individual cities, local authorities and local authority-related organizations were first onto the scene (see Marshall, Chapter 7). Regional organizations tended to 'piggyback' on their efforts (Burch and Gomez 2002).

As the effects of Structural Funding differed acrossEngland, so too did the pattern and extent of activity in individual regions. In the North West, for instance, a North West Regional Association, drawing together all the local authorities in the region, was formed in 1992. In 1994, along with business interests, it formed the North West Partnership – an umbrella body drawing together all North West-focused interest organizations including those covering the voluntary sector, trade unions and further and higher education (Burch and Holliday 1993; Giordano 2002: 86; Jones and McLeod 2002: 181). These developments were directly encouraged by the EU Commission Directorate for Regional Policy (then DG XVI) and were significantly shaped by involvement in Structural Funds activities. In the South West, by contrast, interests remained organized largely on a sub-regional basis reflecting the inherent divisions between Cornwall in the far south west, Devon, Somerset and Bristol in the middle, and Dorset and Gloucestershire further east. Both regions had problems about identity and boundaries, but in the South West these concerns were more acute and the impact of structural funds was not enough of an incentive for players to come together at the regional level.

The EU and changes in processes

Along the process dimension, the EU effect was similarly limited – testament in part to the restricted involvement of the English regions in the UK's EU policy making. There was a varied (across regions) but persistent pattern of change in the processes for disseminating information, handling business and reaching decisions at regional level in England. However, regions were not in any substantial sense an integrated part of the UK government's policy processes. Their input into policy making was largely restricted to the regional development parts of the structural funds. Again, the pattern of involvement varied across regions according to the volume of the structural funds allocated. Even on these matters, representatives of interests in the more engaged regions were largely drawn into the processes for formulating regional plans for the allocation of funds, known as Community Support Frameworks (CSFs). The CSFs set out priority spending areas and financial plans (Bache 1998: 74). Regional players were also involved in implementation processes through oversight committees known as Programme Monitoring Committees (PMCs), a statutory requirement of the regulations, which were set up to oversee the spending of the funds. The power to designate and to take key decisions about the programmes typically rested with central government. But the processes of formulating the CSFs and the operation of the PMCs helped to encourage subnational participation and further encouraged the creation of new, regionally focused policy communities (Bache 1998: 103).

In essence, from 1990 onwards, a more regionalized process for handling structural funds issues had begun to emerge. However, while in keeping with the requirements of the EU, the process was very much run from the centre (that is, Whitehall) downwards. The position of regional players in this process, though it evolved over the period up to 1997, remained tenuous and largely dependent on EU requirements. The distribution of information concerning the formulation of structural funds negotiating strategy (a matter for the Department of Trade and Industry) and the final decisions on CSFs for each region largely by-passed regional players. Indeed, the processes for involving them in these matters tended to be consultative rather than genuinely cooperative.

Nevertheless, the operation of the structural funds programmes and the gradual regionalization of the policy process engendered new networks of players, a development which is said to be characteristic of Europeanization (Kohler-Koch 1999). Regional players were drawn, if rather haphazardly, into the information web from central government and into shaping policy. As well as engaging civil servants from central and regional level, these networks also drew in representatives from interests such as business and local authorities. Yet, again the pattern of networks and the extent to which they were developed varied across the regions. Moreover, these new networks operated at elite level and away from the gaze of the public and the media. Importantly, there was a self-reinforcing effect to the whole set of developments. As the members of this newly galvanized regional elite worked together they developed shared understandings and a collective sense of purpose. This in turn helped to further establish the processes they were engaged in and to cement the personal linkages that increasingly helped to hold the network together.

The EU and regulative changes

The strongest EU effects in the 1990–97 phase are to be found in the regulative aspect of institutional activity. Operating practices changed as a direct result of the obligations imposed by the structural funds regulations. Most significantly, these included rules and guidelines covering both the formulation of spending plans and the allocation of funding. The introduction of the broad guiding principles of programming and partnership (see page 84) was particularly important for the formal involvement of regions in the programmes. All member state governments were required to follow the guidelines laid down in the relevant regulations, though in the English case, the exact interpretation of these guidelines did have a Whitehall spin put upon them. Nevertheless, the broad thrust of these requirements substantially originated in the EU (Regulation 2052/88 EEC). Many of the regulative changes concerned informal regulation: understandings about how things should operate and who should do what. These tended to build up over the period as a result of practice and problem solving amongst those participants from the public and private sector at both national and regional level who were drawn into the operation of the new structures. One consequence of this was that involvement in Structural Funds activities played a significant part in a socializing process that extended into regional working more generally.

The capacity to provide strategic guidance and initiative, however, remained at the national government level, though the GOs' ability to provide some resource towards this task and to give it a regional focus had been enhanced. The extent to which this was exploited depended on how each GO interpreted its role in its region and, in turn, on the responsiveness of local actors. The partnership principle as applied to the Structural Funds was important here, but it was not the only factor. It was more easily developed in some regions than in others depending in part on the extent of prior experience in applying the concept. In the North West, the partnership principle was already part of everyday practice. There had already been a number of partnership-based regeneration schemes especially in relation to Greater Manchester which tried to tie them in to larger schemes such as two bids to host the Olympic games, which were developed from 1985 onwards (Cochrane *et al.* 2002: 99–101). This experience was built on and expanded out into the wider territory of the region. In the South West, there was less of a sense of regional identity and less experience of partnership approaches. Despite the existence of a designated GO, the South West never gelled as a regional entity and retained its sub-regional character throughout the period up until 1997 (Bridges 2002: 97). Unlike the North West, the experience gained from the local level was not transferred upwards. A further factor in determining the extent of regionally based initiative was the attitude of civil servants in regional offices. The appointment of a Whitehall civil servant to head the North West GO from its inception was in part designed to overcome the tendency, as perceived in Whitehall, that staff in the separate departments of the region had 'gone native'. What was emerging was not so much new codes or rules, but rather a set of attitudes and working practices which gave more scope to the regional level, and which were gradually becoming more and more established over time. What was still not clear, however, was the full extent to which the centre would allow this new regionalized approach to flourish.

The EU and the creation of regional institutions: post 1997

The impact of the EU from 1997 onwards was secondary to constitutional change in the UK. Labour's victory in the 1997 general election heralded a series of far-reaching constitutional reforms. Key manifesto pledges to move ahead with devolution to Scotland, Wales and Northern Ireland and to create a Greater London Authority (GLA) were fulfilled while the incoming government's positive attitude towards the EU paved the way for more constructive engagement on European issues (see Bulmer and Burch, Chapter 3).

The launch of the devolution process precipitated an intensive period of institution- building and adaptation. It also gave 'critical momentum' to the development of English regional governance (Burch and Gomez 2002: 776). Yet, the English regions outside London found themselves left behind as the UK began 'to reinvent itself internally' (Morgan 2002: 807). New institutions – Regional Development Agencies (RDAs) and consultative Regional Chambers – were established in Labour's first term, but they fell some way short of the expectations of English devolutionists. The general pattern post 1997 was one of gradual adaptation as the new institutional players came to terms with the European agenda. The structural funds continued to be an important push factor in the changing picture of regional governance and the key source of Europeanization. But after 1997, constitutional change in the UK became the primary driving force behind the emerging English regionalism. European factors remained important but they were secondary to domestically derived pressures and initiatives.

The EU and overall system changes

It is difficult to discern any direct EU effect on the important changes in the overall system of governance that took place post 1997. The most important change in the structure of the state was the creation – in 1999 – of nine RDAs, one for each English region plus London. On paper, the range of powers accorded to these Agencies was modest. The White Paper in which their responsibilities were set out was studiously vague about their European policy functions (Department of the Environment, Transport and the Regions 1997: 45). The document suggested, for instance, that the RDAs should play a leading role in a new round of structural funds programmes but did not lay down clear guidelines about the powers that they might exercise in that area. However, the roles that the RDAs were to play in economic regeneration – they were tasked with drawing up regional economic development strategies – inevitably drew them into the European funding process.

The government also created eight Regional Chambers alongside the RDAs and an elected Mayor and 25-member assembly for London (Department of the Environment, Transport and the Regions 1998). The Chambers – many of which quickly redesignated themselves as Regional Assemblies (RAs) – had few powers and resources. They can be judged to have had only a marginal impact on the structure of the state. The creation of the GLA and mayoral post was, however, an important structural change (Pimlott and Rao 2002). It underlined the already privileged position of London in English policy making and gave the capital's decision-makers new powers and extra resources that could be used to lobby and influence Whitehall.

None of these changes in the system drew directly on European models or requirements, though they have given a more regional slant to English governance and brought it more into line with EU counterparts. In general these innovations, taken alongside the devolution of powers in Scotland and Wales and Northern Ireland, bring the UK closer to the continental European idea of a 'Europe of the regions'.

The EU and organizational changes

The EU effect on organizational change was also secondary to the impact of devolution and decentralization. Expanded GOs retained the lion's share of authority in the evolving regional governance system, reflecting the tight control that Whitehall continued to exercise over the regions after 1997. But the creation of the RDAs, and to a lesser extent the RAs, marked the start of a subtle shift in authority as the new organizations began to exercise and augment their modest range of powers and resources. In particular, they began to absorb and adjust to developments in EU policies and legislation.

Invariably, European funding programmes had the most direct and substantive influence on the EU-related activities of the regional institutions. However, the new political opportunity structures that resulted from the tentative English devolution process provided a platform from which regional players could engage with a far wider range of European issues such as enlargement, transport and environmental policy. Across the English regions, the paths followed by the Agencies and Assemblies diverged as their individual approaches were adapted to the handling of European business and their other statutory and non-statutory responsibilities. Although this process is still unfolding, it is already clear that the organizational dimension of English devolution is characterized by considerable variety.

Of some significance for the handling of European policy was the incorporation in the GOs of a Ministry of Agriculture, Fisheries and Food (MAFF, now Department of the Environment, Food and Rural Affairs or DEFRA) presence from April 2001. Ongoing reform of the EU's Common Agricultural Policy in favour of a more inclusive approach to rural development, with increased funding earmarked for a range of measures identified in regional plans, meant that the GOs took on a range of new functions in the rural policy sphere. The European dimension of environmental policies also impacts upon the work of the GOs (see Marshall, Chapter 7). Implementation of EU regulations on waste management, for instance, requires coordination at regional level.

As in the pre-1997 phase, management of the structural funds remained the dominant EU-related activity of the GOs. Across the board, the GOs again played critical roles in the negotiation of SPDs. The emergence of the RAs and RDAs and the scope for more concerted regional level activity that they offered strengthened the GOs' position as the pivot point between regions and Whitehall departments. In the North West, for example, stronger cohesion among the partners ensured that collaboration with the GO on the SPD was more formalized than had previously been the case (Burch and Gomez 2002: 773). On the implementation side, the GOs retained their status as the designated managing authority for European funding programmes.

Organizational changes in the handling of the structural funds tended to be determined by the level and type of EU funding available to a region. In the South West, the designation of Cornwall as an Objective 1 area attracting the highest level of EU funding led to the establishment of a 'partnership' office in Truro, staffed by three GO officials and officers from the local authority. In the North West, Merseyside's Objective 1 programme continued to be handled largely independently of the overall North West effort and run by a GO Secretariat based in Liverpool. An important development after 1997 occurred in the UK's ESF programme when the decision-making process was significantly altered to give greater scope to the GOs and their regional partners in the operation of the programme. If a pattern has emerged here, it is that the expansion of the GOs' responsibilities *vis-à-vis* European funds has enabled them to become 'more deeply integrated' into regional governance structures (Burch and Gomez 2002: 773).

The lack of clarity about the European policy functions of the RDAs produced considerable regional variations in their internal structures. Most

RDAs assigned staff to handle those aspects of Structural Funds programmes for which they were responsible, although the numbers of staff involved were dependent on the type and extent of European funding. However, the Government's decision to hand over to the RDAs the strategic control of structural fund programmes by January 2001, provided a strong incentive for RDAs to develop their European activities. The North West Development Agency, for instance, appointed a European operations manager to fulfil these functions and a small team of officials to take forward the development of a regional European strategy. Another RDA, Yorkshire Forward, followed a similar path, appointing a strategy team housed in its Strategy and Policy Directorate. All RDAs saw an expansion in the size of their European policy teams and refinement of their internal operations (Gomez and Burch 2002).

It is difficult to discern consistent patterns in the way that Assemblies organize their European activities. Nevertheless, the partnership concept together with the broader incentives to become involved in EU policy has had distinct organizational effects. In several regions, Assemblies were treated by GOs as the source from which local authorities and the 'economic and social partners' were drawn so as to take part in compiling the SPDs for the 2000–2006 round of structural funds. This status as the vehicle for drawing together a diverse array of interests at regional level provided a platform for some to expand their European activities. In the North West, the Regional Assembly established a European Affairs 'Key Priority Group' comprising local authority politicians and officials and business representatives to examine European issues on the Assembly's behalf. In the North East, an 'Assembly Europe Group' was charged with carrying out similar tasks. In other regions, the RAs have been more peripherally involved in European policy. The point here is that the impact of the EU has not been strong enough to direct the new regional institutions towards models or templates for handling EU policy.

Europeanization has been evident in the decisions of both RDAs and Assemblies to establish representations in Brussels close to the heart of EU decision-making. Inevitably, the composition, structure, membership and staffing levels of Brussels offices varied from region to region. In most cases, RDAs and RAs sent their 'own' officials to Brussels, often through jointly funded posts. Few regions, however, have proved able to pull together existing sub-regional representations into a single presence. Only the South West currently operates an office headed by an official that represents the region as a whole. Most have settled for co-location arrangements in which regional officials work alongside officers from local authorities and the economic and social partners.

The dominant theme of organizational change after 1997 is one of more substantial governmental presence in the regions but with great diversity in the way that regions operate in relation to European issues. Domestic pressures were the main driver behind these changes, though regional differences in receipts of structural funds were clearly a factor in accounting for the way organizational structures developed. So too were variations in the management of relationships between the new organizations, local authorities and other sub-regional interests.

The EU and changes in processes

Procedures for handling European policy in the English regions are still 'under construction'. Consequently, it is difficult to assess the extent of Europeanization. Change has clearly been driven from above, most visibly through the Structural Funds regulations and the practice of engaging with Brussels and London on European issues. It has also originated from below as regional players have identified the need to examine a wider range of European issues and have adapted existing processes to cope with a rapidly evolving European agenda. Although there are some common developments in the processes of policy making, principally those relating to the Structural Funds, there are also wide variations as regions have adopted tailor-made solutions to the handling of European business. The overall picture is therefore still quite fuzzy.

The processes for administering and managing European funding programmes have continued to centre on the PMCs. However, growing awareness of the broader relevance and implications of EU policy and legislation coupled with the potentially significant impact of eastern enlargement of the EU on the availability of regional development funding has compelled regional and sub-regional players to establish 'overarching' European policy processes. Their objective is to adopt a more strategic and broad-based approach to EU policy. In this respect, the EU has created a coordination imperative. Regional institutions have adopted procedures both to respond to existing issues and to anticipate future developments. On paper, the PMCs appeared well placed to carry out these tasks. However, they have tended to focus on the operational side of the programmes, leaving space for higher-level machinery to develop. Several regions approached this problem by establishing strategic policy groups, albeit with differing compositions and remits. In the South West, the European and International Vision Group (EIVG) comprising representatives from a wide range of sectors was given a similar remit. The North West, under the initiative of the RDA, established a European Strategy Group (ESG) comprising officials from the RDA, RA, GO, including the DEFRA representative, the PMCs and an academic advisor (Burch and Gomez 2002: 772). All nine regions, including London, now run overarching European policy forums in one form or another.

Europeanization is also evident in the changes that have taken place in the nature of regional lobbies, the focus of their activities and the way they operate. What Tomaney (2002: 728) termed 'quiet regionalization' has accompanied the more visible process centring on the RDAs, RAs and GOs. The generation of regional strategies on a wide range of issues has prompted other government departments, agencies and non-governmental organizations (NGOs) to adapt their structures to reflect their involvement in the preparation and implementation process. On European policy, the implementation of the ERDF, the ESF and various other Community initiatives (that is, smaller-scale funding programmes designed to complement the structural funds) are the primary drivers behind this element of the regionalization process. The networking activity that is a key feature of EU governance has been further consolidated post 1997. Reorganization of the administration and management of the programmes has forced those bodies that seek funding to work with the new regional institutions. The outcome has been that administrative decentralization in England has provided political opportunity space for sub-regional interests, while EU policy has offered them a rationale for filling that space.

The EU and regulative changes

The development of formal and informal rules, regulations and guidance relating to English regional governance has been slow. Unlike Scottish, Welsh and Northern Irish devolution, the limited process of administrative decentralization to the English regions has not been accompanied by the drawing up of codes of conduct for relationships between the different tiers of government. Instead, the emphasis has been on the informal and organic development of procedures for linking together institutions in the region and the centre in a form that is in keeping with the UK's administrative culture. Nevertheless, a small number of rules and regulations have emerged in the handling of European business, many of which stem from EU regulations.

The Structural Funds regulations continue to account for many of the formal rules that govern the handling of European policy in the English regions. Preparation of the 2000–2006 round of programmes saw stricter enforcement of rules by the Commission, especially those associated with the partnership and programming concepts, than had previously been the case. For instance, the strategic objectives included in North West's Objective 2 SPD had to be re-drafted at the Commission's insistence in order to comply with amended rules. Beyond the specific terms of the Structural Funds regulations, other EU legislation has also had a more significant impact on the English regions. One area that has proved particularly problematic in the 2000–2006 round of regional development funding has been the more stringent application of state aids rules. Here, regional players and central government must pay close attention to the compatibility of spending proposals with what has become one of the most highly regulated areas of EU activity.

Turning to the capacity for strategic guidance on European matters, this is still firmly located at the centre, although a more substantial role is being played by regional institutions. However, the settling down of the new organizations – RDAs and RAs – into the existing regional landscape meant that initially, in some regions there was a weakening of the focus of regional efforts with a further proliferation of central government inspired and appointed agencies. It was only once this new pattern of regional provision had been sorted out – through such devices as regional concordats and other forms of agreement about who does what and with whom – that the strategic capacity of regional players began to clarify. The outcome is a strengthened set of resources at the regional level, though how and to what effect these are deployed varies significantly across regions. The most well-organized regions in terms of developing detailed and practical regional European strategies have been the North East and the East of England, though substantial progress has also been made in the North West, and Yorkshire and Humber. The EU effect in this matter, as in others, is evident but varied.

Conclusion

Overall, the EU is an important factor in both phases in the development of English regions. Its effects are often primary and predominant in the first phase and significant but secondary in the post-1997 period. In some ways, in the second period it is more significant in absolute terms in that the sum of EU-related efforts affecting the development of the English regions are far greater, but this is in the context of an overall expansion of regional activities. So that in relative terms, EU-related activities take a bigger slice post-1997, but out of a far larger cake of overall regional activities.

The general pattern of Europeanization in the English regions is one of gradual but variable adaptation of existing and new institutions to the formal and informal requirements of EU legislation, policies and working practices. In the terms of the taxonomy described in Chapter 2, much of the change has involved the absorption of EU influences. However, the extent of Europeanization and its impact on change clearly differs along our institutional dimensions and across and between the English regions. This variety is a prominent feature of the emerging picture of regional engagement on the European issue.

Looked at from an institutional perspective, in the 1990–97 phase much of the substantive change originated within the regulative dimension with new obligations imposed on central government and regional authorities by the structural funds regulations of 1988 and 1993. Here, the EU had a primary effect on institutional arrangements in the English regions. Important changes in processes and organizations within the regions were a direct result of ERDF decision-making requirements. The programming concept helped to both develop and consolidate the regional tier by creating a clear focus for activities and opportunities for engagement and activism on the part of regional players. Formal requirements to operate on the basis of partnership also exerted a powerful regionalizing effect by forcing those actors involved in delivering structural funds programmes to devise new ways of working with subnational interests. The direct EU effect on overall system change in this period was minimal – a reflection of the limited involvement of English regions in UK European policy making and the resistance of the UK's governing institutions to change.

In the second phase, the EU has remained an important influence on the emerging English regional landscape but it has been secondary to central government–led developments. Overall, system change affecting the English regions over this period has been extensive but the EU has played little part in directly driving this. The principal source of Europeanization has continued to be the Structural Funds, which have had the greatest impact in those regions with the largest allocations. Consequently, much of the EU-led change still emanates initially from changes in structural funding rules and regulations, which have then impacted on organizations and processes.

However, as other aspects of European activities and policy have begun to draw in the regions – notably rural development policy and environmental policy – the sources of Europeanization have become more diverse. This has been reflected in the marked increase in EU-related activity within and across the English regions after 1997. Clearly the EU has been an important and persistent factor in the story of English regionalism, though it is too early to gauge the full extent of its (hitherto cumulative) effect.

Drawing on Radaelli's taxonomy in Chapter 2 as a basis for determining the degree of Europeanization proves to be unsatisfactory in one important respect: it does not adequately cover the extent of changes that we identify in our analysis. More specifically, it lacks a category to cover potentially important changes in direction or principles that start small but, if sustained, build up over time to be significant. The taxonomy described in Chapter 2 does not adequately capture the possibility that over time, change may constitute a transformation of how things are done. For example, the adjustment of regional players to the partnership and programming concepts was marginally significant to begin with, but has had a marked effect on patterns and practices of regional governance in the longer term. What might be useful here is a development of the concept of what has been termed 'incremental transformative' change or 'evolutionary transformation' when 'emerging patterns crystallize and become established as a coherent whole which is distinctly different from that which previously existed' (Bulmer and Burch 1998: 605). In other words, there is a dynamic and cumulative quality to change through EU engagement that needs to be integrated into the criteria for evaluating the extent, and especially the scale of Europeanization. The editors return to this point in the final chapter.

At least one other conceptual problem arises out of our analysis. That is the tricky task of distinguishing (or isolating) an EU effect from other factors that have driven change. The experiences of the English regions in handling European business suggest that institutional changes that might be attributable to the EU could also be attributed to a range of domestic and international factors. Consequently, we have had to contend with the issues of causality and causal sequence in order to generalize about the extent of Europeanization. We have in the course of this chapter distinguished direct and indirect, and specific and general effects. We have also noted that there may be outcomes which are in keeping with European models, such as a Europe of the regions, even though the immediate inspiration underlying some developments leading to this end have been primarily domestic. Here, the EU can be seen as having a second-order, contextual presence that has helped to condition the general climate within which changes have taken place. Moreover, consequences become more evident if we consider Europeanization as referring to changes that would not have happened or would not have happened in the way they have if it were not for the existence of arrangements and relationships consequent upon EU membership. Looked at from this perspective, it is evident that the structural fund reforms of the late 1980s set in train a distinct pattern of regional engagement and politics that forms the bedrock of what exists today. Indeed, had such an experience not already been in place, the more domestically driven post-1997 regional reforms would probably have begun with potentially divisive arguments about regional boundaries. There would also have been little in the way of regional elite networks to draw on and to build from. Thus, EU initiatives created the foundations of modern English regionalism and the post-1997 Labour reforms served in part to build on that legacy.

7
Local Governance

Adam Marshall

Introduction

Much of the literature on the Europeanization of Britain has concentrated on national government and Britain's nations and regions (see Bache and Jordan, Chapter 2). However, the EU's impact on local institutions has not benefited from the same level of scrutiny. This is despite the fact that planners, sociologists and political scientists alike emphasize that policies have a different impact at local level than they do at other territorial levels of governance (for example, Harding 1997; Le Galès 2002). Given local authorities' substantial role in implementing EU policy, it seems reasonable to expect to find distinct forms of 'local Europeanization', which exist alongside the better-known national and regional variants in a member state like the UK.

The primary purpose of this chapter is to present a more detailed analysis of Europeanization at the local level in Britain. Empirically, the chapter focuses on the Europeanization of British local authorities, which have undergone significant changes due to increased European activity. It also develops a framework for the systematic evaluation of local Europeanization in Britain, including both local authorities and other key participants in local governance, and argues that additional research is needed to disentangle the European and domestic influences that together have brought about local institutional change.

Three case studies, derived from qualitative empirical research and published studies, will examine the local dimension of Europeanization in Britain. They demonstrate that EU structural funding, sub-national networking opportunities and environmental directives have all had an important impact on local governments across Britain. Involvement in the negotiation and implementation of EU programmes has resulted in organizational and structural change within local authorities, increased joint working between local authorities and other community actors and deepened local engagement with the European Commission. Europeanization, defined as changes in the domestic arena due to actions at EU level (see Bache and

98

Jordan, Chapter 2), has thus become an everyday reality for local authorities and their partners, in cities and rural areas alike.

This chapter mainly assesses the EU's role in catalyzing changes in local authority institutional structures, policy making activities and day-to-day operations. However, it also examines the indirect impacts of EU policies on other relevant local actors, including non-governmental organizations (NGOs), the community and voluntary sector, regeneration partnerships and territorial networks (see also Burch and Gomez, Chapter 6; Chapman, Chapter 11). Thus, the chapter is sensitive to the ongoing transition from more top-down forms of government to a more networked system of horizontal governance, which has been seen as a critical feature of sub-national politics in recent years (see Rhodes 1997; Stoker 1999, *inter alia*).

'Local Europeanization'

The need for a 'local' perspective

Commentators and scholars across the fields of political science, geography, planning and economics all agree that local governance is highly specific, context-dependent and distinct from the broader study of sub-national politics. Although 'new regionalists' and 'new localists' have argued that the emergence of stronger sub-national identities has promoted a reterritorialization of European space (Keating 1997; Deas and Ward 1999; Corry and Stoker 2002), their work has not yet engaged with the broad debate on Europeanization reviewed in Chapter 2. Thanks to huge changes in local governance in Britain over the past twenty years, some of which have been conditioned by EU practices, I argue that it is critical to isolate 'local Europeanization' from its regional and national variants. To that end, the following sections investigate the EU impact on local government – and broader local governance – in Britain.

Defining 'local Europeanization'

The starting point for this discussion is the definition of Europeanization offered in Chapter 2. Additionally, this study assumes that local Europeanization is a path-dependent phenomenon – in other words, the 'reorientation or reshaping of politics' at the local level occurs within a distinct historical context. The arguments deployed here are thus rooted in the new institutionalist tradition within political science, as they emphasize the importance of history in shaping processes of political change. As Vivian Lowndes (2004: 237) has noted, 'the institutions of local governance are shaped by rules that emanate from higher tiers of government (national legislation, EU directives), by institutional templates that circulate in the wider society and economy . . . and by locally-specific cultures and conventions'. In order to properly understand the interaction between UK localities and the EU, researchers must account for local norms and the impact of 'mediating institutions' at regional and national level. Taken together, the path-dependent nature of British local authorities and the 'gatekeeping' role of Whitehall (Bache 1998) ensure that unique and long-standing relationships are not subsumed into a reductionist, 'one-size-fits-all' paradigm.

The four-stage model put forward by Cowles *et al.* (2001) provides a useful framework for analysing local Europeanization. However, I do not share the authors' definition of Europeanization as the accumulation of policy competencies at EU level. Instead, I use their construct within the broader definition of Europeanization first introduced by the editors in Chapter 2 and reiterated above. Modified and adapted to the local policy realm, this model suggests the following pathways of interaction and adjustment, spurred by local engagement with the EU:

Europeanization of local governance in Britain

1. **EU Initiative** (Structural Funding, directives, direct communication) →
2. **Adaptational Pressures** ('degree of fit' between EU/domestic/local norms) →
3. **Mediating Institutions** (regional and national 'gatekeepers') →
4. **Local Structural Change** (institutional shifts/local governance change)

Source: Adapted from Cowles *et al.* (2001).

In this view, the 'mis-fit' (see, *inter alia*, Börzel and Risse 2000) between EU policies (regional, regulatory and environmental) and Whitehall decision-making from the 1980s ensured the creation of adaptational pressures wherever established domestic norms – such as Britain's centralized, top-down administrative structure and the subservience of local authorities to central government – were challenged by EU initiatives. Using the 'local Europeanization' paradigm articulated here, it is possible to examine the ways that local authorities were affected by this mis-fit, despite the continued strength of domestic institutional norms.

Two principal types of change are visible within British local authorities as a result of 'local Europeanization'. The first was sparked primarily by EU funding opportunities:

> *1) Changes in policies, practices, preferences and/or participants within local systems of governance, arising from*
>> *a) the negotiation and implementation of EU Structural Fund programmes, and*
>> *b) the operation of local lobbying offices in Brussels since the mid-1980s.*

These are the most common, and most visible, forms of local Europeanization. Although catalysed by *coercive-indirect* pressures for joined-up working
from the European Commission, namely the strict requirements for partnership working and long-term programming that come with EU structural
funding, these variants have gradually become more *voluntary and indirect*
in nature, with local institutions adjusting their procedures and operations to take full advantage of funding opportunities. Although the regulations surrounding EU structural funding have created some *coercive-direct*
Europeanization – as evidenced by the 1991–1992 Rechar controversy
(McAleavey 1995) – this has occurred principally at the national level.
The case studies presented below show that British localities have adapted
voluntarily – and often enthusiastically – to EU adaptational pressures,
whereas Whitehall did so only under threat from the European Commission in order to safeguard overall structural fund allocations for the UK.
As the case study on local lobbying offices will also show, voluntary-
indirect local Europeanization has also sparked a limited amount of
'uploading' and 'cross-loading' (see Bache and Jordan, Chapter 2). British
localities have used sub-national offices and thematic networks to spread
their preferences and practices to the EU level and to other member
states.

   The second principal impact of Europeanization at the local level is less
voluntary in nature, and has been sparked by the adoption of pan-European
legislation, principally in the form of directives and regulations:

   *2) Changes in policies, practices, preferences and/or participants within local
   systems of governance, arising from the transposition into national law of EU
   directives that require local-level implementation.*

While vitally important in areas such as environmental protection (see
Jordan, Chapter 15), where Britain's local authorities have been forced
to adapt to new EU standards over the past twenty years, this form of
local Europeanization has received far less attention than the variants
catalysed by Structural Funding. The 'mis-fit' between European directives
and *national* legal systems, as well as subsequent processes of transposition, harmonization and adaptation, has been widely researched across
a number of key sectors (for example, Featherstone and Radaelli 2003;
Jordan 2002 in relation to environmental policy). But while Whitehall's
legislative response to new EU requirements has been well documented,
adjustment at the local 'coal face' requires a great deal more attention,
as local authorities in Britain bear principal responsibility for the delivery
of a wide array of EU-mandated policies. The case study describing the
impact of EU environmental directives will briefly outline this form of
local Europeanization.

Local Europeanization in Britain: institutional context

As noted above, local Europeanization in Britain takes place against a backdrop of severe domestic institutional constraints. As Radaelli (2000: 22) notes, these constraints cannot simply be dismissed, since 'the analysis of the effects of European public policy on national policy systems should be conducted in parallel to the investigation of endogenous processes'. Unlike many of their continental counterparts, British local authorities lack constitutional standing, possess relatively few competences and are subject to a restrictive *ultra vires* rule that prevents them from taking action outside those responsibilities expressly granted to them by Parliament. Although they were formerly responsible for the implementation of a wide array of policy initiatives, British local authorities have seen their influence drain away as Quangos and private firms have gradually assumed more and more of their policy implementation and service delivery functions (Skelcher 1998).

Local authorities were also powerless to stop successive Whitehall-led reforms of sub-national government in 1975, 1986 and 1995. These reforms first created and then eliminated (in the case of metropolitan areas) strategic upper tier authorities, with their significant planning and economic development functions. As a result of continuous reorganization, local authorities have often had to develop European engagement strategies and networks in an un-coordinated, reactive and *ad hoc* manner. At the same time, central government has progressively reduced global financial allocations to local government for regeneration and renewal, forcing local authorities nationwide to compete with one another for a slice of an ever-dwindling financial pie (Bailey 1995). To take one example, the relatively generous 1970s' Urban Programme was ended in favour of a smaller, competitive Single Regeneration Budget in the 1990s, and local councils were routinely required to match the funding given to regeneration schemes to an extent that often exceeded their capital budgets (Pierre 1998). Additionally, public–private partnerships became key vehicles for everything from regeneration to day-to-day service delivery, although the type of partnership envisaged by Thatcherite planners was driven solely by fiscal considerations rather than the more social and holistic motives of EU-financed partnership initiatives (Oatley 1998).

The uncertain financial state and limited political independence of British local authorities has been further complicated since the election of New Labour in 1997, despite the latter's commitment to stabilize local government finances. A slew of central government initiatives, emanating from the Office of the Deputy Prime Minister, the Department for Trade and Industry and the Treasury, has constantly moved the goalposts and criteria for regeneration programmes, confusing local actors that depend on central government funding for successful interventions (Hill 2000). This financial 'squeeze' is not the only challenge that local authorities have had to respond to; political devolution to Scotland and Wales, coupled with the now-stalled plan for greater regionalization in England, has also forced local governments nationwide to share many of their competences with new meso-level institutions. In summary, local actors across Britain have had to simultaneously contend with domestic institutional change and EU-inspired opportunities and challenges, making it difficult to disentangle European and domestic causal influences.

The constantly shifting institutional picture surrounding local governance has had a profound impact on the way in which local authorities and their non-governmental partners approach the EU. Local governments seeking to engage with the EU face an array of regional and national bodies, which seek to maintain control over funding and communication with Brussels. British local authorities have looked repeatedly to the European Commission to act as a counterweight to Whitehall and its regional outposts, lobbying for Commission intervention to ensure that EU principles favourable to greater local independence – especially partnership and additionality of Structural Funding – are respected (McAleavey 1995). UK central government efforts to undercut additionality[1] in the 1980s and 1990s actually prompted greater activism by local authorities. Thus, central government efforts to retain absolute control over Structural Funding resulted in increased *voluntary-indirect* Europeanization at the local level. Local authorities that received significant tranches of EU assistance, such as the conurbations of Birmingham and Glasgow, consistently lobbied the Commission for greater local input during the agenda-setting, negotiation, implementation and evaluation phases of EU programmes to counter central government attempts to 'gatekeep' (Bache 1998, 1999; Marshall 2003).

Despite the fact that many British local authorities have looked to the EU for support in their battle for greater subsidiarity and local policy independence:

> the Commission can only go so far in shaping central–local relations in the UK. While it can create networks and encourage others, involve a wide range of actors, and participate itself, the Commission can do little to shift the long-standing power dependencies between central and local government. (Bache *et al.* 1996: 317)

Institutional constraints and the power of central government notwithstanding, it is equally difficult to disagree with John's (1996: 133) assertion that 'the effect of EU directives and finance was to precipitate a growing Europeanization of UK sub-national government' over time. Financial 'gatekeeper' or not, Whitehall has not stopped European notions of partnership and long-term programming from gaining ground among local authorities. While European principles have certainly been adapted to fit the distinct national context into which they are inserted – such as the traditionally strong role of UK central government *vis-à-vis* local actors – they nonetheless have provoked important changes in British local institutions.

EU structural funding

Introduction

The most common variant of Europeanization occurring at the local level – *voluntary-indirect* – owes much to the availability of EU funding for regeneration, economic development, social cohesion and knowledge transfer. British local authorities – especially those in areas eligible for large-scale Objective 1 or Objective 2 structural fund programmes – have willingly changed their organizational structures and working behaviour in order to access much needed EU regeneration and economic development aid. As one local authority chief executive put it:

> local government was showing entrepreneurial drive – they saw the structural funds as useful money, more flexible than what was on offer domestically. (interview with the author, 25 June 2002)

This case study draws on empirical research undertaken in the Birmingham and Glasgow city-regions during 2001–2003, which uncovered significant Europeanization within local authorities and other partners involved in the implementation of EU structural fund programmes (for further details, see Marshall 2003 and 2005).

Europeanization within local authorities

Local authorities in Birmingham and Glasgow demonstrate how the implementation of EU structural fund programmes gave rise to operational and structural changes within local government. Stakeholder interviews, surveys and documentary analysis showed that local councils in both cities voluntarily adjusted to European norms of partnership working, long-term strategic programming and direct lobbying in order to benefit from the 'carrot' of Structural Funding.

Birmingham City Council was one of the first local authorities to mobilize in Europe, opening its first office in Brussels in 1984. It subsequently secured an EU-funded Integrated Development Operation programme and a required change to UK 'Assisted Area' status in 1985 (see Martin and Pearce 1992). The powerful Strathclyde Regional Council, the then metropolitan authority for Glasgow, followed in 1985 and expanded its involvement in ensuing years thanks to activism on the part of leader Charles Gray (McAteer 1997; Colwell and McLaren 1999). The continuing importance of sub-national representation in Brussels is further discussed below.

Back at home in Britain, many local authorities established EU units dedicated exclusively to European working, ensuring continuous flows of information between Brussels and local councils while simultaneously developing the capacity to bid for (and implement) EU-financed regeneration programmes. The early and voluntary adoption of European working by local authorities in Birmingham and Glasgow helped these two conurbations to secure the largest packages of EU structural funding in England and Scotland, respectively, during the 1994–1999 and 2000–2006 programming periods (Marshall 2003).

During the past decade, European working has become part and parcel of everyday business in city council offices in Birmingham and Glasgow – a phenomenon that has also occurred in many non-metropolitan local authorities across Britain, such as Kent County Council (Goldsmith and Sperling 1997). In Birmingham, the City Council's Regional, European and International Division bids for and administers structural fund projects, liaises with other regional actors in the West Midlands, and actively engages with regional, national and international networks in order to promote coordinated regeneration efforts as well as the use of best practice solutions identified elsewhere. Glasgow City Council has incorporated European personnel and resources into an integrated department of Development and Regeneration Services, creating a single division for regeneration projects that links European, municipal and domestic renewal projects together for urban and structure planning purposes.

The establishment of European departments within local authorities goes beyond the simple administration of structural funding. Instead, it reflects the *voluntary-indirect* adoption of EU policy principles, such as programming, which favour holistic and strategic approaches to regeneration and economic development (CEC 1997a, 1998). These departments have subsequently encouraged longer-term, more inclusive thinking on regeneration that has spilled over into other areas of council working. Downward adaptational pressures have caused many local councils to embrace both organizational changes and shifts towards strategic partnership working, despite pressures for centralization and greater oversight emanating from Whitehall. As a prominent Birmingham politician intimated:

> I would argue that Birmingham's European linkage is not simply one of drawing down funding. Instead, it's very much more a process of moving from a parochial city to becoming a city which sees itself in a European league of cities. We talk about our competitiveness and our future in European terms.... (interview with the author, 24 October 2002)

This 're-visioning' has occurred in large part because of the structural funds, which catalyse institutional adjustment within British local authorities, thanks to the strict regulations governing their use.

As examples drawn from Birmingham and Glasgow show, Europeanization within local authorities has taken three distinct forms: organizational change; the development of holistic strategies spurred by partnership and programming requirements; and shifts towards regional working, which I term 're-visioning'. Process-based changes, such as the redistribution of council personnel and resources to strengthen European working, have been accompanied by new strategic, outward-looking initiatives undertaken by local authority leaders and chief executives. This suggests that the structural funds have made a critical contribution to the development of new ways of working in many beneficiary areas – including the development of closer links between local authorities in areas such as the West Midlands, Clydeside, Tyneside and elsewhere.

Europeanization in the local third sector

Local community and voluntary sector organizations throughout Britain have also adjusted their approach to regeneration in a voluntary-indirect manner in response to EU initiatives (for a more comprehensive treatment, see Chapman, Chapter 11). The experience of bidding for European Social Fund monies, coupled with extensive participation on Programme Monitoring Committees in Objective 1 and 2 areas, has given a new prominence to many local community groups. The partnership requirements of EU structural funding created a 'mis-fit' with extant norms in British local governance, and eventually resulted in an enhanced decision-making role for grass-roots organizations in project planning and implementation.

In the words of one interviewee working in the West Midlands:

> the structural funds have transformed the face of Birmingham. The social partners have realised this too . . . There's a lot of networking between all these different organisations. Time and again you meet people with two, three, four, five different hats linked to European activity. (interview with the author, 29 May 2002)

Driven by the participation of local third sector actors in structural fund projects, West Midlands European Network and Regional Action West Midlands were established to express the will of the local community and voluntary sectors in European and domestic policy spheres, respectively. A former chief executive of Birmingham City Council commented that

> absolutely, there is a ratchet effect. That level of investment has increased the pluralism, the number of voluntary organisations, in Birmingham – this is partly down to structural funds input. The security of some of these bodies has also been helped by structural funds money. And it's produced a bigger generation of people used to working in such organisations. (interview with the author, 25 June 2002)

As this example shows, local community groups in many parts of Britain have increased their involvement in agenda-setting and policy implementation thanks to the partnership requirements of the European structural funds. Although often small in budgetary terms, EU grants propelled many neighbourhood and community actors into larger roles in the world of local governance – giving them a coveted 'seat at the table' where strategic decisions are taken.

The increasing participation of non-governmental actors in European structural fund initiatives has also converged with the development of a wide array of local regeneration partnerships across Britain. While partnership bodies have been created and influenced extensively by national policy measures, 'the trend towards local partnership cannot be understood solely in national terms' (Geddes and Benington 2001: 14). In many areas, regeneration partnerships, often organized as limited companies, have become prominent fixtures in the local institutional landscape as a result of voluntary-indirect Europeanization. As a senior local authority officer remarked, EU assistance created 'a widely distributed and enhanced understanding of what works and doesn't work, drawing partners together – in sum, the skills of coalition-building' at the micro level (interview with the author, 25 June 2002). There is a significant degree of optimism that local regeneration partnerships, although started with EU funding, have become broadly institutionalized: 'They have built in structures and partnerships that will live on, operating with the local authorities and the NGOs' noted an interviewee at the Local Government Association, who also insisted that: 'the small community groups are doing the best work – the local authority is saying they have a commitment to these groups, and will divert the money there' (interview with the author, 21 June 2002). Thanks in part to the impact of the EU, local regeneration partnerships across Britain adopted a more joined-up entrepreneurial and international strategy to secure the resources and political backing required to propel neighbourhood regeneration in an era of central government budget-cutting and stringency (see also Martin and Pearce 1994; Geddes 2001).

As this case study of structural funding shows, incentives and pressures for Europeanization have engendered new modes of working within local authorities, local community and voluntary sector organizations, as well as in neighbourhood regeneration partnerships. Over the past two decades, there has been an identifiable process of voluntary adaptation and Europeanization, mediated by extant local and national institutional constraints, in areas benefiting from the structural funds. EU structural policy has thus created new institutions – both structures and less formal 'rules of the game' (Lowndes 2004) – at the local level across Britain.

UK sub-national offices

Introduction

As mentioned above, British local authorities have been opening representative offices in Brussels since the early 1980s, when trailblazers such as

Birmingham, Kent and Glasgow began lobbying the Commission for funding and a greater role in EU policy making (see, *inter alia*, John 1994b). The development of sub-national offices in Brussels and the institutional shifts they have created back home provide a second clear example of *voluntary-indirect* Europeanization affecting British local authorities. Local governments across the UK have developed new modes of interest representation – with the active encouragement of the European Commission – in response to Europeanization from above.

Local authority representation in Brussels

The Audit Commission, writing in its 1991 *Rough Guide to Europe*, argued that most British local authorities did not possess the tools required to engage properly with important EU matters (Goldsmith and Sperling 1997). Representative offices in Brussels were encouraged as examples of 'good practice' for local authorities at European level. By the mid-1990s, Peter John (1994b) found nearly 20 UK sub-national offices in operation. By 2005, the Local Government International Bureau (LGIB) listed some 30 representations on its website (LGIB 2005), despite a high degree of rationalization in recent years. The work of these offices has been a key driver of Europeanization at the local level, as their operation has altered working practices and relationships within the local authorities and regional bodies that they serve.

The restrictive nature of local government financial resources – an important domestic constraint, imposed by Whitehall – led many smaller British local authorities to cooperate in Brussels; for the most part, only large local authorities had the personnel and budget to strike out on their own (John 1994b; Goldsmith and Sperling 1997). Regardless of size and composition, the key goal of nearly all UK local government representative offices in Brussels was, and still is, to secure much-needed EU funding. However, the *regional* application of EU structural fund packages caused many British sub-national offices, and their parent local authorities, to voluntarily shift their focus from local to regional priorities over time (Smith 1999; West Midlands in Europe (WMIE) 2001). As a consequence, many local authorities have adopted new norms that include more regional consultation and strategic planning than before. Brussels offices have served as important stimuli for greater regional working, helping local authorities and their partners to 'download' key European concepts, such as regional partnership, into their everyday operations. This is another clear instance where the 'misfit' between EU requirements and Whitehall conceptions of sub-national governance have resulted, indirectly, in voluntary local institutional change.

Birmingham's European operations exemplify this shift. Originally, Birmingham City Council employed specialist staff at home and in Brussels. Later, this nucleus expanded to handle European relations for all 38 local authorities in the West Midlands region before finally evolving into a fully-fledged partnership body involving the private and community/voluntary sectors as well as local and regional government (WMIE 2001). In a manner that reflects long-standing local institutional norms and identities, offices representing Merseyside, Greater Manchester and nearby rural areas maintain their separate identities, but work together and share a single 'North West England House' in Brussels to facilitate this. Unitary authorities in greater Glasgow continue to work regionally at European level through the West of Scotland European Consortium, despite the abolition of the Strathclyde regional authority by UK Government in 1996.

All these examples show that one of the key impacts of European engagement has been to contribute to more joined-up working among individual British local authorities at regional level. While much of the shift towards regional structures in recent years has resulted from *domestic* institutional changes sparked by central government, Europeanization has also been a key driver of the shift towards a 'new Regionalism' in the UK (Keating, 1997; see also Burch and Gomez, Chapter 6).

Recent developments in UK domestic policy – such as the 'city-regions' approach to economic growth now being touted as a key part of the Government's *Northern Way Growth Strategy* (Centre for Sustainable Urban and Regional Futures 2004; Office of the Deputy Prime Minister 2004) – build upon the history of local authority joint working developed in European affairs. It can be argued that present receptivity and preparedness for city-regional working in the North derive, at least in part, from past joint working encouraged by EU policies during the 1980s and 1990s. Given the defeat of the government's plans for elected regional assemblies by nearly a four-to-one margin in the North East of England in November 2004, this aspect of informal local authority cooperation may become an important new feature in British territorial politics, and thus to the ongoing process of Europeanization.

'Uploading' and 'cross-loading' local preferences

The activities of thirty-odd local authority offices in Brussels have also created bottom-up processes of Europeanization within British local authorities. These include the 'uploading' of local preferences into European policy debates, and the 'cross-loading' or 'transfer' (Burch and Gomez 2003; Dolowitz and Marsh 1996; see also Bache and Jordan, Chapter 2) of proven policy solutions to other EU local actors, through a wide array of thematic networks.

The work of UK sub-national offices has encouraged local authorities across Britain to contribute actively to policy development, such as the consultations on European Commission's Governance White Paper, the future of EU Cohesion Policy and the future European Constitution. As one local government observer noted:

> We know that we can't just say we want this or that from Brussels . . . we
> need to build national and cross-national alliances . . . to 'upload' policy

preferences on to the European stage. (interview with the author, 24 October 2002)

In the field of 'cross-loading', a number of UK local authorities now lend their technical expertise in European affairs to counterparts in the new accession states; others submit to extensive scrutiny of their governance arrangements to distil examples of best practice (see for example OECD 2003, on regeneration and governance in Glasgow).

A more detailed treatment of these forms of Europeanization is beyond the scope of this chapter (but see Benington and Harvey (1998, 1999) on transnational networks; and Marshall (2005) on urban issues).

EU environmental legislation

Introduction

'Local Europeanization' in the area of environmental protection is instigated by the adoption of EU directives and regulations in the Council of Ministers. The 'mis-fit' between these and extant national systems has given rise to adaptational pressures at national and local levels (see Sbragia 2000). As the chief providers of ground-level environmental services, British local authorities have faced the daunting task of adjusting norms, practices and organizational structures to match the new realities created by EU environmental legislation (Lowe and Ward 1998; Weale *et al.* 2000).

Environmental directives and coercive Europeanization

Europeanization in local environmental policy differs significantly from that surrounding structural funding and sub-national lobbying, because EU environmental directives bring with them legal requirements – rather than informal adaptational pressures – for local governance change. Central government's assent to EU directives initiates new and binding obligations for all tiers of government in the UK, with the possibility of legal action in the European Court of Justice in the event of non-compliance. Local authorities have no choice but to change processes and structures to comply with these demands. Hence this form of 'local Europeanization' is both *coercive* and *indirect*.

Since the passage of the Single European Act in 1987 and the release of the Green Paper on the Urban Environment in 1990, which heralded the increased importance of pan-European environment policies, there has been a distinct change in the way that new environmental obligations are implemented in Britain (see Jordan, Chapter 15). Commentators have noted a 'formalisation' of policy implementation (Haigh and Lanigan 1995; Lowe and Ward 1998), with a greater input from central government in relation to target setting and oversight. This contrasts sharply with the previous use of framework legislation and more informal, local authority-specific implementation of new environmental regulations. As Lowe and Ward (1998: 27) have noted:

> Europe has been viewed as a centralising force, where statutory powers have shifted upwards through the governmental tiers. Thus the traditionally strongly devolved nature of environmental administration in the UK has been weakened. Local authorities have been stripped of responsibilities and discretionary authority.

While some observers have argued that this 'formalisation' has been accompanied by increased local authority influence and involvement at European level (for example Morphet 1998), it is clear that EU's dominant role in domestic environmental policy making has resulted in new and more coercive forms of Europeanization at local level. Long-established norms of local environmental governance in Britain, faced with the 'mis-fit' of a more interventionist and formal regime, are steadily being altered in a number of areas in order to ensure national compliance with EU requirements. While domestic forces – including environmental pressure groups and pro-environment industries such as wind power – would in any case have pushed for stronger national policies over time, it is clear that EU requirements greatly speeded up this process, for instance prompting the creation of the UK's Environment Agency in 1996.

Thus, *coercive-indirect* 'spill-over' from the national to the local tier of governance forces councils across Britain to face up to new and uniform obligations in areas such as water, waste management, recycling, environmental assessment, land use and green public procurement. Farcical scenes – such as the highly publicized dumping of unrecycled refrigerators in the wake of one EU directive (see, for example, Williams 2003) – occur whilst national and local authorities reform long-established institutions, with a view to creating new procedures and mechanisms for complying with EU law. The Europeanization of local environmental decision-making seen in recent years is illustrative of the fragmentation of responsibility between various tiers of governance, not to mention local authorities' lack of strategic input into EU-level negotiations *prior* to the passage of directives and regulations (Ward 1995; Morphet 1998). As Jordan (2002) argued, national waste policy is replete with examples of poor coordination and with respect to the anticipation of new EU initiatives.

The requirements of the WEEE (Waste Electrical and Electronic Equipment) Directive, which prompted the 'fridge mountain' issue, led to an enquiry by the House of Lords European Union Committee (House of Lords 2003). This found a high degree of 'mis-fit' between EU, national and local understanding of the Directive, which resulted in the urgent need for local authorities 'to be more proactive in anticipating EU policies and their consequences' (*ibid*: section 99). Whilst the enquiry lauded best practice recycling and disposal schemes resulting from EU pressures, notably in Peterborough and Hampshire, it placed significant emphasis on the coercive pressures and obstacles created by European environmental legislation, and highlighted the need for broad-based changes to policy implementation at local level. The House of Lords report also noted that there were numerous other instances where local authorities were forced to adapt their environmental provision to comply with EU directives – showing that *coercive-indirect* local Europeanization goes deeper than the 'fridge crisis' alone. Additionally, the Department of the Environment (now DEFRA) was historically poor at bringing sub-national viewpoints to the EU negotiating table – a subtle, less conscious form of gatekeeping.

Europeanization and local authority environmental practice

Given the difficulty of implementing environmental directives following their transposition into UK law, many British local authorities have sought assistance from the Commission to ensure their compliance with EU requirements. For example, UK local authorities make up the biggest contingent of successful applicants for LIFE, the EU's Financial Instrument for the Environment, which has been used to speed compliance with the Eco-Management and Audit Scheme (EMAS), green procurement requirements, and water management directives.[2] However, most of these bids come from local authorities with a track record of proactivity on other EU policy areas, demonstrating that the capacity to engage matters.

In recent years, for example, Kirklees Metropolitan Borough Council (2004), Leicester City Council (2003) and Newcastle City Council (1998) have led multi-authority projects that help local authorities to apply the EMAS Directive. Similarly, authorities in the West Midlands have spearheaded a project on sustainable management of urban rivers, given the need to implement EU water directives, while rural local authorities have led projects on land use and waste management that respond directly to Directives in those fields. In all, some 152 LIFE projects have been initiated directly by UK local authorities and partners working with the European Commission. This shows that local authorities are responding to adaptational pressures and the existence of mediating institutions (such as central government budgetary controls and target oversight) in a pragmatic and increasingly joined-up way.

Local authorities' increased activism and cross-national working – as evidenced by their participation in LIFE and other schemes – grew out of the need to implement environmental directives in a manner consistent with the formalized systems enshrined under EU law. As noted above, the Europeanization of environmental policy has resulted in a visible increase in local authority efforts to participate in agenda-setting, not to mention debates over subsidiarity and national compliance. Ward (1995: 120) argues that the dialogue between EU institutions and British local authorities has resulted in mutual legitimation and occasional by-passing of central government, though on balance 'the ability of local authorities to shape the agenda is distinctly marginal'. Others, such as Morphet (1998) and Ward and Williams (1997), highlight the fact that the process of local engagement with Environment Directorate-General and other European institutions is just beginning to take shape, and that these types of communication may serve in the long term to make the implementation of EU environmental directives more cooperative rather than coercive. The EU White Paper on Governance, for example, proposed cooperative 'tri-partite contracts' as a replacement for the present top-down system (CEC 2001).

In summary, EU environmental legislation has had a decisive impact on local governance. The Europeanization of local authority environmental activities, including the implementation of EU requirements and adaptation to a newly formalized system of environmental management, remains very much a work in progress. *Coercive-indirect* Europeanization and interventionist national and regional institutions mean that local authorities and their partners will continue to experience institutional and procedural change as additional environmental competences, such as planning, increasingly become subject to EU-level control.

Conclusions

This chapter argues that EU decisions and initiatives have had a significant influence on local authorities as well as on broader processes of local governance in Britain. While most empirical research has focused on areas benefiting from large-scale EU structural funding, examples of the Europeanizing effect of EU regulatory initiatives indicate that local authorities and their key partners have been affected nationwide. Thus, the local dimension of Europeanization in Britain – and especially its impact on the work of local authorities – is important and deserving of more detailed scrutiny. As the EU accrues new policy responsibilities in areas such as urban policy, spatial planning and environmental management in the coming years, local-level Europeanization will have a significant impact on policy implementation and representative politics.

EU policies have had important effects on local governance – both urban and rural – across Britain. The type of Europeanization witnessed at the local level falls into two principal categories: *voluntary* adjustment to EU norms in order to secure funding, gather information, and improve institutional relationships; and *coercive* pressure for changes in local systems to ensure compliance with EU legislation. Using the case studies above, a typology of 'local Europeanization' can be elaborated, with three main variants:

1. *Voluntary-indirect 'downloaded' Europeanization* in local authorities due to their continuing involvement in EU structural fund programmes, Community Initiatives (Urban, LIFE) and Pilot Projects.

2. *Voluntary-indirect 'downloaded' Europeanization, coupled to 'up-loading' and 'cross-loading', as well as multi-directional Europeanization* through the creation of sub-national offices in Brussels, participation in trans-European networks, and local lobbying.

3. *Coercive-indirect 'downloaded' Europeanization* within local authorities resulting from the implementation of EU directives and regulations, especially those relating to the environment.

The examples discussed above show how *voluntary-indirect* Europeanization has occurred in many local authorities due to the availability of EU structural funds and increasing opportunities for local lobbying in Brussels. At the same time, however, the adoption of EU environmental legislation has created *coercive* pressures for Europeanization among local authorities, who face altered institutional 'rules of the game' and formal targets agreed by Whitehall, often without adequate sub-national consultation. It can thus be argued that British local authorities have been 'winners' as well as 'losers' in the European game-winners, in the sense that voluntary forms of Europeanization have increased their participation in multi-level governance; and losers, where coercive EU directives have imposed politically testing and financially onerous new responsibilities for which councils are often unprepared. On a broader level, local authority officials have also lost some of their professional autonomy to shape policies to fit local circumstances (see Jordan, Chapter 15).

The case studies also clearly show that Europeanization is not limited to local authorities alone. EU initiatives have affected the relationships between councils and third sector actors in local governance, including community groups and contracted service providers. Requirements for long-term partnership working, which feature prominently across EU policy areas, have forced the expansion of the number of players at the local decision-making table, bringing NGOs, representatives from the community and voluntary sectors, business leaders and other social partners into the increasingly complex world of local governance (for more on the third sector, see Chapman, Chapter 11). Their presence alongside mainstream local authorities has, over time, become an increasingly important feature of the more open, fragmented and unstable institutional landscape of local governance in Britain.

However, it is important to note that the partnership approach to economic development, regeneration and environmental management has also been a major element of UK domestic policy change over the past two decades. Therefore, we must be careful not to overemphasize the influence of the EU. Geddes (2001) has argued that the scale and extent of EU programmes have limited their impact on partnership development in the UK. At the same time, he notes that European initiatives have in some cases shifted existing local governance norms. It is clear that more detailed empirical research needs to be undertaken at the local level if we are to systematically separate institutional change due to Europeanization from change that has its origins in domestic policy initiatives.

In sum, this chapter demonstrates that Europeanization most certainly does not stop at the national or regional level in Britain. EU-level policies, practices and preferences have important spillover effects on local authorities and their key partners. The top-down impact of the EU on British local authorities and other sub-national actors is significant, and seems likely to grow ever stronger if and when the Union accrues additional competences in relevant policy areas. Thus, 'local Europeanization' will continue to be an important driver of governance change in Britain's cities, towns and rural areas. Local actors and academic researchers must ensure that Whitehall departments understand that Europeanization is a phenomenon experienced at all levels of the British polity – and take steps to add this *local* dimension into their policy making activities.

Notes

1. The 'additionality' principle requires European structural funds to be additional to – rather than a replacement for – domestic regional and regeneration funding.
2. For more on these projects, see http://europa.eu.int/comm/environment/life/home.htm.

Part III
Politics

8
Political Parties and Party Politics

Andrew Geddes

Introduction

This chapter examines the Europeanization of British party politics. It is within the domain of party politics that debates about the EU have often been at their most intense, yet, compared to particular policy areas, party politics tend not to be the subject of analyses of Europeanization. This is surprising because, as Hix (2005: 180) points out, 'EU politics is party politics' not least because it is the parties that provide a vital link between the national and EU arenas. This chapter aims to address this analytical gap by identifying the domestic consequences of European integration for British political parties.

The chapter's focus is on party political structures and the represent-ation of cleavages, defined by Rae and Taylor (1970: 1) as 'the criteria which divide the members of a community or subcommunity into groups, and the relevant cleavages are those which divide members into groups with important political differences at specific times and places'. Lipset and Rokkan (1967) famously identified the 'critical junctures' centred on church–state, centre–periphery and class relations that provided the social and spatial foundations of European party politics.

As the editors of this volume suggest in Chapter 2, Europeanization need mean neither harmonization nor convergence. Following their definition, the concern here is with the extent to which engagement with the EU has 're-orientated or re-shaped' British party politics. Two arguments are developed. First, that links can be made between two of the domains of Europeanization identified by Radaelli (2000), namely structures of representation and norm-ative and cognitive constraints/change. Ideas, subjectivity and meaning are integral components of the debates about the EU in British party politics because the meaning of European integration in British politics is contested in relation to broader debates about the state, the nation and sovereignty within and between the parties. Second, the powerful, centrist cross-party coalition that linked the centre-left and centre-right of British politics on the issue of European integration has broken down. The Conservatives have

119

become a Eurosceptic party while Labour and the Liberal Democrats, broadly speaking, remain more favourable. A Eurosceptic fringe has also become far more prominent in the form of parties such as the United Kingdom Independence Party (UKIP), which has tended to do well in 'second order' European Parliament elections.

British party politics and European integration

It has been observed that European party systems have been relatively impervious to the effects of European integration (Mair 2000). Aside from the creation of pan-EU party federations, this is not an area where the EU exercises competence. It is also an area where the basic organizational, ideological and communicative tools of political parties remain strongly grounded in national contexts. This does not mean that there is not a European dimension to party politics. There is, and its importance is growing. We can, for example, see a consolidation of party ties beyond the member states, a growing role for the European Parliament, as well as party political ties to transnational federations that themselves have become more meaningful (Hix and Lord 1997; Corbett 1998). Rather, the point is that there are ideological, organizational and communicative constraints on Europeanization as the source of a domestic reorientation of party politics. Moreover, the 'ideological identikit' of British political parties was founded on a two-dimensional left-right dimension rather than the two- or three-dimensional EU space where national-territorial, socio-economic and political-institutional questions associated with European integration challenge these identities (Hix 1999: 78). For example, the Labour Party made a different connection between territory, sovereignty, socio-economic policy and the role of political institutions in the 1970s (when it opposed the EU) and the 1990s (when it adopted an 'open regionalist' position that favoured economic and political integration) (Baker *et al.* 2002).

The EU's effects may, therefore, be more indirect. The EU has possessed the potential to induce a great deal of turbulence within British political parties (Forster 2002). These debates were not necessarily about the EU in some objective sense as though the EU and its effects were some uncontested and clearly defined fact in British political life. Rather, they were, are and continue to be about understandings and interpretations of the EU. Indeed, any attempt to identify European sources of change does raise some methodological issues – not least, disentangling European sources of domestic political change from other sources of change.

This chapter contends that the meaning and effects of the European issue in British party politics are revealed by the ways in which it touches upon core concerns of the state, the nation and sovereign authority; or put another way, the meaning and role of the state, the idea of the nation and the continued relevance of state sovereignty. As parties themselves represent different interests and different ideologies at different times according to internal and external processes, the meaning and effects of the EU within the parties is likely to be contested. Political parties can thus be understood as agents of interests, arenas of conflict, and as forming part of larger arenas of conflict (Panebianco 1988). The result is that the 'European issue' in British party politics does not reveal itself as an objective set of pressures to which Britain must adapt, as suggested by some approaches to Europeanization (see Bache and Jordan, Chapter 2). The party political debate in Britain about Europe is intensely about the contested meaning of Europe viewed through the lens – or perhaps more accurately, the distorting lens – provided by national party politics. This means that the rise of Conservative Euroscepticism or New Labour's more pro-European stance cannot simply be read off from the evolving structures of the EU as the key driver of domestic political change.

Rather, the party political debate in Britain is about the meaning imputed to Europe in domestic politics. The EU may thus be understood and represented as an external constraint in the context of a broader debate about globalization (Dyson and Featherstone 1999; Buller 2000; Buller and Gamble 2002; Buller, Chapter 13). This also means that there may well be less scope for Europeanization as outlined in Chapter 2 of this volume (that is, as a top-down process of construction, diffusion and institutionalization of EU 'ways of doing things'), but this does not mean that European integration has not had an effect on the core roles of political parties. Rather, these effects reveal themselves in the ways that the EU becomes part of a broader debate within and between the political parties and within British politics more generally about the state, the nation and sovereignty.

This argument becomes clearer if we think about the period between the Single European Act (SEA) and the (Maastricht) Treaty on European Union (1992), which had profound implications for practices and ideas concerning the state, nation and sovereign authority within the main British political parties and British politics more generally. During this period the stances of the Conservative and Labour parties were effectively reversed. Labour moved from anti- to pro-EU. The Conservatives shifted in the opposite direction. This reversal in position was in some ways linked to the content of EU legislation as the development of a social and regional policy dimension did provide new political opportunities for the Labour Party and labour movement, while post-SEA 'spillover' in areas of social, regional, environmental and economic policy was seen as a threat to Thatcherism (Rosamond 1998; Forster 2002; van der Maas, Chapter 10). There was, however, also an interpretive element to this re-orientation within both main parties. For the Labour Party from the mid-1980s onwards the EC became an element of party modernization. Meanwhile, for a growing numbers of Conservatives in the 1980s the EC was perceived as a venue for socialist-style re-regulation of the British economy and thus as a threat to the Thatcherite governing project. The backdrop for these perceptions was not only a developing EC role, but also the ascendancy in British politics at that time of Thatcherism, which influenced the strategic and ideological context of British party politics.

Political parties and European integration

The balance of research on Europeanization has tended to be towards the EU's top-down impact on national laws and policies, with rather less attention paid to the EU's impact on political parties and structures of representation. While there is a large literature on both political parties and integration as distinct areas of study 'very little of the literature on integration is on political parties, and very little of the literature on political parties is on integration' (Gaffney 1996: 1). What literature there is tends to focus on attempts to form EU parties (Hix and Lord 1997) or explores the stances of political parties on the EU (Gaffney 1996).

Work on European party politics has focused on the core roles of parties: representation, legislation and government formation. Dalton and Wattenburg (2000: 3) write that an obituary for political parties would be premature, but they do note a decline in partisanship, turnout and party identification which means that there has been a change in the role of political parties and that this trend is apparent across advanced industrial democracies (see also Dalton 2000). The result, they contend, is that while the representational function may have been weakened, the legislative and governmental roles remain intact. One consequence of this can be weaker links with civil society, which in turn is seen as being behind the rise of the 'cartel party' dependent on the state with increased dependence on state funding (Katz and Mair 1995). Overall, Mair (2000) finds that the EU's impact on party politics has been minimal, particularly when compared to other areas such as particular policy sectors where changes have been more profound. He goes on to argue that 'party systems have been most impervious to change' (Mair 2000: 4). More than this, he contends that where the EU has had an effect, it has been largely negative; as marked by a decreased freedom of manoeuvre for national governments, a reduction in policy alternatives for voters because of common EU policies in some areas, and a contribution to the sense that party politics has lost relevance because power and authority are slipping away from national political arenas to the EU level.

The absence of a European party system can also explain the imperviousness of national party systems to the EU's influence. Goetz and Hix (2001: 12) argue that the EU can provide a new structure of opportunities with information and material benefits that can feed into the domestic context. It could even be the case that those most strongly affected by European integration, such as trade unions, some non-governmental organizations, business interests and local authorities, will be much more interested in the

EU than the general public for whom core concerns about health, education, and law and order appear scarcely touched by European integration. Ladrech (2002: 390) suggests a link between the Europeanization of policy and the Europeanization of political parties as the EU works its way into domestic politics in a way that might reframe political opportunities by offering, for example, new funds for regional development. National parties might thus to some extent reorganize their domestic activity to account for this European dimension of national politics. Ladrech (2002) also seeks to introduce more specificity to the analysis of the Europeanization of party politics by oper-ationalizing the concept of Europeanization and then specifying five areas within which the effects of Europeanization on national political parties may be discerned. He specifies European integration as an independent variable with governmental autonomy and interest in politics as dependent variables (Ladrech 2002: 396–400). Then he spells out a research agenda focused on:

- Policy and programmatic content – This can be analysed through the analysis of party manifestos and EU references.
- Organization – Trends towards centralization were mapped by Kirch-heimer (1966). It is useful to distinguish between the party in public office, the party on the ground and the party in central office (Raunio 2002: 408). Katz and Mair (1995) argue that it is the party on the ground that has been weakened by European integration 'emasculating the both-ersome activists' as Scarrow (2000: 148) put it.
- Patterns of party competition – There have been attempts made to capit-alize on the EU issue. This does, though, depend on the salience of the issue. The EU can and has been a *campaign issue* in British elections, but not necessarily a *salient issue* in the minds of voters (Geddes 1997, 2002, 2005a). The *Daily Express* put it more pithily by noting that it was an issue that made the parties swoon and the voters yawn (Geddes 1997: 85).
- Party government relations – Participation at EU level may distance leaders from party programmes as they are pushed towards certain posi-tions or the EU can allow the pursuit of objectives that may not necessarily be in accord with the views of party members. Raunio (2002: 405) explores power relations within parties and points to increased autonomy for party leaders and strengthened agenda-setting capabilities. This is greater in countries with weaker parliamentary scrutiny.
- Relations beyond the national party system – transnational co-operation with pan-European party federations and perhaps too through a transna-tionalization of debates.

Within the literature on European party politics a distinction can also be made between Europeanization understood as more direct EU effects on party politics and Europeanization understood more generally in terms of the social origins of European party politics and the development of party families. These two have been brought together by Marks and Wilson (2000) who, drawing on Lipset and Rokkan's (1967) classic analysis of the formation of west European party systems, analysed the impact of the 'new' issue of European integration. By 'new' they meant in the sense of being beyond the class, religion and state-building basis of traditional 'frozen' cleavages. They asked whether party responses were filtered by historical predispositions rooted in the basic cleavages that structure political competition. They found that European integration is assimilated into pre-existing ideologies of leaders, activists and constituencies and that this process reflects the longer-standing commitment of these parties on fundamental domestic issues. This is because parties have their own 'bounded rationality' that shapes the ways in which they respond to new issues such as European integration. In circumstances where the distribution of individual voters' economic interests is unclear and individual attitudes are 'weakly structured', then political parties will seek to blend the issue into existing patterns of party competition. The conclusion of Marks and Wilson's analysis is that there is more in common between parties of the same family than there is between parties in the same country. Thus, the British Labour Party is more like its sister parties in the Netherlands and Germany, say, than it is like the Conservative Party. To make this argument, Marks and Wilson draw from historical institutionalism, path dependence and what Rokkan called the 'structure of political alternatives' (cited in Marks and Wilson 2000: 437).

If we apply this analysis to the main party families, then social democratic parties will be pulled in two directions. European integration as a liberalizing project could be construed as a threat to national social democracy or could provide the framework of international cooperation to act as its saviour. In contrast, where social democratic parties have been able to attain Keynesian economic objectives and strong welfare states, they may well be sceptical about deeper European integration. Where social democracy is weak, parties tend to be more amenable to European integration and vice versa. There is a problem here in accurately interpreting New Labour's conversion to Europe, in the sense that European integration as a liberalizing project was not seen as a threat to its version of social democracy. This may be because the modernized Labour Party is not easily recognizable in the context of European social democracy (Callaghan 2000; Gamble and Kelly 2000; Clift 2001). If we look at economic management, for example, then the emphasis of New Labour in power has been on forms of European economic modernization that emphasize liberalization and labour market flexibility as a prerequisite for British participation in the single currency (see, for example, HM Treasury 2005).

Parties of the right such as the Conservative Party are pulled in two directions because European integration not only could enhance market efficiency, but can also challenge ideas about the nation, state and sovereignty attached to the territorial state held dear by Conservatives. Marks and Wilson (2000) see neo-liberals as supporting 'negative integration' that deregulates, and opposing 'positive integration' that develops new structures. The problem here is that the division between negative and positive integration is not always clear. The SEA, for example, was, in some senses, a huge exercise in negative integration as it sought to create an area without internal frontiers – a single European market – within which people, services, goods and capital could move freely. At the same time, the SEA introduced new decision-making procedures that strengthened the role of supranational institutions and helped initiate the momentum that led to proposals in areas such as regional, environmental, economic, monetary and social policies in the late 1980s and early 1990s. A problem for the British Conservatives that was linked to the EU, and also to other sources of domestic change, was that the Thatcherite attempt to 'roll back the frontiers of the state' also kicked away some of the central pillars of conservatism in British society (Gamble 1993). There was thus a broader debate within the Conservative Party about state, nation and sovereign authority within which understandings of European integration played a role, but that was more fundamentally linked to the tension between the free economy and the strong state (Gamble 1988). This market/state discourse was, however, strongly focused on Britain. 'Europe' was an opportunity for the projection of Thatcherite values or a threat to them, not some kind of alternative to the territorial state.

Liberals are likely to oppose aggressive nationalism and value decentralized decision-making. This is consistent with a 'small f' approach to federalism found in the Liberal Democrats (Russell and Fieldhouse 2005). The dilemma for the Liberal Democrats is that they are the most consistently pro-European of the main national parties, but attract strong support in areas of Britain where agriculture and fishing are strong and where Euroscepticism is at times quite fierce.

Sub-state nationalist parties such as the Scottish National Party and Plaid Cymru benefit from European integration because the EU creates space for the articulation of sub-state national identities within a European framework, although if these identities are nationalist or irredentist (such as the Lega Nord in Italy) then this would tend to lead to Euroscepticism (Brown 1998; Baker *et al.* 2002). Religion has been most relevant to political life in Northern Ireland. Those parties that identify themselves as Protestant (such as the Democratic Unionist Party and the Ulster Unionist Party) tend to be more sceptical, while those that identify themselves as Catholic, such as the Social Democratic and Labour Party, tend to be more pro-European (Tonge 2002).

These categorizations help make sense of broad party positions on the issues, but we need to drill down a little more deeply if we are to understand the relationship between cleavage structures and meanings and beliefs within the parties. There are often complex traditions within parties.

Moreover, the pro-European alliance that used to exist constructed around the political centre-ground has broken down.

How could patterns of engagement and disengagement with the EU make themselves manifest in British politics? One effect could be a diminished sense of the efficacy of party politics if the freedom of manoeuvre of national governments is seen to have diminished. Another could be increased engagement and increased ties with European-level politicians such as Members of the European Parliament (MEPs) by those most strongly affected by European integration such as trade unions, business interests and local authorities. Another effect if partisan ties are weaker could be electoral volatility with growth in the Eurosceptic fringe as parties such as UKIP seek to profit from a gap between the people and the politicians. It is also plausible that these three patterns of engagement and disengagement could co-exist, as national politics is seen by some to lose relevance, for others to provide new political opportunities and resources, but for Eurosceptics to be a threat.

Dependent and independent variables

A problem with analysing the Europeanization of British party politics in terms of dependent and independent variables is that it is not entirely clear what is dependent and what is independent. There are a range of variables that could affect the relationship between EU and national politics. While key election issues such as health, education, and law and order remain largely within the purview of the national government, political parties have, however, been subject to a squeeze that changes the context within which they operate and changes the nature of the debate within and between the parties. This 'party squeeze' is represented in Figure 8.1 where countervailing national and international pressures on British political parties are identified.

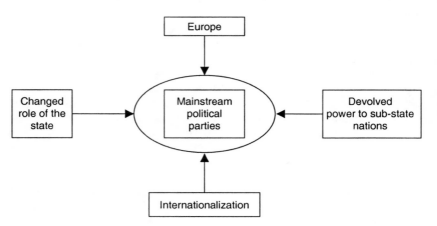

Figure 8.1 The party squeeze

Changing patterns of governance in the UK involve some shifts in power and authority to the EU, which may heighten a sense that normal, state-centred politics has lost some of its relevance. But devolved government, economic internationalization and an increased role for the market in the provision of public services have effects here too. Thus, while we may have the idea that European integration challenges the borders of national political systems, it may also be the case that changes within those systems 'challenge' understandings of European integration as threat or as opportunity. The ways in which Europe is understood may be dependent to some extent on domestic political contexts. If so, it becomes less clear what is dependent and what is independent in this relationship.

Interpreting Europe in Britain

Academic accounts of British relations with the EU tend to emphasize pathologies within the British polity that explain the extent of British engagement understood as awkwardness, reluctance or semi-detachment (George 1992, 1998; Gowland and Turner 2000; Geddes 2004). From the pro-EU side the story is one of failure, by which is meant a failure by the domestic political elite to engage with the EU and thus to promote Britain's best interests (Young 1998). From a pro-EU perspective, and in an allusion to social construction, Baker (2005) refers to 'islands of the mind' as an explanation for Britain's 'defensive' and 'obstructive' engagement with the EU. The arguments of the pro-European camp can be seen to implicitly follow the social constructivist logic as identified by Hacking (2000: 6), in that Euroscepticism and British semi-detachment need not have existed and they are not inevitable. The argument is then extended to contend that a failure to engage with the EU has bad consequences and really should be changed.

The Eurosceptic camp follows the same kind of logic, but in its case it is closer European economic and political integration that have brought bad consequences for Britain and it is this that needs to be changed rather than deficient engagement. The 'social construction' of the EU on the 'Pro' and 'anti' sides points to the idea that there is not some essential notion or 'model' of Europe that is or can be downloaded as a driver of political debates in Britain. Clearly, the EU provides a distinct and challenging legal, political and economic framework; and its effects, whether good or bad, are obviously not entirely imagined. However, while the European issue in British party politics lacks an objective definition, meaning has been imparted to the debate about the EU by its entanglement with broader themes associated with state, nation and sovereign authority.

It is in these terms that we begin to see the outline of the 'islands of the mind' argument that Baker (2005) discusses. Ideas in such terms can be more than *deus ex machina* that cause trouble and then leave (Blyth 1997: 230). They can have power as sources of change because they can 'lend representative legitimacy to some social interests more than others, delineate the accepted boundaries of state action, associate contemporary political developments with particular interpretations of national history and define the context in which many issues will be understood' (Hall 1993: 289). The task is to specify the relevant ideas and the impact they had at particular points in time.

Within the Europeanization literature there has been an influential strand of work that draws from new institutionalist approaches (Schneider and Aspinwall 2001). These approaches have been particularly useful in drawing attention to issues of social embeddedness and the ways in which, for example, domestic change can be in accord with pre-existing logics (Bulmer and Burch 1998). This emphasis on adaptation is a prominent strand in the literature on party politics too (Sartori 1968). Studies of Europeanization have also emphasized cognitive and normative changes/constraints arising from European integration. These draw attention to the beliefs that individuals hold and the ways in which these can alter.

A cognate strand in political analysis has also returned subjectivity to the forefront of political analysis through its emphasis on the need to inter- rogate beliefs and meanings in order to understand changing patterns of British governance (Bevir and Rhodes 2003). This argument implies that 'traditions' and 'beliefs' can exercise some causal power, although the mech- anisms through which this is expressed can be unclear. While we know, for instance, that there may be different interpretations of Britain's place in the EU, how can we explain the rise of Euroscepticism at a particular point in time and attached to particular narrative strands within the Conservative Party? Traditions within political parties as explanatory tools are ambiguous because they appear not only to arise from a set of actions, but also to explain those actions. Finlayson (2004: 152) argues that the need to interrogate the meanings of traditions is important and useful, but that more needs to be said about the formation of ideas and the ways in which they 'constitute action' as well as the ways in which some ideas or beliefs become part of a tradition while others do not. The task then becomes to examine the ways in which the EU enters into the narrative texture of British party politics and to examine when, how and why practices and ideas (and interpretations of them) associated with the EU have had an impact on British party politics.

The European issue in British party politics

It is well known that as the Conservatives party became more Eurosceptic from the late 1980s onwards, Labour became more pro-European. Euroscep- ticism became a distinct and powerful force in British party politics asso- ciated with the Conservative Party. Taggart (1998) saw Euroscepticism as a phenomenon evident on the fringes of party systems and as a way of distin- guishing these (Eurosceptic) parties from mainstream parties that express

Euroscepticism through factions. Taggart (1998: 366) defines Euroscepticism broadly as 'contingent or qualified opposition, as well as incorporating outright and unqualified opposition to the process of European integration' with the result that 'all opponents of the EU are, at least, Eurosceptical, but not all sceptics are opponents'.

Thus, a distinction can be made between Eurosceptic parties and parties with Eurosceptical factions. UKIP is clearly a Eurosceptical party. The Conservative Party is interesting in this respect. Is it now a party with Eurosceptical factions or is it a Eurosceptical party? The conditions the Conservatives placed at the 2005 general election on their engagement with the EU – 'no' to the single currency, 'no' to the constitution, the demand for a fundamental renegotiation of the terms of membership and the repatriation of some powers – would seem to point towards the EU's exit door. The Conservatives have become, to use Taggart and Szczerbiak's terminology, a 'hard' Eurosceptic Party. 'Softer' Euroscepticism has policy and national interest elements, which could be seen to imply that the Labour Party is a soft Eurosceptic party in the sense that opt-outs persist in the key areas of Economic and Monetary Union (EMU) and the free movement of people, while British interaction continues to be dressed up in the language of the pursuit or defence of national interests.

We can now move on to examine more closely the ways in which the European issue has worked its way into the narrative texture of British party politics. If we look at the Conservative party then European integration was integral to the civil war that broke out within the Party in the aftermath of the 1992 general election and Maastricht ratification process. The underlying reason for this was the impact of European integration *as understood* by prominent strands of opinion within the party (and linked to the party, such as in the writings of prominent Eurosceptic journalists) on the Thatcherite governing project. There was no single, consistent strand of thought. Rather, there were a number of stands of thought that drew from particular understandings of the state, nation and sovereign authority, but were to coalesce into a powerful critique of European integration.

The power of ideas can also be discerned in the aftermath of Margaret Thatcher's September 1988 Bruges speech. In terms of the causal power of ideas, it is possible to argue that the substantive content of Conservative Party policy on European integration changed less than the ideas about the EU's effects on the Thatcherite governing project (Geddes 2005b). It was not necessarily the case that Europe's social charter was inspired by Marxist ideas of class warfare, as Thatcher argued, but that the attachment of the Conservatives to the external impetus for domestic modernization provided by European integration was diminished when European integration moved into areas such as social, regional and economic policy and was thus seen to conflict in fundamental ways with the objectives of Conservative governments after 1979. Ideas and understandings of the EU – particularly in the aftermath of Thatcher's Bruges speech – had powerful effects on the Conservative Party. To paraphrase Hall (1993: 289), the Bruges speech leant legitimacy to Euroscepticism as a mainstream rather than fringe concern, delineated the accepted boundaries of state action, associated contemporary political developments in the wake of the SEA and domestic economic, political and social change with particular interpretations of national history, and thus helped define the context in which European issues should be understood.

During this period between 1986 and 1992 when the Conservatives moved to a more Eurosceptic position, the Labour Party changed its stance too. We could read this off as a rational response to the re-orientation of the Conservative party to a more Eurosceptic position and to an EU that moved from being the capitalist club of 1970s' anti-Common Market rhetoric, to a 'Community' with broader social objectives and that, more than this, offered new opportunities for domestically excluded groups such as trade unions to wield influence (via the European back door, as Thatcher put it in her Bruges speech; see van der Maas, Chapter 10). This rational approach would over-determine the EU's role in domestic change. Understandings of the EU were also a component of a broader project of party modernization, that is, to be European was to be modern and to be modern was to be European. This had less to do with the 'nuts and bolts' of the EU. If we look at the single currency, the Common Agricultural Policy (CAP) and the EU's budget, we see that New Labour's stance has not been markedly different from those of other British governments. Rather, European integration became part of a leadership narrative focused on the need to modernize and reform the party. While we can identify EU changes as influencing domestic change, we also have to factor into our analysis the ways in which the domestic content refracted these influences in the context of a broader modernization of the Labour Party (Fielding 2002; Heffernan 2002).

The EU as a campaign issue

The point developed so far has been that ideational variables have been central to understanding the impact of the EU on British structures of representation because they help us understand the distorting lens through which political parties view the EU. We can see this when we examine the EU as a campaign issue in national and European Parliament elections.

The 1997 general election was the first at which European integration was a prominent campaign issue and also demonstrated the grip of party-based Euroscepticism within the Conservative Party. This was particularly evident when John Major appealed during the election campaign to Eurosceptics within his own party: '[w]hether you agree with me, disagree with me, like me or loathe me, don't bind my hands when I am negotiating on behalf of the British people' (cited in Geddes 1997: 85). This was an impromptu party election broadcast replacing the scheduled broadcast with the embattled party leader addressing the nation as though during war time. In fact, the danger came from insurgency from within his own party, as Conservative MPs seemed to assume that their EU obsessions resonated with the electorate as a whole. Unfortunately for the Conservatives, they did not. The EU was a campaign issue rather than a salient concern for voters. Moreover, Labour neutralized the issue during the 1997 campaign by mimicking Conservative positions (most notably Tony Blair's 'why I love the £' article in *The Sun*). We can see this most clearly if we look at the main parties' election manifestos dealing with the EU. We find one party proclaiming that they 'would not allow Britain to be part of a federal European superstate' while another declared that 'an alliance of independent nations choosing to co-operate to achieve the goals they cannot achieve alone. We oppose a federal European superstate' (cited in Geddes 1997: 90). The fact that the former was the Conservative manifesto and the latter was the Labour manifesto indicates that the gap between the official positions of the two parties was not actually that great. They shared a policy emphasis too on enlargement, CAP reform and single market completion. The Liberal Democrats were the most distinct through their support for EMU and for a democratic and diverse EU. There was also Eurosceptic organization during the 1997 campaign within Conservative party candidates in opposition to the formal party position on European integration. A leader of this move was millionaire businessman Paul Sykes who stood down as Conservative party parliamentary candidate for a seat in Barnsley and directed financial support to those Conservatives who would renounce the official 'wait and see' stance and say that they opposed the single currency. Soon afterwards, 237 candidates had received support of up to £3000 each from Sykes (Geddes 1997: 89).

At the 2001 general election, there were further attempts to open clear blue water between Labour and the Conservatives on the EU issue with William Hague's 'save the pound' general election campaign, which veered dangerously close to single issue politics. In 2001, the EU was again a campaign theme but not a salient concern for the voters. Public attitudes towards the EU have certainly been more sceptical in the UK than in other member states with Britain labelled in a Eurobarometer report as the EU's 'don't know, not interested' capital.[1] However, a Eurosceptical public need not mean support for a Eurosceptical party because issues such as law and order and public services are far more important in most people's mind than Europe. Those for whom the EU is an important issue tend to vote Conservative, or for fringe Eurosceptical parties anyway. In 2001, however, differences between the two main parties were more pronounced than in 1997, with the Conservatives edging towards a semi-detached relationship with the EU through what they called a 'network Europe' that would institutionalize this semi-detachment as different countries came together within the EU for different purposes which would require a re-written Treaty framework and certain 'reserved powers' for national governments.

The Conservatives have also been vulnerable to losing support to 'hard' Eurosceptic fringe parties such as the Referendum Party (at the 1997 general election) and since then UKIP. At the 2004 European parliament elections, UKIP won 12 seats and secured 16 per cent of the vote, pushing the Liberal Democrats into fourth place. It could be argued that it is on the Eurosceptic fringe that we see some evidence, perhaps ironic, of the Europeanization of British party politics: but Europeanization as divergence. The resonance of ideational variables centred on the issues of state, nation and sovereign authority can be seen on the Eurosceptic fringe inhabited by UKIP and on the extreme right by the British National Party (BNP). These parties also connect European integration with immigration as threats to the nation, the state and sovereign authority. The Eurosceptic fringe has, however, been more successful at second order European elections where proportional represent-ation favours smaller parties such as the Greens, as opposed to the first past the post system for Westminster elections.

On the Eurosceptic fringe the rhetoric of 'truth-telling' is fundamental to the strategies of both the BNP and UKIP, and has been seen to demonstrate that they are part of the same phenomenon. This 'truth-telling' approach allows them to express solidarity with racism and xenophobia, while also defining themselves as plain-speaking folk who will risk persecution for their defi-ance of liberal hegemony and 'politically correct' laws and attitudes (John, Margetts and Weir 2005). John, Margetts and Weir (2005:15) estimate a poten-tial 20 per cent share of the vote for the extreme right fringe and note that

> [t]he BNP and UKIP are bitter rivals, but they draw from the same reservoir of support, and opinion polls and focus groups suggest they are linked in voters' minds. Though UKIP's main policy position is withdrawal from the EU, its policies link the EU and immigration as closely related nationalist concerns. The party said at the 2005 general election that it would 'put an end to mass EU immigration.

Robert Kilroy-Silk, the former TV chat show host set up the breakaway Veritas party shortly after being elected a UKIP MEP. This party also made clear links between the EU and immigration with Britain supposedly being stolen from its citizens by 'waves' of immigrants.

The Eurosceptic fringe saw its vote crumble at the 2005 general election as the EU barely registered as an issue. According to MORI polling data, the number of respondents who saw European integration as one of the most important issues facing the country was 24 per cent in June 2001, this number fell to less than 10 per cent for the 8 months prior to the dissolution of Parliament and the calling of the 2005 general election. There were three reasons for this. First, the election of Iain Duncan Smith as Conservative leader in 2001 could be seen as the triumph of Euroscepticism within the Conservative party. As soon as he was elected Duncan Smith not only ruled out joining the euro, but also sought to broaden the Conservative agenda. Put simply, the Conservatives stopped talking about Europe. The second reason was that Blair's decision to hold referenda on the draft Constitutional Treaty and membership of the euro meant that the EU debate was extracted out of the party political contest. The third and most telling reason was that EU issues have been consigned to a domain of 'second order politics'. Reif and Schmitt (1980) argued that in second order elections there tend to be lower levels of participation than in national 'first order' elections. Moreover, they provide better prospects for small and new political parties, whereas governing parties tend to do badly. The reason why voters behave in this way is that they know that far less is at stake in a second order election. Indeed, research has shown that European elections are even more second order in the minds of British voters than local elections (Heath *et al.* 1999). This also means that the votes cast at a European election may be more expressive, or from the heart. A vote for UKIP may represent anti-EU sentiment rather than a hard headed decision that a UKIP government would actually be a good idea.

Conclusion

Political parties have been central to European integration as key links between the national and EU arenas, but have not tended to be central to analyses of Europeanization. Indeed, in the terms by which Europeanization is often discussed, there is little evidence of impact because there is no EU template for national party politics, and because the ideological, organizational and communicative practices of British party politics remain fairly strongly rooted in the national context. However, this does not mean that the EU has not affected British party politics. Indeed, it would be a strange reading of recent British political history that argued that it had not.

One effect has been the tension evident as British political parties have sought to reconcile a two-dimensional national political space founded on the left-right dimension and challenges to it such as devolution, with a multi-dimensional EU space where territorial, socio-economic and political-institutional issues associated with European integration create a more complex setting. Another effect has been the breakdown of the centrist, pro-European coalition that used to dominate British politics and united the leaderships of the three main national parties. The Conservatives have now become a 'hard' Eurosceptic party while a Eurosceptic fringe has emerged and enjoyed some success in second order elections.

In order to understand these changes they need to be located in relation to a broader debate about the future of British politics, to which the idea of the nation, the role of the state and sovereign authority therein are central. Temporally, Europeanization was most evident after the Maastricht Treaty. It was particularly evident within the Conservative party and thus was an issue that struck within, rather than between, the main political parties. The mechanism by which this occurred was linked to broader ideational changes in British politics and links made between the EU and the themes of state, nation and sovereign authority within the British polity. The impact of European integration can be seen, and also needs to be balanced by considering the ways in which changes in British politics and its narrative texture affected the political parties and 'challenged' the ways in which they have thought about and responded to European integration.

Note

1. Interestingly Eurobarometer research published in Autumn 2004 showed lower levels of 'don't knows', more interest in the EU and a levelling between those with a positive (32 per cent) compared to those with a negative (31 per cent) image of the EU. Interestingly, while only 14 per cent of UK respondents said that they trusted the British press, 39 per cent said that they trusted the European Commission, although levels of trust in EU institutions are below those evident in other member states (Eurobarometer, 2004).

9
Organized Interests

Jenny Fairbrass

Introduction

Whilst opinion is divided about the precise extent to which organized interests undermine or enhance modern democracy, most analysts find it very difficult to deny that such organizations play an increasingly important role in contemporary political life. In Britain, for example, by the end of the twentieth century they had become one of *the* most significant alternatives to traditional forms of political participation. The degree to which organized interests have become significant actors in the national arena is evidenced by the sustained and substantial growth in the number of organizations and their rising memberships witnessed over a number of decades (Grant 2000). This contrasts starkly with falling political party memberships (Mair and van Biezen 2001) and declining election turnouts (House of Commons 2001: 8).

Employing the definition of Europeanization described in Chapter 2, this chapter explores whether, to what extent and why there may have been a reorientation or reshaping of British organized interests and interest politics. It then considers whether, to what extent and why any discernible changes in the activities of domestic organizations might be a response to the policies, practices and preferences of European-level actors, as advanced through the EU system of governance. To produce such an assessment involves a number of conceptual steps. First, in order to evaluate the extent of the 'reshaping' of British interest politics, this chapter will provide a snapshot of what might be labelled the 'pre-EU' configuration of British organized interests and interest politics (that is, those circumstances prevailing from the 1950s to c.1973). This can then be compared to subsequent developments up to the present to get a sense of the broad scale of the 'EU effect'.

Second, from a 'top-down' perspective it is also necessary to characterize what might be called the 'EU model of interest politics'. This then permits an assessment of the 'goodness of fit' (see Bache and Jordan, Chapter 2) between what might be termed the British model of organized interest politics and the EU's. In order to identify the EU's model, policy papers and strategy documents that specifically address the issue of the role of such organizations (for example, CEC 1992) are surveyed. Where significant changes in British organized interests and interest politics have occurred, this chapter seeks to determine whether and to what extent they have been driven by EU initiatives and decisions, rather than, for example, domestic and/or wider international factors.

Building on the points above, the remainder of this chapter unfolds as follows. Section two reviews some of the major theories and concepts that have been employed to understand organized interests, both in a national and an EU context. Section three then explores the British and EU models of interest representation to establish the goodness of fit between the two. The effect of the EU on the lobbying activities of two contrasting British organized interests (namely business and environmental organizations) are also compared. Section four concludes by relating the main findings of this chapter back to the research questions identified in Chapter 1.

Theoretical approaches and analytical tools

Terminology

Although the study of organized interests is very well established, differences in terminology persist. In effect, many alternative labels exist for what is essentially the same phenomenon. In the academic literature the terms 'interest group' or 'pressure group' tend to be most commonly used. For example, Richardson (1993) uses the term 'pressure group' but lists several alternatives including 'interest group', 'political group', 'lobby', 'special interest group', 'organized group' and 'associational group'. By contrast, the European Commission employs the terms 'special interest group' (CEC 1992) and 'civil society organization' (CEC 2002). The preferred term here is 'organized interests'.

Drawing on the prevailing literature (Richardson 1993: 1; Grant 2000: 14) the term 'organized interests' is used to refer to any organization that seeks to influence public policy by communicating its preferences to those public bodies that possess the power to make authoritative policy decisions. It is worth noting that in much of the existing literature, authors are at pains to distinguish between organized interests and political parties, where the former tend to focus on single issues, whereas the latter normally offer proposals across the full range of public policy. Distinctions are also drawn between the public authorities that the organizations seek to influence and the interest organizations themselves (on the grounds that the latter neither attempt to replace the public body nor seek to form a government). Further differences can be marked out between organized interests and 'social movements' (Grant 2000).

Traditional theoretical approaches

Understandably, early scholars tended to look at interest organizations in the context of the nation state. Traditionally, such research was framed around one of two major contending theories, namely corporatism (for example see Cawson 1978) and pluralism (Dahl 1961). Each has subsequently spawned a number of subtypes, manifesting themselves, *inter alia*, variously as neocorporatism, policy network analysis (see for example, Richardson and Jordan 1979; Peterson 1992) and neopluralism (Smith 1990).

In relation to Europe, since the 1950s, academic research has broadened out to include the study of organized interests in the EU. For example, neo-functionalism (Haas 1958), with its emphasis on the part played by transnational organized interests, represents a variant of pluralism. Corporatism has also been employed as an organizing framework for interest representation at the EU level (see for example, Schmitter and Lehmbruch 1979). Recently, however, some authors have questioned the merit of applying the pluralist-corporatist yardstick to the EU, arguing that while it may be appropriate in the context of a national political system, it makes an unsuitable framework for understanding a unique system of governance such as the EU (see for example, Michalowitz 2002). However, applying the pluralist-corporatist benchmark to the EU as well as Britain does at least allow us to assess the goodness of fit between the two systems (see below).

The existing Europeanization literature

Recently, there has been a certain amount of dissatisfaction with the application of traditional European integration approaches to the study of organized interests in the EU. For example, neo-functionalism (see for example, Haas 1958) treats the ambitions and actions of organized interests allied to those of the supranational bodies (especially the Commission) as the key drivers in European polity building and policy making. By contrast (liberal) intergovernmentalism ascribes only marginal importance to the role of organized interests, downplays the role of supranational institutions and emphasizes the ongoing power of national governments (see for example Moravcsik 1998). Although there is a long-standing and unresolved dispute between supranational and intergovernmental theorists (Jordan 2001a), it does raise useful questions about the role of organized interests in European integration and draws our attention to a particular aspect of Europeanization: that is, the 'bottom-up' process of 'uploading' domestic agendas to the EU level (see Bache and Jordan, Chapter 2).

Clearly, this is well-trodden ground and, while it remains an important part of the debate, our main focus is on the top-down aspects of Europeanization, particular in relation to British environmental and business interest organizations. Some authors (see for example, Jordan 2002) have used a top-down definition of Europeanization to examine the EU effect on national institutions and policy. Whilst there is a growing body of work concerning the Europeanization of organized interests, and business interests in particular, the same cannot be said about work on environmental organized interests in either the UK or the EU (but see Fairbrass and Jordan 2002).

Within the emerging literature, we find a variety of definitions and frameworks. In the past, some authors have equated the Europeanization of organized interests with European integration and the accumulation of policy competences at the EU level. One such major study of business interests (Cowles 1995) which concerns the role of the European Round Table of Industrialists (ERT) in pressing for the completion of the Single European Market detected examples of 'uploading' on the part of business interests. For other scholars (see Lehmkuhl 2000; Eising 2003; Fairbrass 2003; Grote and Lang 2003), the EU is treated as a catalyst for particular types of responses among the national level organized interests. In other words, European integration is seen not as a top-down force *per se*, but more as the creator of political opportunity structures at EU level (see Bache and Jordan, Chapter 2), to which national organized interests respond strategically, structurally and organizationally in line with the organizational capacity/resources at their command. This is one of the most widely adopted approaches to the study of organized interests and the EU.

Identifying Europeanization

In order to test the definition of Europeanization described in Chapter 2, it is vital to compare the 'pre-EU' situation with the 'post-EU' situation. This is achieved by describing British organized interests and patterns of interest politics prior to 1973 and in c.2005. The two images are drawn at two different levels of detail. The first is a survey of broad trends among British organized interests to establish what might be called a 'British model' of interest politics. This is compared with the 'EU model' (insofar as one can be detected) of interest politics, to test for the goodness of fit between the two.

Second, drawing on elements of two extensive but distinct studies (Jordan 2002; Fairbrass 2003), a more detailed analysis is conducted, which examines developments in the activities of British business and environmental organized interests. Such an investigation is accomplished using a variety of organizational indicators including: the *location* of the interest organization (that is, the proximity of the organization's offices to public policy making bodies be they in London, Brussels or elsewhere); its *structure* (have resources such as staff or departments been devoted to monitor and/or influence public policy developments at national and/or EU level?); its *funding* (to what extent does it rely on British and/or EU sources?); and its *policy objectives* (are they oriented towards Britain and/or the EU?).

Whilst some of these features have been explored elsewhere (see Fairbrass and Jordan 2002; Fairbrass 2003), this chapter focuses on two significant facets that reveal a great deal about British interest organizations and interest politics. These are the lobbying *targets* selected and favoured by the interest organizations (that is, which public policy making bodies do they prefer to interact with?) and the interest representation *routes* that they employ to reach them. These features highlight the orientation and shape of British organized interests and interest politics (see Figure 9.1).

Specifically, within the national arena, British organized interests have a number of possible lobbying targets. These include *inter alia*: the public, the media, local government, devolved bodies (in Wales, Scotland, Northern Ireland and England), quasi-governmental bodies such as industry regulators, the judiciary, the legislature (Westminster) or the various components of the executive (that is, ministers and civil servants in Whitehall). Their actual choice is normally constrained by issues such as organizational resources and the likely/actual rewards in terms of meeting organizational objectives (Fairbrass 2002). At the EU level, their functional equivalents can be targeted, subject to similar constraints.

Similarly constrained choices operate with regard to lobbying routes. British organized interests may make direct contact with policy makers at the national and EU levels. Alternatively, they may employ intermediaries (that is, organizations or bodies that act as a channel or interlocutor for the organized interest such as a government department). In the national context, there are clearly fewer types of intermediaries available, although it is conceivable that a business association or an environmental group may want to lobby through, for example, local government in addition to making direct contact with central government, as a way of reinforcing their message. In the EU, there are a greater number of intermediaries available. For example, national organized interests may use government bodies or European groupings to act as a conduit for the articulation of their interests.

The Europeanization of British organized interests

Broad patterns of interest politics in Britain

Public policy making and the role of organized interests in Britain in the post-war period up to the 1970s were dominated by a tripartite relationship between the government, the Confederation of British Industry (CBI) and the Trades Union Congress (TUC) (Grant 2000). Cowles (2001) describes this as a form of 'weak corporatism' (see Figure 9.2). Whether these patterns amounted to corporatism or not, it is clear that business interests (especially producer organizations, employers' associations and employees' groups) have traditionally played a major role in the British polity (Wilson 1991: 102; Grant 2000: 2). By contrast, other organized interests, such as environmental groups, have been largely marginalized. Even with regard to environmental policy making, environmental organizations have been in a relatively weaker position compared to a powerful alliance comprising the Ministry of Agriculture, Fisheries and Food (MAFF) and the National

140

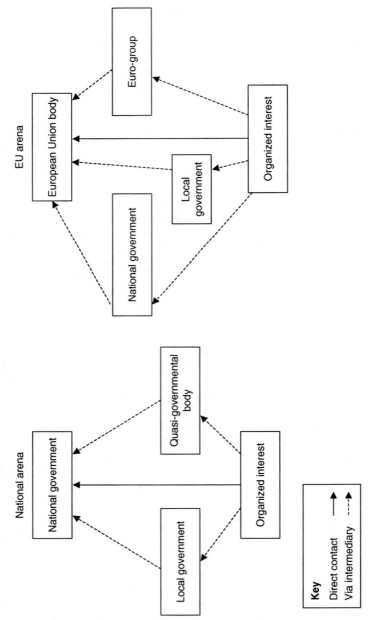

Figure 9.1 Intermediaries: the national and EU context compared

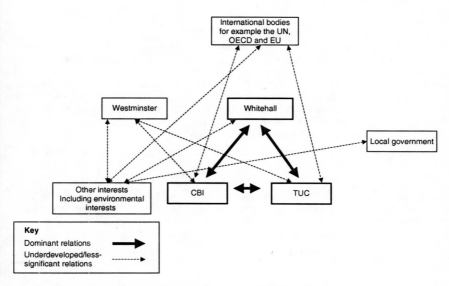

Figure 9.2 Pre-EU patterns among British organized interests

Farmers' Union (NFU) (Cox *et al.* 1986: 183–184; Smith 1993: 101–103) that formed the so-called agricultural policy community. Moreover, influential land owning interests such as the Countryside Land and Business Association (CLA) and the then Department of the Environment (DoE)[1] have not been nearly as central to environmental policy decisions (see Jordan (2002) for further details).

After 1979, a succession of Conservative governments attempted to dismantle the earlier tripartite arrangements, for example, by sidelining the CBI and including other organizations in public policy making such as the Institute of Directors (Grant 2000). However, there was some continuity, at least in terms of the routine relationships between government departments and organized interests (Grant 2000). Nevertheless, from the 1980s onwards, British interest politics appear to have become less corporatist in nature; by the 1990s Britain was described as 'elite pluralist' (Cowles 2001) or even 'pluralist' (Eising 2003) by some commentators. Significantly for this study, in the period following the 1970s, it has been suggested that British environmental organized interests became more powerful, playing an increased role in national policy making as national public policy 'greened' (Rawcliffe 1998) (see Table 9.1).

Looking at the British political system during the 'pre-EU' period, a number of domestic features were crucial to the development of a British style of organized interest politics (see Table 9.2). The 'pre-EU' situation comprised a unitary structure with a strong centralized and stable government in combination with a weak but well disciplined Parliament (Richardson

142

Table 9.1 British and EU interest politics

	British interest politics	EU interest politics
'Pre-EU' (1950s–1970s)	*Corporatist* tendencies: public policy making dominated by tripartite relations between Government, the CBI and the Trades Union Congress (TUC).	Intention to create *corporatist* relations (based on the German model) but actual pattern was largely pluralist.
	Environmental groups at the margins.	Business interests powerful. Environmental groups at margins.
Subsequent developments (1970s–2000)	Greening of the political agenda – growing importance of environmental arguments/groups.	Greening of the political agenda – growing importance of environmental arguments/groups.
	Pluralist or 'elite pluralist'.	Pluralist or 'elite pluralist'.

Table 9.2 British and EU political systems compared

	British political system	EU political system
'Pre-EU' (1950s–1970s)	Unitary state with strong government, weak local government and weak parliament.	Initially powerful 'executive' (that is, the Commission and the Council of Ministers) and relatively weak Parliament. Federalization/regionalization commences.
	Interest representation focused on Whitehall.	Multi-level decision-making introduced. Interest representation focused on the Commission and the Council of Ministers.
Subsequent developments (1970s–2000)	Largely unchanged domestic conditions until devolution which created new tiers of government below central government and above local government.	Increasingly powerful Parliament, declining power of Commission. Growing regionalization/federalization across EU.
	EU membership led to increasingly multi-level decision-making. Provided additional or alternative lobbying targets.	Increasingly multi-level decision-making. Additional/alternative lobbying targets.

1993) (the EU was somewhat similar, with its relatively weak Parliament). Consequently, it has been argued (Richardson 1993) that British organized interests would be compelled to take account of these domestic factors and orientate their main interest representation efforts towards Whitehall rather than Westminster (or the national political parties, the judiciary or local government).

This domestic unitary structure remained largely unaltered until the devolution programme of the late 1990s, when, with the creation of devolved bodies in Wales, Scotland, Northern Ireland and the England, a more multi-tiered administration began to appear. Crucially, even before the EU emerged on the radar screen of most British organized interests, wider international forums, such as the Organisation for Economic Co-operation and Development (OECD), European Free Trade Association (EFTA) and the United Nations (UN) were targeted. In summary, therefore, during the period under discussion, British organized interests were faced with an increasingly multi-level, pluralist arena, both within the domestic system and beyond it.

How good was the 'fit'?

The difficulties encountered in trying to characterize the British situation are repeated with respect to the EU. Nevertheless, some attempts have been made. For example, Coen and Dannreuther (2003) argue that owing to the origins of the EU (that is, very much influenced by the German Christian Democrat model of politics), early business–government relations attempted to foster continental corporatist arrangements based on national sectoral and peak associations. Whether or not corporatist arrangements really existed, business organized interests do seem to have had an equally prominent role in the EU as at national level (see Cowles 1995). As for environmental interest organizations, much like their British cousins, the EU environmental groups found themselves sidelined by the EU institutions in favour of agricultural organized interests. It was not until the 1970s that environmental groups gained ground nationally and, later, in the EU (Jordan 2005).

For several authors, the EU also subsequently developed along much more pluralist lines. Coen (1998), for example, recently used the term 'elite pluralism' to describe the functioning of the EU. For Richardson (1993), the profound absence of hierarchy and monopoly, the wide variety of players of uncertain status naturally led the EU towards the American model of 'disjointed pluralism' or 'competitive federalism' organized across three territorial levels (the region, the nation state and 'Brussels').

Given the apparent similarities between the British and EU models of organized interest and interest politics, it would seem that little adjustment would be demanded of the British organizations in coming to terms with the EU system that is, the goodness of fit between the two should have placed little pressure on British organized interests to adapt their core approach to selecting lobbying targets (and hence the choice of lobbying routes).

British organized interests could employ similar tactics at both the national and EU levels of governance, preferring to lobby the 'executive' (that is, Whitehall/the Council of Ministers and the Commission), while affording other actors (such as the Parliament) a much lower priority. In fact, the lessons learnt in managing interest representation in one context could well be fed back into the other. The next two sub-sections examine whether these tactics were actually adopted by British interest organizations.

Targets

Existing research reveals that during the 1970s, British business interests did indeed tend to give preference to contact with those Whitehall departments with a direct relevance to business activity, in preference to Parliament and other public bodies. As Grant and Marsh (1977) report, the CBI favoured its contacts with Whitehall and especially the then departments of trade, industry and, to a much lesser extent, employment (Grant and Marsh 1977: 109). By contrast, whilst British environmental interest organizations may have wished to build stronger relationships within Whitehall, they found Westminster to be much more receptive to their demands (Lowe and Goyder 1983). That said, they did find that some parts of Whitehall were more accessible (for example departments such as environment, education and science) (Lowe and Goyder 1983: 65).

After 1973, within the national arena there appears to have been no major reshaping of the preferred targets among the British organized interests. Whitehall continued to dominate the thinking of the majority. Business interest organizations continued to target department such as trade, the Treasury and the Cabinet Office (Fairbrass 2003). Environmental organizations continued to prefer contact with the DoE and its successors (Fairbrass and Jordan 2001a,b), although access was also sought to (but not denied by) MAFF, the Department of Trade and Industry (DTI) and territorial offices such as the Scottish Office. Perhaps the one significant change to emerge in relation to environmental interest organizations was that some of the less accessible central government departments became less hostile as policy and politics more broadly 'greened' in the 1980s (Jordan 2002).

Therefore, during the period up to the late 1990s, although the EU did not appear to directly alter the lobbying priorities of the British interest organizations (that is, they continued to focus on Whitehall), it caused some reorientation in their overall pattern of interest representation with respect to targets (and routes) (compare Figures 9.2 and 9.3). In a way that is reminiscent of neofunctionalist predictions (Haas 1958), there was some shift in the focus of British organized interests towards EU bodies. Crucially, this process predated British membership. Accession in 1973 only served to reinforce the desire of business and environmental interest organizations to secure and sustain contacts with EU actors, sometimes in preference to national level policy makers (Fairbrass 2003).

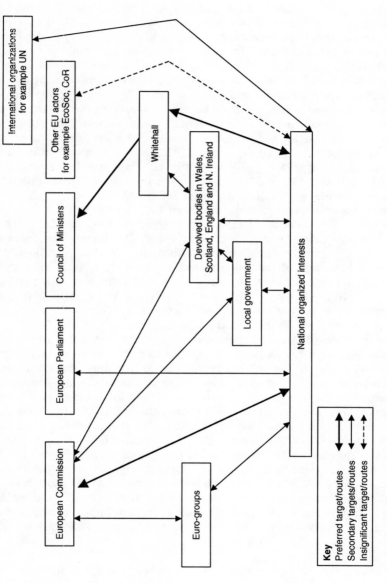

Figure 9.3 British organized interests c.2000

By the late 1990s, British interest organizations had become more discriminating in their choice of targets and routes. Business and environmental interests were selective in terms of the Directorates General (DGs) and individual Members of the European Parliament (MEPs) that they targeted. This replicated their activities at national level (where they had selectively targeted particular Whitehall departments and Parliamentary Committees). Meanwhile, British business interest organizations carefully nurtured their relationships with relevant parts of the Commission. For example, the Association of British Insurers (ABI) treated the DG responsible for the internal market as its prime target. For the Association of Electricity Producers (AEP), contact was most highly sought with the DGs responsible for energy and competition policy; for the Federation of Electronics Industries (FEI), the DG managing information society policy was regarded as the primary target; and British Telecom's (BT) main targets were the DGs dealing with information society and competition policies. Within the European Parliament, individual MEPs were picked out for their personal interests and their membership of particular Committees (Fairbrass 2003).

Environmental organizations also treated the European Parliament as a very important target and found it more receptive than some other parts of the Commission. Within the Commission, DG Environment was the most sought after target, although relations were developed with the DGs responsible for agriculture, fisheries, transport, the EU budget and regional policy. The environmental organizations also sought access to particular MEPs within the European Parliament who had shown a personal commitment to environmental issues or who played a significant role in its environment committee (Fairbrass and Jordan 2001a,b).

For both sets of interest organizations, access to the Council of Ministers would have been highly desirable but was not feasible given its relatively closed nature (see Bache and George 2006: 276–93). Instead, the British organized interests had to rely on their pre-existing links to national government departments. Not surprisingly, given its limited influence, neither the environmental nor the business interest organizations placed much weight on the relatively weak Economic and Social Committee (Fairbrass and Jordan 2001a,b). In spite of these similarities, there were also some striking differences in relation to the European Court of Justice (ECJ). For several of the environmental groups, access (albeit indirect) represented a major target because of its role in enforcing the implementation of EU legislation (see Fairbrass and Jordan 2001a,b). It was seen as much less important by business organizations, who perceived Britain's record at implementing relevant directives to be much more favourable to their interests (Fairbrass 2003).

Routes

Academic research concerning business interests suggests that they will choose to exploit one or more of three potential routes to gain access to EU-level targets (that is, policy makers): the 'direct' route, the 'national' route and the 'European' route (see Grant 1989). British business interests exploited all of these, although the evidence suggests that they preferred to make direct contact whenever possible. Nevertheless, they did not dismiss the use of intermediaries. Individual firms would work via national trade associations and the national government officials. National trade associations would channel their demands via European groupings (Fairbrass 2003). Similarly, the evidence shows that the environmental interests tended to seek out and gain access to EU-level policy-makers mainly via two main routes. They established direct contact with EU officials and placed significant weight on lobbying via European environmental groupings (Fairbrass and Jordan 2001a,b).

However, one difference between the environmental and business interests lies in their use of European groupings. For the environmental organizations, the European groupings have been a source of solidarity and support, whereas for the British business interests, membership was born out of a perceived need to stifle or circumvent opposition to their preferred policy developments (Fairbrass 2003). For the British business and environmental interests organizations, the decision to channel their demands through intermediaries such as the European groupings was partly driven by resource considerations. However, it was also partly a function of the EU institutions' needs.

Following the explosion in lobbying at EU level in the 1980s, EU-level actors publicized their preference for working with and through Euro-groups (CEC 1992), rather than nationally based groups (compare Figures 9.3 and 9.4). This stated intention was, at least in part, an attempt to manage their rapidly increasing workload resulting from the growing volume and frequency of contact from organized interests.

However, despite indications to the contrary (CEC 1992), EU-level actors such as the Commission made increasing use of direct contacts with national organized interests, rather via Euro-groups. This was partly born out of the shared view among the EU-level actors (the Commission and the Parliament) and national groups that the Euro-groups were largely ineffectual (Grant 1993; McLaughlin and Jordan 1993; Coen 1997). It is evident that when the Commission believes Euro-groups to be weak, it tends to prefer to consult with national associations (or even individual firms).

Nevertheless, McLaughlin *et al.* (1993: 199–202) have noted that the European Commission has not entirely sidelined Euro-groups because it needs to be seen to be 'even-handed' (that is, not favouring particular companies or countries). In addition, given that the European Commission is a small and relatively under-resourced bureaucracy, it often needs Euro-groups to supply technical information and to assist with implementation. However, these are benefits that the national organized interest can also supply. What marks out the Euro-groups is their potential to act as an 'international referee'. For instance, the Euro-groups have been able to smooth

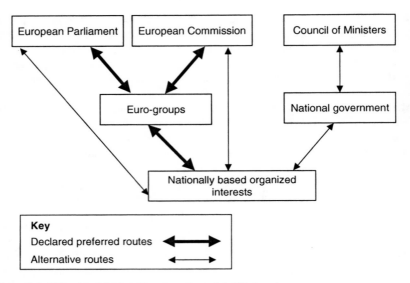

Figure 9.4   EU actors' declared preferred model of interest

over national differences, before proposals reach the European Commission (Fairbrass 2003). The Commission is more than happy to be relieved of such an irksome task. As a result, the Commission has continued to encourage the establishment of Euro-groups as conduits through which national organized interests could channel their demands (McLaughlin and Greenwood 1995: 150).

Conclusions

This chapter has explored the top-down impact of the EU on British organized interests and interest politics. In so doing, it has used a broadly defined notion of the 'British model' and contrasted it with the 'EU model', in the period c.1950–2005, to indicate the goodness of fit between the two systems. It has made these comparisons in relation to two particular types of British interest organizations, namely business and environmental interest groups. This in-depth analysis has concentrated on two of their organizational features: their selection of lobbying targets and their choice of routes.

   To conclude, the evidence suggests that there are elements of continuity during the period of study. Broadly speaking, in the national arena, British organized interests have continued to focus their lobbying on Whitehall in preference to other public bodies, although with varying degrees of access. For business interests, Whitehall has remained the most highly prized target. For environmental organizations, greater reliance has had to be placed on

Westminster, although Whitehall has proved to be less impervious with the passage of time.

However, some significant changes have occurred too. The most discernible alteration is the growing importance of organized interests within the British arena, to the extent that they are arguably now some of the key participants in domestic policy making. This trend is partly a function of the increased numbers of organized interests and their growing memberships, and partly because other (and more traditional) forms of political participation have declined. Other broad differences include the shift from the tripartism of the 1950s, 1960s and 1970s, to the elite pluralism of the 1980s and 1990s. Interconnected with this development is the shift in the relative influence of business and environmental groups. The latter have gained authority as part of a more general 'greening' of society and government. Clearly, the EU is not the only factor here; British organized interests have also found themselves being drawn into the transnational and global activities of organizations such as the UN and the OECD.

Whilst it is difficult to disentangle many of the causal factors above, the staff working for British business and environmental interests reveal that the EU almost certainly has played a significant part in reshaping and reorientating their interests and activities (Fairbrass and Jordan 2002). Adaptation to EU interest politics among British interests began as early as the 1950s, pre-dating British membership of the EU. From that time on, British organized interests have been 'Europeanized' in the sense that they began to approach EU-level policy making targets and reorient their lobbying routes via Euro-groups as part of their preparations for UK membership. Whilst it is difficult to pinpoint exactly when the EU became a major issue for British interest organizations, it is clear that their remodelled activities altered significantly during the frenzied, dynamic years of the 1980s, when EU-level lobbying targets and routes grew considerably in their importance. Clearly, major steps on the part of the EU to legislate in the areas of environmental and industrial policy contributed to this change, motivating both business and environmental interest organizations to strengthen their relations with EU actors (Fairbrass and Jordan 2002).

Through its very existence, the EU has presented new lobbying targets and routes. Herein lies one of the crucial differences between the British environmental and business organizations. Decisively for the environmental interests, the EU provided an *alternative* set of lobbying targets, particularly when national government pursued environmentally damaging objectives (Fairbrass and Jordan 2001a,b). Importantly, British environmental organizations were able to ally themselves to key EU policy makers such as DG Environment and the European Parliament's environment committee. By contrast, British business interest organizations broadly shared the objectives of both the British Government and the European Commission in relation to the core objectives of the EU's market liberalization strategy. This meant that EU actors such as the Commission provided an *additional*, rather than an alternative, set of lobbying targets for most British business organizations (with the main opposition coming from member states such as France and Spain (Fairbrass 2003)).

In one sense, perhaps one of the more surprising features of the Europeanization of British organized interests is that domestic interest politics have not been more deeply affected. Recall Haas' prediction (1958) about the shift in expectations, activities and loyalties to the EU level, it might have been anticipated that British organized interests would (almost) entirely re-orientate their lobbying activities towards the EU, given that it was fast becoming the major source of regulation. However, in recognition of the continuing power of the Council of Ministers in EU policy making (and hence of national government), British interest organizations have continued to focus as much effort on influencing the national government as on EU institutions. Even the Commission's efforts to reshape the landscape of national interest politics, by formally elevating the Euro-groups in their consultation process, have had little impact. This was particularly because the Commission and the national interests colluded, in effect, to by-pass the Euro-groups.

Overall, the evidence assembled here shows that the same patterns established within the national arena have been re-created at EU level. Perhaps learning from their experience within the domestic political system, British organized interests have tended to devote more effort to their relations with the Commission (in parallel with their focus on Whitehall) than to any other EU institution. Evidently, in both the national and EU contexts, it is a question of 'shooting where the ducks are' (Richardson 1993: 89–9). Drawing on experience gained in the domestic arena, British organized interests appear to have adjusted with ease to the EU polity. This smooth adaptation may also be a result of the goodness of fit between the two systems. Operating in the increasingly pluralist environment of the British arena may well have helped British organizations to prepare for the pluralist conditions encountered at the EU level. As a result, it is argued that British organized interests have had to do no more than accommodate the EU's model of interest politics. Even though the British organized interests have added EU targets and routes to their portfolio, the core features of their lobbying activities remain largely intact. By comparison, organized interests in some other EU member states have faced much greater pressures to adapt (Fairbrass 2003). For example, French organized interests have been accustomed to operating within a more state-dominated political system (Schmidt 1999; Fairbrass 2003). Accordingly, they have found the pluralist nature of the EU to be much more alien. For them, the EU effect has tended to require 'transformation' rather than simply accommodation.

In addition to the points above, a number of other EU effects can be posited. Given the existence of the EU, there is arguably greater uncertainty and complexity facing organized interests, as more and more organizations have been drawn into the policy making game. Overall, it could be argued that the EU policy process has become slightly more legitimate in that a growing range of actors are now consulted during policy drafting/formulation. Conversely, it should also be noted that most of the consulted organizations are privileged, relatively well-resourced bodies creating what amounted to 'elite pluralism' (Coen 1997, 1998). Consequently, the Europeanization of British organized interests has had no discernible improvement in the transparency of national or the EU's decision-making.

One of the more difficult aspects to assess in terms of organized interests and interest politics is whether Europeanization has produced any identifiable 'winners' or 'losers' over time. However, it could be argued that the provision of alternative lobbying routes and targets at the EU level of governance have helped to make national environmental groups the main winners. Similarly, the business interests could also be seen to be 'winners' in the sense that market liberalization has extended beyond national boundaries, thus creating greater opportunities and more favourable politico-economic conditions for them too.

Finally, it is worth emphasizing that although this chapter has primarily examined the Europeanization of British interest organizations using a top-down perspective, it is obvious that other interpretations have some merit. Specifically, given that British organized interests have contributed to the creation of new EU powers by successfully 'uploading' their ideas to the EU level (Category 2, Chapter 2), one might also say that European integration has created a new, European lodestar of domestic politics (Category 3). What is less clear is whether there has been any horizontal transfer or 'cross-loading' of organized interest politics between states (see Category 4): some member states (for example, France) have proved to be resistant to the sort of lobbying activities that are the norm in Britain and the EU (see Fairbrass 2003). Perhaps most significantly, what this chapter indicates is that there is an increasingly dense, two-way pattern of interaction between states and the EU (Category 5).

Note

1. In 1997, the DoE was superseded by the Department of the Environment, Transport and the Regions (DETR), and then, in 2001, by the Department for the Environment, Food, and Rural Affairs (DEFRA).

10
Trade Unions

Erin van der Maas

Introduction

Trade unions have long played an important role in the politics of member states and were seen as a potentially significant driver of European integration by the earliest theorists on the subject. Haas (1958) envisaged trade union responses to market expansion as a key *spillover* mechanism extending European integration from markets and economics into labour regulation and political fields. This classic neo-functionalist expectation matched earlier theorizing in the field of industrial relations. Commons (1909), for example, made similar claims regarding the nationalization of trade unions in his research on the extension of markets from local to national level in the USA. The basic premise is that in order for trade unions to be effective wage bargainers and carry sufficient political weight to influence the wider political economy, the scope of their organization must match the scope of the market. In European terms, this means that national trade union organizations must extend their bargaining scope to be congruent with the single European market. What is quite clear from even a cursory study of industrial relations is that European-level collective bargaining is conspicuous by its absence. However, a shift to collective bargaining at the European level is not the sole indicator of trade union Europeanization, as will be discussed here.

A commonly accepted definition for trade unions was put forward by the Webbs, pioneer commentators in the study of British trade unionism and social welfare organizations, in 1894: '[a] Trade Union, as we understand the term, is a continuous association of wage-earners for the purpose of maintaining or improving the conditions of their employment' (Larson and Nissen 1987: 188). This definition is non-prescriptive with regard to how trade unions are to go about improving their members' lot, which probably explains why the definition is both enduring and commonly accepted. Trade unions across Europe have employed various strategies, based on their identity and ideology, in order to represent their members' interests (Hyman 1997, 2001). Marks and McAdam (1996: 97) suggest that the rigid distinctions between pressure groups, social movements and trade unions do not apply outside of the national context: all of these groups 'share the status of "challenging groups" which hope to contest and shape the emerging institutions and philosophy of the EU'.

The development of an industrial relations regime at the EU level has not replicated the earlier development of national regimes of industrial relations. Dølvik (1997: 20), for example, argued that:

> (historically contingent) specific forms of trade union articulation known from the nation-state experience is not necessarily an appropriate reference model for the kind of trade union policy-formulation and organisation that is evolving in the very different EU-polity.

If the pattern of development at EU level is unique, then so too is the Anglo-Saxon conceptualization of trade unions as market-based actors engaging primarily in collective bargaining. Unlike some of their continental counterparts, British trade unions have, in general, eschewed political entanglements as far as was possible, concentrating instead on collective bargaining with employers as a means of improving their members' conditions of employment.

This chapter explores the responses of British trade unions to the growing importance of the EU. Specifically, in the context of this volume, it refers to the reorientation of trade union activities through engagement with the EU. It should not be presumed that Europeanization has taken place but investigated with reference to a number of questions. In the case of this chapter, these are as follows. Have trade unions reoriented their activities as a consequence of EU membership? Is the EU akin to a 'lodestar' that trade unions have found impossible to ignore? In what ways have trade unions enhanced their 'organizational capacity' through EU membership? (Here, organizational capacity refers to the ability of the union to monitor and intervene in the EU policy process, what Hyman (1997: 519) refers to as 'intelligence, strategy and efficacy'.) Have trade unions adapted existing, or created new, capacities for monitoring and disseminating information on EU developments? These questions are addressed in a case study of the response of British unions to the policy of Economic and Monetary Union (EMU) and, specifically, on the diverging responses of two unions with similar membership constituencies. However, before addressing these questions it is important to set out briefly why European integration, under the auspices of the EU, matters for trade union organizations.

European integration and trade unionism

The first question to ask is why is there an EU dimension to trade union activity? Trade unions are, and traditionally have been, organizations that operate almost exclusively within national boundaries, although international work has generally been an important factor for the Trades Union Congress (TUC), which represents 69 affiliated unions with over 6.5 million members, and bigger affiliated unions. Explanations of the Europeanization of trade union activities are usually couched in terms of different *push* and *pull* factors (Visser 1998). This categorization correlates with the well-worn debate in European integration studies between neofunctionalists (who emphasize the pull of supra-national solutions) and the intergovernmentalists (who suggest that supranational solutions are only an option for member states when national solutions are no longer viable – 'push').

Push factors emanate from the domestic environment trade unions operate in and do not necessarily connect to the EU: 'unions may be pushed or forced to seek co-operation across national borders because they no longer find allies, protection or rewards within national arenas' (Visser 1998: 231). On this view, globalization has eroded the regulatory capacity of national institutions operating only in the national arena. The methods by which nation states mediate globalization pressures vary from state to state and the approach taken in Britain provided a *push* for trade unions that has arguably been more pronounced than for many member nation-states of the EU.

The policies pursued by the Thatcher governments after 1979 did a great deal to push British trade unions to forge links with the EU. As their domestic influence was waning, the unique ability of the EU to make law binding on member state governments provided British trade unions with a particularly welcome opportunity to bypass national institutions and exploit new political opportunities. Thatcher sought an end to state intervention in the market and previously sacrosanct national goals such as full employment were sacrificed to the free functioning of the market. The consensual approach of the previous Labour government, via tripartite incomes policy bargaining at national level, was abandoned. State support for industrial relations institutions were withdrawn, the legal immunities of trade unions eroded and the labour market transformed. Far from 'rolling back the state', the Thatcher government sought to exclude trade unions from hindering the free working of the market and did so by a series of legislative initiatives. Paradoxically, therefore, the British state became much more involved in deciding how trade unions should operate both internally and externally. As Hyman (2001: 104) explains:

> From one of the least legalistic industrial relations systems in the world, Britain became one of the most legally prescriptive; and in a form bearing asymmetrically on workers' organisations as against employers.

However, it was the TUC that was hardest hit by the shift in policy post 1979. The TUC represents its affiliated trade union organizations in the political sphere. With the Labour Party out of office, and a Conservative administration refusing to have any dealings with the trade union movement, the relevance of the TUC to its affiliates seriously waned. Throughout the 1980s and 1990s, the Thatcher and Major governments dismantled almost every tripartite institution in Britain. These activities constituted the 'bread and butter' of the TUC's workload. Its loss of status has had a significant impact on the Europeanization of British trade unions.

The significance of *push* factors in the British context is not seriously contested. In part, trade unions in Britain have been subject to similar pressures that their sister union organizations in other member-states have had to withstand. However, the British union movement also faced a hostile and ideologically driven government that was determined to crush the trade unions' power rather than engage in the sort of consensual decision-making that feature in some parts of continental Europe.

These *push* factors provide a clear message for British trade unions: national industrial relations institutions are no longer as relevant as they once were, even where they are still in operation. Yet, while transnational cooperation now appears crucial for the continuing survival of British trade unions, it does not necessarily imply that they should reorient their activities to the EU. If national industrial relations actors and institutions have been challenged by globalization, it is valid to question why transnational action should take place at the European rather than other levels, for example through the United Nations (UN) or the International Labour Organisation (ILO). The simple answer is that the EU, and the European Commission in particular, has been keen to *pull* trade unions into the European integration project. The 'carrot' of EU regulation (pull) complements the 'stick' provided by the paucity of domestic opportunities (push). The Commission has good reasons for pulling trade unions into EU decision-making. Independent pressure groups are seen as a legitimizing aspect of decision-making that, to some extent, lessen the oft referred to 'democratic deficit' within the EU. It is in this context that corporatist and/or pluralist interest representation from independent pressure groups has been seen as particularly important to decision-making legitimacy in the EU context (Andersen and Eliassen 1996: 255). The inclusion of the European labour movement in social policy formation under the Maastricht Social Chapter provisions represents part of the EU's strategy to bring the decision-making closer to the peoples of Europe and thus provide it with a more 'human face' (Lodge 1989). Including groups from civil society in the formal structures of EU decision-making thereby provides an opportunity for the Commission to expand the scope of its policy competences, increase the legitimacy of its decisions and thereby move EU decision-making one step closer to the peoples of Europe.

These *push* and *pull* factors set out a rational-choice explanation for the Europeanization of trade union activities. However, the opportunities and threats deriving from EU integration are very difficult to determine, and trade unionists are no closer to consensus on the advantages and disadvantages of EU engagement than many other participants and commentators.

Conceptualizing the EU

The Single European Act and subsequent Treaty alterations have deepened market integration in the EU by removing both tariff and non-tariff barriers to the free movement of goods and services. This has been achieved by relaxing the intergovernmental decision-making process and allowing for qualified majority voting (QMV) in the Council of Ministers in policy areas concerned with market making. One consequence has been that previously nationally bounded firms have now become Euro-companies with their corporate governance, in addition to macro-economic, financial and political governance, shifting to the European level.

For trade unions, the neo-liberal core of the European integration project has important implications for the achievement of their aims and objectives. Member states of the EU can no longer pursue independent national strategies of macro-economic management, and therefore trade union achievements, linked as they are to the nation-state, are threatened. In addition, the QMV arrangements, crucial to facilitating integration, do not generally extend to the relevant social policy fields; there is an asymmetry in EU governance. The build up of social democratic elements (positive integration) at European level is *de facto* a harder task than implementing market liberalization policies (negative integration) (Geyer 1997; Scharpf 1996; Streeck and Schmitter 1991).

The Maastricht Social Agreement (MSA), although limited, has provided a potential mechanism at the Euro-level for trade union participation in social and labour market policy making. The EU has delivered some important new social and labour market directives, especially in areas such as health and safety and industrial democracy. Optimistic and pessimistic assessments of the prospects for trade union participation generally hinge on their interpretation of the EU social dimension. For some, the neo-liberal core of the EU, intergovernmental decision-making, employer opposition and cross-national trade union diversity preclude the possibility of the EU developing a comprehensive social dimension to balance the predominance of the free-market (for example, Streeck 1995; Dølvik 1997).

However, others point to the pivotal role of the Commission in politically constructing 'spillover' from market making to social policy and labour regulation. Pierson (1996) argues that EU integration is a path-dependent process that can create gaps between the intentions of the original institution builders and the long-term development of those institutions. Pierson's study of the social dimension recognizes its limitations but he suggests that it has developed more significantly than anticipated by those using a straightforward rational explanation.

Trade unions as rational actors?

Until this point it has been assumed that trade unions can adapt themselves to changing external events in a rational manner. However, as most students

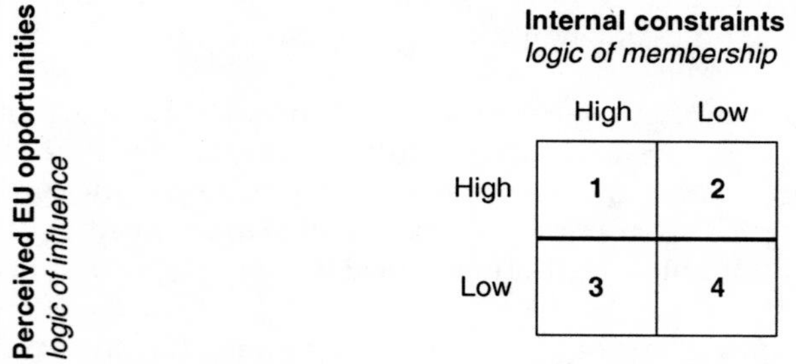

Internal constraints
logic of membership

		High	Low
Perceived EU opportunities *logic of influence*	High	1	2
	Low	3	4

Figure 10.1 Internal and external conditions of European interest organizations
Source: Dølvik 1997: 22.

of industrial relations would argue, trade unions do not always act in a rational manner maximizing their material interests. The rationalist 'logic of influence' drawing trade unions into political engagement in Brussels is balanced by the 'logic of membership', in which the composition of individual trade unions can limit 'rational' action (Dølvik 1997) (Figure 10.1).

Marks and McAdam (1996: 103) qualify the assumption that changes in the location of institutionalized power will inevitably lead to a shift in the location of mass politics, arguing that the ability of trade unionism to interact with the EU political environment is

> more a function of its internal characteristics. Of particular relevance here is the way inherited institutions and ideologies may constrain a group's ability to exploit whatever EU-level opportunities are available. That the link between political opportunity and movement response is not at all reflexive.

On occasions, trade unions have to manage a tension between these two logics. The extent of Europeanization is dependent not solely on the perceived EU opportunities ('logic of influence') but is also subject to internal organization constraints ('logic of membership'). Trade unions are, after all, democratic organizations that have to reconcile both effectiveness and legitimacy (Dølvik 1997). Debates on the trade-off between democracy and efficiency in trade union governance are by no means new, and each and every organization must manage this tension. Undy *et al.* (1981: 23), in an expansive work on analysing change in trade union organizations, finds that external changes might have little or no effect at all.

> It seems to us that these external agents of change have done little more than present union leaders and their allies with additional problems to

solve. Such change agents usually allow union leaders a variety of alternative responses, including, on some occasions, the alternative of inaction.

Strategic choice is possible and responses are the outcome of 'internal discussion, debate and often conflict' (Hyman 2001: 170). The internal dynamics and constraints of the organization are another potential variable mediating Europeanization. Responses to European integration are mediated by intra-union institutional/ideological struggles and decision-making processes.

It is in the context of pull and push factors and the often conflicting logics of influence and membership that the Europeanization of trade unions has to be understood. We now turn to the British case specifically.

Europeanization: the TUC

Many commentators have suggested that the 1980s and 1990s witnessed a profound change in the TUC's attitude towards European integration. The British referendum on membership of the European Economic Community (EEC) in 1975 saw the TUC opposed to membership, not just on the terms renegotiated by the Wilson Government but also in principle (TUC 1975). Nairn (1972) claims that attitudes at this time were dominated by a chauvinistic 'little Englander' mentality, while other writers emphasize the peculiar British situation and the predominance of Commonwealth and Atlantic concerns in foreign policy (Geyer 1997). Given that the TUC has been especially active in international trade union structures, including the establishment of the European Trade Union Confederation (ETUC), Nairn's findings are perhaps overstated.

The 1975 referendum result meant a thawing in attitudes towards the EEC, even among the most ardent opponents of European integration such as Jack Jones of the Transport and General Workers Union (T&G). TUC Officials began to explore ways to use EEC structures to achieve international objectives. However, official TUC policy (as set by Congress) was highly volatile in the period 1973–1988, shifting between pragmatic acceptance and outright hostility on numerous occasions. The TUC Congresses of 1981 and 1983 even called for a future Labour Government to withdraw completely from the EEC favouring the domestically oriented 'Alternative Economic Strategy' proposed by the Labour Party under Michael Foot (TUC 1981, 1983).

Yet by 1988, the European Commission President Jacques Delors received a standing ovation from TUC delegates after setting out his vision of a social dimension to Europe that included a role for trade unions as social partners. This 'astonishing conversion' of the TUC to a pro-EU position was a major feature of British politics in the late 1980s (Rosamond 1993: 420). For the majority of the TUC General Council, the mood was one of pragmatism rather than one of Euro-optimism. However, the switch to a pragmatic rather than hostile position is an important one. As the President of the TUC at the time put it:

> It is no secret that many of us have been sceptical about there being any benefits of the European dimension . . . You could argue that the European Council of Ministers has procrastinated for ten years or more on the question of workers' participation and industrial democracy. In the short term we have not a cat in hell's chance of achieving that in Westminster. The only card game in town at the moment is in a town called Brussels. (Todd, in TUC 1988: 572)

Key to the TUC's increasingly favourable assessment of the EU was the social dimension, which was added to by Delors speech to Congress in 1988. His emphasis on the importance of trade unions and workers' rights as integral parts of a healthy modern economy stood in stark contrast to the closed-door policy of the Thatcher government. Thatcher's response given in a speech in Bruges shortly afterwards (see Nelsen and Stubb 1998), stating that Britain would not accept the EU promoting 'socialism through the back door' was probably just as important in encouraging the trade unions. That is, if Mrs Thatcher was worried by EU developments, there were probably sound pragmatic reasons to investigate them more closely.

Since this marked turnaround in official TUC policy, the TUC began to develop a strategic response to the EU, which meant that individual Europhilic officials no longer had to work in the shadows. The moves towards a single European market provoked a serious assessment of EU issues within the union movement: until the mid-1980s just one member of staff within the TUC's International Department dealt with the European issues. Yet, the dramatic drop in union membership and abolition of the tripartite institutions in Britain led the TUC to reorganize itself into a more streamlined campaigning organization. However, as part of this restructuring, the TUC set up 'Network Europe' with two aims: to influence decision-making in Brussels; and to act as a trade union information-gatherer, educator and coordinator on EU issues.

In 1993, the TUC opened an office based in the ETUC building in Brussels, aimed at improving its lobbying and information services. The TUC is represented at the monthly meetings of the European Parliamentary Labour Party in Strasbourg and has contacts with Members of the European Parliament (MEPs) from all member-states. The office in Brussels is made aware of the views of TUC affiliates via the *Europe Monitoring Group*, which is a subcommittee of the General Council. The presence in Brussels allows the TUC to react quickly to events on the spot. One example is the Transfer of Undertakings and Protection of Employment legislation (TUPE) revision that the Major government sought to weaken. The TUC official in Brussels was well placed to work with the Danish, Swedish, Austrian, Finish and British

Labour MEPs and union bodies in order to defend the TUPE legislation. In short, knowing when, where and how to intervene requires a presence and a profile.

In addition to a number of educational courses run for trade union representatives and the publishing of educational materials on the EU, the TUC also coordinates a monthly meeting of trade union officials with EU responsibilities. The *Network Europe Contacts Points* (NECP) brings together representatives of various affiliate organizations. Organizationally and politically, the TUC's journey into Europe is significant. Without it, the TUC had a limited future as an arbiter of inter-union squabbles. Not surprisingly, TUC officials grasped this opportunity quickly and effectively.

Europeanization: TUC affiliates

Economic and Monetary Union has been a key issue for trade unions and provides an important illustration of how Europeanization of trade union activities has taken different forms within the British context. Dyson (2002: 14–16) identifies four prevalent discourses on EMU that contextualize the issue within wider debates on the significance of European integration and globalization.

1. EMU as a means by which the EU internalizes the economics of neoliberalism and globalization. Consolidating the 'Anglo-American' business model at the core of the EU and thus a threat to the European social model.
2. EMU viewed negatively as a means to dissolve national policy autonomy, national identity and sovereignty.
3. EMU as a means to resist the US model of globalization and entrench and protect the European social model.
4. EMU as a way to adapt and modernize the European Social Model to the realities of globalization, using the neo-corporatist social dialogue and not simply the free market as a way of managing transition.

Table 10.1 shows the policy response of some of the major TUC affiliates and notes the discourses predominantly utilized as explanations and justifications for their policy positions.

Bieler (2003) suggests that the nature of the industrial sector represented plays an important role in shaping trade union policy on the EU. His findings suggest that manufacturing unions who are exposed to the competitive pressures of globalization are much more likely to support further European integration than public sector unions. Public sector unions are more likely to oppose EMU because it undermines the national policy autonomy upon which they depend. Manufacturing unions are more acutely aware that they have lost control of capital at the national level and the EU is one way of clawing back control over free-market dynamics. Table 10.1 illustrates this

Table 10.1 EMU policy positions and discourses*

Trade Union	Policy position	Discourses
Unison	Anti-EMU	1
T&G	Anti-EMU	1 & 2
ASLEF	Anti-EMU	1 & 2
RMT	Anti-EMU	1 & 2
AEEU	Pro-EMU	3 & 4
GMB	Pro-EMU	3
GPMU	Pro-EMU	3
CPS	Pro-EMU	3
CWU	Undecided	Undecided
TUC	Pro-EMU	3 & 4

* Unison and the PCS (Public and Commercial Services Union) are public service unions, ASLEF (Associated Society of Locomotive Engineers and Firemen), RMT (National Union of Rail, Maritime and Transport Workers), AEEU (Amalgamated Electricians and Engineers Union), T&G and the GMB are general workers unions, GPMU (Graphical Paper and Media Union), CWU (Communication Workers Union).

almost conclusively. The manufacturing unions (AEEU, GPMU) are both pro-EMU, whereas those unions with membership in the sheltered sector of the economy are decidedly anti-EMU (Unison, ASLEF). The CPS union, representing civil servants and public sector workers, is the one exception to the rule.

The most interesting cases are those unions that have members in both the sheltered and exposed sectors of the labour market, the two general unions (T&G, GMB[1]) and the Communication Workers Union (CWU). The CWU has intentionally remained officially undecided on the issue of EMU. However, the T&G and the GMB, which have very similar membership constituencies, have responded in very different ways both to EMU and to the wider process of European integration. Examining diversity between two trade union organizations in one national context, which have similar compositions of membership, provides an excellent opportunity to illustrate the organizational factors that shape the nature and extent of Europeanization.

The General Unions: explaining diversity

The GMB has over 700,000 members, organizing in both the exposed and sheltered sectors of the economy (namely clothing and textiles, commercial services, construction and furniture, timber and allied, energy and utilities, engineering, food and leisure, and public services). The GMB union has traditionally been positioned on the centre-right of the labour movement. This has meant that a supportive policy towards European integration has been a long-term feature of union policy: a position inherited by the incoming left-leaning General Secretary John Edmonds in 1986. The GMB was a key actor in turning both Labour Party and TUC policies on the EU from hostility to pragmatism.

As noted above, Thatcher's unrelenting hostility made the EU an attractive alternative to domestic exclusion. The closed doors of Whitehall and Westminster contrasted with the open doors at Brussels 'where arguments were taken on their merit' (John Edmonds, interview with the author, 2004). The GMB was instrumental in setting up *Trade Unions for Europe* (TUFE) in the mid-1990s, as it was unhappy with the overemphasis on economic, financial and market integration from the 'Britain in Europe' group and the lack of emphasis on securing workers rights in the EU. The GMB has been keen to stress the construction of the social dimension as a key plank of the integration project and Edmonds felt that the Britain in Europe was dominated by business interests and concerns with EMU.

The T&G represents approximately 900,000 members and organizes in a number of industrial sectors or 'trade groups' (namely food and agriculture, manufacturing, services, and transport). It has traditionally been positioned on the left of the British Labour movement; Teague (1989) situates it in the anti-European camp. The 1972 TUC Congress saw the T&G vote to oppose Britain's impending membership of the EEC. Throughout the 1970s, this anti-EEC position was maintained with Jack Jones (General Secretary) being a strong opponent of the common market. The T&G remains a Euro-sceptic trade union. The respective policy positions of the GMB and T&G on EMU are explored below to illustrate diversity responses to the EU.

Press releases and newspaper articles written on behalf of the T&G leadership (T&G 2001, 2003a,b) would suggest that a pragmatic balancing act has been formulated on its EMU policy; a 'yes but not yet' policy response. The emphasis appears to be on the Chancellor's five economic tests being met and ensuring a favourable sterling/euro exchange rate on entry. It would seem that the timing of entry is the most important issue for the T&G, and it is the economic tests that determine the criteria of entry.

This presentation of T&G policy positions it identically with that of the Labour government. However, closer examination of the union's official position on EMU opens up caveats, which illustrate both the sectoral influence of the trade groups within the union and the political influence of the 'broad left' faction. Two political factions operate within the T&G: the broad left has held the General Executive Council of the T&G since the two factions emerged in the 1980s, except for a brief period in the late 1980s when the 'centre left' faction held control.

Official T&G policy posits EMU as a threat to both manufacturing and public sector workers. The EMU Stability and Growth Pact (SGP) is cited as an unacceptable restraint on public service provision, threatening both jobs and conditions of employment for public sector workers. The provisions of the European Central Bank (ECB) are interpreted by the T&G as a threat to its manufacturing workers. The rules of the ECB allow it to intervene in the economy if inflation is running high; however, no provision exists for the ECB to intervene if growth is stagnating or in the negative. This deflationary bias leaves a hypothetically recessionary Europe with no mechanism for intervention, democratic or otherwise (see also Buller, Chapter 13). The likeliest losers in this scenario are manufacturing workers, as shrinking growth would impact on both employment figures and work conditions, as demands for flexibility increases. These arguments are broadly similar to Dyson's first discourse (above) that interprets EMU as a neo-liberal threat to the European social model. However, it is not simply the specific provisions of EMU that concern the T&G: concerns are also expressed that question the legitimacy of EMU in eroding national policy autonomy and sovereignty (Discourse 2). The timing of British membership of EMU is therefore of no consequence whatsoever to the T&G as membership of EMU appears to be ruled out on political rather than economic arguments.

The GMB has been a consistent supporter of EMU. Its position on EMU is very rarely presented in isolation from the wider context of European integration (GMB 1992a,b, 1993). EMU is framed as being part of the wider package of European integration. Although, critical of a number of the specific provisions of EMU, the GMB does not view these criticisms as impediments in the way of overall support. The primary reason underpinning support for British entry to EMU is that it is a crucial component driving the development of the European social dimension and entrenching European norms regarding the legitimate status of trade unions and the provision of a comprehensive social wage in Britain. This argument suggests a 'varieties of capitalism' argument comparing the European and US models: the latter being the fall-back position if the EU stalls.

The GMB policy also illustrates the perceived longer-term costs of EMU non-membership: that Britain's role in the EU will be incrementally undermined the longer it decides to remain outside. Here, the view is that if the GMB, and the UK more generally, is to retain influence in Brussels its partners must view them as credible. An approach that asks for the benefits of the social dimension without also supporting Euro membership is not a credible strategy. The UK must be part of the inner core of economic policy making and this means joining the Euro. The longer the uncertainty remains, the more isolated the UK will become (GMB 2001).

> [I]ndifference is not an option. We cannot stand back from the issue of the single currency. If we fail to prepare for entry we risk a disaster. Can we be an important member of the EU and stay outside the Euro? Almost certainly not. The slogan I have seen. 'Europe yes, the Euro no' is a con. (John Edmonds, in TUC 2000)

The UK entry into EMU would bring with it easier trade and travel, protection against currency speculation and increased employment due to higher inward investment. Inward investment is projected to decrease in the near future due to the uncertainties of UK membership and exchange rate fluctuations (TUFE 2002). However, the major fault-line for divergent interpretations between the T&G and the GMB relates to the likely impact of the SGP. The GMB, in stark contrast to the T&G, places less emphasis on the potential impact of the SGP on public spending and, as evidence for this argument, points to the member-states of EMU who have higher public spending on public services than Britain. The T&G framed its policy quite differently, spelling out the potential costs of EMU membership.

The two very divergent policy positions speak volumes about the internal processes of interest aggregation in each organization. At first glance there are many similarities in their governance structures. Both organizations decide policy at a biannual delegate conference and both have an executive committee to oversee the work of the leadership between conferences. However, the composition of the various representative bodies within the two unions varies greatly.

The T&G was formed in the 1920s from an amalgamation of various trade union organizations with divergent industrial orientations. In order to govern these diverse interests, and to encourage growth by further mergers, the T&G adopted a governance system that allowed a degree of independence for its trade groupings. Each trade group is entitled to representatives on the Executive Council and provides delegates to national conference. In addition to the *de jure* control over the executive from the trade groups, political factionalism within the T&G amounts to a *de facto* internal constraint. This to a large extent explains the *Janus* policy stance on EMU: policy has to be acceptable to both the dominant left faction and the various trade groups.

The GMB was initially established for workers in the various municipalities in the UK and so has always included a substantial public sector membership; one that Bieler (2003) suggests should mean the GMB is less favourable to EMU. Although trade groups are a feature of the GMB, the governance structure is predominantly designed to represent regional interests. Regional groups, and especially their leaders who have often been likened to Barons, are a significant *de jure* constraint on national leadership autonomy. However, in the case of EU policy making, the regional delegates and leaders have not proved a *de facto* internal constraint on leadership initiative and policy making. Research has indicated that the General Secretary is able to lead on matters European (interviews with the author, 2003). Political factions do not feature at the national level as a constraint on discretionary decision-making. Edmonds has exploited the lack of constraints on his leadership to initiate an engaging pro-EU approach. As one GMB official put it (interview with the author, 2003): 'to be quite honest I think the General Secretary had an easy run on matters European, there was never any strong opposition to the union's formal stance'.

In terms of the development of organizational capacity, the two union organizations again adopted widely divergent approaches. The T&G, under the leadership of Ron Todd, was one of the first trade unions in the UK to appoint an official with responsibility for European matters. It appeared that although the T&G approach shifted between pragmatism and hostility, its national leadership acknowledged that the EU was going to have an important impact in the domestic arena; as such, the ability to monitor developments and respond to them appropriately would be a necessity. Based in London, the official developed contacts with MEP and officials from the other EU institutions. The post of EU Coordinator was made redundant in the mid-1990s, during Sir Bill Morris's tenure as General Secretary. Subsequently, European issues have been dealt with by the various trade groups, with no officer specifically responsible for overall coordination, lobbying and information-gathering. By failing to coordinate EU responsibil-ities and removing the position of European Coordinator, the organizational capacity of the T&G to monitor, respond and intervene in EU policy making is diminished. One indication of the difference in the importance attached to EU issues between the two unions is that the GMB European Officer travels back from Brussels each month to attend NECP meetings, while the T&G does not send an official the short way across London from Transport House to Congress House for similar meetings. Organizational inertia at the national level of the T&G has meant that organizational capacity is severely limited.

In general, the organizational response of the GMB to the EU has been internally innovative and externally engaging. The overall strategy to Europe has been termed 'going over and under', referring to UK governments of both persuasions that rarely support EU social legislation. As General Secretary, John Edmonds was largely responsible for the key changes. Soon after taking over, Edmonds brought in a new Research Director who was to oversee a European 'experiment'. In 1991, the GMB appointed a European Officer to work initially out of the office of a sympathetic MEP. Within 18 months, the GMB had managed to secure a permanent office in Brussels. At this point, even the TUC did not have a permanent office in Brussels and the GMB remains the sole TUC affiliate to locate permanently in Brussels.

The Brussels office has enabled the GMB to gather information on and respond to developments in the EU. The office enables the GMB to keep up with UK government and other important actors' positions. A monthly *European News Bulletin* is published by the office outlining the relevant information from Brussels. Not only is the bulletin sent out to relevant or interested GMB officials and activists, but also it is disseminated to the network of contacts and lobby targets established by the office since the early 1990s. The information disseminated from the Brussels office is presented to GMB officials, activists and members in a user-friendly format, translating 'Brussels speak' into a more accessible language. Interviews with regional offi-cials indicate that this is a much-valued resource as it clearly and concisely sets out EU developments and their implications for the GMB.

The office provides a direct feed to EU officials, MEPs, other trade union organizations located in Brussels and other lobbyists. The GMB has been active especially with regard to the raft of health and safety legislation and industrial democracy initiatives in the 1990s. The European officer in Brussels is able to connect GMB (trade group) representatives with relevant EU officials when necessary, and has been extremely successful in developing a wide network of contacts and allies outside the traditional paths trodden by trade unionists at the international level.

The GMB leadership also made important domestic organizational changes that enhanced its capacity to receive and aggregate interests before projecting a coherent response to EU initiatives. A European steering group was established to provide an informal forum for senior officials (national trade groups and regional officials) and representatives of the GMB to meet, put together the information they had gleaned, and exchange experiences. As it stood, the steering group did not have any direct authority to direct matters and had an unclear relationship with the GMB Central Executive Committee's International Committee. Subsequently, this Committee became the European and International Committee, absorbing the steering group. Half of all meetings were to be EU related and the Brussels-based official also regularly attends.

The 'double whammy' of strong trade group influence and political factionalism within the T&G appears to be largely absent from the GMB. In the determination and execution of EU priorities, the regional characteristics of the GMB also prove a *de facto* negligible internal constraint on the discretionary decision-making of the General Secretary. Subsequently, the centre of the union organization has been both able and willing to lead and innovate in order to respond to the threats and opportunities of the EU.

Conclusion

In the context of globalization, the capacity of nation-states and national industrial relations institutions is eroding due to the competitive pressures brought on by the expansion of international markets. This threatens the previous achievements and processes of trade unionism in the domestic context. While there is an opportunity to (re-)regulate markets at the EU level, the structural bias in the European integration process favours market liberalization. Despite this, if national trade unions (such as those in Britain) are to effectively represent the interests of their members, it is a logical step for them to engage with and make representations to the EU.

However, this rational approach to understanding the European strategies and policies of British trade unions has its limitations. Trade union leaderships are often unable to adopt 'rational' strategies of response due to the internal constraints of their particular organizations. Developments at the EU level do not comfortably map on to the traditional ideologies and identities of the British trade union movement and so it is likely that only in times of perceived crisis will Europeanization seem an attractive option. Since 1988, the TUC has been able to project a rational response driven both by domestic push factors and by a corresponding pull from the EU. It has overcome previous ideological opposition to the EU and reoriented some of its activities to enhance its role at a time of limited domestic opportunities.

The study of two unions, however, illustrates the problems of interest aggregation in the context of multi-sectoral unions who have different perceptions of the opportunities presented by the EU. The study demonstrates that the degree to which trade union activity is reoriented through engagement with the EU varies according to a number of factors that include internal organizational structure, internal politics and ideology.

More generally, the traditional orientation of British unions towards collective bargaining at the workplace does not make them particularly well placed to take advantage of the developing EU regime of industrial relations. Adapting to this regime is especially difficult where the procedures and practices of a union leave little scope for leadership autonomy. And, while it is not the intention here to question the positions decided democratically within trade union organizations, there is clear evidence that the growing importance of the EU to the interests of trade unionists should have elicited organizational responses aimed at amplifying their organizational capacities. At the time of writing, only a handful of British trade union organizations have a political profile and presence in Brussels. In this regard, the clear losers in this Europeanization process are those unions, such as the T&G, that have failed to reorientate their activities in proportion to the opportunities afforded due to internal organizational constraints.

Note

1. The Union began as the Gas Workers and General Union, which was formed in March 1889 in East London, and later became the General, Municipal and Boilermakers (GMB) Union. Subsequent mergers with other unions meant that since 1989, it is now known simply as 'GMB – Britain's General Union'.

11
The Third Sector

Rachael Chapman

Introduction

The third sector encompasses a wide range of organizations that are non-profit distributing, self-governing, significantly voluntary and have some formal institutional existence (for a succinct definition, see Kendall and Anheier 1999). For the purposes of this chapter, trade unions (see van der Maas, Chapter 10) and employers associations are excluded from this definition. Third sector groups are engaged in a diverse range of activities from service provision, self-help and mutual aid to community development, advocacy and representation. The contribution that the sector makes through these activities has been increasingly recognized by European institutions and the British government. This has led to the opening up of new opportunities for third sector organizations to act as vehicles for citizen and community participation and representation in policy making within both domestic and EU systems (see Taylor *et al.* 2004). More importantly for our purposes, it raises the intriguing possibility that domestic third sector activity in British might have been Europeanized by EU-level policies and law-making activities.

Despite this possibility much of the academic research on the third sector to date has focused on domestic policy contexts, with only a few studies examining the third sector's involvement in the EU-level policy process (Kendal and Anheier 1999; Armstrong *et al.* 2002a; Bouget and Prouteau 2002; Cook 2002; Etherington 2002; Evers and Laville 2004). Even fewer studies have examined the Europeanization of the third sector in British. This chapter draws on both previous research and new empirical findings to analyse the Europeanization of the British third sector. In applying the definition of Europeanization set out in Chapter 2, it focuses on changes in British third sector interest representation and participation in the EU policy process arising from relevant EU-level policy developments, regulations and programme agreements. In adopting this approach, however, it is recognized that initiatives and developments 'downloaded' from the EU can themselves be influenced by member state domestic policies and practices that are 'uploaded' to the EU (Bache and Jordan, Chapter 2).

The remainder of the chapter is structured as follows. Section two reviews some of the challenges posed in researching the third sector and sets out a model for understanding the Europeanization of third sector–governmental relations. Section three utilizes this model to examine the extent, nature and mechanisms used by the third sector to shape the EU by 'uploading' ideas, policy proposals and concepts. Section four examines the significance of uploading in relation to downloading, by drawing on a specific case study of the implementation of the EU structural funds. The final section (five) concludes by assessing the nature and extent of the Europeanization of the British third sector.

Conceptualizing third sector–governmental relations

It is widely recognized that the impact of EU-level pressures on the domestic polity is difficult to untangle from other causal factors. In relation to the third sector, particular difficulties arise from the complexity of third sector–governmental relations and from the recent emergence, fluidity, ambiguity and instability of many EU policy developments in this area (see Kendall and Anheier 1999: 300–302). Added to this is the fact that many of these policy developments have co-evolved with similar national policy preferences, making it increasingly difficult to separate out and quantify distinctively national or EU-related pressures.

In view of these difficulties, this chapter draws on a range of tools to disentangle cause and effect relationships. In addition to utilizing the concepts and tools outlined in Chapter 2, it draws on a model of third sector–government relations, which is adapted from Bouget and Prouteau (2002) (see Figure 11.1).

As can be seen, this (admittedly) simple model illustrates the links between third sector organizations and networks operating in Britain and at the EU level. Each link is represented by a two-way arrow, depicting a potentially dialectical relationship between the actors. When applied to the British third sector, this diagram illustrates different routes through which third sector organizations and networks can, in theory, pursue their interests in the national and EU policy processes. For example, they may seek to influence policy making directly through supranational institutions (relationship 5), and/or indirectly through, or in alliance with, EU-level third sector organizations/networks (relationships 4 and 2) or national government (relationships 1 and 3).

Projecting Bache and Jordan's definition of Europeanization on to this model suggests that Europeanization of the British third sector arises where changes in any one of these *sets* of relationships reflect the policies, practices

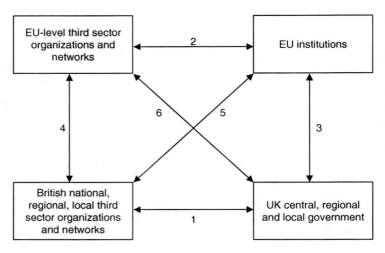

Figure 11.1 A model of third sector and government relations
Source: Adapted from Bouget and Prouteau (2002)

and preferences of European-level actors, as advanced through the EU system of governance. Crucially, these changes may take place at either the policy-shaping *or* the policy implementation stages.

Inevitably, third sector–governmental relations are, in practice, unlikely to be as simplistic as the above model depicts. Despite this, it does offer a useful starting point for examining the impact of the EU on third sector activities. In particular, it can be used to highlight changes in relations across multiple levels, policy actors and routes and can, therefore, help guide investigation of *how* EU membership has impacted on patterns of third sector engagement. With this in mind, the remainder of this chapter explores and attempts to explain how and to what extent the British third sector has been Europeanized.

EU-level policy shaping

Patterns of third sector engagement

A review of the existing literature indicates that British third sector organizations have been Europeanized insofar as they have reoriented their activities to exploit additional opportunities provided by the EU. This can be seen as part of a more general growth in recent years of third sector involvement and interest group activity in EU-level policy making (see Mazey and Richardson 2001; Bouget and Prouteau 2002: 33; Etherington 2002: 131; Fairbrass, Chapter 9).

An application of the third sector–governmental relations model outlined above reveals that engagement takes place via a number of routes. First, there is evidence that third sector organizations and groups have established direct relations with, and have participated in consultation opportunities offered by, the European Commission and European Parliament (Warleigh 2000, 2001; Kendall 2001: 5). Fairbrass and Jordan (2004: 162) provide specific examples of this, highlighting direct contacts between environmental groups, such as the Royal Society for the Protection of Birds (RSPB) and British World Wildlife Fund (WWF), and European Commission and European Parliament officials.

Second, there is evidence that nationally based third sector organizations and groups have increasingly worked with, or through, Brussels-based and/or Europe-wide third sector networks as a means of advocating their interests in EU policy making (Bouget and Prouteau 2002: 33; Kendall 2001: 5). As stated in a National Council for Voluntary Organizations (NCVO) briefing document:

> Brussels-based non-governmental organization networks act as an effective bridge between organizations active at the national level and the EU institutions, thereby ensuring effective and co-ordinated campaigning and lobbying activities vis-à-vis EU decision-makers. (NCVO, 2001: 1)

In fact, this route is potentially significant given claims that the Commission is more likely to recognize the legitimacy of, and therefore listen to, interest groups and networks organized at EU level, as opposed to those functioning exclusively at national or sub-national levels (see Michalowitz 2001; Warleigh 2001: 622; Mahoney 2004: 453). Again, Fairbrass and Jordan (2004: 162) provide examples of British environmental voluntary sector organizations that have successfully exploited this route.

Third, there is evidence that third sector organizations have successfully worked in partnership with, and/or have lobbied, the British government in an attempt to shape EU-level agreements. Examples of this can be seen in EU structural fund negotiations, which involved the Commission, national and sub-national governments and third sector organizations; although the latter have been regarded as by far the weaker partner (see, for example, Armstrong *et al.* 2002a: 18–20). In addition, Fairbrass (2002) confirms that British voluntary sector environmental groups have sought access to national officials as a means of shaping EU policy, although she concludes that many of them failed to gain an adequate hearing from national government departments.

Among the different routes of engagement, Warleigh highlights differing participatory tendencies according to organizational size and resources. In particular, he suggests that, 'smaller NGOs [non-governmental organizations] tended to be heavily reliant on umbrella organizations at the

EU-level, often leaving much of the EU-level campaigning work to them' whereas 'nationally-based NGOs tended to focus their campaigning work on national actors, hoping thereby to feed their concerns into the EU policy making process' (Warleigh 2001: 630). In the context of urban policy, Armstrong *et al.* (2003: 8–11) confirm that national third sector umbrella organizations continued to focus primarily on the national government, although they acknowledge that many organizations also developed EU representation and alliances.

So far, the discussion indicates that third sector involvement in EU-level policy and programme negotiations has grown. However, the continuing importance of third sector–governmental relations in the national arena on both domestic and EU-related matters should not be underestimated. As Kendall states, 'it is well established in the UK that the primary tier of the state to which the third sector relates for policy purposes is local government' (Kendall 2003: 9). This is, perhaps, unsurprising given that the majority of third sector organizations are relatively small in terms of funds and staff, or are entirely voluntary (Cook 2002: 63). From this perspective, the Europeanization of the British third sector, understood as the reorientation of activities towards EU institutions, is likely to be heavily constrained by the fact that the natural point of contact for many third sector organizations remains with local authorities. Furthermore, variations in third sector engagement across policy sectors indicate that the extent of such Europeanization is likely to be more significant in some EU policy areas than others. European institutions are perceived to be of high salience to third sector organizations within a small number of policy fields, particularly environmental policy and overseas development (Kendall 2001: 9).

To summarize, EU membership has reshaped patterns of British third sector engagement through the participatory opportunities provided by European institutions. However, to understand Europeanization as discussed and defined in Chapter 2, it is also necessary to investigate causation in the relationships between EU decisions and initiatives and changes in third sector relations at the national and sub-national level in Britain.

EU initiatives and decisions relating to the third sector

A number of 'horizontal'[1] EU-level developments and trends can be identified that may help explain the emergence of new opportunities for third sector engagement in policy shaping. First, there have been several calls since the late 1980s for greater and/or improved co-operation between EU institutions and third sector organizations. Such requests were embedded in the 1987 Fontaine Report, produced for the European Parliament, which called for the Commission to see the non-profit sector as an important ally in building a 'new Europe'. They are also present in

Declaration 23 attached to the 1993 Maastricht Treaty, which called for co-operation between the EU and (social welfare) charitable associations and foundations.

Second, the Commission has taken various steps to promote the engage-ment of NGO transnational networks at the EU level. One aspect of this is the direct funding of transnational organizations and networks by the EU (Kendall 2001: 5). Another is marked by the Commission proposals in 1991 and 1992 to establish a European Association Statute with the aim of easing transnational network mobilization. Although these proposals met with limited success (see Kendall and Anheier 1999: 289–91), they indicated a desire within the Commission to more actively mobilize NGO transna-tional networks.

Third, the Commission has published a series of documents proposing measures and guidelines for improving its relations with voluntary organiz-ations/NGOs specifically, and with interest groups more generally. The first of these documents took the form of a Communication published in 1997 entitled 'Promoting the Role of Voluntary Organizations and Foundations in Europe' (CEC 1997b). This examined the contribution made by third sector organizations to European policy making, and identified steps that could be taken to improve it. At the EU level, this included proposals for the Commis-sion to improve consultation and dialogue with the non-profit sector and to ease transnational network creation and mobilization. Three years later, the Commission published a discussion paper on NGOs, entitled 'The Commis-sion and NGOs: Building a Stronger Partnership' (CEC 2000). This docu-ment provided an overview of existing Commission–NGO relationships, followed by proposals for a more structured and coherent Commission-wide framework of co-operation. These proposals entailed measures to improve Commission–NGO dialogue and consultation, restructure and rationalize EU budget lines and improve the management of NGO grants. They were designed by the Commission to give impetus to an ongoing debate for estab-lishing a more coherent and efficient approach to its relations with NGOs, which was seen as part of the overall process of administrative reform to improve transparency and accountability.

Since then, the Commission has adopted a Communication setting out general principles and minimum standards for consultation of interested parties, including NGOs, that apply to the EU policy-shaping phase. This Communication, published in December 2002 (CEC 2002), stipulates that the consultation process should be governed by the principles of participa-tion, openness, accountability, effectiveness and coherence. More specific-ally it suggests that:

- Clear and concise information should be provided in communications relating to consultations.
- Relevant parties should have an opportunity to express their opinions.

- Consultations should be published widely in order to reach target audiences.
- Participants should be given sufficient time to respond.
- Acknowledgement and adequate feedback relating to consultations should be provided.

The publication of these principles and minimum standards for consultation form part of the follow-up to the 2001 European Governance White Paper. This Paper falls under the fourth category of EU-level policy developments, in which discussion of EU–NGO relations has been integrated into broader debates on European governance and civil society (Etherington 2002: 135). In the White Paper, the Commission promised to open up the policy making process and get more actors involved in shaping and delivering EU policy (CEC 2001: 15). Here, reference is made to civil society organizations, which the Commission defines as a broad range of groups that includes voluntary and community sector organizations as well as social partners (for example trade unions and employers associations), and consumer organizations. These organizations are seen as important for promoting civil dialogue, for example by giving a structured channel for citizens to voice their criticisms.

More recently, Article I-47 of the draft Treaty establishing a Constitution for Europe contained provisions for establishing a legal basis for consultation through civil dialogue. This Article provides for the maintenance of open, transparent and regular dialogue between the European institutions and civil society and for appropriate opportunities to be given to citizens and representative associations to express views on all areas of EU action. It also requires the Commission to carry out broad consultations with parties concerned in order to ensure the EU's actions are coherent and transparent.

So far, the patterns of engagement and EU-level initiatives and decisions concerning the third sector have been explored. The next section discusses the significance of these, with a view to discussing the nature, extent and mechanisms of any Europeanizing effects that have flowed from them, especially in Britain.

The nature, extent and mechanisms of Europeanization

Taken together, the EU-level trends and developments outlined above have emphasized the development of transnational NGO networks, improved dialogue and consultation between EU institutions, and the role of NGOs and third sector groups, as agents for enhancing EU participatory democracy. These developments appear to correlate with increased third sector engagement directly with EU institutions, and through EU-level NGO organizations and networks. As such, they may serve as EU-level mechanisms through which 'windows of opportunity' are opened up to allow for a deeper Europeanization of the British third sector.

Even so, the relative importance of formal Europeanization pressures, as advanced through 'horizontal' EU policy developments, rather than more informal 'vertical' Commission policy preferences within particular sectors, is unclear. As the 1997 Commission Communication notes (CEC 1997b: 6), 'European institutions have a long history of contacts and informal consultation with the voluntary sector', albeit on an ad hoc and sector-by-sector basis. In other words, consultation and participation were taking place on a sector-by-sector basis prior to the development of more formal Commission/EU-wide frameworks on third sector and civil society engagement, indicating that informal EU-level preferences are significant in shaping participatory opportunities. With respect to this, the 1997 Communication gave examples of pre-existing third sector relations with Commission DGs responsible for development, employment, industrial relations and social affairs, environment and enterprise policies at EU level (CEC 1997b: 6).

Furthermore, the extent and nature of Europeanization of third sector engagement depends not just on 'top-down' political opportunities available to third sector organizations from the EU, but also on domestic factors shaping their responses to these opportunities. As Casey (2004: 249–50) highlights:

> To a certain extent, third sector organizations are masters of their own destiny in that their capacity to influence, and the strategies they choose, will also depend on factors internal to the organization. First, third sector organizations must choose to participate; second, they often have a choice between alternative strategic options; and third, they must have the organizational skills and resource capacity to bear the transaction costs of their choices.

Applying this to EU-level policy making, the fact that third sector participation is not mandatory seems to suggest that any Europeanization of British third sector engagement that has occurred would tend to be voluntary rather than coercive in nature. With respect to this, Dunkerley and Fudge (2004: 245) point out that 'many interest groups have now begun to see the European Commission in greater terms as an opportunity structure and an agenda-setting institution that is more permeable and open to negotiation than many national governments'. Even so, limited resources, information and interest, together with the localized or highly specialized focus of many smaller third sector activities, are key factors limiting the extent to which British third sector organizations seek to influence EU-level policy making (Armstrong *et al.* 2003: 22), and, therefore, the degree of Europeanization of third sector interest representation. More generally, these factors encourage third sector organizations to establish contacts with local and, to a lesser degree, regional and national government in their quest for policy influence. As such, the domestic political environment is likely to be highly significant in shaping the extent, nature and significance of third sector engagement in EU policy processes.

To summarize, the British third sector has been Europeanized in accordance with Bache and Jordan's definition insofar as it has taken advantage of political opportunities to engage in EU policy shaping emerging from EU-level decisions and initiatives. In this sense, the extent and nature of Europeanization appears to be largely voluntary and is shaped by the availability, frequency and nature of specific participatory opportunities, together with third sector resources, knowledge, interests and strategies. Even so, the fact that the local government remains a key point of contact for many third sector organizations, suggests that the Europeanization of the British third sector relating to direct relations with EU institutions is relatively limited.

EU policy implementation

So far, this chapter has explored Europeanization in relation to EU-level policy shaping (or 'uploading'). This section focuses on policy implementation, which relates to the notion of 'downloading'. It draws specifically on a case study of the EU structural funds. There are three main reasons for adopting this policy area as a case study. First, the structural funds provide one of the most significant sources of EU financial support for the third sector (Home Office 2001; Kendall and Anheier 1999). As funding has traditionally been a significant constraint on third sector activity, its provision, in theory, creates a fertile context in which Europeanization might occur. Second, notions of social exclusion and community economic development, which have been closely linked to greater opportunities for third sector engagement (see Bache 2001; Armstrong *et al.* 2002a,b, 2003) have become increasingly important in the implementation of the structural funds, again suggesting a rich potential for Europeanization. Third, by taking a case study approach it is possible to examine policy sector–specific developments in detail, which may provide deeper insights into the nature and extent of Europeanization. In short, this case is one in which the prospects for Europeanization might be expected to be relatively good.

The EU structural funds consist of a number of programmes providing financial assistance to targeted EU regions to enhance economic and social cohesion. The discussion here focuses on mainstream structural fund programmes, particularly Objectives 1 and 2 that support the economic and social conversion of regions whose development is lagging behind or experiencing structural difficulties. In Britain, these two programmes amount to 11,970 million euros (at 2004 prices) over the 2000–2006 period. The next section examines patterns of third sector engagement in these programmes. This, together with a subsequent review of relevant EU initiatives and decisions, forms the basis of a discussion concerning the nature, extent and mechanisms of Europeanization.

Patterns of third sector engagement

A review of current literature and policy documentation suggests that third sector engagement in mainstream structural funds has grown, particularly from the 1990s onwards. In particular, two recent evaluations report an increased role for third sector organizations in Britain's Objective 1 and 2 programmes between 1994 and 1999 (Kelleher *et al.* 1999: 96–97; ECOTEC 2003: 129). Similarly, Armstrong *et al.* (2002a: 17) highlight the growth of third sector participation in connection with the introduction of community economic development (CED) priorities towards the latter half of the 1994–99 Objective 2 programming period. More recently, a review of the current four 2000–2006 Objective 1 programmes revealed that third sector engagement is now widespread, with the sector being a partner on each of the Programming Monitoring Committees (PMCs), that is, the partnerships responsible for overseeing programme implementation, as well as on partnerships set up to formulate and/or implement policy strategy.

An application of the third sector–governmental relations model described above reveals that formal third sector engagement in structural fund implementation primarily takes place in partnerships. In the case of PMCs, this entails direct dialogue with Commission officials, national, regional and local government representatives, social partners and private sector representatives. Third sector relations have also arisen with regional and local government officials, social partners and the private sector in sub-partnerships set up to formulate and implement policy strategy. In the model, these relationships are, in part, illustrated by the dialectical arrows between British third sector organizations, EU institutions and UK central, regional and local governments (relationships 1, 3 and 5) . However, the model does not reflect the true complexity of changing relationships due to the absence of social and private sector partners and the aggregation of EU institutions and domestic governmental and third sector institutions, both of which mask complexity.

Leaving aside this criticism, examples of extensive third sector engagement in structural fund partnerships can be found in the South Yorkshire and West Wales and the Valleys Objective 1 programmes. In West Wales and the Valleys, for example, the composition of the Programme Monitoring Committee and 15 local partnerships were established on a so-called 'three-thirds' principle, with equal representation from the public, private/social and voluntary and community sectors (see CRG 2003: 13). In South Yorkshire, the third sector was designated the lead partner on the partnership established to implement the Programme's CED Priority,on which voluntary and community actors accounted for around one-third of the total membership (Programme Directorate 2001: 7). In order to facilitate this lead role, the South Yorkshire Open Forum, a sub-regional third sector umbrella organization that evolved during the programming negotiations, secured Objective 1 funding to act as the key co-ordination point for wider voluntary and community sector engagement and interest representation in the delivery of the Programme. Community sector organizations also played a lead role in developing and implementing 39 local community action plans that sought to build capacity and tackle economic and social exclusion in targeted areas. With respect to South Yorkshire, research by Chapman (2004) concluded that third sector partners were, within certain parameters, influential in shaping policy outcomes, particularly with respect to formulating detailed policy strategies and in upholding underlying notions and beliefs concerning the delivery of CED.

Together, these findings reveal that EU membership has shaped patterns of British third sector engagement in policy implementation through the creation of new participatory and funding opportunities. The next section outlines a number of EU-level mechanisms that help to explain these developments.

EU initiatives and decisions relating to the third sector

Since their introduction, the structural funds have undergone a series of reforms that help to explain the emergence of new participatory opportunities for the third sector in Britain. Two such developments are examined here. The first is the introduction and extension of the EU partnership principle. This principle, introduced in the 1988 Structural Fund Reforms, requires close consultation between the Commission, the member states and competent authorities at national, regional and local levels in both the development and implementation of structural fund programmes (Regulation EC/2052/88). This principle is seen by the European Commission as a means of improving the effectiveness of the structural funds by promoting the inclusion of regional and local actors deemed to be most familiar with the problems and priorities of targeted areas. The partnership principle was later extended in the 1993 structural fund reforms to include economic and social partners, thereby formally opening up opportunities for the inclusion of non-governmental actors. Whilst not explicitly mentioned as a partner in these regulations, the inclusion of third sector actors is implicitly supported, and, in some cases, actively encouraged by the European Commission (see also Armstrong *et al.* 2003: 5; CRG 2003: 13).

The second policy development considered is the inclusion of CED priorities in mainstream structural fund programmes. The origins of CED in structural fund programmes can be traced back to Merseyside's 1994–99 Objective 1 Pathways Areas initiative. The approach, which was subsequently set out in the 'Lloyd Report' (CEC 1996), entails targeting programme resources on the most disadvantaged communities, with the eventual aim of linking them back into mainstream social and economic activity. More specifically, it involves a 'bottom-up' approach to economic and social development that emphasizes the engagement and empowerment of communities in capacity building and tackling social and economic exclusion (see Bache 2001). Third sector organizations are regarded as key agents in this process, based on their localized knowledge and potential to engage with, and represent communities in, policy making and implementation. CED approaches have since been incorporated as a priority activity within all British 2000–2006 Objective 1, and the majority of Objective 2 programmes (Europa 2005). CED priorities were also introduced in the previous 1994–99 Objective 2 programmes, primarily at the instigation of the European Commission (Armstrong *et al.* 2002a: 15). As such, CED offers significant potential for greater third sector engagement in economic and social development in Britain. The next section explores the significance of these developments more fully, with a view to establishing the nature, extent and mechanisms of Europeanization.

The nature, extent and mechanisms of Europeanization

Together, EU-level trends and developments favouring partnership and CED appear to open up windows of opportunity for greater third sector involvement in economic and social regeneration. As noted by Armstrong *et al.* (2003: 7), the role the third sector could play in the development and delivery of structural fund programmes, particularly with respect to tackling social and economic exclusion in CED priorities, had become 'an accepted part of the EU structural policy thinking by 2000'. As such, these policy trends appear to correlate with the growth in third sector participation in programme implementation, indicating a potential EU-level Europeanization mechanism.

Even so, existing research reveals that EU-level pressures and mechanisms do not shape all policy outcomes at the implementation stage. Thus, whilst EU programmes and policies promote institutional designs that favour particular outcomes, there is often scope for domestic actors and institutions to interpret them flexibly at the implementation stage. Some evidence of this was found within the South Yorkshire Objective 1 Programme, in which decisions made and driven forward by domestic actors at the programme delivery stage were significant in shaping the precise nature, extent, take-up and continuation of participatory opportunities available to the third sector (Chapman 2004: 23). In particular, Programme Directorate officials, including staff from the Government Office for Yorkshire and The Humber, were key actors influencing a partnership restructure. This led to the replacement of the partnership responsible for CED strategy development, on which the third sector was designated lead partner and accounted for around one-third of the total membership, with broader thematic partnerships and task-specific groups. In addition, the motivation and choices made by key third sector actors to engage in both programme development and delivery was clearly important in explaining the degree and nature of Europeanization. Factors influencing such choices are, in some cases, EU related, depending on EU funding participation, in others, factors internal to the organisation – culture, ideology, history and resources – are more important.

As discussed in Chapter 2, the notion of adaptational pressure emphasizes the 'goodness of fit' between EU-level changes and existing domestic structures, policies and practices. According to this top-down view of Europeanization, a poor fit creates strong pressure on national systems to adapt to EU requirements. When compared to national government support towards third sector engagement in regional policy specifically, adaptational pressure from the EU appears stronger prior to 1997 but has since weakened. As Armstrong *et al.* argue (2003: 4), the commitment of national government between 1994 and 1997 to engage the third sector in regional policy was weak, which suggests that the EU was a key source of encouragement behind the growth of third sector participation in regional structural fund programmes in the 1990s. Even so, it is widely recognized that the nature and structure of structural fund partnerships in Britain and other member states tend to follow domestic institutional traditions and preferences (see Bache 2004: 166–74; Hooghe 1996). Similarly, there is evidence that the introduction and promotion of CED, which is strongly associated with growth in third sector participation, was actively supported, and in some cases led by local and regional domestic actors, particularly in Merseyside and Yorkshire and The Humber 1994–99 Objective 2 Programmes (see Armstrong *et al.* 2002a: 17, 2002b: 2). In fact, the experiences of the Merseyside Pathways Areas initiative informed the development of the European Commission's own model of CED, indicating a degree of 'uploading' to the EU.

Viewed from this perspective, EU-level adaptational pressures towards deeper third sector engagement originating from the partnership principle and CED appear relatively weak within some British regions and, where they existed, were subject to significant voluntary adaptation and interpretation by domestic actors. Furthermore, the weakening of adaptation pressures is likely to have become more prominent following the election of the Labour Government in 1997, in which bottom-up approaches and the engagement of the third sector in policy making gained increased support within the governments' own policy priorities and preferences (see Taylor *et al.* 2004: 69). Indeed, there is evidence in the 2000–2006 South Yorkshire case study suggesting that domestic actors and the domestic political environment have facilitated deeper third sector involvement and influence (Chapman 2004).

To summarize, the discussion above suggests that EU-level pressures arising from the EU partnership principle and inclusion of CED priorities in structural fund programme agreements *have* helped to open up windows of opportunity for third sector actors in Britain to engage in policy implementation. This suggests that a degree of Europeanization has taken place according to Bache and Jordan's definition. However, the relative importance of domestic actors and the domestic political environment in interpreting and delivering structural fund policy and programmes suggests that the precise role, nature and extent of third sector engagement at the implementation stage – and thus the degree of Europeanization – is very heavily modulated (and to some extent determined) by domestic factors. In this sense, there is more evidence of voluntaristic than coercive forms of Europeanization as set out in Chapter 2.

Conclusion

This chapter has drawn upon a review of the existing literature and original research to discuss the Europeanization of the British third sector. It has focused in particular on third sector representation and participation in the EU policy process. In doing so, it has focused primarily on the definition of Europeanization set out by the editors in Chapter 2. In relation to this definition, Europeanization arises where changes in third sector–government relations reflect the policies, practices and preferences of European-level actors, as advanced through the EU system of governance. The main findings on the third sector are summarized in Table 11.1.

The analysis presented above suggests that Europeanization has taken place; to the extent that the British third sector has exploited new and additional opportunities for engagement arising from EU-level policies, preferences and programmes. Examples of this at the EU policy-shaping stage include opportunities arising from the Commission's emphasis on improved co-operation and dialogue between European institutions and third sector/civil society organizations, and the promotion of transnational network creation and mobilization among third sector groups. Third sector policy preferences have also been advanced through informal Commission–voluntary sector contacts and consultation, conducted on an ad hoc and sector-by-sector basis. More recently, a number of more formal Commission initiatives and documents have emerged calling for improved Commission–NGO relations across all EU policy sectors. Together, these developments appear to correlate with increased third sector mobilization in policy making direct to EU institutions and through EU-level third sector networks. At the policy implementation stage, third sector organizations have increasingly taken part in structural fund strategy development and delivery. This trend correlates with EU-level decisions that place increased emphasis on partnership working and, in particular, on the role of CED within structural fund programme agreements.

Table 11.1   The Europeanization of the British third sector

	Policy shaping (uploading)	Policy implementation (downloading)
Key EU-level developments	• Calls for transnational NGO network development. • Improved dialogue between the third sector and EU institutions from late 1980s onwards. • Increasing emphasis at EU level on role of third sector groups in enhancing participatory democracy.	• Introduction and extension of the EU partnership principle (1988 onwards). • Commission support and encouragement for third sector inclusion. • Introduction of CED priorities in mainstream structural fund programmes.
Patterns of engagement	• Growth in third sector participation/representation at EU level (for example via direct third sector contacts with EU institutions, European NGOs and UK government).	• Growth in third sector participation in structural fund partnerships, particularly from the 1990s onwards.
Extent of Europeanization	• Some reorientation of third sector activities towards shaping EU decisions/initiatives. • Much direct political contact for third sector organizations remains with local government.	• Some reorientation of third sector activities through EU policy opportunities. • Domestic factors remain crucial in shaping precise role, nature and extent of third sector participation.
Nature of Europeanization	• Largely voluntary.	• Largely voluntary.

While presenting some evidence of Europeanization, this chapter confirms the findings of earlier Europeanization studies that stress the relative importance of domestic factors in shaping outcomes. With respect to the third sector, a number of domestic factors seem to be particularly significant. First, the response of third sector organizations to participatory opportunities, which may be shaped by organizational strategies, interests, culture and capacity, is clearly important in shaping the extent and nature of Europeanization. With respect to this, many smaller British third sector organizations are unlikely to engage significantly in EU-level policy shaping due to lack of interest and/or resources: for many such organizations the sub-national and, to a lesser degree, national levels remain the primary point of contact.

Second, the fact that EU-level policy and programme agreements concerning the third sector tend to be broad, vague and under-specified has left considerable room for manoeuvre and interpretation by domestic actors at the policy implementation stage. Domestic actors have, in turn, played a key part in shaping the precise role, nature and extent of third sector engagement. For example, in the case of the South Yorkshire Objective 1 Programme discussed above, Government Office for Yorkshire and The Humber officials were instrumental in determining the participatory opportunities available to third sector actors.

To conclude, while the EU creates new opportunities for the third sector to become involved in policy making and policy implementation, the precise extent to which it engages in uploading and downloading can only be satisfactorily explained by investigating the role of domestic factors. Domestic factors appear to explain the variance in the degrees of engagement of different third sector actors and, as such, are crucial to understanding the highly voluntaristic nature of Europeanization in this particular sector of contemporary British policy making.

Note

1. The term 'horizontal' is used here to depict third sector policy developments and trends that cut across traditional policy sectors, as distinct from 'vertical' policy developments and trends taking place within specific policy sectors (see Kendall 2001).

Part IV
Policies

12
Foreign Policy

Tim Oliver and David Allen

Introduction

In recent years, British foreign policy has engaged in many European foreign policy frameworks, from the Western European Union (WEU) and Nato to the European Free Trade Association (EFTA), the Council of Europe, and the Organisation for Security and Cooperation in Europe (OSCE). However, this chapter will concentrate on the growing role of the EU in British foreign policy and assess the extent to which this constitutes Europeanization as defined in Chapter 2 of this volume.

We will argue that since the end of the Cold War, Britain has, to a limited but growing extent, engaged more closely with the EU and that this has been built on the relations developed in the previous decades. During this time, Britain took an active lead in the area of European Political Cooperation (EPC) (Nuttall 1992; Allen 2005) and in doing so shaped EU foreign policy as well as being shaped by it. Nevertheless, Britain retains a high degree of ambivalence towards adding a European dimension to its foreign policy, with ongoing worries concerning sovereignty, relations with the United States, independent capabilities and the national policies of Britain's EU partners – especially France. Thus, while Britain has actively engaged with both EPC and now the Common Foreign and Security Policy (CFSP), an element of ambiguity with regard to wholehearted commitment remains.

This chapter is divided into three sections. The first section gives a brief chronological analysis of Britain's fifty-year engagement with European integration and the impact this has had on British foreign policy. In this section, the major focus is on the post 1973 period of EU membership with a particular focus on the period since 1997. In the second part, we concentrate upon the key questions about Europeanization that shape this book (see Chapter 2). The final section summarizes our main conclusions.

Although this is not the place for a detailed discussion of the nature of foreign policy (see Hill 2003), this chapter recognizes that Britain continues to pursue unilaterally what it thinks of as foreign policy and that Britain is also a key member of the EU, which itself claims to have established a common foreign and security policy. There is, therefore, a possibility that Europeanization is taking place whether this is conceived of as the EU impacting on British foreign policy or Britain impacting on European foreign policy (see Wong 2005 for an excellent general discussion of the Europeanization of foreign policy). However, most analysts of foreign policy (in particular, see Webber *et al.* 2002; Hill 2003) would also argue that foreign policy in general has been transformed in recent years and so it remains difficult to isolate the impact of the EU on British foreign policy from the impact of other factors such as interdependence, globalization or the 'blurring of boundaries' between the foreign and the domestic. We explore this issue more fully below.

From three circles to two

As a victorious world power with imperial and global interests and an economy to match, it is easy to understand why, in the immediate postwar era, the general feeling within Britain was that it could and should stand aloof from European integration. The idea of pooling Britain's defence and key industries of coal and steel with European allies so soon after narrowly surviving the Second World War and at a time of a growing Soviet threat seemed a mistake. Whilst welcoming such moves on the mainland of Western Europe, Britain itself was not prepared to engage with Europe alone, preferring also to look to the Commonwealth and the United States. As Churchill told it, Britain stood at the heart of these three overlapping circles; but in retrospect, perhaps, British policy makers were attempting the impossible – maintaining commitments within all three circles (see also Chapter 4).

The United States seemed to offer everything that a war-torn Europe could not; it had emerged victorious from the war with its political, economic and military power enhanced and, as the Soviet threat developed, appeared to be an essential ally for Britain in an increasingly dangerous European and international system. A habit of cooperation between Britain and the United States had grown up during the war that was of a different quality to that enjoyed by Britain and its other allies either during or after the war.

It was with the decline of the Empire that Britain faced its starkest choice. The independence of India saw the disappearance of the manpower provided by the British Indian Army; the Korean War showed the limits of British military strength; Australia, New Zealand and Canada began to look to the United States for leadership; economic growth and links were slow; and the entire structure, despite attempts to transform it into a Commonwealth, came under challenge from within and without.

Suez

It was the key imperial issue of Suez that so dramatically challenged the idea of three circles. US anger at the Franco-British-Israeli collusion to intervene against Egypt's nationalization of the canal led to massive US economic pressure upon Britain and France forcing them to withdraw. The relative decline in British (and French) power could not have been more clearly demonstrated but, whilst this probably helped to convince France of the imperatives of European integration, it made the British all the more determined to rebuild relations with the USA. Suez persuaded France that continued global influence would only follow if France, in association with West Germany, embraced the European concept. The British seemed to believe that preserving a special relationship with the United States required a firm rejection of such Europeanization and so refused all invitations to be positively associated with the European Economic Community (EEC) when it was established in 1958.

Suez could have indicated the end of the US special relationship as a viable basis for British foreign policy, and shortly afterwards the Commonwealth 'circle' too was under challenge. Prime Minister Harold Macmillan's 'winds of change' blew not just across Africa but across the entire former Empire from which Britain beat an orderly retreat. It had failed to provide the platform for Britain in the post-war world but left Britain with an international outlook and many global commitments. Britain remained eager to fulfil these and develop her international role, but, ironically, given the initial stern rejection of the EEC, it was to Europe that Britain now began to turn. The relative economic success of the EEC suggested that Britain had been mistaken in her rejection and it was thus the economic potential of membership of the largest trading bloc in the world that led Britain to move towards Europe in the early 1960s. However, the eventual application to join the EEC did not represent a British conversion to the French idea that a united Europe would provide a counter or balance to US and Soviet power; for Britain, the attraction of the EEC was the opportunity it provided to make Britain economically strong enough to maintain alone its status as a global power. Britain wanted to join the EEC, but it did not at that time accept that this would or should entail the Europeanization of its foreign policy.

The late convert

This late conversion to the European project aroused suspicion amongst European allies, most notably the French, with fears that Britain would prove to be an American 'Trojan Horse' and likely to challenge French leadership. Thus, it was not until 1973 that Britain was admitted and appeared, at least under Heath's leadership, to commit itself both to European economic integration and to foreign policy cooperation under the newly established EPC procedures. EPC complemented both European and British aims; Britain as a key international player was central to making the process work and provide for a larger role for Europe in the world. For Britain, this was an area in which it could naturally lead and in doing so face key Anglo-American problems such as Vietnam. Furthermore, the determinedly intergovernmental nature of the agreed EPC procedures seemed to offer the opportunity for a less painful Europeanization than that suggested by the supranational procedures of the European Community (EC) proper. Britain liked the idea of foreign policy cooperation precisely because it could be presented to a domestic audience as designed to preserve rather than challenge British sovereignty. EPC represented the acceptable face of European integration to both the British government and the British public because it seemed to offer the advantages of foreign policy cooperation without the attendant dangers of supranationality.

Heath as Prime Minister was more prepared than all his predecessors (and successors) to advocate both the supranational (EC) and intergovernmental (EPC) strands of integration and to prioritize European over American foreign policy positions where these were perceived to clash. Wilson, Callaghan and, most spectacularly, Thatcher preferred the intergovernmental over the supranational and saw continued support for the special relationship with the United States as a choice that clashed with wholehearted support for European foreign policy cooperation. It should be noted, however, that the necessity for Britain to choose between the EU and the United States was never seriously accepted in Washington (Allen 2005: 122). The United States has usually expressed a preference for a Britain influential within the EU rather than resistant to it, with most US administrations frustrated by Britain's reluctance to fully engage with Europe. Whilst the British resisted Europeanizing their foreign policy because they believed it to be a potential obstacle to the continuance of the special relationship with the Americans, the Americans for the most part seemed to regard it in a more positive light.

The special personal relationship that Mrs Thatcher cultivated with President Reagan, however, could not disguise the significant differences that existed with the USA and the large areas of agreement that were emerging with the Europeans within the EPC process. Although Mrs Thatcher engaged in Cold War diplomacy without any real reference to EPC, and dealt with the future of Hong Kong on a strictly Sino-British basis, Britain did opt for a European approach in a growing number of areas. Before Mrs Thatcher came to power, EPC had provided the framework for Britain to take the lead in a distinctly 'European' response to political change in Greece, Spain and Portugal. After 1979, as the EC struggled in the doldrums, EPC flourished partly because of pragmatic British reforms (such as the London agreement that provided for an EPC crisis reaction mechanism) and partly because the British were prepared to develop their foreign policy within a European framework. In the Middle East, the EU position, as developed in the 1980 Venice Declaration, reflected British concerns that the US-led Camp David process was too restrictive and failed to properly recognize the legitimate rights of the Palestinians. Relations with South Africa were dealt with on a European as opposed to Commonwealth basis. EPC proved helpful not only with the Falklands (where the EU's diplomatic support was instantaneous in comparison to America's initial indecision), but also when seeking to avoid uncomfortable situations with the Americans in Central America or as with the US invasion of the Commonwealth island of Grenada (Hill 1996).

The issues of the Iranian fatwa on Salmon Rushdie and the Tiananmen Square massacre were similarly dealt with through European channels. Whilst Britain in the mid-1980s accepted only very reluctantly that the single market required EU procedural reforms (the use of QMV and increased powers for the European Parliament), Mrs Thatcher's government enthusiastically both proposed and embraced attempts to improve the EPC procedures. The fact that foreign policy cooperation was developing along transgovernmental rather than intergovernmental lines did not seem to inhibit the British who remained transfixed by the dangers of supranationality (see Wallace (2005: 87–89) for an elaboration of transgovernmentalism as one of five EU policy modes).

The implications of 1989

It was the events of 1989 (and the collapse of Communism in particular) that provided the stimulus for a further key change in European foreign policy cooperation and British engagement. The developments of the previous two decades had left EPC ripe for further evolution. The procedural framework now drew many diplomats, ministers and institutions into a network of meetings, discussions and reports all together representing a highly advanced form of cooperation based on pragmatic and informal discussions which suited and was shaped by Britain. As these procedures became transgovernmental, the potential for Europeanization became much greater. However, because EPC, and subsequently the CFSP, were still perceived as intergovernmental, they did not stimulate the sort of resistance in Britain that the supranational procedures experienced.

The fall of the Berlin Wall and the reunification of Germany, and the reunification of Western and Eastern Europe, propelled foreign, security and defence policy to the heart of EU discussions. German reunification, monetary union and CFSP were all intertwined as part of a package drawn up for the 1991 intergovernmental conference (IGC). Britain in particular resisted moves, as it had done over the Single European Act, to bring the intergovernmental framework of EPC under the Community Method. British hostility to any integration of foreign and defence policy into the Community proper led to the enhancement of the Pillar model with CFSP, and JHA, outside the EU framework. Here Britain succeeded in preventing what it perceived as the further Europeanization of European foreign policy cooperation. Britain, however, found itself at odds with France over the future of the WEU which France, and to a limited extent Germany, hoped would acquire an operational capacity and in turn develop into an alternative European defence organization to Nato rather than the institutional bridge the British hoped would link the two. In response to these various tensions, Britain succeeded in ensuring that the 1992 Maastricht Treaty provided more a modification of existing foreign policy arrangements than a fundamental change, although the possibility that foreign policy cooperation might eventually extend into defence cooperation was accepted by Britain – a development that could be interpreted as the potential for indirect Europeanization.

The collapse of Yugoslavia thus came at a time of institutional change and growing expectations of what Europe might achieve in foreign policy (Hill 1993). US indifference did not provide a stimulus for collective EU action but it did point to significant differences between Britain and the United States, which suggested that Britain would be more likely to meet its Balkan interests within a European rather than transatlantic framework. Over time, it developed into a painful learning process for Britain, the United States, and the rest of the EU. While all were frustrated at the failure and incoherence of the EU, the UN, and the OSCE and, in the long run, even Nato offered no better chance of success. That said, the experiences of the former Yugoslavia did shape British attitudes towards working with France and vice versa with the result that a confidential but active Franco-British defence dialogue began in 1993. At the same time, in Brussels, the CFSP institutional machinery was expanding as the member states' foreign ministries became increasingly adept at working together (see chapter on the FCO) and more willing to do this in Brussels rather than national capitals (see Allen 1998 for a discussion of this process of *Brusselsization*).

The 1990s

Throughout the 1990s Britain's key partners in the CFSP remained Germany and France. With Germany undergoing a gradual normalization in its approach to foreign policy, Britain and France appeared to be converging in their attitudes towards the European versus Atlantic frameworks based on similar military capabilities and frustrations over the US attitude to Yugoslavia. Thus, in the negotiations for the Amsterdam Treaty (1997), Britain and France agreed on the creation of a High Representative for CFSP, a measure Britain viewed as practical and safely based within the intergovernmental structure of the Council. Such convergence, however, registered little in the domestic debate where the continuing problems within the Conservative party and the British media's hostility to Europe obscured any real progress or discussion. Indeed, even the new Blair government, which accepted so much at Amsterdam that its predecessors would not have, felt the need to publicly deny that any progress – albeit limited – had been made on the defence issue.

The election of Tony Blair in 1997 brought a government more committed to Europe and more secure in office but lacking any real experience or discussion of foreign policy (see Kampfner 2003; Seldon 2004). However, the government was from the beginning constrained by a vehemently Euro-sceptical media and a politically frustrated but ambitious Chancellor who blocked moves towards the euro and thus a more whole hearted British parti-cipation in the EU (see also Buller, Chapter 13). The new Labour government was also committed to ensure that Britain would pursue a stronger role in the world beyond Europe (as had been the Major government) and the Atlantic Alliance; indeed, the 1997 Manifesto said more about British foreign policy towards the Commonwealth than the USA. Robin Cook's announcement in the first few days of the Labour government of an 'ethical dimension' to foreign policy and the establishment of the Department for International Development signalled a determination that Britain would be seen as a force for good in the world, and one which in turn would shape European and US approaches. Blair found it personally easy to be at home on both sides of the Atlantic, with close relationships with both the then President Clinton and the then Chancellor Schroeder, underpinned by a series of Third Way discussions on both sides of the Atlantic.

In comparison to the Conservatives, the new Labour government seemed far more committed to the EU in general but initially had shown no greater specific or substantive interest in the CFSP than the Major government. Over time, a growing interest in European foreign and defence cooperation emerged. This is nicely illustrated by the change from the Labour govern-ment's first Strategic Defence Review, which almost entirely ignored the European dimension, to Blair's December 1998 commitment to the Franco-British St Malo Declaration (Howorth 2005: 185). For Britain and Blair, this was not only a commitment in compensation for lack of progress on the euro but also reflective of a desire to be seen to be 'leading' in Europe never-theless (see Dover 2005). Britain now accepted that the EU should provide the framework for a European pillar in the Atlantic Alliance combined with a French acceptance that this should complement and not replace or duplicate Nato structures. St Malo led to the development of a 'Rapid Reaction Force' within the framework of a European Security and Defence Policy (ESDP) and was intended to overcome the 'capabilities–expectations gap' identified by the Yugoslav experience (Hill 1993). The Helsinki European Council in December 1999 set targets for the Rapid Reaction Force, established an EU Military Committee as well as a Political and Security Committee and an EU Military Staff – the latest in a long line of British-inspired institutional innovations in the foreign policy area.

Despite Britain's continued commitment to operating with the Americans in the Gulf (where she participated in Operation Desert Fox in 1998) and to pursuing a wider global role, relations with the United States were strained by the experiences of Kosovo, where American reluctance to commit ground forces drove forward British and European desires for more substance in EU foreign and defence policy capabilities. Kosovo also saw Blair set out his own – and some would argue very personal – approach to foreign policy in his

Chicago speech entitled 'The Doctrine of the International Community' (see Kampfner 2003; Riddell 2003; Oliver 2004; Seldon 2004). It encapsulated the tensions inherent in Britain's approaches to Europe, America and the rest of the world. The doctrine was a foreign policy programme that encouraged and supported American military engagement in support of ambitions that were beyond Britain's reach. It expressed renewed confidence that British foreign policy could bring together Europe and America, that there was a continuing community of values across the Atlantic and that Britain could hold the two sides together (Wallace and Oliver 2005). Reconciling these ambitions was never going to be easy, even when Clinton was in the White House, with the Prime Minister often relying on his own rhetorical skills and approach to carry cabinet, Parliament, the Labour Party and British people with him.

On a range of issues, Britain and the EU continued to develop close relations. One such area was Zimbabwe where Britain's approach to sanctions required and was based on the support of the EU (Williams 2002). At the same time Britain continued to pursue its own bilateral and multilateral initiatives in other domains such as the Commonwealth and the UN. Policy towards Africa has for most of the post-war era been characterized by competition with France but in recent years attempts have been made to work with France although not necessarily towards the development of a European policy.

It might have been expected that the victory of George W. Bush in the 2000 US Presidential elections would have given a further stimulus to a greater European dimension to British foreign policy. However, the easy relationship that developed between Bush and Blair reaffirmed the belief in London – and especially with the Prime Minister – that Britain could continue to play the role of a transatlantic 'bridge' despite indications that American foreign policy under Bush junior would take a more unilateralist turn

September 11 and beyond

British, American and European foreign policy was transformed by the events of September 11. Britain undertook a role supporting the United States that was militarily, diplomatically and politically substantial. At the same time, the attacks provoked an unprecedented reaction by the EU with all the main EU institutions adopting a joint declaration on September 14 leading to movement on such things as a European arrest warrant and measures to combat terrorism (see Blair 2004). However, the EU was not formally present in the Afghanistan conflict; rather it was the member states such as Britain and Germany that contributed. And, in a sign of things to come, it was the leaders of the EU's 'Big Three' (Britain, Germany and France) that were to sit down for an informal dinner in Downing Street on November 4, organized by Britain despite London not holding the EU Presidency. Although the dinner rapidly expanded to include the Dutch, Italian and Spanish Prime Ministers as well as the High Representative for CFSP, its original conception suggested that for the British in the EU, like the Americans in Nato, not all member states were regarded as of equal importance. For Britain, and Blair, it was a pragmatic means of reaching agreement and coherent action in an enlarged EU (see Kampfner 2003; Riddell 2003). But it suggested a greater partiality for 'uploading' rather than 'downloading' in part, of course, because there seemed to be little foreign policy of any substance to download from the EU.

The approach to the war in Iraq appeared to further fuel feelings that Britain's commitment was to the United States and not Europe and that a choice had to be made contrary to Blair's initial aspirations. Yet, the logic by which Britain went to war in Iraq was significantly different to that presented by the United States, with an emphasis upon international law for both domestic and European purposes. Britain was also not as isolated within the EU as might have been suspected, but the support of Italy, Spain and the applicant states from Eastern Europe only served to deepen the divide within the EU. Britain's decision to follow the Bush administration in attacking Iraq was as much a result of the Prime Minister's own personal convictions that the action was morally correct and necessary as it was the continuation of a policy that would always see the United States privileged over Britain's European partners (see Wallace and Oliver 2005). However, this was not how it was seen by France and Germany, in particularduring the first half of 2003.

Yet, the April 2003 mini-summit in Brussels involving just France, Germany, Belgium and Luxembourg showed how hollow EU foreign, security and defence policy would be without Britain and significant efforts were made during the latter part of the year to repair relations both between the two sides within the EU and between the EU and the United States. Indeed, throughout the crisis, Britain, France and Germany continued to engage in a trilateral relationship over defence and foreign policy issues. Transatlantic trade and economic links continued to show considerable growth and appeared largely unaffected (CEC 2004a). The publication of the EU's Security Strategy Document (ESS) (European Council 2003), written in large part by Robert Cooper, a former FCO adviser to Blair, was heavily based on British and French thinking. Its positive reception in Washington delighted London, again demonstrating the British desire for Europe to support and not counter the United States. Yet, when compared with the American National Security Document, the ESS in many regards symbolized the differences of European and British approaches to security-related questions (Kissack 2004: 19). The ease with which tensions between Britain and France over Iraq were overcome symbolized the very strength and commitment of Britain to European foreign policy cooperation. At the same time as the EU published its strategy documents, the FCO and MoD published their own national strategy documents, and, although not forming a coherent British version of a national security strategy, they could be seen as symbolizing a movement away from a purely pragmatic approach to a foreign policy based more on national strategic concerns within a European context.

The European Constitutional Treaty was also being drafted during the Iraq crisis and contained significant implications for EU and British foreign policy. The proposal to create a European Foreign Minister and a European External Action Service was accepted by Britain as the logical next step in developing the position of the High Representative and the external capability of the EU, albeit one based firmly within the Council of Ministers. Nevertheless, the suspicion remained (particularly in the light of the demise of the Constitutional Treaty) that the transgovernmental procedures of the CFSP and ESDP would become increasingly problematic in an enlarged Union. Foreign and security policy is an area where Britain has little to fear from moves either towards 'enhanced cooperation', multi-speed Europe or an adversarial *directoire* of the other major states, as no serious development in this issue area is worth contemplating without British participation.

Indeed, it is within the *directoire* of Britain, France and Germany that EU policy is largely forged on issues such as Iran, North Korea, China and especially on defence policy. Britain has made it clear that she will retain (as has France) a Permanent Seat in the UN Security Council. The emergence of a EU Foreign Minister or an External Action Service poses as much of a challenge to the Commission's view of how foreign policy should be managed at the European level as it does to Britain. All of which suggests that whilst Britain under Blair has moved towards the EU on foreign policy matters the EU is also changing so as to become more agreeable to Britain in this policy area. In other words, there are both aspects of downloading and uploading.

For instance, both Britain and the EU have developed an increasing interest in state intervention in the face of failing states in what Robert Cooper refers to as the 'pre-modern world' (Cooper 2003). Britain's engagement in Sierra Leone matches similar French-led interventions in the Great Lakes region of Africa and Ivory Coast (Badie 2004). Ongoing plans to operate EU battle groups in Northern Africa not only signal the EU's progression from the situation in the early 1990s as exemplified by the Yugoslavian fiasco, but suggest a coming together with Britain's own interests in Africa and Blair's own personal approach to foreign affairs. They also reflect the growing military capability of the EU. In December 2003, the member states of the EU achieved, almost unnoticed, their 1999 aim to make ESDP operational (see Giegerich and Wallace 2004), with forces today operating in Bosnia, Macedonia and Central Africa. As Giegerich and Wallace (2004) point out, rhetorical declarations followed by unease and inadequate implementation has long been part of European integration, yet the European forces have increased their scale, distance and diversity of external operations over the period 1999–2004. As Giegerich and Wallace (2004) also note, it is remarkable that European governments have been able to collectively double the number of troops deployed abroad within the past decade, with so little national or Europe-wide debate. Britain is a major participant in these military developments, suggesting that the Europeanization of British foreign and security policy has taken place to an extent as yet unappreciated by the British electorate during the Blair years.

Like so many other British prime ministers in the post-war era, Tony Blair became increasingly preoccupied with trying to knit together close relations with the United States and Europe, committed to a multilateral international order and determined to play a more positive role in the European and international affairs whilst still trying to preserve the illusion of Britain as an independent major power. Blair's approach did not shake this approach, nor did it undermine the gradual evolution of Britain's relationship with its European partners, although both the European and American dimensions of British foreign policy continued to lack domestic support.

Evaluation: the incremental Europeanization of British foreign policy

From the above account, we can see how various aspects of British foreign policy have experienced varying degrees of Europeanization and in turn address the key questions guiding this book. When accounting for the extent of Europeanization we must appreciate that British foreign policy has been shaped in large part by a number of aims that have the potential to be both contradictory and complementary. On the one hand, Britain has sought to support the USA and ensure the future of the 'special' transatlantic relationship. On the other, Britain has actively encouraged and engaged in the construction of a European foreign policy provided that it remains based on the consensual coordination of the national foreign policies of the EU member states. Although British positions on numerous foreign policy issues show evidence of adaptation to a European norm, Britain has, on a number of occasions, refused to be bound by European positions whilst nevertheless doing its utmost to maintain European solidarity over issue areas, such as the Middle East, where it judges that British influence can be enhanced by collective European action. As a result there can be no clear or consistent sequence to the process by which Europeanization has occurred.

That said, the process has only been possible and taken forward in large part by the active engagement of Britain. Despite many bitter arguments with its European partners, the result of an active engagement in EPC/CFSP for over thirty years has been the evolution of a reflex towards sharing foreign policy concerns with its European partners in international relations. Nevertheless, the degree of loyalty or reflex varies. In key areas, such as intelligence, European cooperation is strained by the perceived benefits of working closely with the United States. Similarly, the British remain reluctant to work closely with their European partners in the area of diplomatic representation. The problem, of course, is that the nature of the CFSP and ESDP makes it quite possible for national foreign policies to show signs of both accommodating and resisting Europeanization at the same time.

We can see clear examples of what has been Europeanized – and to some extent when this happened – in the increasing numbers of staff dealing with CFSP (see Allen and Oliver, Chapter 4), the increased sharing of information through the *Correspondant Européen* (COREU) network, the regular meetings of Political Directors and their ambassadorial deputies in Brussels and the development of the Permanent Political and Security Committee (PSC). Each of these developments equates to a certain Europeanization (not to mention Brusselsization, which, for the British, obsessed with integration theology, is regarded as a form of Europeanization) in the organizing and implementation of policy. The experience of working closely with EU partners (especially in regard to the Former Yugoslavia) in recent years and the recent problems posed by the United States are all reflected in the shared international outlook to be found in the European Security Strategy. It is this shared European perception of the current state of international society that has led the British to make their European commitments, such as that to further defence cooperation or to working with France and Germany to try and find an agreeable alternative to US policy on Iran.

Despite these changes, the imagery of British involvement in CFSP has not changed, with Britain continuing to resist Europeanization through supranational means by preserving the intergovernmental framework, whilst at the same time being prepared to accept a degree of Europeanization in practice by actively promoting institutional change, such as the creation of the High Representative and through 'Brusselsization'.

Because EPC existed as a consensual process outside the constitutional framework and then the CFSP was handled within a separate pillar, European foreign policy has evolved only very slowly and without recording any dramatic or symbolic integration advances at specific times. Thus, the starting point for Europeanization in this areas has been, as Ginsberg notes, the 'process by which CFSP, and EPC before it, moved closer to EC norms, policies and habits without EPC/CFSP becoming supranationalised' (Ginsberg 2001: 37). Such advances as have been made have essentially been at the behest of the major players (in particular, Britain, France and Germany) who have been able to control the extent, sequence and pace of the uploading dimension of Europeanization. The Anglo-French St Malo declaration was an example of this, representing an uploading of British and French foreign policy concerns. One of its key aims was to further engage Germany on foreign and defence issues by using the EU framework to effectively 'crossload' foreign policy concerns.

Co-operation at the EU level has not, however, simply resulted in output that might be described as non-Europeanized because it reflected the lowest common denominator. Luddecke (2004) has shown that a number of processes have been at work, such as socialization of officials and ministers, which have led to significant changes in national positions including those held by Britain. Not only has there been a centralizing effect within the EU, but international pressures have also played a key role in bringing about Europeanization; in particular pressures from the USA, the Commonwealth, the UN and other external third parties who have increasingly – especially since the 1990s – looked first to the European Union as a collectivity rather than to a single member state, even an important one like Britain. Finally, internal battles for the control of British European and foreign policy between Downing Street and the FCO have themselves given rise to a degree of Europeanization that the FCO alone might have been able to resist (Forster and Blair 2002).

Britain, as a significant power amongst the EU member states, has been able to upload to the EU level some of its extra-EU foreign policy commitments, such as those that arise from its particular role in the UN, its close relationship with the USA, its links with the Commonwealth and its global military and diplomatic interests. At the same time Britain's diminishing capabilities at a time of increasing global demands and expectations make it susceptible to the attractions of sharing responsibility with EU partners. It is worth noting the coincidence of Europeanization and periods of crisis. While the examples of Iraq, Bosnia or 9/11 do not immediately engender images of a united European foreign policy or British commitment to it, these crises have tended to stimulate further action at the EU level that has been both initiated and supported by Britain. The drafting of the ESS document at the time of the crisis over Iraq is an example of crisis-sponsored Europeanization that was initiated by the French and Germans and then actively promoted by Britain.

In general, the extent of Europeanization of British foreign policy has been based upon a slow acceptance of changes to the institutional dimension to increases in European capabilities in the foreign and military spheres and an evolving shared outlook with regard to strategic concerns and foreign policy priorities. Domestically this has been the product of the demand to maintain a clear British role in the world but one that has been reluctant to admit to the progress made in CFSP.

Christopher Hill identified Britain's contradictory aims towards EPC as being to exercise leadership and extract benefit from it without making a serious commitment to carrying it forward (Hill 1996: 77). However, it has proved difficult for Britain to resist Europeanization in this manner, and exercising leadership and extracting benefit has only been possible to the extent that a serious commitment to the development of European foreign policy has been demonstrated. The result is that most areas of British foreign policy are now subject to some degree of European influence. Indeed, a high degree of coordination with the EU has become part of the organizational and cultural outlook of British foreign policy with many key issues being referred to the European level. For some years now, the EU has been Britain's point of departure when considering its dealings with the rest of the world rather than the neighbour that Britain encountered first when considering its external environment. This does not mean that Britain is limited to working through the European option; in many respects the EU has enhanced the opportunities and mechanisms through which Britain pursues its foreign policy aims and the CFSP is anything but a 'zero sum game' (Forster 2000). Indeed, many prime ministers have found that EPC/CFSP can be made to work to Britain's advantage (see Hill 1996). In doing so, British foreign policy concerns have not been replaced by European ones, rather they have been adapted, shaped by and influential on collective EU foreign policy concerns

Conclusion

To return to an issue we raised at the start, the evolution of the EU in recent years has increased the 'blurring' of the distinction between European and national foreign policy making it all the more difficult to assess the degree of Europeanization at any one point of time. In Britain, 'theological' resistance to and lack of public sympathy for the further advancement of European integration has made successive governments reluctant to publicly acknowledge, or even semi-privately take stock of, the degree to which British foreign policy has been Europeanized. Thus, Britain continues to pursue a foreign policy through the EU that is characterized by ambiguity, seeking on the one hand to use the EU as a foreign policy platform, but unwilling to accept any limits this might impose upon Britain's other multilateral and bilateral relations. However, with time, the constraints of participation in collective foreign policy making and activity have been more willingly accepted and adopted, a process made easier by the successful uploading of British concerns to the EU level. As Paul Williams (2002: 1) noted, 'a distinctly British and European foreign policy should not be thought of in mutually exclusive terms. Rather, although there are significant areas of overlap, European foreign policy does not exhaust British options on the international stage'. However, what may well limit British options in the future is a perception in the outside world that British foreign policy is more Europeanized than British foreign policy makers are willing to recognize or accept. It is now ten years since Dr Henry Kissinger was invited to make the keynote address at an FCO conference entitled 'Britain and the World'. He perhaps more accurately reflected the true extent of British foreign policy Europeanization when he failed, throughout his forty-minute speech, to distinguish between Britain and the European Union.

13
Monetary Policy

Jim Buller

Introduction

Governments utilize monetary policy in order to affect macro-economic variables such as economic output, employment and inflation. They do so by attempting to control the quantity of money in existence through a number of policy instruments, including interest rates and the exchange rate. Since the 1970s, monetary policy has played an increasingly important role in the macro-economic management of Britain. According to monetarists, if a climate of low and stable inflation could be achieved, it would stimulate investment, growth and employment. To operationalize this policy, the Thatcher Government published a Medium Term Financial Strategy (MTFS) (1980), which contained targets for the growth of £3M (the preferred measure of the money supply at this time), as well as interest rates and public expenditure (Lawson 1992). There was no target for the pound, which was allowed to float and find its own value on the financial markets.

Historically, the policy making process in this area has been highly centralized within Britain, with a small elite centred on the Prime Minister, the Chancellor of the Exchequer, and the Treasury taking the key decisions. Since 1997, the Bank of England has been given operational independence to implement monetary policy in accordance with an inflation target set by the Chancellor. However, it is very important not to view monetary policy simply as a series of technical measures formulated and implemented by this core group. The operation of instruments such as interest or exchange rates has always impacted directly on the prosperity of industry, as well as the electorate more generally. In addition, some aspects of monetary policy have hugely symbolic importance for many sections of the British public. Not only is the management of sterling perceived to be one of *the* defining qualities of a sovereign government, the existence of the pound (complete with the Queen's head) is also closely associated with British identity. Understood in these terms, we might therefore expect any attempt to Europeanize monetary policy to be especially controversial.

The Europeanization of British monetary policy has proved to be a highly contentious experience. While in formal policy terms, it only lasted two years, we shall see that it was in part responsible for the resignation of one prime minister and several senior cabinet ministers, and helped to bring to an end the Conservatives' long run in power (1979–97). While paying lip service to future membership of the euro, since 1992 the Treasury has gone about carefully constructing a domestic institutional framework for confronting issues and problems in this particular policy area. In other words, the focus of this chapter is not just on the Europeanization of British monetary policy, but also on why the process became so contentious over the last decade or so.

The Europeanization of British monetary policy

In Chapter 2, Bache and Jordan defined Europeanization as:

> *the reorientation or reshaping of politics in the domestic arena in ways that reflect policies, practices and preferences advanced through the EU system of governance.*

According to this definition, two things are required to demonstrate that Europeanization has taken place. First, we need to show that the EU has developed its own institutions, policies and norms in this area. Second, it needs to be established that these have been incorporated into the decision-making process at the domestic level.

What has been Europeanized?

It is certainly possible to argue that the EU has developed its own monetary policies, practices and preferences and has advanced these through European-level initiatives and decisions. 'The Snake' – an agreement for the joint determination and collective defence of fixed exchange rates – represented the first concrete move in this direction. It was set up in 1972 in response to a feeling that common EU policies were increasingly being undermined by disruptions on the foreign exchange markets. It only allowed currencies to fluctuate 2.25 per cent either side of a central parity. Unfortunately, the combined effect of continuing volatility in the value of the dollar, deepening world recession and the quadrupling of oil prices in 1973–74 led to the gradual fragmentation of this system. Britain left it less than two months after joining (de Guistino 1996: 214–16; Blair 2002: 53).

At the end of the 1970s, EU member states decided to revive this attempt at creating a European-wide exchange rate policy as a way of insulating their economies from the destabilizing impact of the dollar. The main policy instrument used to achieve this objective was the European Monetary System (EMS), of which the Exchange Rate Mechanism (ERM) was the most important component. Like 'the Snake', the ERM contained a *parity grid* representing a set of cross exchange rates among all participating currencies. As before, each currency was allowed to fluctuate 2.25 per cent either side of its parity (although Italy and Spain enjoyed 6 per cent fluctuation margins). When the limit of the margin between any two currencies was reached, both central banks were obliged to intervene in the foreign exchange markets to maintain this central value. In certain circumstances, participants were allowed to devalue or re-value their parities. Indeed, this practice was quite common in the first half of the 1980s (Grahl 1997: 63–70).

In 1987, member states adjusted the rules and procedures of the ERM through the negotiation of the Basle-Nybourg Agreement. The short-run defence of parities was strengthened in two ways. First, central bankers agreed to make use of so-called intra-marginal intervention rather than purchasing the currency of a country when it had reached the edge or margins of its fluctuation bands. Second, in the event that a country's currency did come under pressure, it was now expected that national governments would also attempt to undertake supporting domestic policy measures to correct the situation (Grahl 1997; Mayes 2001). These changes in part reflected the fact that government defences against financial speculators had become much weaker with the gradual abolition of exchange controls throughout the 1980s. As it was, these reforms failed to provide adequate defence against the forces of global finance capital. In July 1993, the ERM collapsed temporarily after a massive run on the French franc forced France out of the system. Later in the year, it was reconstituted with new 15 per cent fluctuation bands.

When did Europeanization occur?

In formal policy terms, the British government took a decade to incorporate these European institutions and practices into its domestic decision-making process. As already noted, when the Conservatives came to power in 1979, they developed an alternative policy of 'domestic monetarism' to control inflation. However, in October 1990, Britain finally joined the ERM at a rate of DM2.95 (with 6 per cent fluctuation margins). Moreover, although this Europeanization of monetary policy only lasted two years, it was implemented with a dedication that horrified even those that supported it. On the eve of 'Black Wednesday' (16 September 1992), Norman Lamont (the then Chancellor of the Exchequer) raised interest rates to 15 per cent, despite the fact that the British economy was experiencing an economic recession. At the same time, the Bank of England spent approximately £3 billion of taxpayer's money trying to defend sterling's central parity. When this policy collapsed, ERM membership came to be held responsible for a balance of payments deficit that topped £1 billion, an unemployment rate standing at 2.8 million, and increasing levels of negative equity in the domestic housing market (for a good discussion, see Stephens 1996).

While the Thatcher Government took a decade to incorporate the rules and norms of the ERM into the monetary policy process in Britain, the *idea* of Europeanization found its way much earlier into the *discourse* in this area. By 1985, Nigel Lawson (the then Chancellor) was publicly advocating the benefits of ERM membership in Cabinet. It was asserted that the ERM had a better record of achieving stability in nominal exchange rates, while Geoffrey Howe (a former Chancellor and Foreign Secretary) and other Conservative leaders made a connection between this reduction in exchange rate volatility, and larger trade volumes, higher investment, output and employment. At the same time, low and stable inflation would be assured by Germany's dominance within the system. The German economy's post-war record on inflation was second to none in Europe and it was felt that the independence of the Bundesbank would guarantee that it remained the case (Heseltine 1991: 69–73; Lawson 1992: 494–95). Finally, if sterling continued to experience fluctuation problems, the advocates of Europeanization said that arrangements were in place that required central banks to support one another's currencies (see above).

One of the reasons it took time for this discourse to be reflected in the decision-making process was because these arguments were resisted at the elite level throughout the 1980s. Most notably, Margaret Thatcher employed the arguments of her economic adviser, Alan Walters, in her sharp disagreements with Lawson, Howe and their supporters. According to the 'Walters critique', using the exchange rate to control inflation presented a dilemma. It meant de-coupling interest rate policy from domestic conditions, as this instrument would now be required to regulate the price of sterling. In practice, this arrangement did not matter as long as the pound joined the ERM at a rate consistent with stable non-inflationary growth. The problem was that economists differed in their conception of what the 'right' rate was. The problem was that the 'Fundamental' or 'Natural Real Exchange Rate' for sterling at any moment in time could rapidly change as Britain's economic circumstances altered. In short, the possibilities of an exchange rate misalignment were very real. There was also no guarantee that ERM membership would augment the counter-inflationary credibility of British monetary policy (Walters 1990: 35–37; Thatcher 1993: 688–89). As the 1980s wore on, these concerns were magnified as it became clearer that the ERM was being incorporated into a fledgling proposal for Economic and Monetary Union (EMU) (see below).

This resistance to ERM membership at a discursive level meant that the Europeanization of monetary policy was delayed for another five years. Lawson kept up the pressure by pursuing a surrogate policy. From 1986 to 1988, he instituted a strategy of trying to control inflation by shadowing the Deutschmark DM within an unpublished band of DM2.90–3.00, until Thatcher roundly put a stop to it. On the eve of the Madrid European Council (1989), Lawson and Howe both threatened to resign unless the government made a more positive effort to join the ERM. Thatcher begrudgingly agreed in principle, providing certain conditions were met, including: the abolition of all exchange controls; the convergence of British inflation with other EU member states; and the creation of a free market in financial services (Thompson 1996: 141). In the end, Lawson resigned anyway in 1989 when further progress was blocked. Howe followed in 1990, citing Thatcher's euro-scepticism as the main reason for his departure. When Major (who replaced Lawson as Chancellor) and Hurd (who replaced Howe as Foreign Secretary) continued to lobby for the Europeanization of monetary policy, a weakened Thatcher consented, knowing full well that she could not afford to lose another Chancellor and Foreign Secretary in such a short space of time. Many of the conditions she had stipulated at Madrid were now conveniently ignored.

Why did Europeanization occur?

In one sense, it is not clear why the Europeanization of British monetary policy (as well as the discourse surrounding this area) took place. Monetarism appeared to reduce inflation from 21.9 per cent in 1980 to under 4 per cent in 1983, a level at which it stayed before rising again into double figures at the end of the 1980s. However, on closer inspection, this achievement had little to do with monetarism as it was practised. Targets for the growth of £3M were consistently overshot and ministers complained that no reliable relationship could be found between any measure of the money supply and the movement of prices in the economy (Lawson 1992: 413–22, 447–55; Pepper 1998: 37–44). Instead, this outcome probably had more to do with the fact that Britain experienced a severe recession in the early 1980s, which helped to squeeze inflation out of the domestic economy. One of the contributing factors to this recession (and indirectly, the record on inflation) was the high value of the pound, which had been artificially inflated by rising North Sea Oil revenues (Alt 1987; but see also Walters 1986).

In this context, the Europeanization of British monetary policy did not take place as a direct result of a misfit between EU and domestic institutions or policies. Instead, Conservative leaders and the Treasury in particular came to perceive ERM membership as a way of injecting some credibility into their domestic monetary framework. Howe and Lawson had already begun to focus more on the exchange rate as an instrument for helping to achieve non-inflationary growth, despite remaining publicly committed to the MTFS and the monetary targets within it. Although growth of £3M was exceeding its monetary targets, the Treasury cut interest rates from 16 to 12 per cent in the period from 1980 to 1981 in an attempt to bring down the value of the pound which, as we have seen, was hampering the performance of British exporters (House of Commons 1983: 399). However, the growth of the euro-dollar market, and its emergence (in the absence of the US-dominated Bretton Woods system) as the main institution regulating the flow of global credit, meant that this policy instrument became increasingly vulnerable to shifts in 'opinion' or 'sentiment' on the currency exchanges that bore little relation to actual developments in the economy (Bonefeld *et al.* 1995). The sensitive nature of the relationship between global capital and national policy could be observed directly by the mid-1980s. In June 1984, the value of the pound was dragged upwards in the wake of a rising dollar, boosted by figures showing a significant rise in economic growth. By July 1985, sterling was falling to the equivalent of $1.10 and threatened to slip below $1 after Bernard Ingham, Thatcher's press secretary, foolishly let it be known that the Prime Minister would accept parity if that was what the markets decreed (see also, Heseltine 1991: 72; Lawson 1992: 467–71). Faced with these implementation problems, the ERM appeared to offer 'sanctuary' from turbulent global financial forces.

How did Europeanization occur?

It should be clear from the above discussion that the Europeanization of British monetary policy was, in formal terms, a voluntary process involving conscious choices made by key individuals at the domestic level to download EU institutions, procedures and practices. Indeed, if we take into account the institutional origins of the EMS, this conclusion is not altogether that surprising. The EMS was created through an extra-legal resolution of the European Council rather than an amendment to the Treaty of Rome. In this sense, it was highly unusual as an EU policy. Only member states could participate, and none were formally obliged to do so (Dinan 2004).

In reality, the mechanisms of Europeanization involve a combination of both voluntary and coercive elements. In fact, this chapter goes further in suggesting that what counts for voluntarism and coercion can in itself become a matter of interpretation and discursive construction at the domestic level. According to Europhiles, the Conservative government had little choice but to submit to the Europeanization of monetary policy after monetarism became discredited. Euro-sceptics, on the other hand, resented the argument that 'there was no alternative' to membership of the ERM. They warned that the institutions of this system could unnecessarily constrain the hands of ministers, while proclaiming that the preservation of some freedom of manoeuvre was always preferable in the economic matters (see Ridley 1992: 188–9, 193; Thatcher 1993: 700, 707). Therefore, not only are the notions of voluntary and coercive Europeanization best understood as ideal types (as suggested in Chapter 2), but the *reality* of these categories can in themselves become the subject of dispute between different actors in the decision-making process.

So far, it has been argued that membership of the ERM can be conceptualized as the Europeanization of British monetary policy according to the definition offered in Chapter 2. While EU institutions, procedures and practices only reshaped the conduct of monetary policy for approximately two years, the EU's involvement had a more sustained impact on the discourse in this policy area. It has also been asserted that, in formal terms, the Europeanization of monetary policy represented a voluntary process in response to the perceived need by Lawson, his advisers and other members of the Cabinet to inject some credibility into domestic decision-making after the failure of monetarism in the first half of the 1980s. Yet, while adaptational pressure from the European level (as a result of a top-down misfit) appears to have played little or no role, Europeanization was the product of considerable domestic pressure from within the government and the Conservative Party more generally. In other words, formally, membership of the ERM may have reflected a conscious choice. But in reality it was the product of a complex *melange* of voluntary and coercive factors that can only be accurately understood through the perspectives of those actors taking part in the decisions.

What factors explain the domestic reaction to Europeanization?

Even though the Europeanization of British monetary policy only occurred briefly at the start of the 1990s, this experiment generated a significant amount of domestic controversy. For some commentators, much of the Euro-scepticism that hampered Major's leadership throughout the early- to mid-1990s can be traced back to this event. Other academics suggest that it was chiefly responsible for Major losing the support of influential Tory newspapers during this time (Seldon 1997: 288–89, 707–13) More generally, 'Black Wednesday' (as it is now known) became increasingly identified as the most important factor in the 1997 election defeat of the Conservatives.

Why did the Europeanization of monetary policy become such a controversial topic in British politics? It is tempting to assert that the answer to this question is self-evident given its symbolic importance. Bearing in mind, some of the perverse effects that ERM membership conferred on the conduct of British monetary policy (noted above), it would be surprising if dissent and anger did not arise at the domestic level. Yet, in at least one important sense, the Europeanization of British monetary policy proved to be a success. When Britain joined the ERM in October 1990, inflation stood a 10.9 per cent. On the eve of Britain's exit (16 September 1992) it had dropped to 3.6 per cent. Moreover, while it is true that the UK was left with various problems (see above), these cannot be blamed solely on the ERM. Of more significance was the fact that an increasing constituency of Euro-sceptics *perceived* that the ERM was to blame and resented the loss of British sovereignty that it seemed to represent. Moreover, it coloured many observers' perceptions of the EU's drive for a single currency.

In order to better understand this argument, it is necessary first to provide a brief discussion of the resurgence of European integration in the late 1980s and early 1990s. By 1987, international financial forces had impacted on the ERM in a way that led to complaints about German dominance of the system. Having been a source of instability because of its persistent strength in the first half of the 1980s, the managed devaluation of the dollar as a result of the Plaza Agreement (1986) presented a new set of problems for EU countries. The dollar's descent led to an appreciation of the Deutschmark, which had the effect of dragging the French franc and other currencies within the system upwards in its wake. Rather than accept this unwelcome tightening of monetary policy, the French Government eventually let the franc fall through the floor of its ERM band (Thompson 1996: 73–74; Grahl 1997: 71–72). A postmortem undertaken in Paris concluded that only the construction of supranational institutions would effectively dilute the power of the Bundesbank over economic policy.

Developments at the geopolitical level served to broaden and entrench this view. The collapse of the Soviet Union provoked widespread concern that an imbalance of power existed within central Europe. The re-unification of Germany in 1990 re-awakened fears that the EU's biggest economic power would begin to take advantage of this security vacuum to develop its political and economic power. In response, members of the EU decided to negotiate a three-stage plan for EMU as a way of addressing this 'German Question' (Dyson 1994; Baun 1995/96: 610–12). EMU became one of the central policy planks of the Maastricht Treaty, which also included aspirations to create a Common Foreign and Defence Policy, as well as measures to forge a common citizenship. ERM membership thus became an integral part of the single currency process, as set out in Stage One of a three-stage timetable. Because of the explicit link between ERM and EMU, existing member states were now less tolerant of changes to parities in case they undermined the single currency project as a whole. In short, the ERM was now a much less flexible system than it had been in the first half of the 1980s.

What compounded this problem from a British perspective was that the economies of the UK and Germany (the Deutschmark was the anchor currency of the ERM) had also begun to diverge significantly. As already noted, Britain was experiencing a recession at this time and the Treasury desired low interest rates to help stimulate production and consumption. Conversely, the German economy was beginning to overheat, partly as a consequence of reunification after 1990. In July 1992, the Bundesbank raised its discount rate from 8 to 8.75 per cent, causing sterling to slip to the bottom of the ERM.

In September 1992, the British public was confronted by the sight of a Conservative government that had boxed itself into an unsustainable course of action. It watched incredulously as the Cabinet stuck religiously to its European commitments, while apparently presiding over a policy that seemed to worsen the domestic economic plight of millions. At the same time, the Major leadership was pushing through the ratification of the Maastricht Treaty, which contained provisions for EMU and eventually

a single currency. Warning of the dangers of this continued Europeanization of monetary policy, Conservative Euro-sceptics in Westminster began
to make apocalyptic statements about the future of representative government in Britain. Chris Gill, speaking in a House of Commons debate on the
Maastricht Treaty, probably, best summed up their message:

> stripped of power to influence or decide matters of state, we shall have
> created the classic recipe for failure: responsibility resting with a body of
> people who do not have the authority to discharge that responsibility in
> full measure. This will result in public disillusionment with politicians
> and with people's capacity to obtain satisfaction through their elected
> representatives. In the fullness of time that disillusionment will turn to
> frustration and anger, which will lead ultimately to the rejection of estab-
> lished political leadership, traditional party loyalties and the whole body
> politic. (*Hansard* (Commons), vol. 201, 18 December 1991, col. 415)

Writing on the challenge of EMU, John Redwood prophesied that Britain's
membership of this policy would lead to precisely the same consequences
as 'Black Wednesday':

> the electorates will want to make their views known. In this system
> (Economic and Monetary Union) there will be no way of letting the
> pressure out. The valve in the pressure cooker will have been soldered
> over, and as the temperature rises, as people become more disenchanted
> with the economic and monetary policy being pursued, the pressure will
> build up. (Redwood 1997: 187)

In short, 'Black Wednesday' became a hugely controversial episode in the
history of British monetary policy. Not only were the economic costs of exit
dramatic, but the event also seemed to symbolize the growing emasculation
of British sovereignty, an issue that was already a source of growing debate
in British party politics.

What have been the effects of Europeanization?

This chapter concludes by arguing that the effects of this controversy over
Europeanization have led to retrenchment in the area of monetary policy .
That is to say, since 1992, decision-makers have consciously attempted to
develop new national policies that diverge in certain ways from EU requirements. It is important to note a qualification to this argument before it is
outlined in more detail below. A discourse still exists at the elite level that
advocates the merits of Europeanization in the area of monetary policy.
However, this case now focuses on the benefits of single currency membership for the British economy and it contains the following themes: if the

Blair Government joins the euro it will eliminate transaction costs for British firms, leading to increased trade with the EU; it will also eradicate currency fluctuations and encourage more investment among British companies looking to take advantage of a stable and more predictable financial climate; EMU will result in greater price transparency and more competition, and these changes will help to increase productivity and reduce inflation; and so if Britain wants to enjoy the full benefits of the single market, it needs a single currency (for examples of this argument, see Radice 1996, 2003; Haseler and Reland 2000; Beetham 2001; Layard *et al.* 2002).

For the Europhiles, the problem with the ERM was that it was a semi-fixed exchange rate system *after* its time. These currency regimes (for example Bretton Woods) worked reasonably well in the 1960s because capital controls were still in existence. However, as we have noted, the increasingly expanding and more liquid capital markets that emerged in the 1970s and 1980s made the defence of exchange rate parities increasingly difficult. In a new world of globalized financial markets, only two choices remain: either a fully floating regime or a full currency regime.

Despite these arguments, no British government after Black Wednesday has attempted to develop a narrative putting forward the positive case for euro membership. Indeed, 'Britain in Europe', the organization set up by New Labour to lead such a drive, was reduced to making the more general case for Britain's continuing membership of the EU, rather than the single currency itself. Similarly, the Confederation of British Industry announced that it would cease promoting membership of the euro until a more positive lead was given by Labour politicians (*The Financial Times* 30 May 2001). Yet, when we remember that opinion polls have consistently shown two-thirds of the public to be opposed to EMU, the absence of a more proactive policy is perhaps understandable (Banducci *et al.* 2003).

Under Labour, the euro-enthusiasts have not been helped by the attitude of the Treasury. As Gordon Brown has constantly asserted, the five economic tests are the ultimate guide to if and when Britain should join the euro. To mount a campaign before these tests have been passed would be to undermine the government's central claim that entry into the single currency will only take place when it is 'clearly and unambiguously' in the UK's economic interests to do so. In short, Treasury control has suffocated all attempts to create a discourse proposing a return to Europeanization strategies in the area of monetary policy.

In the period after Black Wednesday, the process of retrenchment proceeded as follows. From 1992, the Treasury set about constructing an alternative counter-inflationary framework that was domestically based. The origins of this framework can be found in certain reforms brought in during the Major government. After the collapse of the ERM, Lamont implemented a new policy to control inflation that moved away from a concentration on one specific target or rule. Instead, a whole series of policy instruments were set up to monitor and control price rises in the economy, including: an inflation target of 1–4 per cent, a new attachment to the importance of charting house and asset prices, and a confirmation of the importance of the exchange rate (although no formal target for the level of sterling was set) (Lamont 1999). At the same time, the Bank of England's role in the conduct of monetary policy was made public as a result of changes made by Kenneth Clarke, Lamont's successor. Of particular importance was the decision to publish the minutes of the monthly meetings between the Chancellor and the Governor of the Bank of England. For the first time, the electorate had an opportunity to compare and contrast the views of these two prominent policy makers, and to trace these opinions through to the execution of observable outcomes. Of course, Clarke remained formally in charge of both the formulation and the implementation of policy. But the effect of this development was to heighten the profile of the governor of the Bank of England and give the strong impression that the governor was an equal partner in the making of monetary policy decisions.

These arrangements were formalized soon after the new Labour Government took office, when Gordon Brown granted operational independence to the Bank of England. While the Chancellor remained chiefly responsible for formulating the objectives of monetary policy (in this case an inflation target of 2 per cent, measured by the harmonized Consumer Prices Index), a new Monetary Policy Committee (MPC) consisting of independent experts was charged with implementing them. The Bank would be held accountable via a number of mechanisms. For example, the governor of the Bank would be required to write a letter of explanation to the Chancellor in the event that the inflation target was missed. The minutes as well as the individual voting records of the MPC would be published shortly after each meeting, and the record of the Bank would be scrutinized by Parliament. In certain exceptional circumstances, the Chancellor retained the right to give directions to the MPC if it is deemed in the public interest to do so (Balls and O'Donnell 2002). As a result, some freedom of manoeuvre was maintained in the hope that the Treasury would not again find itself locked into an unsustainable course of action.

On the fiscal side, the search for counter-inflationary credibility was buttressed by the development of two rules designed to remove suspicion of political interference in this area. The 'Golden Rule' stated that on average, over the economic cycle, the government would only borrow to invest and not to fund current spending. The 'Sustainable Debt' rule stipulated that debt would be held over the economic cycle at a 'stable and prudent' level. The stipulation 'over the economic cycle' is crucial here. This condition was designed to give the Chancellor a certain amount of flexibility to vary fiscal measures in a way commensurate with economic circumstances. These reforms were not free from criticism. Some commentators suggested that the fiscal rules represented little in the way of a genuine constraint on political interference in this area because real differences existed within the academic and policy community concerning how to measure the beginning and end of an economic cycle (Portillo 2000; Howard 2002; Daneshkhu 2004). They certainly allowed the Treasury to accommodate large rises in public spending after 1999; so much so, that the Blair government claimed to have reversed decades of underinvestment in Britain's public services.

Why, then, has been Labour so disinclined to join the euro? And why did the Europeanization of British monetary policy not continue after Black Wednesday in 1992? After all, in many respects, the institutions of the euro-zone would appear to be very well suited to the purpose of entrenching anti-inflationary growth at the domestic level. In particular, the responsibility for the pursuit of low and stable inflation was devolved to an independent central bank, which had its independence enshrined in EU law. Article 107 of the Maastricht Treaty explicitly forbade the European Central Bank (ECB) from taking instructions from any other organization or body. At the same time, the rules of the EU's Growth and Stability Pact were designed to prevent national politicians from manipulating fiscal policy in a way that might affect the maintenance of price stability in the eurozone. In particular, it required that a government's budget deficit should be close to balance or surplus and certainly not exceed 3 per cent of GDP (although, as we shall see, was subsequently been revised). At the same time, a country's ratio of government debt to GDP was not to exceed 60 per cent (Radice 2003).

Treasury publications on EMU after 1997 revealed that it considered that there were subtle, but important, differences between these two frameworks, and that they were sufficient to represent a barrier to membership of the euro. One perceived difference centered on the independence of the ECB. Not only was the Bank responsible for the implementation of monetary policy, it also had a policy formulation role. Article 105 of the Maastricht Treaty stated that the prime objective of the ECB was the maintenance of price stability: no numerical target for the level of inflation was specified. Initially, the Bank committed itself to an asymmetrical figure of 2 per cent or less, although this was subsequently revised to 'close to, but below 2 per cent' (*The Financial Times* 9 May 2003). One problem with such a goal was that, unlike the Treasury's symmetrical target, it ran the risk of producing policy with a deflationary bias. As long as the ECB retained this independ-ence, it was likely to be judged not only on its ability to hit this target but also on the underlying suitability of this reference value. In the first paper to be published by the Blair Government on the case for single currency membership, David Currie (1997: 21) highlighted the problem:

> In time, though not quickly, continued high unemployment could weaken the position of the ECB and lead to pressure for change. The future of EMU and of the EU will depend on how European leaders respond to this challenge. A failure to respond could generate national pressures,

and lead to a slow unraveling of EMU and possibly eventually the EU itself. The wrong response, such as trying to pressure the ECB to adopt a looser monetary policy, with the consequences of higher inflation, could be equally destructive for the future of the EU. Yet the unaccountable nature of the ECB leaves it a target for such pressures. Indeed, evidence of such discontent is now widespread in the eurozone, with many EU countries, such as France, Germany and Italy publicly exhorting the ECB to cut eurozone interest rates in response to sluggish economic growth. (HM Treasury 2003: 44)

Of course, the existence of such criticism would not matter as long as the ECB could be held account for its actions. But here lies the second perceived disparity between eurozone arrangements and New Labour's domestic monetary institutions: the ECB's legally enshrined independence. According to Article 107 of the Maastricht Treaty, the ECB is forbidden to take instructions from any other organization or body, including EU Finance Ministers. Changing this mandate would be difficult and might involve the negotiation of a treaty amendment at an Intergovernmental Conference. If 'Black Wednesday' conferred one lesson on the Treasury, it was to ensure that decision-makers retained some freedom of manoeuvre to react to policy mistakes and unanticipated events. Unless national politicians obtained a stake in eurozone institutions (and enjoyed some autonomy within them), the feeling was that any further Europeanization of domestic monetary policy would provoke too much controversy in British politics. For Edward Balls (1992: 17), the Chancellor's economic adviser (1994–2004), one of the key differences between New Labour's reforms and the monetary framework of the eurozone was that the Bank of England remains directly answerable to Parliament.

'Independence' does not mean independent of the political process. It does not mean transferring the power to set interest rates from an elected official to an unrepresentative and unaccountable group of bankers who need pay no attention to the wider economic consequences of their actions (see also Keegan 2003: 159).

Finally, it should be noted that the legitimacy of the EU's framework has actually been challenged by some member states. What is interesting is that much of the pressure can be found in the area of fiscal policy: the one part of the euro zone framework where national governments still retain a role. For example, in June 2002 (six months after the introduction of euro notes and coins), national governments reneged on a commitment to run balanced budgets by 2004. Moreover, in October 2003, France and Germany admitted that they would break the 3 per cent deficit rule for the third successive year in 2004. Then, in November 2003, member states suspended the sanctions mechanism of the Growth and Stability Pact, which had been designed to enforce fiscal discipline on all participants. The Commission has subsequently accepted the need to take into account factors like debt levels and the economic cycle before making judgements about the budgetary position of a country.

At the time of this writing, recent drafts of a revamped pact also suggest that some member states have been pushing for a list of other items to be excluded from budgetary calculations. These include: higher research spending, higher investment spending, pensions and health reform and defence expenditure (*The Financial Times* 8 March 2005; 9 March 2005). Ironically, these putative reforms appear to suggest a 'loosening' of the pact in a way that conforms to British theory and practice. This raises the intriguing prospect of an 'Anglicization' of European monetary policy in the none-too-distant future.

Conclusion

Although this chapter has argued that the formal Europeanization of British monetary policy only took place for a short period of time, broader theoretical conclusions have emerged from this story. Most significant, perhaps, is that our understanding of the *reality* of Europeanization cannot be separated from the *discourses* that surround it. It has been argued that membership of the ERM was in large part a voluntary process, driven by a particular group of actors with a particular narrative promoting the benefits of Europeanization in this context. Similarly, part of the reason why this process was resisted in the early 1990s was that the experience of ERM membership gave succour to a counter (Euro-sceptical) narrative that warned of the dangers that European integration posed for British systems of governance. We might also add that several key themes of this Euro-sceptical discourse appear to have influenced the Treasury, which has become one of the major obstacles to further Europeanization in this area.

Underpinning this conclusion is a constructivist approach to the understanding of political phenomena. As Risse (2004) has noted, constructivism is not in itself a theory of European integration or Europeanization. Instead, it represents a more general ontological stance which asserts that social reality is not a given, but can be shaped by human agency (individuals and groups) with their own ideas, beliefs and normative commitments. This is not to suggest that agents exist independently from the structures that surround them (or vice versa). Indeed, the day-to-day experience of working through material institutions may, in turn, feedback into (and change) the attitudes and values of those actors. That said, through a process of communicative action, individuals and groups have the potential to reproduce and change the environment within which they live. Agents and structures are mutually constituted in a dialectical relationship that unfolds across time and space.

The conclusions reached in this chapter also problematize the dominant way that we think about Europeanization. As Chapter 2 discussed, this process is often presented as the product of institutional/policy misfit and adaptational pressure from the European level. At times, the literature implies that these properties can be *objectively* defined. As long as the interested researcher charts the degree of material incongruence between European and domestic institutions and policies in a given policy area, he or she can investigate the potential for Europeanization. To be fair, as Chapter 2 has also noted, this adaptational pressure will be 'mediated' by domestic political factors. This chapter has gone further in suggesting that notions of fit/misfit and adaptational pressure *can actually be constructed and disputed* at the domestic level. This argument will not be applicable to all instances of Europeanization. In areas where EU institutions enjoy substantial competence (for example the environment or the single market), real top-down pressure will exist to bring domestic structures and practices into line. But constructivism does remind us that in many cases, Europeanization cannot be accurately understood without reference to agents and their differing narratives about European integration.

14
Competition Policy

Michelle Cini

Introduction

In market economies, competition policies are important as they create regulatory frameworks allowing governments to maintain or promote competition (and sometimes other objectives too). Competition policies tend to be based on the assumption that competition is a 'good thing' – an efficient way to ensure that high quality goods and services reach consumers in sufficient quantity and at reasonable cost. All EU member states have competition policies, and most have policies that resemble those of the EU. This is no coincidence. The EU policy, which was set out in the 1950s, pre-dated almost all other European competition policies (with the exception of those of Britain and West Germany). The EU model (or system) of competition policy is highly supranational, involving substantial decision-making powers for the European Commission and an important judicial role for the European Court. It is founded on the principle of 'prohibition', which means that there is an in-built presumption that certain types of agreement or conduct by firms are *de facto* anti-competitive. Prohibition is not, however, the only distinguishing characteristic of the EU model of competition policy. The EU model is also noted for: its impressive powers of investigation; its far-reaching rights for third parties (that is, those affected by anti-competitive conduct) to seek damages; its tough enforcement and, particularly, its fining policy; and the procedural form in which investigations occur, supported by what is now a substantial body of competition case law.

In all these respects, until very recently at least, British competition policy differed substantially from that of the EU. Britain's policy evolved incrementally over the post-1945 period. Despite these revisions, Britain's post-1945 model (or system) can still be characterized as one based on a pragmatic, case-by-case approach to decision-making. It relied on an administrative style of investigation, which privileged the 'public interest' over 'competition' as the prime criterion for decision-making. Moreover, and also in contrast to the European model, it was characterized by weak enforcement mechanisms. The involvement of ministers in decision-making served only to emphasize still further the discretionary, flexible and, indeed, often politicized nature of British competition decisions.

It was only in 1998 that a comprehensive revision of the post-1945 competition policy model was undertaken. The conventional wisdom is that these recent reforms were in large part triggered by EU pressures (see Kon and Turnbull 2003: 70). This seems to make sense when we look at the content of the 1998 Competition Act. But to what extent have these reforms really been driven by some (perhaps perceived) need to adapt to European norms and rules? The fact that it took 25 years, from accession to the EU, for a British government to introduce a reform of this kind suggests, at the very least, that other factors may have been important, in explaining the *timing* of the reform.

This chapter identifies the factors that were important in shaping both the timing and the nature of Britain's reforms in the mid- to late-1990s. Taking as its starting point the existing legal, economic and political literature on Britain's competition policy reform, it begins by introducing Britain's competition policy and, more specifically, the background to the Competition Act of 1998, and some subsequent developments. The second section then looks first at the factors that have been important in determining the timing of these reforms and then the factors that have shaped their content. Finally, a brief conclusion suggests that British reforms were driven by two government agendas. The first was indeed that of compatibility with the EU model; the second was the creation of an effective, modernized policy, inspired as much by the United States as the EU. Related to this, the conclusion reflects upon the extent to which the British model of competition policy has been Europeanized, as defined in Chapter 2, and what factors contributed to this process.

The British competition model prior to 1998

Britain was the first West European country to introduce competition legislation at the end of the Second World War. For much of the post-1945 period the policy provided a good example of 'British exceptionalism' (Wilks 1996: 140, 1999: 7). The 1948 Monopolies and Restrictive Practices Control and Enquiry Act was the first piece of legislation to enshrine the 'public interest' principle and to establish that investigations into competition cases would be undertaken administratively on a case-by-case basis in line with British cultural preferences for non-adversarial regulation (see Wilks 1996: 143). Yet, it was the legislation of the 1950s and 1960s that really established the framework for competition policy in this period, creating (through the Restrictive Trade Practices Act (1956) and the Monopolies and Mergers Act (1965)) a more formal, judicial-based policy that became inextricably linked to the post-war settlement.

The longevity of this legislation did not mean, however, that the policy was left unchanged over the decades that followed. As governmental (and indeed, business) approaches to industrial policy altered, so too did the application and focus of the competition rules. Yet, discretion remained at the heart of the British system of control in the form of a political dimension, which endowed the 'Secretary of State for Trade and Industry with an important role at the policy's political apex' (Eyre and Lodge 2000: 66). The 1973 Fair Trading Act strengthened this administrative framework, setting up an independent agency, with its own substantial discretion embodied in the person of the Director General of Fair Trading (DGFT). This shifted the balance back towards a more informal approach, though restrictive trade practices remained largely judicial in character. By contrast, the 1980 Competition Act did little more than streamline existing provisions to allow for the investigation of anti-competitive practices by individual firms (that is, monopolies).

In all, then, 'Britain's policy on competition has been shaped by a pragmatic evolutionary approach, which relies on an administrative investigative style'; over time, the policy became 'sporadic, haphazard, sometimes contradictory, and increasingly complex' (Wilks 1996: 139), with the 'public interest' criterion opening the door to a discretionary form of decision-making, privileging economic over legal considerations (Eyre and Lodge 2000: 66). It was not until the 1998 Competition Act that fundamental domestic reform was introduced.

Although Britain joined the EU in 1973, Britain's competition policy was not altered in line with European norms, despite the fact that 'British policy . . . [was] "divergent"' (Wilks 1996: 179). Although serious competition reform was not introduced until the late 1990s, it had been mooted well before then (Suzuki 2000: 3). Indeed, the Department of Trade and Industry (DTI), under a Conservative government, set up a team to review restrictive practices and mergers policy in June 1986, as a response to growing criticism of domestic policy, initiating a decade of discussions on this issue. In 1989, the DTI produced a White Paper (DTI 1989) which proposed a fundamental reform 'largely modelled on the European system' (Suzuki 2000: 3–4). However:

> Although the government would normally form White Paper recommendations into a new bill and present it to the Parliament, it failed to do so on this issue "for reasons which have never been fully explained, though many have speculated" [Robertson 1996: 211]. . . . Generally speaking, competition policy officials and consumer groups supported the introduction of EU-based monopolies control in which market dominance was prohibited in principle, whilst big business opposed to [sic] that idea. A clear consensus was not found among academics, presumably because the European model based on Article 86 [now Article 82] of the Treaty of Rome was not viewed as successful . . . .(Suzuki 2000: 4)

In another (1992) Green Paper entitled 'Abuse of Market Power', new options for reform were proposed (Suzuki 2000: 4). These were: (i) to strengthen the existing legislation; (ii) to replace the British system with the European system; and (iii) to introduce the European system, while keeping the monopoly provisions of the 1973 Act. Eyre and Lodge (2000: 68) pointed out that an earlier draft had only suggested adopting the prohibition approach, but that this was deemed 'too European' by John Redwood MP, then a Junior Minister at the DTI, even though he supported the idea of a strong competition policy. It was also opposed by the Confederation of British Industry (CBI) at the time.

Ultimately, the first option – that of strengthening the existing law – was agreed: an outcome which led many to view it as a 'wasted opportunity' to make it more compatible with that of the EU (Pratt 1994). By 1996, the government's rather restrictive approach to competition reform seemed to shift substantially. However, while the government showed itself more amenable to a reform of restrictive practices policy in line with EU policy in its 1996 Green Paper, its position on monopolies remained unchanged. And once again no draft bill was introduced to Parliament, as had been promised, 'without giving any clear reason' (Suzuki 2000: 6). We can assume that Eyre and Lodge (2000: 69) are correct in pointing to the imminence of the 1997 general election as a crucial factor, though Wilks (1996: 140) also identifies the low political saliency of the issue and the relative lack of political pressure on the government for reform, as factors providing an explanation for why this legislation was not prioritized.

Since the Conservatives had failed to take action, it was left to the newly elected Labour Government in 1997 to alter this state of affairs. A commitment to competition reform was included in Labour's 1997 election manifesto. Soon after coming to power, the Blair government introduced a Competition Bill, which both sought to reinforce merger control and reduce ministerial involvement in competition decisions. This was more than just the inherited draft from the Tories, as it had been revised following a new round of consultations (Eyre and Lodge 2000: 69). Perhaps as a consequence, the Conservatives opposed the Bill on a number of grounds, and were successful in delaying it, though the changes they secured were rather marginal (DTI 1996).

The new legal framework

The Competition Act of 1998 came into force in 2000 (see Gordan 2001). On the surface at least, it bore a remarkable similarity to the competition provisions found within Articles 81 and 82 (formerly 85 and 86) of the EC Treaty (see Scholes 1998). As Eyre and Lodge (2000: 69) stated: 'The adoption of the European competition model marks a fundamental shift in the core characteristics of the traditional British policy. For the first time, monopoly and restrictive practices policy have been combined in one piece of legislation, and as one policy'.

Like the EU's competition provisions, the Act was divided into two (that is, Chapters I and II), the first of which dealt with cartel policy (restrictive practices), and, the second, monopoly policy (abuse of a dominant position). These[1] resembled very closely the European treaty provisions. In both cases, the fundamental change was the introduction of a 'prohibitive approach'. In other words, instead of dealing with competition issues on a case-by-case basis, the Act made it clear that *all* cartels and abuses by monopolies were banned. In the case of the former, the Act also stated exemptions, as in Article 81.

The new legislation also brought British legislation into line with the kinds of investigative powers held by the European Commission's Directorate-General for Competition: an essentially voluntaristic process of Europeanization. The Act allowed officials to enter premises and engage in 'dawn raids', whilst also introducing civil penalties (of up to 10 per cent of turnover) for the first time. It also extended the rights of third parties to challenge companies and seek damages. These revisions echoed the existing European rules, which provided for all these elements, albeit not quite in the same form that they took in the new British legislation.

The 1998 Act also restructured the Monopolies and Mergers Commission, renaming it the Competition Commission, and supplementing it with a Competition Commission Appeals Tribunal (CCAT). Yet, it conspicuously excluded merger control, as advisers to the government claimed that to introduce a prohibitive approach in merger regulation was a more difficult exercise than for monopolies and restrictive practices. The government was to come back to this aspect of competition policy at a later date, after further consideration had been given to the issue. What the Act did, however, was to remove almost all ministerial influence from (non-merger) competition decisions. This was significant as it suggested a de-politicization of decision-making in competition cases.

Especially important was Section 60 of the Competition Act. This read as follows:

> so far as is possible (having regard to any relevant differences between the provisions concerned), questions arising ... in Community law in relation to competition within the United Kingdom are dealt with in a manner which is consistent with the treatment of corresponding questions arising in Community law in relation to competition within the Community.

Section 60 gave some cause for concern for lawyers during the drafting process, as they saw it as contributing to uncertainty about the conditions under which EU law might be relevant to a British case, and when it might not. It is, nevertheless, a very important clause in that it demonstrates the explicit relationship between the EU model and the new British model.

Once the 1998 Act had come into force in 2000, the Office of Fair Trading (OFT) was quick to make use of its new powers. Its first fining decision under Chapter I concerned the sharing out of bus routes in Leeds. In this case, one company involved in the case (Firstgroup) obtained 100 per cent immunity from fines, as it had complied fully with the investigation from the outset, leaving the other (Arriva) to pay a fine of £200,000 (OFT 2002).

There were also a number of cases falling under Chapter II of the Act. The first fining case under Chapter II was that of *Napp Pharmaceuticals,* with a decision taken by the DGFT on 30 March 2001. This case was important as it dealt with the issue of excessive pricing as a form of abuse of dominant position. An appeal was made against the decision to the newly formed CCAT. Although the DGFT decision was upheld in the main, the CCAT reduced the fine. The second fining decision under Chapter II also concerned predatory pricing by a dominant firm, in the *Aberdeen Journals,* decision of 16 July 2001. The newspaper firm in question was accused of pricing advertising space within the *Aberdeen Herald and Post* at a level intended to squeeze a competitor paper out of the market. This led to the imposition of a fine of £1.3 million on the offending firm. In this case, the CCAT threw out the decision on the grounds that there was insufficient reasoning in the decision. In a restated decision issued on 16 September 2001, the DGFT expanded its reasoning in line with the CCAT's requirements (Kon and Turnbull 2003: 70).

Eyre and Lodge (2000: 71) suggested that:

> British competition policy was finally 'Europeanized' with the passing of the Competition Act, transforming the very essence of the traditional approach... The emphasis on pragmatism in policy development and an administrative investigative style has changed towards policy development by case law and procedural investigation. At the same time, the role of the OFT had to change, moving away from routine oversight of commercial activities to a more focused approach on anti-competitive behaviour, also requiring a reorganization along the lines of DG IV.

These provisions are said to have moved the British competition model 'in just three years from one of the feeblest anti-cartel systems in the developed world to one of the most ferocious' (Joshua 2002: 231).

However, the 1998 Act and its implementation were by no means the end of the story. The British government continued its efforts to create a 'world class competition policy' by producing a White Paper in July 2001 (DTI 2001a). This eventually led to the 2002 Enterprise Act. The new Act dealt with mergers, removing ministerial involvement from merger cases in all but exceptional circumstances, so that all decisions are now taken by the OFT and the Competition Commission. The public interest test is replaced by a new criterion – whether a merger would result in a substantial lessening of competition (Miller 2002: 68). The 2002 Act also allows for the prosecution of individuals who are found to be responsible for setting up, or even condoning, cartels, providing a new deterrent against hardcore cartels.

Explaining the timing of reform

Adapting to European legal norms, whether in competition or other policy areas, has always posed problems for Britain because of the very different legal principles that underpin the EU's legal system. Whereas Britain has its common law, the EU is founded on a system of Roman Law. The challenge for the legal community in Britain has been to understand the differences between these two ostensibly incompatible systems, and then to find a way to make the incompatible compatible.

One might imagine that familiarity over time would facilitate a gradual adaptation to the EU approach. Thus far, this has not happened to any great degree, illustrated by the fact that, amongst senior judges, resistance to using 'Euro-arguments' in English legal cases has, according to one well-informed commentator, become entrenched (Maitland-Walker 1999: 1). In the field of competition reform, this resistance has been an important factor in holding back the reform of the post-1945 model – at least in any European direction. However, there is little evidence that the judges themselves *actively* hindered reform, though the competition law community has been vociferous in pointing out the practical problems associated with the application of European case law (and, indeed, precedents established within Commission Decisions) to competition cases in Britain.

One example of this in the Competition Act of 1998 concerned the overlapping nature of the two jurisdictions. As Eyre and Lodge noted:

> The adoption of the European prohibition approach was less of a problem of wording than a problem of drafting enabling legislation owing to conflicts with existing powers and methods. In particular, the adoption of European case law into the English legal system caused potential problems as the European policy has often been driven by political rather than legal motives. The CBI was worried about the impact of adopting the stricter European legal interpretation into the domestic context . . . (Eyre and Lodge 2000: 70).

This issue of the appropriateness of the import of European case law into the domestic arena related in particular to the single market (Scholes 1998: 45). It was not clear how Britain's model would be able to disentangle those aspects of the case law that were relevant to the British arena, from those that really only ought to apply to the European level. Even so, issues such as these were generally not seen as a barrier to reform, but as a puzzle to be clarified, initially by government legislation, and then subsequently within cases brought before the English courts.

Broader factors did serve as barriers to reform, however. In contrast to the majority of EU member states, Britain already had an extremely well-developed system of competition regulation when it joined the EEC. Initially, at least, there was a complacency of the 'if it ain't broke...' variety amongst the British political elite. Indeed, a residual attachment to this kind of thinking persisted even up to the late 1990s. However, by that stage, the British model had been much criticized in the financial press by specialist lawyers and by economists (Wilks 1996: 140; Peretz 1998) to the extent that the policy 'was held in widespread disrepute and arguments for change were promoted by almost all actors in the policy domain, ranging from the former [DGFT]..., former officials..., lawyers..., to Parliament...' (Eyre and Lodge 2000: 68). In addition, even '[b]usiness in the UK shared the perception that the established UK approach had become increasingly dysfunctional and therefore favoured a shift to the EU model' (Eyre and Lodge 2000: 76). The DTI used this emerging consensus on the discredited British policy as a justification for reform.

It seems, then, that this particular institutional constraint imposed by the pre-existence of Britain's competition model was undone by a whole range of actors willing to argue for its dismantling (Suzuki 2000: 14). The most important of these shifts in position was undoubtedly that of the CBI. The CBI was deeply opposed to the reform of competition policy when it was first mooted in the late 1980s (see above), and it lobbied the government intensively at that time, particularly over the issue of fining policy (Suzuki 2000: 10–11). However, by the mid-1990s the CBI's position had altered, and it came to favour a Europeanization of the existing rules.

These changes came at a time when the European Commission had already proved itself an activist player in matters of competition regulation. This activism had not arisen from any change in the European legal framework, but was, rather, a consequence of the increasing influence of neo-liberal ideas (see below) within the Commission, and the role of specific competition Commissioners in operationalizing those ideas through a more robust enforcement of the existing regulations (see for example Cini and McGowan 1998). It was not until the credibility of the EU model improved that arguments for competition reform in Britain became convincing. Coming at the same time as the discrediting of the British framework, it seemed obvious that the British legal community would turn to the increasingly successful EU model as an alternative tried-and-tested approach.

The success of the European competition model only served to increase the 'anxiety of Euro-sceptics' (Suzuki 2000: 13) within the Conservative Party, however. Indeed, even though the British policy was discredited, there was no small measure of reluctance within the Party to engage in any reform that involved importing a European model into Britain. There was some tension here, however.

In Britain, the long process until the final acceptance of the prohibition approach was mainly caused by the Conservative Government being torn between its preference for a non-discretionary approach as part of its neo-liberal economic policy agenda and its hostility towards adopting anything 'European' (Eyre and Lodge 2000: 76). The importance of ministerial leadership and preferences cannot be ignored in this respect. While in the case of the 1984 pro-competition 'Tebbit Doctrine', the Europeanization – or possibly more accurately, the convergence process – was unintentional; under Michael Heseltine, with his more activist interpretation of industrial policy, the reform of British competition policy was not viewed as a priority (see Eyre and Lodge 2000: 69). It might be argued convincingly, then, that the Europeanization of the Labour Party, that is, the Party's commitment to playing a more positive role in European affairs (see Chapter 1), was a necessary condition for the reform of British competition policy.

More generally, some of the drivers of the 1998 reform can be seen as:

> the case of an old DTI agenda, often using the CBI to test its proposals, which met the neo-liberal economic policy agenda of the Conservatives and Labour's desire not only to fulfil demands expressed by business associations, but also to make "New Labour" more credible by reducing ministerial discretion in competition issues. (Eyre and Lodge 2000: 76)

These shifts within the British political system also came at a time of much discussion in the competition sphere about international convergence and the creation of a global competition policy. This was driven by concerns about the competition effects of a massive growth in cross-border trade and direct investment (Suzuki 2000: 7). The influence of international organizations in this debate has been particularly important (especially, the Organisation for Economic Co-operation and Development (OECD) and the World Trade Organisation). Although one might expect this agenda to have been led by the United States, even under Clinton its preferences were much more supportive of bilateral, rather than multilateral, agreements. Indeed, it was the EU's competition officials who were most active in setting up new international initiatives, such as the Global Competition Forum website and the International Competition Network (see Murphy 2002).

Substantive influences: explaining the form of reform

There is no evidence that EU institutions played an active or aggressive role in promoting a particular type of reform within the British competition model (Eyre and Lodge 2000: 70). However, at the same time as Britain was reforming its legislation, the EU was also initiating its own reform (or 'modernization') process. This took the form of a complete review of policy enforcement, with an emphasis particularly placed on decentralization. With this, came serious concerns at the EU level about the degree of variation that still existed across the member states, particularly with regard to the consistent application of EU norms in competition enforcement. If there was little external *pressure* to change existing systems in line with certain aspects of the EU system, there was some encouragement to do so. It is fair to claim that the timing of these developments post-dated Britain's reform. But what is also clear is that the interest in decentralization began well before the Commission's 2000 White Paper on modernization. Increasingly, the Commission's DG for Competition expected national competition policies to act as part of a federalized system (or network) of competition regulation. And in adopting such an approach, issues of (in)compatibility had to be addressed if the system as a whole was to remain effective. For governments keen to maintain a strong pro-competition line, there was little choice but to adapt home-grown systems to European principles, norms and rules.

Moreover, for the British government to influence EU policy (as it engaged in its own reform process), it was important for it to have a policy compatible with that at the European level. A post-1998 example of how this might happen can be gleaned from the *Napp Pharmaceuticals* case (see page 221). The new British model allowed Britain not only to deal with the case in a way that was compatible with the EU model, but also to make a contribution to the shaping of EU policy (Kon and Turnbull 2003: 70). This was possible as the case dealt with excessive/predatory pricing, a phenomenon on which there is little existing case law at European level.

The best evidence for a direct EU effect on reform comes, however, from looking at the legislation itself. There were quite staggering similarities between the new British model and the European system of competition regulation. Moreover, the reforms dealt explicitly with the issue of compatibility between the two systems. Competition lawyers pointed in particular to three aspects of the EU model that were imported into the British system (Barr 1998: 139):

1. the prohibitions, which are closely based on Articles 81 and 82;
2. the European principles clause, which provides for the interpretation of the British prohibition in a manner that is not inconsistent with the principles and case law which would apply in a like manner under EU law;
3. the 'parallel' approach, with provision for the automatic application of EU exemptions in Britain (parallel exemptions), and the obligation on the DGFT to consider fines imposed at EU level in assessing domestic penalties.

However, '[i]n some senses, the Bill is even more European in approach than a straightforward description of these three areas might suggest' (Barr 1998: 140). The following are all worthy of note: the lack of domestic definitions, which is likely to lead by default to the introduction of European legal language into domestic law; the import of European (for example single market) policy objectives into the domestic context; and the provision of positive assistance by the policy, and national competition officials to be given to the Commission carrying out an investigation in Britain. Yet, despite this, Britain's approach still managed to differ substantially from the EU model, in that it was 'tailored to meet the UK's own special requirements . . . [whilst having been] designed to improve upon the problems encountered at EU level . . .' (Barr 1998: 141). This was especially the case in relation to the introduction of criminal sanctions for anti-competitive agreements into the British policy, something that had not been possible at the EU level.

Part of this 'tailoring' involved drawing upon North American experience. This was particularly evident in the reforms in the 2002 Enterprise Act allowing for the imprisonment of individuals in competition cases. Andrews (2002) suggests that one reason for the adoption of a US-style approach to penalties had been the (successful) crackdowns on hardcore cartels in America. Not surprisingly, the reaction of the business community to this development was negative.

But, as Joshua (2002) pointed out, aside from this expected opposition, there were also important legal and political reasons why this new approach should be treated with caution. Joshua identified issues that are likely to be crucial to the viability of the new British legislation. First, there are the questions to do with the compatibility of British and EU approaches to competition enforcement: he suggested that 'the [UK's] go-it-alone attempt to deter cartels with jail sentences may yet be thwarted by concurrent EU legislative developments in Brussels to which the British Government has already in principle signed up' (Joshua 2002: 231). Further, the Commission's 'modernization' agenda, which recommends the implementation of a single system of competition control for transnational cartels at the European level, may well 'inhibit or even preclude separate criminal prosecution' (Joshua 2002: 231).

Second, even if it does not preclude criminalization *per se*, Joshua wondered whether:

> the British Government have really considered fully the implications of operating a separate system of criminal law investigations in tandem (or competition) with the E.C. administrative enforcement measures in the same case. If the criminal regime in Britain hampers or impedes the uniform operation of E.C. competition rules, it could still run foul of obligations under the Treaty. (Joshua 2002: 232)

Important questions about the compatibility and consistency of the British and the EU model made it clear that the British reform was not simply the import of an EU model. It could equally be understood as an Americanization of competition control – at least in the sphere of cartel policy. In a peer review of the British policy produced on behalf of the DTI by PriceWaterhouseCoopers in April 2001 (DTI 2001b), Britain sat in the top half of the list of OECD countries benchmarked. The United States and Germany, and maybe also a couple of others (Australia, for example), ranked above Britain. The report claimed that the 'UK regime is also seen to be more effective than the EU but not by a wide margin' (DTI 2001b). Applying a sort of league-table approach to competition policy suggested that it was to the US and German models that Britain was looking, as competitors in the 'best in class' game.

The key question here is whether it has been possible for Britain to both Europeanize and Americanize its competition policy at the same time. Not only is it important to ask whether it is possible to import US-style solutions to large cartels into the EU, but the question becomes all the more resonant when one remembers that the EU (at least at the time of this writing) does not have the power to introduce a European-level criminal law, thus precluding the import of a 'criminalization' approach. As a consequence, '[t]here are . . . valid concerns that the Government's plans suffer from a lack of "joined-up thinking"' (Joshua 2002: 245).

The form that the new British system has taken has been strongly set in the context of neo-liberal assumptions about economic management; assumptions that entered the mainstream in the 1980s via a competition law epistemic community (van Waarden and Drahos 2002: 933), and which have taken a specific form in the case of competition regulation. These ideas have influenced both European level and British thinking about competition policy, helping to bring the two models together. One manifestation of this convergence has been the newly developed role of economic analysis in European competition decisions, a development that is now supported in European Court judgements (Hildebrand 1998).

The alignment of the European and British models began in the mid-1970s: 'Both systems changed from a structural approach for judging the effects of monopolies on markets towards stressing the importance of entry barriers and competitive process' (Eyre and Lodge 2000: 68). This alignment was accelerated in 1984 by Norman Tebbit, when he redefined the notion of 'public interest' along competition lines in merger cases; although in this instance, Europeanization was purely an unintended consequence. 'Further factors facilitating similarity were the evolving close relationship between UK and European Community officials . . . secondments to DG IV by UK officials and increased communication flows between various competition authorities' (Eyre and Lodge 2000: 68). One might see this as a form of Europeanization, or as a consequence of much broader transnational ideational transformations that impacted both on the EU and Britain.

Conclusions

The primary objective of this chapter has been to identify the extent to which the British competition model has been Europeanized and the factors that have driven this process. This has been done by unpacking the timing and substance of recent policy reforms. Whereas on first sight these appear to present a rather straightforward case of Europeanization, a closer look suggests a gamut of additional factors that have been important in shaping the outcome. Taken together, they explain why, despite the adoption of certain elements drawn from the EU, the British approach continues to differ substantially from the EU's: 'Where there has been, at a superficial level, convergence towards and utilization of the European model, detailed and qualitative evidence of the domestic policy processes provide a picture of limited "fungibility" leading to a "hybridization" of policies' (Eyre and Lodge 2000: 77).

As a case of Europeanization, British competition reform raises interesting questions about the causal relationship between EU and domestic policy, and about how Europeanization relates to the themes of convergence and lesson-drawing. Beath (2002: 234) notes that since the 1998 Competition Act came into force, there is now 'some consonance between US, UK and EU competition law', thereby claiming convergence without necessarily implying causality. Eyre and Lodge (2000: 75–80) seem to concur when they state that 'it is difficult to find a "European" cause' for the reform, though the 'European "theme"' was used to propose alternatives to perceived domestic weaknesses in competition policy.' They do, however, all identify a process of Europeanization, which is indirect and inadvertent, as opposed to direct and intentional on the part of the EU. One might go so far as to claim that, rather than this example of Europeanization involving a 'push' from the EU level, it is a case that rests on a 'pull' effect from within the domestic political arena. In other words, and given the support for the reform from within Britain, one might see Europeanization as a consequence of a voluntaristic embracing of the EU model.

This does not mean, however, that the EU's impact is likely to be marginal. It is also difficult to draw firm conclusions about the long-term effect of the Europeanization of Britain's policy, given that the changes have been relatively recent. However, it is not inconceivable that what we are witnessing in this case is an example of *transformation* (see Bache and Jordan, Chapter 2). What is interesting is that this kind of transformation can come about through indirect and voluntaristic mechanisms. One might otherwise have hypothesized that where transformation takes place, states would have been forced to comply with EU rules in a much more direct and less voluntaristic fashion. In explaining transformation in this case, the fact that the EU is only one driver of change must surely enter into the equation.

Although support for change was widespread by the mid-1990s, where there was resistance to Europeanization this came from the political class, and in particular from the Conservative Party, where a Eurosceptic distaste for EU-inspired reforms at times rode roughshod over its other policy objectives. A reluctance to replace the traditional British approach with a European model of competition regulation became less tenable, however, even within the Conservative Party, once the European approach was deemed to be successful (in the main), and given that the changes proposed were broadly in line with neo-liberal thinking.

For Labour, both during the run-up to, and after winning, the 1997 election, two main agendas motivated the post-1998 reform. The first was discretely European, and concerned the *compatibility* of the British model with the EU's system of competition regulation. This has to be understood in the broader context of the (soft) pro-Europeanism of the party at this time. The second was Labour's modernization agenda. Whilst incorporating a European dimension, this agenda was really about credibility or policy *effectiveness*. The two agendas are, as these things often are, inter-related in the sense that the first is a necessary condition of the second. In other words, the modernization of the British competition model could not be successful if there was an awkward mismatch between the British and EU approaches. But to talk of 'lesson-drawing', as do Eyre and Lodge (2000), is to say something different. My point here is that, in striving for a 'modernized' British competition policy, lessons may be drawn from a number of different sources, including the United States as well as the EU. Lesson-drawing may mean that some elements of the old system (regarding the regulation of complex monopolies, for example) remain in place, even if they are out of step with the EU. With the DTI now accepting that the EU model is no more effective than the post-1998 British model, Britain has to look beyond the EU – to the United States, or possibly in future to Germany – for ideas on how to toughen up British policy.

What broader insights can be drawn from this case that might contribute to a richer understanding of Europeanization? As already mentioned above, Europeanization in this policy area is voluntaristic and indirect. This would seem to be a necessary condition for the 'cherry-picking' approach to the EU model, demonstrated by British authorities. Although Europeanization does involve a top-down impact (with the EU model being adopted – if only in part – at the national level), there is also some indication of bottom-up influences, and even a suggestion that Europeanization might, in future, involve much more in the way of horizontal cross-fertilization. However, given the influence of the US model globally, defining such horizontal influences as Europeanization does not seem particularly helpful, as to do so would be to ignore a crucial driver of policy change. Indeed, internationalization may be a more appropriate term to reflect the multi-directional ideational and policy influences evident in the extremely cosmopolitan field of competition policy.

To conclude, it is possible to draw from this case two inter-related lessons for the study of Europeanization. First, researchers working in this field must take care to consider hypotheses other than those drawn from the Europeanization literature when examining the drivers of domestic change. The moral is that if one goes out looking for Europeanization, one may well find it (see Chapter 2). Second, this case demonstrates some of the difficulties facing researchers as they seek to disentangle the factors driving change within domestic arenas. For example, in this chapter, the distinction between Europeanization and modernization effects is made. While, analytically, one might satisfactorily divorce one from the other, one must also be aware that Europeanization and modernization may not be entirely separable, but may have worked together in a mutually dependent way. Thus, while this chapter emphasizes the importance of Europeanization, it also serves as an important warning to those who seek to examine the *kind of* Europeanization taking place, before asking *whether* what they are researching is in fact Europeanization.

Note

1. Namely, Clause 2, Chapter 1 (Article 81 EC); and Clause 18, Chapter 2 (Article 82 EC).

15
Environmental Policy

Andrew Jordan

When Britain[1] first considered the case for joining the EU (then EEC), environmental considerations were at best secondary to what were widely perceived to be more pressing national interests, such as trade, agriculture and parliamentary sovereignty. When the decision to join was finally taken in 1972, there was still a widespread view in Britain, that British environmental policy would thereafter formally be 'in Europe', but European environmental policy would not conceivably ever be 'in Britain'. Or, to put it slightly differently, membership would offer Britain an opportunity to share its long experience of dealing with environmental problems with other member states, but British policy would not be systematically Europeanized by the EU.

Why was this? First, even by the late 1960s, environmental policy constituted an *extremely* minor aspect of EU affairs (Jordan 2005). There was, therefore, very little policy that could conceivably Europeanize Britain or any other member state. Second, there was a very widely shared view within Britain that British policy was inherently better than the policies of continental states or anything that the EU might conceivably produce. For most British people 'the issue [of membership] was seen essentially to do with joining a trading bloc' (Lowe and Ward 1998: 11). By the early 1970s, Britain had amassed plenty of experience about how to achieve its 'non'-domestic environmental concerns (for example safeguarding the survival of endangered species such as tigers and elephants as well as migrating birds) (Lowe and Ward 1998: 9) by working through international bodies such as the United Nations (UN). Therefore, most British environmentalists assumed that if EC membership had any environmental implications, the dominant flow of influence would run the other way that is, from Britain to other member states via Brussels.

However, these early expectations proved to be spectacularly wide of the mark. Today, almost all 'national' environmental policy is made by, or in close association with, the EU (Jordan 2002). The EU's influence vastly exceeds that of the UN and the Organization for Economic Co-operation and

Development (OECD). This puzzle provokes a number of analytical questions. First, what were the traditional features of national policy prior to the EU's involvement (that is, *what* has been Europeanized)? Second, through which phases have British–EU relations in this sector passed? Third, which changes in domestic thinking and policy practice can be causally related to the EU's involvement (that is, *how much* Europeanization has there been)? Finally, what do the events in this sector reveal about the wider themes raised in Chapters 1 and 2?

The remainder of this chapter is structured around these questions. Thus, the next section describes what British environmental policy looked like prior to the EU's involvement. This chapter differentiates between the *content*, *structures* and *style* of national policy. Following Hall (1993), the *content* of national policy is divided into three different sub-aspects or 'levels'. The first level comprises the overall goals that guide policy. These goals operate within a policy paradigm or a 'framework of ideas and standards that specifies not only the goals of policy and the kind of instruments that can be used to attain them, but also the very nature of the problems they are meant to be addressing' (Hall 1993: 279). The second covers the instruments or techniques by which these policy goals are attained, for example direct regulation, fiscal instruments, or voluntary agreements. Finally, the third level measures the calibration of these policy instruments, for example the level of an emission standard or tax, and so on. Meanwhile, national *structures* range from formal bureaucratic organizations with staff, budgets and buildings, through to more informal phenomena such as codes, conventions and other socialized ways of looking at the world (Peters 1999: 146). Finally, the section on the *style* of national policy draws upon what Richardson (1982: 2) originally described as society's 'standard operating procedures for making and implementing policies'. By that, he meant: (1) the dominant approach to problem solving, ranging from anticipatory/active to reactive; and (2) the government's relationship to other actors, characterized by their inclination either to reach consensus with organized groups or to impose decisions.

Having constructed this baseline, the third section briefly describes the historical evolution of national and EU policy. Then, section four identifies how the EU has affected the content, structure and style of national policy. The final section (five) investigates what the events in this sector reveal about Britain's role in Europe and Europe's growing involvement in British affairs.

The traditional features of national policy

The dominant style

'Voluntarism', 'discretion' and 'practicability' are the words that are commonly used to describe British environmental policy prior to the

EU's involvement (Weale 1997). As new problems emerged and became important, new laws were enacted and new agencies put in place to administer them. In operational terms, environmental regulation proceeded on the basis of courteous negotiation between polluters and regulators operating in exclusive policy communities of experts (what Weale *et al.* (2000: 181) term 'club government').

As it was sold to foreigners by British politicians (Waldegrave 1985), 'the British approach' was predominantly reactive rather than anticipatory, tactical rather than strategic, pragmatic rather than ambitious, and case by case rather than uniform. In practice, it was really a pragmatic 'trial and error' search for the most cost-effective (that is, to business) solutions to policy problems. Influential policy elites genuinely believed that 'muddling through' problems was inherently superior to the EU's preference for strategic, long-term planning, which they viewed as being far too rigid (Ashby and Anderson 1981). This attitude of mind sprang from the British legal system (which relies heavily on common law with its constant interplay between precedent and interpretation), its informal and constantly evolving constitution, and the widespread desire to optimize pollution rather than minimize waste emissions regardless of their environmental impact (see below).

The main structures

When it joined the EEC, Britain had some of the oldest and most innovative policy structures in the world. In 1863, Britain created the first industrial permitting agency in the world, known as the Alkali Inspectorate (which has since been merged into the national Environment Agency – see below). In 1970, it created the world's first environmental ministry – the Department of the Environment (DoE). Although these structures of government have changed since 1970, their guiding philosophy has remained largely unchanged. This holds that central government should only ever set the broad legislative or policy framework, leaving the detailed aspects of policy either to specialist agencies (such as the Alkali Inspectorate) or to local government officials. By contrast, the EU tends to develop highly specific policy proposals, which are then passed down to the national level to be implemented. Finally, legal structures (that is, a mixture of statute and common law; no environmental court or tribunals, or a constitutional commitment to environmental protection) were also consistent with Britain's common law traditions, its unwritten constitution and consensual policy style (for example very few environmental disputes ever reached court).

The content of policy

It is difficult to identify an overall philosophy or *paradigm* of British policy other than that pollution should be optimized by limiting its effects on the environment, rather than minimized at source (Weale *et al.* 2000: 177). Lowe and Flynn (1989: 256) concluded that British policy was little more than a pragmatic 'accretion of common law, statutes, agencies, procedures and policies'. Traditionally, the underlying principle of policy has been that standards should be 'reasonably practicable' that is, tailored to reflect local conditions and circumstances, the economic costs of abatement and the current state of technical knowledge (Jordan 1998: 180–81). This approach was assumed to be more effective and more economically efficient than forcing all polluters to attain the same (that is, harmonized) statutory standards.

Britain was reluctant to set long-term *policy goals*, especially whose achievement could not be guaranteed. Instead, the preference was for targets to be developed incrementally by technical agencies working together with industry. The 'technology forcing' element of German policy has never really taken root in Britain. Where long-term goals were set, they tended to be associated with distinct geographical areas (that is, they were environmental quality objectives or standards), as opposed to the emission limits favoured by continental European states.

In terms of the *policy instruments* used, regulation was generally preferred to taxes, subsidies and formal voluntary agreements (Jordan *et al.* 2003, 2005). Crucially, British regulatory instruments were somewhat different to those used in continental European states and the EU. Whereas the latter preferred fixed legislative standards and deadlines to ensure comparability of effort and to simplify the process of monitoring and enforcement, Britain opted for non-legislative guidelines and flexible implementation systems (see above).

British policy – a summary

These three aspects of policy fitted closely together. Thus, the allocation of tasks between the main structures reflected the dominant style and the 'contextual' paradigm of British policy (see below), the finer details of which could not have been determined by civil servants working at desks in London. Close, secretive and collaborative relationships between regulator and regulated provided an effective means of making the subtle trade-offs required to optimize pollution. And as a rule, regulators working in specialized agencies preferred not to set standards which could not be complied with.

There are several other features of national environmental policy and politics prior to 1973 that stand out. First, the British tended to view 'environmental policy' in slightly narrower terms than other northern European states. They focused on problems that bulked large in a relatively crowded island state like the UK that shares no land borders with other states (for example heritage and landscape protection, land use planning and nature conservation). Second, British elites were immensely 'proud' of these arrangements (Hajer 1995). In the late 1970s, the DoE[2] (DoE 1978: 1) claimed that it was already 'at a comparatively advanced stage of development and adoption of environmental protection policies', the implication being that the Commission's help was not required. The DoE therefore informed the Commission that it should not invest too much time in designing common policies, because Britain was 'well placed to cope with its own environmental problems' (in Evans 1973: 43).

Finally, almost from the outset, there was an obvious misfit between what many continental European states regarded as being the most immediate priorities (that is, the pollution of shared water courses such as estuaries and rivers) and Britain's twin specialisms, namely: international environmental diplomacy (that is, primarily exercised through the organs of the UN), and remedying its own 'domestic' environmental problems. Crucially, while the former required detailed and intensive intra-EU collaboration, the latter could (and, Britain believed, *should*) be pursued through international (that is, supra-EU) or local means. In a sense, then, Britain and the rest of the EU were almost destined to conflict with one another, because they had different policy aims and ways of implementing them.

Europeanization: a short history

The 1970s: small beginnings

It did not take long for conflict between the EEC and Britain to occur. A proposal issued by the Commission in 1974 to reduce the emission of dangerous substances to water was a very early trigger. A Directive (EEC/76/160) containing extensive exemptions for Britain was only agreed in 1976 after protracted wrangling. This episode soured relations for years to come. Part of the problem was that the British did very little to upload its policies to EU; therefore the Commission tended to base its thinking on other countries' priorities (Jordan 2002: 31–32). There were, of course, areas where the DoE successfully took the initiative in Europe – or at least supported European solutions – but they were far 'fewer than might have been expected of a country with such a well established environmental policy' (Haigh 1984: 302). Instead, Britain tried to steer EU environmental policy from the margins by blocking policies that misfitted with its settled domestic traditions (Jordan 2003). Extensive state ownership and/or sponsorship of key polluting industries such as water, energy and farming provided Whitehall with many reasons to resist the environmental investments demanded by more environmentally ambitious states such as Germany and the Netherlands.

The creeping Europeanization of national policy did not, however, trigger much societal debate. The only people, who seemed aware of what was happening, were law lords. Very early on, an influential House of Lords select committee produced a very detailed report that questioned the EC's growing competence in areas (such as the environment) that did not sit within its formal remit. Their Lordships believed that 'the... transfer of sovereignty should be defined and the Community should keep within its powers', because it 'causes an irreversible removal of legislative power from [Britain]' (House of Lords 1978: 16–17). Interestingly, not one witness – not even the DoE – could say precisely how much legislation had actually been adopted, let alone assess what impact it had had.

The 1980s: growing conflicts

During the mid- to late-1980s, EU environmental policy entered a new and much more energetic phase (Jordan 2005). The DoE's failure to upload British policy ideas to the EU, combined with the national environmental movement's increasingly strident demands for the existing rules to be implemented, combined to generate a series of sizeable policy misfits. During this period, the DoE tried to limit Europeanization by employing its veto in the Council of Ministers, typified by the five-year battle against the Environmental Impact Assessment (EIA) Directive even though it merely formalized existing best practice (Jordan 2002: Chapter 10). It also made every effort to neuter legislation that was passed, typified by the highly selective implementation of the directives on bathing and drinking water (Jordan 1999). To make matters worse, the Commission vigorously opposed Britain's attempts to close these and other misfits informally, by initiating infringement proceedings. These culminated in several far-reaching judgments by the European Court of Justice (ECJ) in relation to non-compliance in Britain, which forced the British government to radically alter its view of EU law and implement costly remedial works.

By the mid-1980s, Britain was markedly out of step with the rest of Europe. It was also under attack from normally very moderate domestic actors including the House of Lords Select Committee on the European Communities, the Royal Commission on Environmental Pollution, and the Royal Society for the Protection of Birds (RSPB). Moreover, attempts to neuter Europeanization by blocking and/or subverting directives not only conspicuously failed to correct the misfits but also lumbered Britain with a reputation for being *the* Dirty Man of Europe. As the impact of EU policies escaped from the narrow confines of the 'environmental' parts of the DoE and began to intrude into much more politically important areas of its core business, principally water and later energy privatization, demands increased for a much more fundamental re-think (Jordan and Greenaway 1998). With the Prime Minister's backing, the DoE won a number of important interdepartmental battles on issues such as acid rain (1986), North Sea pollution (1987) and ozone depletion (1987) that helped to realign Britain with the rest of the EU. But even these were not enough to stave off a minor political crisis in 1989 when the Green Party achieved an unprecedented 15 per cent share of the national vote in European Parliamentary elections. Thereafter, the (then Conservative) government re-doubled its efforts to present a much greener face to the domestic electorate and the rest of the EU.

The 1990s: from policy taking to policy shaping

By the early 1990s, the Europeanization of national policy had progressed so far and the political conflicts it had generated had become so distracting that continuing to 'take' policy from Brussels in the hope that it could be either blocked in the Council of Ministers or watered down at the implementation stage was no longer a viable political strategy. With the added push of greater majority voting in the Council, Britain really had no other option but to engage much more proactively in EU environmental policy making (Jordan 2003). Thus, starting in the late 1980s, Britain embarked on a comprehensive strategy to shape the EU by uploading more policy ideas to the EU.

Today, Britain is to be found exporting domestic environmental ideas to Brussels with a passion that would have been unimaginable even fifteen years ago. Britain is no longer perceived as *the* Dirty Man of Europe (other states now perform this role); on the contrary, in some areas (for example climate change) but by no means all (for example waste management, recycling and renewable energy generation), it leads the rest of Europe. In fact this strategy has been so successful, that traditional environmental lead states such as Germany are now to be heard complaining that EU policy has become *too* Anglicized (Wurzel 2002)!

How much Europeanization has occurred?

Policy style

The style of national policy

There are two aspects to policy style: the style of British policy in Britain, and the style in which the British conduct themselves in the policy business of the EU. The style in which contemporary British environmental policy is enunciated and implemented is undeniably very different to that of the EU described above, that is, consensual and reactive. I have already noted the secular trend in Britain towards greater explicitness, more formalism and greater proaction. However, there are many factors behind the emergence of what Weale (1992) has described as a 'new politics' of the environment in Britain, of which the EU is only one. For instance, the politicization of environmental politics (itself accelerated by Europeanization) has perturbed the quasi-secretive world of pollution control, as has the advent of public registers of information, mechanisms of judicial review and (most recently of all) the formal adoption of the European Convention on Human Rights. New public management has also ushered in a much more open and formal style of regulation, although arrangements are still in a state of flux. For example, there are now independent utility regulators that openly challenge the basis of environmental policy decisions on water treatment and climate change. In so doing, they help to create a more open and publicly accountable system of regulation, which forces central government departments to lay bare the financial calculations underpinning environmental standards. At the same time, industry has realized that tougher and more independent regulation plays well with customers, employees, shareholders and potential investors. Many large companies are beginning to divulge information voluntarily as part of corporate social responsibility initiatives, although smaller companies still have a long way to go.

Overall, therefore, the domestic policy style has changed significantly since 1973, but it has not been transformed and there is no obvious shift towards an adversarial style; informal negotiation and game playing are still the lifeblood of domestic environmental regulation. Court proceedings are, in any case, expensive and judicial review procedures are long, expensive and uncertain as to their outcome. That British environmental groups have often found it more productive to exploit the lobbying opportunities available in Brussels is a good indication that 'club government' (Weale *et al.* 2000: 181) is still alive and well in Britain, albeit in a political system transformed by Europeanization.

The British policy style in the EU

To a large extent, the British have carried their style of working into Brussels (Christoph 1993). The British like to think that they are hard negotiators but dutiful implementers of EU legislation (Wallace 1995). The British believe that they inject a dose of administrative common sense into EU policy making, while other, supposedly more 'European', states slip into an 'easy rhetoric' about the merits of deeper European integration (Wallace 1995: 47). The British have, for example, successfully advocated the use of a more formal style of working in the EU, using white and green papers, as well as broader framework directives, and economic appraisal techniques, to strategize more effectively while at the same time clarifying the underlying principles of policy making.

In other respects – and particularly during the early years of EU membership – the British were forced to adopt a new and somewhat more adversarial policy style in order to resist the demands made by other, more pro-environment states and the European Commission. However, on many occasions, it was left looking distinctly 'awkward' and anti-environmental. In fact, some commentators have gone as far as to suggest that many of Britain's European problems stem not from substantive interstate differences but from contrasting styles of bargaining and coalition building (Buller 1995). For a variety of reasons (see above), the British do find it difficult to speak the language of European integration. To a large extent, they still see the EU as a zero-sum game played between sovereign states. Consequently, they still tend to spend more time trying to defend a fixed national position in the Council (a task to which the highly polished but somewhat inflexible interdepartmental coordination mechanisms are ideally suited), instead of employing more subtle negotiating tactics to create broad alliances or shape the all-important pre-negotiation stages of the policy process.

However, under the Blair government there were signs that the British had started to learn a new, much more *communautaire* policy style in Brussels. Labour's politically more engaged stance certainly made it easier for the environment department to work inside the EU political system to upload policies, than when John Major was Prime Minister. Interestingly, the unexpectedly deep and politically painful Europeanization of environmental policy had forced the department to adopt this more 'European' style already in the early 1990s, that is, well before the arrival of Blair. This shift was made mainly for pragmatic reasons – the department realized that it had to get a firmer grip on EU policy, or risk many more policy misfits. Being more proactively engaged meant uploading more policies to Brussels, using more *communautaire* language ('yes, but' in response to Commission proposals rather than an unequivocal 'no') and engaging in more 'corridor diplomacy' (Jordan 2002) to achieve its departmental objectives. In making these changes, the DoE successfully transformed itself into one of *the* most European departments in Whitehall (Buller and Smith 1998).

Policy structures

Legal structures

The impact of the EU has been particularly evident in relation to domestic legal structures (Macrory 1987, 1991), which have become more formalized and much more specific in terms of the overall objectives to be achieved. In fact, national law was probably one of the first elements of British life to be Europeanized, although the overall extent still surprised many lawyers (Nicol 2001). The government was to an extent to blame for this because during the 1970s it set out to reduce the depth of change by employing administrative circulars to implement EU rules rather than secondary legislation. This practice had to be discontinued following adverse rulings by the ECJ. Of course, the written word of EU law only represents one dimension of change; it has to be interpreted and implemented by national enforcement bodies to have any real effect. Therefore, any assessment of the Europeanization of legal structures must also take into account changes in the overall style of national policy making (see above).

Governmental structures

It is considerably harder to identify a clear 'EU effect' on other national structures. The most obvious changes include the creation of a permanent representation (UKRep) in Brussels, the creation of some new regulatory agencies (for example the National Rivers Authority – now a part of the national Environment Agency (Jordan 1998)), the establishment of a

European coordinating unit in the DoE, the appearance of new procedures to secure agreement across Whitehall, and the creation of parliamentary committees to oversee the core executive's activities in the EU (see Bulmer and Burch, Chapter 3). However, these are actually quite modest impacts. If anything, the characteristic features of policy making in Whitehall remain essentially undiminished. For instance, the 'Rolls Royce' system of inter-departmental coordination still operates much as it always has. Westminster, meanwhile, has developed new procedures to scrutinize the Whitehall departments, but they are strikingly similar to those governing national policy. EU pressures most certainly added to the need for parliamentary reform (for example the creation of select committees) (Giddings and Drewry 1996), but they were certainly not the sole cause (Rasmussen 2001: 158).

However, those who have looked in much greater detail at the Europeanization of organizational cultures suggest that the EU has made some Whitehall departments more 'European' in their attitudes and expectations (Buller and Smith 1998). Research reveals that the DoE has indeed 'learnt' new, more *communautaire* tactics, established new alliances and, most profoundly of all, adopted a new (that is, more environmental and more European) 'departmental view' (Jordan 2002: 211). Ironically, Europeanization has greatly strengthened the hand of the DoE within Whitehall battles, even though it did not consciously set out to achieve this outcome.

Central–local government relations

Turning to the relationships between central and local government, Nigel Haigh's (1986) thesis that EU Directives have centralized power in Britain is still extremely apposite, but it does need to be seen against the backdrop of a series of important domestic and international drivers of change. So while it is almost certainly true that the logic of European integration has shifted more policy making from local levels to Whitehall and the EU (thereby eroding the power of local government and technical agency officials), the organizational landscape would have changed regardless of Europeanization, not least to fit the new public management aspirations of successive governments since 1979.

The content of British policy

Policy goals and paradigms

In terms of *policy paradigms*, the EU has forced Britain to adopt a more preventative, source-based policy paradigm. The need for change first arose in the long and acrimonious battle to agree the 1976 Dangerous Substances Directive (see above). No sooner had this philosophical conflict been apparently resolved than a similarly bitter conflict erupted over the application of emission limits (this time enshrined within the principle of best available technology (BAT)) to acidic gases. This time, Britain was forced to back down in the teeth of concerted opposition from other states. In the course of these and many other battles (for example the dumping of waste at sea), the EU made the objectives of national policy more environmentally ambitious, specified the instruments to be used to achieve them, and even the manner in which they should be applied.

There are, however, three reasons for rejecting the simple view that the EU has forced Britain to adopt a more precautionary policy paradigm. First, to paraphrase Albert Weale (1997: 105), Britain has lost important aspects of what used to be referred to as 'the British approach', but it has still not found a new 'approach' or paradigm. So while it is more environmentally ambitious, Britain is not wholly committed to the philosophy of ecological modernization and feels distinctly uneasy about adopting strongly precautionary policies – other than when it is economically or politically favourable (for example, climate change) to do so. A more accurate characterization is therefore one of deep change with important elements of continuity. We can see this reflected in the way that Britain succeeded in shaping the integrated pollution prevention and control and the water framework directives to incorporate elements of British thinking.

Second, the depth of change varies greatly across the various sub-sectors of British environmental policy (Lowe and Ward 1998: 290). So, for example, air, noise, water and chemicals policy now follow the EU's preference for strong source-based controls, whereas land use planning and biodiversity protection still – although by no means exclusively – reflect the contextual approach of gradually negotiating targets, rather than specifying *a priori* some absolute level of environmental protection.

Finally, it is debatable whether the pre-existing British approach was ever a paradigm in the sense of a narrow, confining cognitive framework (Jordan and Greenaway 1998). It is probably more accurate to view it as a set of politically and economically expedient activities, which were only worked up into a broader 'philosophy' by British officials seeking to justify the *status quo* to the EU (cf. Haigh 1989: 22). In other words, we might say that for a period of time (c.1974–1988), Europeanization exacerbated the paradigmatic differences between British and EU policy, which led – temporarily – to a period of retrenchment (see Chapter 2).

Policy instruments

In terms of *policy tools*, the EU has led directly to the adoption of more source-based controls as well as more formal environmental quality standards for certain types of pollutants. These reflect the EU's preference for more harmonized and precautionary-based policies. However, for reasons that are widely known, the EU's toolbox is still predominantly regulatory (Jordan *et al.* 2003). Consequently, domestic and international drivers provide the dominant source of pressure behind the recent appearance of 'new' environmental policy instruments such as voluntary agreements and eco-taxes and so on.

The calibration of policy instruments

The precise calibration of policy instruments has been clearly and very directly affected by the EU. The EU has created many new emission standards, tightened existing ones and formalized their achievement by setting strict deadlines. The style in which instruments are calibrated has also changed, as has the organizational context in which the calibration takes place. In the past, the ability to constantly fine-tune policy instruments process to reflect local needs and circumstances was highly prized by local technocrats. Their freedom has decreased dramatically as more and more standards are set within the EU. This trend has eroded the administrative discretion once enjoyed by local and technical officials.

Analysing domestic change

A new British environmental policy?

The last thirty years have arguably witnessed the appearance of new forms of environmental policy and politics in Britain. In terms of the *content* of policy, a more consistent and formal system of administrative control has emerged which is increasingly based upon fixed standards and timetables of compliance, rather than administrative rules of thumb. There are many more source-based emission controls, and a much more explicit set of guiding principles and objectives such as precaution, prevention and sustainability. Policy makers are also more willing to experiment with non-regulatory instruments such as environmental taxes and, more recently, tradable permits (Jordan *et al.* 2003). In terms of policy *structures*, many powers have gradually shifted from officials working in local government and technical agencies to civil servants working at higher (for example EU) levels of governance. New structures have been created within central government to coordinate the increasing amount of policy work done at this level. Finally, the *style* of environmental regulation is considerably more transparent with greater public involvement. The most marked change is to be found in the regulation of public utilities such as energy and water, which are now regulated at arms length from government, by non-departmental public bodies.

However, the overall process of change has been evolutionary rather than revolutionary. Thus, if we look at the *content* of many policies, there is still a marked preference for the traditionally British approach of informal 'gentlemen's agreements' and non-quantified standards. Central government is still reluctant to set clear and legally binding targets other than those specifically required by EU or international legislation. Environmental taxes and voluntary agreements are beginning to appear (Jordan *et al.* 2005), but regulation still forms the bedrock of national policy. New departmental *structures* have been created (for example the fusion of the departments of transport and environment in 1997), but the extent of change should not be exaggerated. In relation to Richardson's (1982) schema, the *style* of British environmental policy is still overwhelmingly consensual and reactive, reflecting traditional patterns.

How much domestic change is Europeanization?

Not all of the changes in British policy are, of course, wholly or even partly associated with the EU's influence. Many are symptoms of the increasing maturity of the environment as a policy issue and a defined area of policy making. Of the 'domestic' drivers the most salient are, *inter alia*: the growing demand amongst the public demand for higher levels of environmental quality; pressure exerted by independent bodies (for example the Royal Commission on Environmental Pollution) and Parliamentary select committees; the activities of an increasingly large and sophisticated network of environmental pressure groups; the ideological preference (by and large maintained under Labour (Barry and Paterson 2004)) for market competition and the modernization of the state; and recent constitutional changes such as devolution, freedom of information legislation and, possibly, the creation of a supreme court on the US model. Meanwhile, the most important 'international' drivers are probably international agreements brokered in the UN, international bodies like the OECD and the mega international environmental conferences held in Stockholm (1972), Rio (1992) and Johannesburg (2002) (Seyfang and Jordan 2002). Together, these have helped to disseminate new ideas and concepts as well as more specific emission-reduction targets and timetables. Importantly, these drivers would almost certainly have destabilized the domestic environmental policy system in Britain irrespective of EU membership.

However, so many of the changes noted above are to be found in other comparable member states that there must be some EU involvement, if only an indirect and contingent one (Jordan and Liefferink 2004). One way to disentangle the EU drivers from the 'non EU' ones is to engage in some counterfactual analysis; that is, what might national environmental policy have looked like if Britain had not joined the EEC in 1973? Regardless of the EU, Britain would almost certainly have been forced to modernize its environmental policy by international pressures arising from continental Europe. However, the EU strengthened the arm of those ambitious states (like Germany, the Netherlands and Denmark) that set out to 'win' the regulatory competition to set EU environmental standards. If the EU had not existed, they would not have been able to exert nearly as much leverage over states such as Britain that had less environmentally ambitious priorities and their own, unique and relatively inward looking policy arrangements. Consequently, the pace and depth of domestic change in Britain would in all probability have been significantly less than that which has occurred since 1973. Crucially, any domestic change that occurred independently of the EU would almost certainly taken a different form to what we see today that is, far fewer unequivocal timetables, binding targets and explicit standards.

To conclude, therefore, the 'EU effect' is most clearly inscribed upon the content of national environmental policy. Its effect on national policy structures and policy styles has been heavily modulated by domestic factors, although the EU remains an important trigger of national action and a significant constraint upon the ability of national actors to pursue 'domestic' policy objectives.

Modes of Europeanization

In Chapter 2, it was suggested that Europeanization could adopt four distinct forms, depending upon the immediacy (direct or indirect?) and experience of change (voluntary or coercive?). On balance, it is probably more meaningful to allocate individual items of environmental policy into Table 2.1 (Chapter 2) than to try and allocate the whole sector to one or more cells. Having said that, Europeanization in this sector has gradually changed from being a predominantly externally imposed process (that is, coercive) to being much more voluntary in nature. This shift corresponds to the changing way in which Britain – defined broadly to include the lead department (the DoE), as well as British Members of the European Parliament, environmental and business pressure groups – engages with the EU environmental policy system. That is, the shift noted above from a fairly negative form policy of policy 'taking' from the EU to a much more proactive form of policy 'making' in Europe.

With hindsight, the British clung to the 'British approach' to environmental problem solving too doggedly, believing it was innately better than anything developed on the continent. Instead of selling its model (or 'approach') to the rest of the EU, Britain chose instead to dig in its heels and resist policy innovations proposed by other member states and the European Commission. Very little sustained effort was put into uploading policies to Brussels. Because of this, Britain suffered the fate of those that consistently download policy from the EU – namely mounting implementation problems, significant policy misfits and, eventually, painful political crises (Cowles *et al.* 2001: 8–9). Therefore, the outcome has been quite paradoxical: although EU membership was never originally pursued for environmental reasons, it has nevertheless transformed many aspects of national environmental policy, often in highly unexpected ways (Jordan 2002).

Prominent winners and losers

Who have been the main winners and losers to emerge from the Europeanization process? Thus far, Europeanization has created two main losers: national parliament (which struggles to audit policy making in Brussels) (Armstrong and Bulmer 1996: 275) and local level technocrats, who used to enjoy working in relatively closed professional policy communities away from the public gaze. In particular, Europeanization has greatly circumscribed their professional discretion and influence.

By contrast, Europeanization has undoubtedly altered and empowered the DoE. Through its engagement with EU policy making, the DoE has altered its *internal management*, its *tactics* and, most radical of all, its *identity and political interests*. Its bargaining power in Whitehall has grown. Ironically, the DoE initially set out to thwart Europeanization by forestalling European integration. It would have been a less environmental and a much less powerful department today had it succeeded in this endeavour (Jordan 2002).

Europeanization has also greatly empowered national environmental groups, offering them a higher authority to which they can now appeal (Lowe and Ward 1998: 295; Fairbrass, Chapter 9). In the 1980s, the Commission's Environment Directorate General actively courted these groups to legitimate enforcement actions arising from the growing misfit between EU and national policy. More radical groups such as Greenpeace and Friends of the Earth first used this new point of leverage in the late 1980s. More recently, less confrontational 'insider' groups such as the RSPB and the World Wide Fund for Nature (WWF) have successfully exploited EU nature conservation legislation (that is, the wild birds and habitats Directives) to challenge economic developments on or near protected sites in the courts (Fairbrass and Jordan 2002). Europeanization has also helped to make the standard setting process more transparent, by inserting fixed standards where administrative rules of thumb and gentlemen's agreements used to be the norm. Through the mechanism of Directives dealing, for example, with public access to information, environmental impact assessment and bathing water, the EU has also helped to produce and disseminate much more detailed environmental information to pressure groups and the public. In all these different respects, Europeanization has pushed Britain further and faster towards what Weale (1992) has termed 'new' and much more openly contested forms of environmental politics.

Conclusion: conflicting interpretations of Europeanization

At a very general level, it is possible to explain the Europeanization of British environmental policy in top-down terms. This would emphasize the determining influence of the deep-seated misfit between the model of environmental protection pushed by continental states and the Commission, and the one preferred by island member states such as Ireland and the UK. This misfit produced an underlying source of pressure on Britain to make its environmental protection system more like that of continental member states. The last thirty years could, on this view, be portrayed as one long struggle to overcome the 'first mover disadvantage' of having innovated earlier and differently to other EU states. The 'British approach' (that is the pre-commitment to externalize waste into the sea and the air through careful negotiation with business interests) was, in fact, doubly disadvantageous. Not only was it fundamentally different to continental models, but it could not easily be imposed on continental states via the EU because these states had similar legal systems and shared many policy problems through their strong geographical links.

While top-down models provide an intuitively appealing rationale for Europeanization in this sector, they do not explain everything. For example, some have argued that notions of 'fit' and 'misfit' are sometime inaccurately presented as though they can easily be read off from a 'snapshot' comparison of national and EU policy. In fact, 'fit' in this sector proved to be a constant and recursive process of interaction between many different sub-elements of 'policy' as well as activities at many different levels of governance (Dyson and Goetz 2003). That is, the flow of influence was not entirely or unremittingly top-down. Thus, European integration generated common policies that Europeanized national political systems, which in turn altered the domestic circumstances in which national actors formed their national preferences during subsequent rounds of policy making. The British state (led, of course, by the DoE), struggled to anticipate – let alone control – these processes and, in the end, was itself subtly transformed by them. Having, therefore, once been a reluctant 'taker' of policy determined in Brussels, the deep and politically painful Europeanization of national policy (Jordan 2002, 2003) has gradually forced Britain (and in particular the DoE) to invest more time and resources to positively 'shape' EU policy in its own image. This gradual, temporal shift and the associated interactions which recursively connected many different levels of governance, is difficult to reconcile with a simple top-down model, even though the basic misfit was the underlying trigger for change.

Second, the rather static misfit concept that lies at the heart of top-down models can easily fool the observer into thinking that EU and national policy are, to large extent, independent, and that the EU's influence is gradually making these separate national policies more similar over time. In the case of UK environmental policy, some have convincingly argued (Lowe and Ward 1998: 18–19) that the 'British approach' was never as coherent – or as logically set out – as it is described in section two of this chapter. They argue that it 'came to be defined in reaction to the incursions of EC environmental policy' (Lowe and Ward 1998: 18–19). They continue: in 'emphasizing Britain's distinctiveness . . . the differences with the Community's approach were stressed to the point of caricature, and a coherence and commitment was claimed for British practices and procedures – that was not entirely warranted' (Lowe and Ward 1998: 18–19). This suggests that the differences (that is, the misfit) between British and continental practices may not be as different as is sometimes claimed (that is, both are to an extent discursive constructions). If true, it also implies that – for a period at least – EU pressure exacerbated the differences between British and continental policy (that is, policy diverged, not converged).

These suggestions point to a third weakness in top-down approaches: they tend to overlook the many ways in which fits and misfits are *socially constructed* by different actors. These actors either (as in the case of the Commission) sought to recover ground lost at the negotiation stage or (as in the case of national pressure groups) adapted themselves to exploit the new political opportunities created by EU policy implementation. They did so by seizing the opportunities afforded by the formal site designation process under various biodiversity and water directives, and the public particip-ation provisions of the EIA Directive. More importantly, they bound all these activities together using a narrative that successfully portrayed Britain as '*The* Dirty Man of Europe'. Those adopting a constructivist perspective (for example Hajer 1995) have shown how successful this was in changing other actors' perceptions of the overall effectiveness of British environmental policy. So, while the misfit concept appears to work quite well in relation to environmental policy, analysts should not overlook the many ways in which social actors helped to realize misfits, which might otherwise have remained latent.

Notes

1. As this chapter is mostly concerned with events in England, and, to lesser extent, Scotland and Wales, I use the term 'Britain' rather than United Kingdom.
2. From 2001, the environment department became known as DEFRA – the Department for Environment, Food and Rural Affairs.

16
Regional Policy

Thomas Conzelmann

Introduction[1]

Regional policy is one of the areas covered by this book in which the impacts of European-level policy have been debated quite strongly in the past two decades. The principles of 'partnership' and 'programming' which feature prominently in the EU's structural policies have profoundly transformed the national–regional link in Britain (on local effects, see Marshall, Chapter 7). Burch and Gomez (Chapter 5) demonstrate how these principles were instrumental in galvanizing regional awareness in England and in advancing the more recent moves towards English regionalism. In a similar vein, the 'additionality' principle in EU structural policy has helped local authorities to challenge the funding regime that evolved under the Conservative government from the early 1980s onwards (Bache 1998, 1999).

While much of the attention during the 1990s focused on the Europeanization (or not) of political processes and territorial relations in Britain, other relevant facets have been neglected. In particular, there have been relatively few contributions on how regional policy activity at the European level has moulded the corresponding domestic regional policy instruments, such as the spatial coverage of regionally differentiated investment support, or the delineation of activities that are publicly funded in order to help restructuring 'old industrial' regions (for example recovering polluted areas, (re)building infrastructure or training jobless people). This seems odd, given that: (a) European level influences on the content of national regional policy are a primary concern in many other EU member states (Wishlade *et al.* 2003); and (b) the EU is relevant for domestic regional policy decisions both through its own regional funding activities and through the control it exerts (via its single market powers) of regional state aids. These topics are also highly relevant politically, since decisions on regional assisted area coverage and eligibility criteria for regional funding impact directly on the life chances of individuals living in affected regions. Thus, regional policy is one of the areas of British policy and politics reviewed in this book, where 'Europeaniz-ation' seems especially likely to be experienced by ordinary citizens in a very direct way.

Against this background, this chapter asks whether and to what extent membership of the EU has transformed both the instruments of regional policy in Britain,[2] and also the ways in which those instruments are used. This chapter starts by outlining in more detail the opportunities and constraints that both the EU's regional funding and the operation of regional state aid control by the Commission pose to domestic policy-makers. It continues with a brief discussion and critique of the concept of Europeaniz-ation. The remainder of the chapter is then devoted to an assessment of the 'Europeanization' of British regional policy. The discussion focuses primarily on changes in British regional policy from the early 1980s until 1997. This seems appropriate for two reasons. First, the mid-1980s was the period in which the EU's regional policy began to transmogrify from its roots as a mechanism of budgetary redistribution into a much more socially trans-forming instrument. This new autonomy manifested itself most clearly in a number of reforms introduced in 1988 (see below). Second, the fact that the Conservatives were in power during this period is important in that it helps to exclude one very obvious non-EU-related explanation of change in domestic policies (that is, change in domestic political leadership) from the analysis. It is, of course, important to ask whether a possible reorientation of policy instruments or of their political use during the period of Conservative government does extend into the period of Labour-led governments from 1997 onwards. To that end, more recent changes in British regional policy are also discussed. To contextualize the findings, illustrative comparisons are also made with developments in Germany (for a fuller discussion, see Conzelmann (2002)).

Regional policy in a multi-level polity

It is important to make clear at the outset the different ways in which EU regional policy may become important for its domestic counterparts. As mentioned above, EU regional policy is understood here to comprise both the field of regional funding policies of the EU as well as the control of regionally differentiated state aids by the Commission. In this section, each aspect is described in further detail.

Funding policy

In the period since 1975, EU regional policy has increasingly become a second layer of regional policy in the member states. In that year, a new European Regional Development Fund (ERDF) was installed alongside the already existing funds for vocational training (namely, the European

Social Fund – the ESF) and for the restructuring of agricultural economies (the Guidance Section of the European Agricultural Guarantee and Guidance Fund – the EAGGF). The basic objective of the early ERDF was to support the regional policies of member states. In practice, this meant that projects pursued by member states received financial backing from the EU without the Commission enjoying much influence over the way in which money was spent. Building on several experiments with giving the supranational layer a greater say, the crucial 1988 reform installed for the first time autonomous assisted areas of the ERDF (whereas formerly use of the ERDF was delimited to domestic assisted areas), and introduced a new management scheme that loosened the control of national governments over the use of resources. Funds were now disbursed through multi-annual programmes that included monies from the ERDF and other funds, and gave the Commission as well as regional and societal actors a say through the so-called 'partnership' principle (Bache 1998).

A further important development to be observed, which has occurred ever since the very first ERDF reform in 1979, is the increasing differentiation of the uses to which ERDF money can be put. While the ERDF (like more 'traditional' regional policy schemes; cf. Bachtler and Yuill 2001) up to the present date focuses on productive investment leading to the creation or maintenance of jobs and infrastructure development, there are virtually no restrictions on what counts as 'infrastructure' and 'industrial investment'. As explained on the Commission's regional policy website, 'all development areas are covered: transport, communication technologies, energy, the environment, research and innovation, social infrastructure, training, urban redevelopment and the conversion of industrial sites, rural development, the fishing industry, tourism and culture' (CEC 2005). This rather broad set of eligible funding areas is supported by the third ERDF priority of developing regional endogenous potentials, which was introduced in 1984 and mainly seeks to create a business environment that is conducive to the success of small and medium-sized enterprises (SMEs).

The broad eligibility criteria of the ERDF and the emergence of the EU's own assisted areas have no clear effect upon member state policy. In order to understand the reorienting effects of the structural funds on domestic policy, it is important to note that member states cannot access European funding unless they provide 'matching funds' from domestic sources. Member states are, in principle, free to decide from where to take these funds, but an obvious strategy is to 'couple' ERDF funding and domestic regional funds in an attempt to increase the effects of domestic regional policy. Thus, when EU and domestic instruments (assisted areas and eligibility criteria) are incongruent, the question arises whether one set of instruments should be adapted in order to link smoothly with the other. Second, due to their broad eligibility criteria and their integrated management structures, the EU structural funds are seen by many as relatively innovative means of helping disadvantaged regions and as an instrument for systematically organizing the exchange of best practices and policy transfers between individual levels of decision-making (Heinelt 1996; Tömmel 2002). Thus, there is also reason to consider the extent to which the development of policy instruments at domestic level has been influenced by 'learning' from the structural funds model. Finally, drawing down ERDF funding comes at a price – the Regional Policy Directorate of the Commission and subnational actors are suddenly given a legitimate say in how European funds and, by implication, the domestic matching monies are used by member states. The Commission is in a crucial position here, since it can unilaterally withhold the final approval of the spending plans drawn up by the member states. During the 1990s, it did sometimes use this competence to make strict demands regarding the substance of policy or the process of consulting with subnational actors (Hooghe and Keating 1994; McCarthy and Burch 1994; Conzelmann 2002).

Control of regional state aids

Since regional aid policies often make heavy use of direct subsidies to firms, they raise the question of compatibility with the notion of a single European market. Although the treaty allows member governments to provide state aids when they are used for regional policy purposes, the ultimate decision on this remains with the Commission. Thus, some aspects of member state regional policies may be declared irreconcilable with single market rules, which makes the adaptation of domestic policy obligatory.

Supported by the rise of the cohesion objective in the context of the Single Market Programme and a number of European Court of Justice (ECJ) rulings during the 1980s, the relevant Commission directorate (DG Competition) has increasingly taken intra-Community cohesion as its point of reference in making judgements; that is, it has used European, and not national, criteria in determining whether state aids may be given for regional policy reasons (see Conzelmann 2002: 91–101; Wishlade, Yuill and Méndez 2003: 11–12). Due to the inherent difficulties in determining the competition-distorting effects of specific regional policy schemes, the Commission has resorted to the size of assisted areas and the aid intensities available therein as rough proxies for assessing deleterious effects of national regional policies on intra-EU cohesion. In wealthier member states, it has pressed for the reduction of aid intensity and for a smaller area coverage of national regional funding (Cini and McGowan 1998: 148; Wishlade, Yuill and Méndez 2003). Consequently, these states have had to accept that they may be unable to help regions they consider to be in need of support if, according to Community criteria, these regions are too wealthy to justify domestic regional aid.

There are a number of exemptions and loopholes within the EU's regional state aid regime that allow governments to pursue regional policy measures

even if the Commission has disapproved of certain types of aid or the inclusion of a particular region in the assisted areas' maps. One is the so-called
de minimis rule, which generally tolerates smaller state aid (grants of not
more than 100,000 euros over three years) no matter whether they take
place within or outside of the national regional aid areas. Another important
escape route are 'horizontal' (that is, not spatially targeted) state aid schemes.
Examples are aids to SMEs, for research and development and for environmental improvements. Although higher rates are available in assisted areas,
horizontal aids are principally permitted in the whole territory of the EU.
This is particularly true for aid to SMEs, where outside of domestically assisted
areas the aid intensity can be as high as 15 per cent of the total investment
costs.

Contested governance in regional policy

Both state aid control and the regional funding policy of the EU take
the policy objective of community-wide cohesion and the EU territory as
their starting points. The operating assumption is that the EU's territory
can be understood as a single economic space within which individual
regions are faced with a permanent locational competition. At the same
time, the Commission has been able to develop relatively autonomous
policy paradigms that are rooted in the notion of the European space as
the relevant reference point for judging the legitimacy of national regional
policy initiatives. The resulting situation is one where European eligibility criteria and policy paradigms increasingly contest those institutionalized in member state regional policies. Both the salience of regional
problems ('Is the problem severe enough to justify public intervention?') and
policy conceptions ('Which measures constitute an appropriate response to
perceived policy problems and which actors should legitimately take part in
solving the problem?') are subject to this contestation. (Conzelmann 2002:
101–108).

In principle, national policy-makers have three options to react to EU
decisions and initiatives, namely (1) adaptation, (2) evasion and (3) resistance. If one takes the broad eligibility criteria of the ERDF as an example,
national regional policy-makers may either *adapt* national criteria to the EU
ones in order to increase the compatibility between the two and to facilitate the flow of funding into domestic regional policy (rationalist variant)
or to improve the perceived quality of policy (learning variant). Under
the condition of incongruence of European and domestic policy, a second
alternative is to take the matching domestic funds from a broader range of
funding programmes than just 'traditional' regional policy. While such a
move would not necessitate an adaptation of regional policy instruments,
it would diminish their relative importance vis-à-vis other instruments and
would constitute a potential threat to government branches in charge of
'traditional' regional policy instruments (*evasion*). A third option would be

resistance, that is, to retain as much policy autonomy as possible. An example would be tough negotiation over ERDF programmes in order to push through domestic policy priorities and to reduce incongruence by rolling back the EU influence. Renouncing part or the whole of the ERDF money (if at all feasible under the conditions of strained public finances) would be the most extreme form of this strategy.

Similar scenarios may be developed for the case of state aid control. Although (coercive) *adaptation* (that is, a Commission-imposed decrease in assisted area coverage and aid intensity) seems to be a likely outcome in wealthier member states, these may to some extent resist and/or evade the directives from Brussels. As concerns *evasion,* one possible strategy would be to scale down regional policy instruments that are viewed critically by Brussels and expand others that are less vulnerable by state aid control (for example to step up SME support to the detriment of large investment support). Moreover, it is easy to overestimate the powers of the Brussels bureaucracy vis-à-vis the member states. While experience shows that the prospects of successfully challenging a Commission decision at the ECJ are bleak, decisions by the Commission are usually preceded by extended negotiations between Brussels and the national capital. During these nego- tiations, the member state concerned will be able to *resist* at least to some of the demands of DG Competition; the reasons being the obligation of the Commission to consult member states and to listen to their arguments (Articles 87 and 88 TEC), the limited control capacities of the Commission and, finally, the necessity for the Competition Commissioner to get approval for the interdiction of state aid measures from their colleagues (Conzelmann 2002: 94). Thus, both sides are locked into a negotiation system that puts a premium on consensus and coordination between the domestic and the European level. As a consequence, member states increasingly pre-negotiate assisted areas' maps or amendments to regional policy instruments with Commission staff, thus giving DG Competition a relatively influential role in shaping domestic policy decisions (Smith 1996; Wishlade *et al.* 2003).

A case of Europeanization?

To what extent are these policy dynamics constitutive of 'Europeanization'? According to the editors of this book, Europeanization denotes:

> *the reorientation or reshaping of politics in the domestic arena in ways that reflect policies, practices and preferences advanced through the EU system of governance.*

The definition is useful in that it clearly delineates the 'subject' of Europeanization (what is Europeanized?) and also suggests a clear causal mechanism through which Europeanization occurs. It also thankfully avoids the rigidities implied by the prominent 'goodness of fit' discourse

(Risse *et al.* 2001), which seems to work best where domestic adaptation is a reaction to integration by EU law. As shown above, both the EU's regional funding regime and the operation of regional state aid control do not add up to a prescriptive EU policy model, against which the 'goodness' or 'badness' of fit' could be gauged. In the field of regional funding, the policy consists of a number of general procedural rules to be followed during the implementation of regional policy schemes that are co-funded by the ERDF. The substantive content of the policy emerges only after the Commission has agreed with national and regional administrations in individual member states on how EU funds are to be spent. Similarly, the field of regional state aid control consists of a number of general treaty paragraphs and a universe of principles and decisions developed by the Commission in order to assess funding policies of individual member states. The effect of that policy is to exclude certain options from the range of national policy choices after case-by-case negotiations with the Commission, but not to impose a certain more or less prescriptive policy model upon the member states. Hence, at first blush, the understanding of Europeanization advanced by the editors does appear to apply to the field of regional policy due to its focus on initiatives and decisions advanced through the EU system of governance rather than on policy prescription.

The focus of this book is on the domestic effects of EU membership, whether they be top-down or interactive. Simple top-down models posit two distinct sets of actors on the European and the domestic level, with the latter taking into account the policies, preferences and practices of the former and then reacting accordingly. Europeanization, therefore, is a phenomenon that is caused by a set of constraints and opportunities posed by initiatives and decisions of the European level actors. A critique of this perspective is not only that the vectors of influence may also run from the domestic to the European level ('uploading'), but, even more important, that an analytical separation of 'European' and 'domestic' actors is unable to properly account for the multi-level character of the European polity in regional policy (see below). I return to this argument in the conclusion.

The Europeanization of British regional policy

The 1970s

Regional policy has a long and chequered history in Britain (see Damesick 1987; Taylor and Wren 1997). Probably the most radical change happened in 1979, when – after some initial reforms during the Callaghan years – the new Conservative government of Margaret Thatcher radically broke with the post-war consensus that regional policy could be used to mobilize underused resources and bring about a more sensible distribution of economic activity across the country. The period of large and automatically released government grants for investment in Britain's disadvantaged regions came to an end and gave way to selective and much smaller forms of support. Ideas of a 'passive' regional policy (that is, solving the problem of regional unemployment through migration) became more influential, while the DTI in a 1983 White Paper on regional industrial policy argued that:

> expenditure on regional measures imposes a burden on taxpayers throughout the country... In addition, industrial development controls... and regional incentives may have encouraged investment in locations that were not the best for the companies: the national economy may have suffered in consequence. (DTI 1983: para. 8)

These new policies sat somewhat uneasily with the increasing emphasis on regional policies at the European level. One of the main triggers for the creation of the ERDF had been the need to redistribute European monies to Britain in order to compensate for its disadvantageous position under the Common Agricultural Policy. In consequence, although the government did not firmly believe in the value of regional policies as such, the objective of continued accessibility of EU funds necessitated the retention of some forms of regional policy.

The 1980s

In that context, it became important that from 1984, the ERDF used percentage ranges instead of fixed quotas in order to determine the distribution of resources among the member states (see Bache 1998: 58–62). In order to reach the upper limit of funds that could be given to any one member state, it became important for policy makers to avail themselves of a relatively large and differentiated pool of projects that could qualify for co-funding from the ERDF. A set of reforms of British regional policy in 1984 consequently expanded the assisted area coverage of British regional policy (from 27.5 to 36.4 per cent of the UK population) in order to increase the pool of projects that could be used as match funding for the ERDF. At the same time, aid intensity was drastically reduced for many assisted regions while high intensities were still available in the most deprived regions. This move reflected the outcome of consultations in the aftermath of the 1983 White Paper (DTI 1983), during which 'views on overall coverage tended to favour a tightly drawn inner tier in order to focus resources on the areas of greatest need coupled with the widest possible outer tier to facilitate access to ERDF aid' (DTI 1984: para. 12). At the same time, the so-called 'Regional Development Grant' (RDG), one of the most important regional policy instruments at the time, was reformed. The changes meant that a higher premium was put on job-related investment and that support for industrial replacement investment was terminated. While the first part of this reform helped the RDG to qualify for monies from the ERDF, the latter part happened in reaction to a Commission complaint about the automatic and not job-related nature of the RDG (see Conzelmann 2002: 207–10 for an extended discussion).

Post 1988

After 1988, the underlying logic of policy changed due to a number of factors. The first important trigger was the 1988 reform of the EU structural funds mentioned above. The decision to introduce autonomous assisted areas and eligibility criteria for the ERDF (hence, to partly 'decouple' the ERDF from national regional policies) meant that one of the Britain's rationales for retaining national regional policies vanished. Although matching funds from national coffers were still obligatory, they did not need to stem from regional policy instruments *per se*, but could instead come from 'horizontal' (that is, not regionally differentiated) schemes. Second, 1988 brought the end for the RDG as the longest standing instrument of regional policy in Britain, while the importance of Regional Selective Assistance (RSA) as the other pillar of regional industrial policy in Britain was greatly enhanced. In practice, RSA (which was eventually terminated in 2004) was focused mainly on larger-scale investment by internationally mobile capital, although it also offered some support for SME activities. Because the use of ERDF resources for supporting such forms of regional policy was (and is) viewed critically both by the Commission and by Whitehall, the importance of RSA as a source of matching funds for European monies began to decline, while more ERDF and other structural funds monies were diverted into the second branch of British regional policy, the so-called 'regional regeneration policy' (see Temple 1994; RPC 1996 and below). At the same time, maybe *the* most important rationale for regional industrial policy became the attraction of inward investment to Britain (Armstrong 2001). Although no conclusive assessments of this have been made, it seems that the continued existence of some form of regional industrial policy was motivated at least in part by the desire to maintain a competitive subsidy regime in Britain. As explained by a high-ranking former DTI official, 'but for the existence of other European countries' ability to attract industry, probably the British Government would not have had a regional industrial policy' (interview with the author, March 1998). In a similar vein, the British government argued in a 1995 White Paper that 'the Government will continue to press the European Commission to limit subsidies to prevent competitive bidding for internationally mobile projects. Where it has been essential, Regional Selective Assistance has been made available . . . to secure projects' (DTI 1995: para. 11).

Ironically, then, the EU's state aid regime may have served not to curb but to maintain a certain level of regional industrial policy in Britain during the 1990s. Within the parameters set by Brussels, the British government sought to use regional industrial policy mainly for national objectives. One indication of the importance of the inward investment (as opposed to regional development) rationale for British regional industrial policy was the 1993 reform of the RSA area map. This map only marginally reduced the assisted area coverage, but shifted assisted areas from the north of England and Scotland to the south of England and some inner London areas. *The Guardian* (26 June 1992: 2) had strong claims when it complained that 'Heseltine [had] move[d] money to Tory-voting regions' immediately after the 1992 general election. However, it is important to note that this move was consequent on the desire of the British government to provide inward investment aid in economically more feasible locations. It was also encouraged to do this by a changing Commission practice concerning the approval of member state regional aid maps. In the early 1990s, the Commission increasingly began to allow member states more flexibility in selecting regions for state aid purposes according to domestic criteria, as long as the overall coverage remained within a certain ceiling and some regional economic rationale could be given for the delineation exercise. This approach was later (in 1998) formalized in a communication of the Commission to the member states, but had been established Commission practice during the years before (Wishlade *et al.* 2003: 15–18).

DG Competition and Whitehall: an increasingly uneasy relationship

While overall relations between the British government and DG Competition were relatively untroubled during the 1990s, there were a number of minor tussles. One case in point was the rather abrupt end of the Thatcherite experiment of so-called Enterprise Zones under John Major. Within Enterprise Zones, a very generous funding and taxing regime operated for a certain span of time. These zones were viewed unfavourably in Brussels, since the total value of state aid (expressed as a grant equivalent of the different benefits available) in the zones was almost impossible to calculate. While the government claimed that the reason for ending the zones in 1992 was the difficulty in getting new zones approved by Brussels due to their lack of aid transparency, the government itself viewed the instrument critically due to its high costs and relatively low effectiveness in creating new jobs. Thus, DG Competition served more as a scapegoat rather than being the crucial trigger for elimination of the scheme (see Conzelmann (2002: 236–39) for a thorough discussion). Generally speaking, if there were instances of contention between Whitehall and DG Competition during the 1990s, the debate related more to 'public problems rather than real problems, because . . . the Conservative Government in most cases has been quite happy to be fairly tough [on state aid]' (DTI official, interview with the author, March 1998).

A clear example of divergent interests, however, was the July 2000 exercise in redrawing the assisted areas' map in Britain. With Eastern enlargement of the EU looming, the Commission imposed a cutback of RSA areas from around 35 per cent down to 30.7 per cent of the UK population. This was the first time that the EU-imposed discipline on regional state aids could be felt in Britain. Partly in anticipation of this move (but also in connection with the new Labour Government's emphasis on strengthening regional policy), the DTI had introduced a new regional policy scheme called 'Enterprise Grants' (EGs) in 1998. These are targeted at SMEs and, although available within RSA assisted areas as well, are chiefly intended to 'soften the blow a little for some of the areas losing their RSA eligibility' (Armstrong 2001: 252). The introduction of EGs and the accompanying creation of a new category of assisted areas ('Tier 3' areas in which only SME aid is available) can be interpreted as a strategy of bowing to EU pressures concerning assisted area coverage while at the same time creatively using the loopholes that are left by the EU's regional state aid regime. As explained above, support for SMEs is deemed acceptable under the Commission's state aid rules, but at the same time constitutes a shift away from traditional focal points of regional industrial policy. A similar development of Commission-imposed decreasing assisted area coverage and increasing use of SME support as a consequence can be observed in Germany (Conzelmann 2005a).

A parallel regional policy

As mentioned above, there is a second branch of regional policy in Britain, namely regional regeneration policy, which became the principal source of matching funds for the ERDF post 1988. It aims at the renewal of inner city areas, improvements of infrastructure, cleaning-up of the environment and helping SMEs to thrive. The main instrument of regional regeneration policy in England; and one of the most important sources of ERDF matching funds, is the Single Regeneration Budget (SRB). The instrument was introduced in 1994/95. As its name suggests, it is little more than a budget: that is, no strings are attached as concerns territorial or substantial eligibility criteria, but it does follow rather strict procedural rules. This is partly due to the fact that at the time of its inception, the SRB was the result of merging a host of smaller instruments with largely different eligibility criteria into one budget, and partly due to an increasing dissatisfaction within the Department of the Environment (DoE) with formal eligibility criteria (interviews with the author at DoE, February 1998).

In consequence, the basic approach of the SRB was to let subnational partnerships come up with whatever project they considered worthwhile pursuing and then letting the government decide whether to make assistance available. From the beginning, local authorities criticized the criteria for being opaque. Moreover, there was criticism during the early years of the instrument that it was rather the 'professionally packaged and polished' bids that stood the best chance of profiting from the budget (as opposed to less polished bids coming from areas of genuine need) and that the bidding process entailed a lot of wasteful competition (see RPC 1996: 52–54, quote on p. 53). The government's approach invited this critique by initially specifying only very roughly that bids should demonstrate their potential for genuine regeneration in areas of need, and should lever in monies from sources outside the SRB. Subsequently, SRB objectives became more detailed. Successful SRB projects must now demonstrate that they contribute, for example, to improving employment prospects, address social exclusion or promote sustainable regeneration and growth in local economies (ODPM 2005a).

In the context of the present discussion, it is important to note that the ERDF (and the other structural funds) tends to play a rather important role for SRB projects. First, there was (and is, up to the present date) an explicit stipulation by the government that bids for assistance should be designed in a way to attract maximum European funding (ODPM 2005b: paras 1.6.7. and 1.6.12). Second, SRB-funded partnerships are asked to relate their proposals to strategic development plans for their individual regions, which did not really exist outside the area of EU structural funding during the 1990s. Third, it has been argued that partnerships that have developed within EU-assisted regions are both more experienced in drawing up plans that stand a good chance of receiving SRB funds and are at the same time more capable of managing large-scale regeneration projects in an appropriate manner (House of Commons 1995, paras 64–65). In sum, not only has the SRB become the main co-financing source for ERDF money in England; there are also a number of indications that its use was strongly influenced by the European funding regime during the 1990s (Conzelmann 2002: 222–25).

The net result of the developments discussed above was the emergence of a two-tier regional policy in Britain during the 1990s. On the one side, there were regional regeneration activities that obtained their spatial dimension partly through government decisions, but inevitably also through the designation of eligible areas for ERDF purposes. On the other side, regional industrial policy continued within domestic assisted areas with little European influence apart from the increasing constraints imposed by EU state aid control. Due to the development of this two-tier regional policy, there was no longer such a strong need to make the domestic assisted areas and the ERDF areas congruent. Consequently, more than 40 per cent of the UK population who currently live in an 'Objective 2' area designated for ERDF purposes are not part of an RSA area. Again, matters will change in the foreseeable future, as the Commission has begun to put much more emphasis on the congruence of ERDF areas and the nationally assisted areas (Wishlade *et al.* 2003: 17–20; European Commission 2004). If a greater congruence would be achieved from 2006 onwards, this would mean that the instruments used as matching funds for the ERDF, in particular the SRB, may become targeted on the areas where RSA also is available. This would leave behind the ability of the SRB to act as a spatial complement to the instruments of regional industrial policy.

Conclusions

The situation of contested governance in regional policy has resulted in characteristic forms of 'Europeanization' appearing in the area of regional policy. Coming back to the three scenarios of adaptation, evasion and resistance mentioned above, we find a complex mixture of all three. It is clear that *adaptation* to European prerogatives was the most common strategy in Britain during the 1990s. This can be explained by the priority of Whitehall to tap the ERDF funds as fully as possible rather than to preserve the conceptual integrity of policy (as happened in Germany, see Conzelmann (2005a)). Instances of policy adaptation can be found in the 1984 reforms, but also in the high degree of policy flexibility and the invitation to adjust SRB-funded regeneration strategies to places and activities where European funding is available.

The most significant effect of the presence of the ERDF in Britain has been the emergence of an EU-supported regional policy that runs in parallel with established domestic policies rather than transforming them. This process has enhanced the role of regional regeneration policy and has led to a relatively strong focus of regional industrial policy on inward investment – a priority that, as a matter of principle, is not co-funded by the EU instruments. Thus, the EU's most prominent effect is not so much to change national policy instruments, but rather to affect their application and relative significance (as is the case of the RSA). It is important to note that this result is mainly caused by the lesser degree of 'coupling' between European and domestic policy instruments that emerged after the crucial 1988 reform of the structural funds. The reform made it possible to operate a European regional policy in the EU member states with very little direct relation to traditional forms of regional policy (that is, large-scale infrastructure and investment support in peripheral or otherwise disadvantaged regions; cf. Bachtler and Yuill 2001). If national governments (as in Germany) insisted on a tight link between European funding and traditional domestic regional policy, conflicts over funding priorities and the congruence between European and domestic assisted areas became much more intense (Conzelmann 2002: 146–59). This did not happen in Britain due to the more adaptive approach of the Conservative government and also its lesser belief in the merits of regional policy. A further reason why such perturbations could not be observed in Britain is the peculiar institutional structure of its political system. During the 1980s, Conservative governments were able to effectively insulate national policy making from any regional or local influences.

Evasion has become a more common strategy recently due to the mounting pressure of DG Competition on British assisted area coverage. While during the 1990s the European state aid regime did not really serve as a constraint, but rather as an incentive to retain some form of regionally differentiated subvention of industry, things have changed with the advent of the Blair government and the impact of Eastern enlargement. Much as in Germany (cf. Conzelmann 2005a), the new British government reacted with a strategy of introducing new regional policy schemes (the EGs) and a new third tier of assisted areas that allow an active form of regional policy, but are less thorny from a competition policy point of view. It may well be that what can be observed here are the future contours of a 'Europeanized' regional policy. Recent Commission thinking (CEC 2004b) indicates that in the future assisted area coverage for RSA could go down to less than 10 per cent of the UK population in order to compensate for Eastern enlargement (Wishlade 2004: 20). Should these plans materialize, only a few areas of the UK territory would still qualify as national assisted areas under EU rules. For all others, regional policy would be possible only in the less significant form of small-scale 'horizontal' aid (Conzelmann 2005b).

Resistance is to be observed mainly in relation to procedural issues, for example the implementation of the partnership and additionality principles mentioned above. However, it can also be observed in the 1990s practice of 'top slicing' a certain amount of ERDF monies and distributing them not according to need or European priorities but through a competitive 'challenge' process (Hoppe and Voelzkow 2001: 203–206). Other than in Germany, resistance has not been very prominent in the state-aid field until recently. Although European state aid policies have effectively constrained policy makers (as in the case of EZs and in the 1984 changes to the RDG), these requirements were rather welcomed by Whitehall officials: either because Brussels could be used as a scapegoat for terminating a politically prestigious, but expensive and ineffective, instrument (the EZs), or because Whitehall and DG Competition thinking largely went into the same direction (the RDG case). Thus, up to 2000, the constraints of state aid control did not really bite due to the comparatively unfavourable economic situation of Britain during the 1980s and early 1990s and the largely market-liberal policies of the Conservative Government. The first real point of contention that emerged between Brussels and Whitehall was the 2000 reduction of assisted area coverage against the background of imminent EU enlargement. As pointed out above, this struggle is likely to continue into the future (cf. HM Treasury, DTI and ODPM 2003: paras 3.17–3.23).

While the discussion on the three strategies of adaptation, resistance and evasion may evoke the impression of unswerving domestic policy autonomy under the conditions of European integration, they should rather be seen as forms of strategic reorientation of policy under changing circumstances. Europeanization of domestic regional policies is the result of an inter-active and iterative process, characterized by the legitimate participation of additional (European or domestic) actors in domestic policy making. Once the national governments decide to tap European resources, actors at the domestic level have to subject the use of ERDF *and* domestic monies to decisions taken in a cross-level negotiation system comprised of European, national and subnational actors. The existence of alternative policy paradigms and eligibility criteria as institutionalized in the European funds henceforth cannot be simply ignored, in particular since the Commission through its power to co-decide on the use of the funds has a unique veto potential. In addition, the broad eligibility criteria of the ERDF and the partnership principle may trigger demands from actors that are not typically part of decisions on regional policy to influence the content and/or the implementation of regional policy schemes in order to receive funding for own priorities. At the same time, DG Competition uses EU rather than domestic criteria in assessing the legitimacy of domestic regional policy initiatives, thus opening up a second conduit through which 'Europe' becomes relevant for domestic policy making. As in the case of funding policy, the Commission has become an important actor in domestic policy making in its own right (for example by means of extended consultations with national officials *prior* to changes in domestic instruments). In addition, the presence of the European state aid regime has been advantageous for those actors at the domestic level that view more traditional forms of regional policy critically, thus dynamizing domestic policy conflicts and advancing certain policy options to the disadvantage of others.

In consequence, although formally there still exists a 'domestic policy' and a 'domestic arena' of policy making, these are more and more permeated (and not just constrained or influenced) by European actors and European policies. The field of regional policy is inescapably multi-level and requires a 'second generation' understanding of Europeanization (as discussed by the editors in Chapter 2). A distinctive feature both in Britain and in Germany is that policy contestation happens less among the 'European' and 'domestic' levels, but rather among different actor networks that span these levels and that are organized around competing policy paradigms. The two principal points of contention between them are whether the national or the EU space should be the legitimate point of reference in making decisions on eligibility for regional funding; and the extent to which and in what form public money should be spent in order to help disadvantaged regions thrive.

Notes

1. I am indebted to Brigid Laffan, Randall Smith and the two editors of this volume for useful comments on earlier versions of this chapter.
2. I do not focus on Northern Ireland due to the largely different regional funding regime operating there.

Part V
Comparative Conclusions

17

The Europeanization of British Politics

Ian Bache and Andrew Jordan

Introduction

In our opening chapter, we surveyed Britain's relationship with the EU since the Treaty of Rome, and highlighted some of the popular characterizations of Britain as a 'reluctant', 'semi-detached' or 'awkward' partner in Europe. We also noted an imbalance in the literature on the broad topic of 'Britain and Europe'. It tends either to look at the behaviour of Britain *in* Europe, or to treat British politics and policy making as processes in which the EU is a supranational body, disconnected from daily life in Westminster and Whitehall. Conspicuously missing from the existing literature is systematic analysis of the deepening interconnections between political processes at the national and EU levels. Our focus on the Europeanization of British politics brings these interconnections to the fore.

In Chapter 2, we surveyed the existing literature on Europeanization for analytical tools that could help us to understand better the interconnections between Britain and the EU. We concluded that there are still neither clear definitions nor theories that are fully agreed upon, and that the field of enquiry remains inchoate. We then identified a number of uses of the term 'Europeanization', before explaining why our empirical focus would be primarily on the domestic effects of EU membership. In doing so, we outlined a straightforward definition of Europeanization as 'the reorientation or reshaping of politics in the domestic arena in ways that reflect policies, practices, and preferences of European-level actors advanced through the EU system of governance'.

We highlighted the EU mechanisms likely to promote domestic change, and identified a range of possible outcomes, from transformation to retrenchment. We also described a number of ways in which the impact of the EU might be measured and disentangled from other possible influences, both domestic and international. Having highlighted these various definitions, mechanisms and taxonomies, we then asked our authors to reflect on their utility for their case studies.

To facilitate comparison with other country studies, we divided our contributions according to the categories of polity, politics and policy. In examining their cases we encouraged contributors to use our definition of Europeanization, alongside and in comparison with others where appropriate, but in doing so to focus on a common set of questions. Our aim here was to stimulate a discussion of the core themes, issues and effects that might not have been quite as obvious had they all used different analytical frameworks. We re-state the common set of questions here:

- What has been Europeanized and to what extent?
- When has Europeanization occurred and in what sequence?
- How and why has Europeanization occurred, and via what EU-level mechanism?
- Were there winners and losers through Europeanization?
- What factors explain the domestic response to Europeanization pressures and how should the process be characterized?
- Has Europeanization had any other important long-term effects?

Our starting point for analyzing the empirical contributions is to draw comparisons across the three dimensions – polity, politics and policy – and to assess how this matches with received wisdom.

The remainder of this chapter is structured as follows. In the next section, we assess the relative degree of Europeanization across our three domains of polity, politics and policy, and compare our findings with existing scholarship. In section three, we seek answers to the six questions outlined above to gain a more complete and detailed understanding of the Europeanization process. In section four we reflect on the significance of our findings for existing research on Britain's relationship with the EU and, specifically, consider the degree of continuity and change under the New Labour government since 1997. In light of this, we assess how far Britain is still an 'awkward partner' in the EU. Finally, we reflect on how our findings compare with other studies of Europeanization and also on the value of adopting a Europeanization lens in our study.

The Europeanization of British polity, politics and policy

In surveying the existing research, we highlighted the emerging consensus that Europeanization was more marked in the policy domain than in relation to polity or politics. In their study of Germany, Dyson and Goetz (2003: 386) identified a contrast between 'progressively Europeanized public policies, a semi-Europeanized polity, and a largely non-Europeanized politics'. How does this compare with the British findings?

Polity

Our first major finding is evidence of a higher degree of the Europeaniza-tion of the British *polity* than the existing literature would suggest. In all the chapters covered in Part II of this book, there were significant institu-tional changes that could be traced back to the EU's system of governance, whether it be directly or indirectly. A key feature here is the gradual and incremental process of change: what Bulmer and Burch term a 'quiet revolu-tion' in the way in which Whitehall manages Britain's formal input to and representation in EU institutions. This change encompasses formal structures, such as offices and machinery of government, and less-tangible aspects such as opportunity structures and organizational values. However, this does not imply that Whitehall is structured or operates in the same manner as the governments in the other 24 member states. On the contrary, Bulmer and Burch found an attitude of 'Europeanization yes, but on our terms'.

Within Whitehall, the Foreign and Commonwealth Office (FCO) has responded by creating new high-level co-ordinating posts, adapting its struc-ture to a more functional format and diverting more of its human resources to interfacing with the EU. More subtly, the FCO has been forced to redefine its role, from gatekeeper of the lines of communication between Whitehall and Brussels, to what Allen and Oliver refer to as an 'interested department' operating in an ever-widening network of actors who feel that they have a stake in foreign policy making.

Beyond Whitehall, distinct EU effects can be detected in the Scottish institutions, the English regions and local governance. In the first of these, Smith also identifies changes to departmental structures, working practices and working cultures, which he claims is evidence of administrative 'fusion' between EU and Scottish administrative practices. While Burch and Gomez found variation in effects across the English regions, they also suggest that the EU has been central to the emergence and development of the regional tier of governance. Indeed, they go so far as to claim that 'EU initiatives created the foundations of modern English regionalism.' At a more local level, Adam Marshall identifies wide-ranging EU effects on many aspects of local governance, including ways of working and influencing others, finan-cing regional development activities and dealing with local environmental problems. Moreover, the EU's effects extend beyond the formal sphere of local government, to include the many other actors involved in delivering services, such as voluntary and community groups.

Politics

The Europeanization of the *politics* dimension was found to be more variable, but discernible. Geddes argues that, as a political issue, the EU has affected all the major parties, none more so than the Conservatives. However, the

EU's effect has not corresponded to the formal top-down model of Europeanization, where a preferred model of domestic politics descends downwards from Brussels and puts adaptational pressure on – in this case – the party political system or the internal organization of parties. Rather, the EU's effects are of an indirect or second-order nature, in that EU membership has challenged established notions of the nation, state and sovereign authority within British political debate. These have, in turn, led all the parties to re-examine how they understand these ideas and how they communicate their positions on them to the broader public. More broadly, while there is no clear EU template of party competition or political organization 'coming down' from Brussels, the existence of the EU as a new centre of power for British political actors has challenged the traditional two-dimensional space of British party politics based on socio-economic class and left-right terminology with the more complex multidimensional European political space in which territorial, institutional and socio-economic issues mesh together in complex multi-level interactions. The emergence of a new political party (UKIP) is the main *direct* consequence of EU membership. Otherwise, the Europeanization of political parties has been indirect and complex, but significant.

In the case of the three other types of political actor covered in Part III of the book – namely, organized interests, trade unions and third sector bodies – there has been more straightforward and direct Europeanization. Many organizations, particularly sub-national ones, have voluntarily reoriented at least a part of their activities towards the EU. In most cases, this has also led to a reshaping of organizations to allow them to make more effective representations at the EU level or to tap into EU sources of funding. The variations in the nature and extent of Europeanization among such organizations are only understood through the detailed bottom-up research designs used by our respective contributors. Fairbrass, for example, explains the different degrees of reorientation and reshaping that have occurred within business and environmental groups by relating them to the evolving structure of incentives and political opportunities provided at the EU level compared to those at the domestic level. She finds that organizations were largely instrumental in their choice of targets and the routes they followed to hit them most effectively.

In his chapter on trade unions, van der Maas identifies how what would appear to be 'rational' organizational responses to the changing structure of incentives and opportunities brought by EU membership, are actually constrained by internal organizational structures, internal politics, and the political values and ideologies of key individuals. Specifically, in the case of the TGWU the constraints placed by established organizational procedures and the political-ideological 'take' on European integration prevented it from taking advantage of EU opportunities in the same way as did the GMB, whose pro-European leadership was less encumbered by organizational constraints on its actions. Thus, while there has been direct Europeanization of some trade union activity, variation between unions shows the degree of voluntarism in this process.

Chapman also emphasizes the importance of various institutional factors, specifically those internal to particular organizations, both in terms of their political culture and their capacity for action (for example staff resources, skills and so on). She sees such factors as crucial to understanding the degree of Europeanization in third sector voluntary and community groups. Although she could not find a clear and constraining EU model of third sector activities, there is undeniably a coherent EU approach to involving third sector bodies – expressed in white papers and communications – which has a direct effect on the activities of third sector groups. Chapman found clear evidence of third sector organizations being mobilized in response to EU policies, and in some instances being created where none existed previously. Europeanization, therefore, corresponds more to the 'framing' (Knill and Lehmkuhl 1999) or 'facilitated' (Bulmer and Radaelli 2005) forms described in Chapter 2, than to classical top-down models of Europeanization.

Policy

As with the polity dimension, our findings on policy do not sit easily with the standard findings on the degree of Europeanization in this domain. Even where there is superficially a strong EU policy-competence in an area, this does not equate straightforwardly with Europeanization in relation to the reorientation or reshaping of policies in the domestic arena. The effects, in short, are much more nuanced. There is a spectrum of Europeanization here that is approximately equal to the extent of EU competence, but only approximately.

If we start with environment policy, which is the probably the most Europeanized of the five policy areas covered, we find that some aspects of British policy have been deeply transformed by the EU's growing involvement; but not all of them have. So, while the content of national policy has been challenged, the style and structures of national policy have remained relatively resilient to the EU's incursions. The overall pattern is partly accounted for by changes in the nature of EU policies flowing down from Brussels, but also by the rhythm of international policy making and by the growing willingness (post-1987) of the British environment department to proactively shape Europeanization by uploading policy ideas to Brussels. Jordan concludes that British environmental policy would have evolved significantly regardless of the EU's involvement, but that EU membership directly influenced the shape and form it has adopted.

In the area of competition policy, Cini detects a 'voluntaristic embracing of [an] EU model', which on the face of it is quite surprising given that a free, open, integrated European market is very much the EU's *raison d'etre*. An EU model long pre-existed the major change in national legislation in

1998: however, this change came from shifts in domestic politics rather than from EU pressure. That the EU's preferred policy model was successfully resisted for so long illustrates the importance of these domestic shifts. The policy that emerged was one with clear 'extra-EU' influence – particularly from the United States. Indeed, Cini describes competition as an extremely 'internationalized' and 'cosmopolitan' area of policy making.

Regional policy is also more complicated than one might first expect, given the increasing involvement of the EU in the rehabilitation of Britain's poorest areas and the growth of the EU's budget for regional policy to around a third of all EU spending. This is an area where it is particularly important to distinguish between 'domestic politics' and 'politics in the domestic arena', because, as Conzelmann argues, important aspects of British regional policy co-exist relatively unchanged alongside EU policy. Since the late 1980s, increased EU funding for regeneration projects within the regions has produced significant effects in the domestic arena. However, there is still a distinct domestic domain of national regional policy, which focuses on the provision of state aids to ailing industries in targeted areas. Moreover, while there has been co-existence of EU and British regional policies, this has been characterized by contestation, in particular over the legitimate space for making decisions over regional policy.

Our remaining policy chapters covered two of the most controversial areas of British–EU relations, namely foreign affairs and monetary policy, where Britain has been generally reluctant to participate in EU initiatives, arguing strongly for intergovernmental forms of co-ordination. Nonetheless, Europeanization is evident in both areas. For example, Oliver and Allen relate how there has been a blurring of the distinction between European and domestic foreign policy and a gradual acceptance in key parts of the British state, particularly the FCO, of the need to collaborate with other EU partners. The effect goes beyond the deployment of staff and resources in Whitehall: the EU's growing involvement has gradually inculcated in British civil servants a more European view of international affairs, to the extent that Britain increasingly uploads policy ideas and initiatives to the EU, such as those contained in the St Malo declaration.

In terms of monetary policy, Buller also finds some support for a top-down interpretation of events. However (and here there are strong parallels with competition policy), he characterizes the British experience as the voluntary importing of an EU model, to provide a 'sanctuary' from global economic forces. More than that, he makes a strong argument that the 'reality' of Europeanization cannot be separated from the discourses that surround it. In other words, while in a formal sense the Europeanization of British monetary policy lasted little over two years (1990–92), before Britain crashed out of the ERM, the dominant political discourse that emerged from that troubled experience constructs a significant misfit between EU policy requirements and British preferences. The validity of this construction is contestable. Buller argues, for instance, that the EU's model is actually being 'Anglicized', albeit through no conscious uploading of British ideas by the Treasury, which remains extremely wary of EU involvement. But the existence of the single currency undeniably acts as a real and enduring constraint on the options facing British governments as they continue to sit outside Euroland. Therefore, it is undeniably an EU effect.

Understanding Europeanization

In Chapter 2 we outlined six research questions, which we asked all the contributors to assess in their chapters. In this section we seek to distil their responses and look for general patterns in the depth, extent and timing of Europeanization.

a. What has been Europeanized and to what extent?

One thing that emerges very strongly from the previous section is that the EU's impacts range widely (although by no means uniformly) across the three domains of polity, politics and policy. With regards to *polity*, our chapters detect changes in relation to the formal institutions of the state and their internal working procedures, through to the more informal governance strategies of local authorities in the field of economic regeneration. The *politics* domain has also changed as a result of EU membership. This shows up in a number of forms, some of which (for example changes in the lobbying routes of organized interests) are more tangible than others (for example revisions of the 'idea' of nationhood and sovereignty and of political narratives and discourses). In relation to *policy*, changes to policy paradigms, to policy goals, to policy instruments, and to the calibration of instruments are all evident. We return to categorizing the extent of Europeanization below (see section 'e').

b. When did Europeanization occur and in what sequence?

This question is important in helping us to trace and disentangle the causes of domestic change. The first observation is that no area study shows a sharp and immediate change immediately after accession in 1973. Generally, change has been gradual, albeit with periods of acceleration (and braking) at various points. For example, there was a marked increase in the Europeanization of trade unions and interest organizations in the 1980s and early 1990s, partly because of the increasing opportunities available to these actors at the European level, but also (at least in some cases) because of diminishing opportunity structures within domestic politics. In some cases, there were key moments (monetary policy in 1990, competition policy in 1998), although not all of the key moments were necessarily or wholly connected to the EU. Obvious examples of (other) international effects on foreign policy and the foreign office are the collapse of communism and the 2001 terrorist attacks.

Changes within Whitehall in relation to the organization of EU business also had a distinct domestic influence in the form of a change of government, a point to which we return below.

c. How and why has Europeanization occurred, and via what EU-level mechanism?

Inevitably there is no straightforward answer to questions of how and why Europeanization has occurred. In a sense we are dealing with the answers to these questions throughout this chapter. While descriptions and typologies of various mechanisms are outlined in Chapter 2, no obvious pattern emerges linking a particular EU mechanism (for example governance by negotiation, governance by hierarchy) with a particular outcome at the domestic level (for example transformation, retrenchment and so on). Rather, the nature of particular mechanisms relates more clearly to the extent to which domestic change takes place through a primarily voluntaristic or primarily coercive process (below), which then provides a fuller explanation of how and why Europeanization has occurred.

d. Has Europeanization created an identifiable pattern of winners and losers?

The short answer to this question is 'not really'. One problem in addressing it is that of establishing the counterfactual. What would have happened in the absence of Europeanization? Thus, for example, we might observe that the role of the FCO has clearly been challenged and has probably diminished because Europeanization has promoted the role of other domestic actors in foreign policy making. Yet, it is equally possible to argue that without Europeanization British influence over world events would be less – and thus the role of the FCO would have diminished further. A further complication is the issue of weighing up what some actors may have gained in one sphere of Europeanization, against what they might have lost in another. Thus, local authorities may have been offered new financial resources and political opportunities through EU regional policy, but they have lost a degree of autonomy through the Europeanization of environmental policy (Marshall, Chapter 7).

Perhaps the most clearly discernible pattern is that Europeanization has offered opportunities for a wider range of British political actors to influence policy making. The mobilization of trade unions, interest groups, and the voluntary and community sector adds weight to arguments that the EU is characterized by multi-level governance. Local authorities, the devolved institutions of England, Scotland and Wales, as well as individual ministries of central government might also be added to the list of British institutions and actors who have developed an independent relationship with the EU as a means of exercising influence. Again, we are faced with the difficult question of establishing the counterfactual. However, it is clear that in at least some of the cases covered (for example, environmental groups, the voluntary and community sector) this mobilization has had tangible benefits for the actors concerned.

e. What factors explain the domestic response to Europeanization pressures and how should the process be characterized?

In Chapter 2 we distinguished between direct and indirect Europeanization and set out a voluntary-coercive continuum. These distinctions proved useful in a number of cases. On the former, Bulmer and Burch, and Burch and Gomez emphasized the importance of indirect or 'second order' EU effects on domestic national and regional institutions. While some cases suggested direct change had come about through responding to a clear EU role or requirement (for example partnership and programming requirements for the structural funds), Europeanization often came through less clear EU requirements or models, particularly in the case of interest groups, trade unions and the third sector. The most indirectly influenced area is that of political parties, where no formal requirements for change exist but where there is a distinct EU impact on an ideational level. Finally, some areas demonstrate a shift from direct effects to indirect effects, monetary policy being the most obvious case, but also environment policy.

In terms of the voluntary-coercive continuum, we tend to find a mix of responses in each case. Bulmer and Burch's description of the Europeanization of Whitehall being on 'our terms' fits well with the polity dimension generally. In all areas, EU membership has required some adaptation, but this has occurred gradually and largely in keeping with established practices. In the established academic discourse, it is 'Europeanization with national colours'. In terms of interest groups, trade unions and the third sector, there was a marked voluntarism albeit with obvious incentives to Europeanize. As Fairbrass points out, the trend is for interest organizations of all types to 'shoot where the ducks are'. Our policy case studies revealed some coercive elements (for example EU environmental legislation, state-aid law), but also a large degree of voluntarism, with competition policy being in something of a surprise position at the voluntaristic end of the spectrum. Marshall adapted our distinctions to elaborate a typology of 'local Europeanization' with three main variations: *voluntary-indirect 'downloaded' Europeanization* in local authorities due to their continuing involvement in EU structural fund programmes; *voluntary-indirect 'downloaded' Europeanization, coupled to 'up-loading' and 'cross-loading', as well as multi-directional Europeanization* through the creation of sub-national offices in Brussels, participation in trans-European networks, and local lobbying; *coercive-indirect 'downloaded' Europeanization* within local authorities, resulting from the implementation of EU directives and regulations, especially those relating to the environment.

Applying the second set of categories, this time to capture the effects of Europeanization, proved more problematic. These were the taxonomic distinctions between transformation, accommodation, absorption, retrenchment and inertia. A number of our contributors preferred other descriptions: Bulmer and Burch refer to a 'quiet revolution in Whitehall', Allen and Oliver to 'fine-tuning' in the FCO, Smith to 'fusion' in the case of Scotland. Cini identifies 'transformation' in the case of competition policy, but is clear that this was not only through EU effects. Geddes's study of political parties finds the main effect of Europeanization to be the creation of a multidimensional political space; this is perhaps closest to transformation, but it is not a comfortable fit. In short, the categories were useful in prompting our authors to think specifically about the nature of domestic change, but too restrictive for most cases to be easily accommodated within them. Burch and Gomez's argument that the taxonomy does not really capture change that is both gradual and transformative – the type of change that is evident in many of our case studies – illustrates the general point well.

More specifically, a recurring theme in many of our case studies was the concept of resistance in relation to EU pressures, a category not found (or at least not explicitly) in the established taxonomy. Resistance on some issues sometimes accompanied adaptation or accommodation on others within a single case study, but across different issues (for example foreign policy, regional policy); or it was evident in some periods of EU membership but not others (for example trade unions, monetary policy). We suggest that this concept may have particular importance in the British case, given the domestic sensitivities over the EU, and its absence in extant Europeanization models reflects the dominance of institutional approaches developed in less politically sensitive contexts. We return to this issue in the concluding section.

f. Has Europeanization had any other important long-term effects?

Most of the specific effects of Europeanization have been covered in the sections above. More generally, we might observe also that Europeanization has undoubtedly added to the complexity of British politics and governance by bringing new actors into the policy making process, challenging the role of established actors, and reshaping aspects of both elite and public discourse. In this sense, the landscape of British politics has been transformed, albeit unevenly across time and domain. This has not merely been a period of post-membership flux – that is, a time-bound period of adjustment through which each member state has to pass before eventually emerging with a changed but essentially stable set of core features. Rather, it is an ongoing state of affairs in which complexity and change is a recurring feature. In this context, both European and domestic actors have to seek, and have begun to develop, new tools through which to govern and, increasingly, new mechanisms through which complex governance might be made more transparent and more accountable.

Continuity and change in Britain's relationship with the EU

Identifying continuity and change has been an important theme in the study of British politics. Addressing this theme challenges us not to take at face value the claims of political actors. It has proved a useful theme here. We use it in two ways: to consider the extent to which, in general terms, the domestic effect of EU membership has been characterized by continuity or change; and to consider the extent to which the post-1997 period under New Labour has significantly altered the relationship with the EU in broad terms and specifically in relationship to the Europeanization of British politics. Recall that in Chapter 1 we noted the Blair government's declared intention to take Britain closer to the 'heart of Europe'.

We have a helpful point of reference in addressing this first issue, which is the earlier study on British adaptation directed by George (1992). This study suggested that much of the adaptation had taken place on a 'technical level' as 'civil servants and interest groups learned how to operate in the EC process, rather than resulting from or leading to a political conversion among political actors in favour of the EC' (George 1992: 203). Our findings largely echo this earlier finding and thus suggest a strong element of continuity in the Europeanization process. There is much evidence of civil servants 'getting on with it', and, in the case of Scotland, some evidence of 'apolitical enthusiasm' for the EU. Similarly, interest groups generally adjusted their activities pragmatically to a new, more European centre of gravity in British politics. In some instances there is evidence of 'conversion' to the EU in a more ideological sense, the leadership of the GMB being a case in point.

There is a temporal effect evident here that distinguishes the degree and nature of Europeanization. Compared to the 1992 study, there is clearer evidence that at least some political actors have gone beyond simply strategic interaction with the EU to a more normative commitment to Europeanization. The effects of the 1980s, when a number of key political actors turned to the open doors of Brussels when they found the doors of Whitehall firmly closed, had not worked their way through the political system by 1992. Actors who were then marginalized in British politics – environmentalists, trade unionists, Labour local government leaders – have since become more central, in the latter cases as a direct result of New Labour's 1997 election victory, and have become torchbearers for deeper European integration. There is irony in the thought that some of the more entrenched features of the Europeanization of British politics have their origins in the years of Thatcherism.

To turn to another question from George's 1992 study, do these developments amount to Britain being less awkward or less semi-detached? The answer to this is helped by our focus on continuity and change. Britain's most co-operative stance was then on the single market programme and on this nothing has changed: governments of both parties have remained leading advocates of removing barriers to free trade. Of course, in 1992 the related project of monetary union was a distant and uncertain prospect, but Britain's reluctance to participate in it has not changed. Perhaps we would not have expected much change in the period 1992–97, but we might have expected some under a New Labour government that was seeking a 'step change' in Britain's relationship with the EU. It is to the change of government we now turn.

New Labour

There is little argument that the New Labour government's approach to the EU has been the most positive since that of the Heath government that negotiated entry. In some of our cases we can identify a distinct change as a result of New Labour's approach. Bulmer and Burch identify a number of initiatives launched by New Labour in the areas of labour market reform, economic competitiveness, defence and asylum, and suggest overall a 'considerable shift in pace and direction'. Within Whitehall specifically, an observable change has been a structural improvement in Britain's ability to project its preferences in the EU: the 'uploading' dimension of Europeanization. Allen and Oliver note a distinct shift towards greater willingness within the FCO to try to influence EU affairs. Beyond the centre, New Labour's policy of devolution has, in Smith's words, allowed the Scottish Executive to go further on aspects of Europeanization than the Scottish Office ever could. In the English regions, New Labour's policy has built on the nascent institutions created primarily by EU structural funds and subsequently strengthened the position of the regions to assert themselves further in a European context, albeit primarily on matters of economic development.

In policy terms, New Labour's impact has been decidedly mixed. On foreign and defence policy, New Labour has moved close to the EU on some issues, but not so on others. More significantly perhaps, Allen and Oliver identify the two-way dynamics of this relationship as important, with the EU in some respects moving closer to Britain's foreign policy position. Monetary policy has seen no substantive change in the British position, despite continued speculation over the prospects of joining the single currency. Competition policy is an area in which New Labour has taken things forward and, Cini argues, has gone further than any of the blueprints being considered by the Conservatives. In doing so, New Labour has gone closer to the EU model without fully Europeanizing this sector: another case of nationally directed adaptation. Much of the Europeanization of environment policy took place before 1997, so Jordan does not single out the change of government as particularly important in this sector. In terms of regional policy, the most important development post-1997 is the proliferation of domestic initiatives alongside those of the EU. The main change is that British and European approaches to regional policy (and indeed commitment to it) now sit more easily alongside each other than in the past.

Not surprisingly perhaps, given the degree of reorientation of interest group activities from the 1980s onwards, the change of government in 1997 has had a particular impact on these patterns. Environmental and business groups, trade unions and, increasingly, third sector organizations have well-worn paths that now lead them simultaneously to Brussels and London (and indeed elsewhere within and beyond the state). In terms of parties, the nature, intensity and effects of the debates on Europe are similar and have not been significantly affected by the change of government.

Still awkward?

Britain under New Labour lives more easily with Europe. In many respects, Britain can no longer be considered Europe's awkward partner. Issues of profound difficulty for Britain remain, the euro being the most obvious. Here there is continuity in that the Treasury remains the least Europeanized department. In areas not covered in this book, agriculture being a key case, Britain has continuing difficulties that have led to tension with key players in the EU. However, in both cases it is important to note that Britain does not stand alone. Moreover, the evidence assembled here is that in a number of areas the relationship has evolved substantively, despite the context of continuing public distrust of the EU. It is also important to note that Britain's record of awkwardness has always related as much to style as to substance. The 'winner take all' tradition of British politics contrasts with coalition and consensus-building in much of continental Europe, which often leads to a confrontational British political style that was most forcefully evident under Mrs Thatcher. There is no doubt that whatever the continuities in substance in Britain's relations with the EU, there has been a change of style – or perhaps more accurately, a change of tone. Rhetorically in particular, Britain is no longer so awkward.

Conclusion

We conclude by reflecting on how this study of Britain compares with studies of other states, and on the utility of Europeanization as a concept. In our opening chapters we identified three common themes of Europeanization research. The first was the argument that polities and politics are relatively resilient in the face of Europeanizing pressures, whereas national policies have been much more deeply transformed. The second was that Europeanization does not imply convergence: although some elements of national systems could be said to be converging, others seem resilient to centripetal forces, thus producing a highly differentiated pattern – what Cowles *et al.*, (2001: 1) referred to as 'domestic adaptation with national colors'. The third theme was that, despite the focus on the downward impact of the EU on member states, Europeanization is a two-way process, in which states also seek to upload their preferences to the EU level.

On the first of these themes, there are similarities between the findings on Britain and the conventional wisdom on the polity, politics and policy dimensions. However, we need to point out the bluntness of this threefold categorization because of the considerable variation within each of the domains. For example, within the 'polity' domain, there is a perceptible difference in the impact of the EU on national and sub-national institutions, with the role of local authorities and the English regions generally being more profoundly affected. Within the 'policy' domain there is a clear contrast between the degree of Europeanization in environment policy, in monetary policy and in competition policy. Perhaps most significantly in highlighting dissimilarities with the conventional wisdom, the notion of a 'non-Europeanized politics' is much more questionable in Britain. There has been no marked change in the structures of either the party system or internal party structures. On an ideational and discursive level, however, there has been significant change. Moreover, if we think of politics beyond the parties – as we surely must – then we have seen a significant reorientation of the activities of interest groups, trade unions, and voluntary and community groups. Temporally, policy was generally the first of the three domains to experience Europeanization, but the indirect effects of this were gradually experienced to varying degrees in the other domains. Moreover, while change has generally been gradual, gradual change can be transformative.

In short, none of our three domains can be easily categorized as Europeanized, semi-Europeanized or non-Europeanized. It is an interesting observation that what works as a short-hand, and admittedly simplified, description of the domestic effects of the EU in Germany works significantly less well for Britain. On this comparison, a further observation can be made. Dyson and Goetz (2003) suggest that Germany's relationship with the EU has moved from co-existence and co-evolution to co-evolution and contestation, signalling a more problematic relationship developing. In some respects, Britain's relationship has moved in the opposite direction: partly as it has come to terms with the requirement of EU membership, and the necessary adjustments and adaptations; but – and related to this – partly as it has sought to play a more constructive role and shape the future of the EU at both an individual policy level and on matters of grand design, such as the Draft Constitutional Treaty. While this may be partly a conscious and deliberate strategy, it may also be that other pressures are being brought to bear on the EU and its member states that are leading to convergence between the established British political economy and that emerging on the continent. We cannot resolve this question here, but we raise it to identify again a contrast between Europeanization in Britain and elsewhere.

In terms of Europeanization as a concept, there are evident strengths and weaknesses. There is merit in both top-down and interactive approaches and, as the EU increasingly relies on less-formal governance mechanisms such as OMC, then the horizontal dimension is likely to become more important. The top-down approach is of most value when the EU's obligation is clear and firm (that is, embedded in legislation) than when it is not. However, across many domains, Europeanization clearly operates as a two-way or cyclical process involving repeated interactions between national and European arenas, involving actors across different sectors and levels. Such is the complexity of these territorially overarching networks that, as Conzelmann suggests, it is increasingly difficult to separate what is purely 'European' from what is purely 'domestic'. Thus, the task of isolating particular causal factors when there are mutual interacting flows and multiple pressures emanating from different EU (and non-EU) sources is difficult and likely to become more so. As such, the notion of misfit between EU and domestic models becomes more difficult to apply.

To complicate matters still further, there is increasing awareness of the way that the notion of misfit is (or can be) constructed and then contested, and sometimes reconstructed, in the context of political debate. Indeed, the whole political dimension comes out particularly strongly in the British case. Perhaps this is because of the distinctively sensitive nature of Britain's relationship with the EU. However, we will only know this if future studies of Europeanization set out to test the importance of the political dimension more than present studies do. While the Europeanization literature has begun to adopt the tools and language of the literature on policy transfer to emphasize the horizontal dimension, it has to date underplayed the concept of *policy resistance*, which is a politically focused complement to the institutionalist literature. This concept highlights the importance of domestic political relationships in the process of transfer and illustrates how, through the development of 'hidden transcripts', the outward agreement and co-operation of domestic actors disguises strategies of non-compliance and obstruction (Bache and Taylor 2003).

More generally, our findings have important implications not only for the academic debate on Europeanization but also for research and teaching on British politics. The EU is not an optional extra in the study of British politics, although it has often been treated as such. Rather, our analysis suggests that it penetrates to the very heart of Britain's governing institutions, shapes major policies directly and indirectly, and has influenced the discourses, preferences and actions of a range of political actors. It remains, as Gamble (2003: 114) argued, the most important issue for the future of British politics.

Bibliography

Allen, D. (1998) 'Who Speaks for Europe? The Search for an Effective and Coherent External Policy', in J. Peterson and H. Sjursen (eds), *A Common Foreign Policy for Europe? Competing Visions of the CFSP*, London: Routledge.

——(2004) 'So Who Will Speak for Europe? The Constitutional Treaty and Coherence in EU External Relations', *CFSP Forum*, 2 (5), 1–4.

——(2005) 'The United Kingdom: A *Europeanized* Government in a *non-Europeanized* Polity', in S. Bulmer and C. Lesquesne (eds), *The Member States and the European Union*, Oxford: Oxford University Press.

Almond, G. (1990) *A Discipline Divided*, Sage: Beverly Hills, CA.

Alt, J. (1987) 'Crude Politics: Oil and the Political Economy of Unemployment in Britain and Norway, 1970–85', *British Journal of Political Science*, 17 (2), 149–99.

Andersen, S. and Eliassen, K. (1996) *The European Union: How Democratic is it?* London: Sage.

Anderson, J. (2002) 'Europeanization and the Transformation of the Democratic Polity, 1945–2000', *Journal of Common Market Studies*, 40 (5), 793–822.

——(2003) 'Europeanization in Context: Concept and Theory', in K. Dyson and K. H. Goetz (eds), *Germany, Europe and the Politics of Constraint*, Ch. 2. Oxford: Oxford University Press.

Andrews, P. (2002) '"Modernisation" – Irish Style', *European Competition Law Review*, 23 (9), 469–73.

Armstrong, H. (2001) 'Regional Selective Assistance: Is the Spend Enough and Is It Targeting the Right Places?', *Regional Studies*, 35 (3), 247–57.

Armstrong, H., Wells, P. and Woolford, J. (2002a) 'Research Working Paper Number 1: The Role of the Third Sector in the Governance of Regional Policy in South Yorkshire', Sheffield: University of Sheffield.

——(2002b) 'Research Working Paper Number 2: A Comparison of the Role of the Third Sector in the Governance of Regional Policy in Yorkshire and Humber and the North West Region', Sheffield: University of Sheffield.

——(2003) 'Multi-Level Governance, Regional Policy and the Role of the Third Sector: The Emergence of New Policy Networks in the United Kingdom?', paper presented at the Regional Studies Association Conference on Reinventing Regions in the Global Economy, Italy, 12–15 April.

Armstrong, K. (2002) 'Rediscovering Civil Society: The European Union and the White Paper on Governance', *European Law Journal*, 8 (1), 102–32.

Armstrong, K. and Bulmer, S. (1996) 'The United Kingdom', in D. Rometsch and W. Wessels (eds), *The European Union and Member States: Towards Institutional Fusion?* Manchester: Manchester University Press.

Ashby, E. and Anderson, M. (1981) *The Politics of Clean Air*, Oxford: Clarendon Press.

Bache, I. (1998) *The Politics of European Union Regional Policy: Multi-level Governance or Flexible Gate keeping?* Sheffield: Sheffield Academic Press.

——(1999) 'The Extended Gatekeeper: Central Government and the Implementation of EC Regional Policy in the UK', *Journal of European Public Policy*, 6 (1), 28–45.

——(2001) 'Different Seeds in the Same Plot? Competing Models of Capitalism and the Incomplete Contracts of Partnership Design', *Public Administration*, 79 (2), 337–59.

——(2003) 'Europeanization: A Governance Approach', paper presented at the EUSA 8th International Biennial Conference, Nashville, 27–29 March.

——(2004) 'Multi-Level Governance and European Union Regional Policy', in I. Bache and M. Flinders (eds), *Multi-Level Governance*, Oxford: Oxford University Press.

Bache, I. and Flinders, M. (2004): 'Multi-Level Governance and the Study of British Politics and Government', *Public Policy and Administration*, 19 (1), 31–52.

Bache, I. and George, S. (2006) *Politics in the European Union*, 2nd edn, Oxford: Oxford University Press.

Bache, I., George, S. and Rhodes, R. (1996) 'The European Union, Cohesion Policy and Sub-national Authorities in the United Kingdom', in L. Hooghe (ed.), *Cohesion Policy and European Integration: Building Multi-Level Governance*, Oxford: Oxford University Press.

Bache, I. and Taylor, A. (2003) 'The Politics of Policy Resistance: Reconstructing Higher Education in Kosovo', *Journal of Public Policy*, 23 (3), 279–300.

Bachtler, J. and Yuill, D. (2001) 'Policies and Strategies for Regional Development: A Shift in Paradigm, Regional and Industrial Policy Research Paper 46', Glasgow: European Policies Research Centre at the University of Strathclyde.

Badie, B. (2004) 'Sovereignty and Intervention', in W. Carlsnaes, H. Sjursen and B. White (eds), *Contemporary European Foreign Policy*, London: Sage.

Bailey, N. (1995) *Partnership Agencies in British Urban Policy*, London: UCL Press.

Baker, D. (2005) 'Islands of the Mind: New Labour's Defensive Engagement with the EU', *Political Quarterly*, 76 (1), 22–36.

Baker, D., Gamble, A. and Ludlam, S. (2002) 'Sovereign Nations and Global Markets: Modern British Conservatism and Hyperglobalism', *British Journal of Politics and International Relations*, 4 (3), 399–428.

Baker, D., Randall, N. and Seawright, D. (2002) 'Celtic Exceptionalism? Scottish and Welsh Parliamentarians' Attitudes to Europe', *Political Quarterly*, 73 (2), 211–26.

Baker, D. and Seawright, D. (eds) (1998) *Britain For and Against Europe: British Politics and the Question of European Integration*, Oxford: Clarendon Press.

Balls, E. (1992) *Euro-Monetarism: Why Britain was Ensnared and How it Should Escape*, London: Fabian Society.

Balls, E. and O'Donnell, G. (2002) *Reforming Britain's Economic and Financial Policy: Towards Greater Economic Stability*, London: Palgrave.

Banducci, S., Karp, J. and Lodel, P. (2003) 'The Euro, Economic Interests and Multi-level Governance: Examining Support for the Common Currency', *European Journal of Political Research*, 52 (5), 685–703.

Barr, F. (1998) 'Has the U.K. Gone European: Is the European Approach of the Competition Bill More Than an Illusion?', *European Competition Law Review*, 19 (3), 139–44.

Barry, J. and Paterson, M. (2004) 'Globalization, Ecological Modernization and New Labour', *Political Studies*, 52 (4), 767–84.

Baun, Michael J. (1995/96) 'The Maastricht Treaty as High Politics: Germany, France and European Integration', *Political Science Quarterly*, 110 (4), 605–24.

Beath, J. (2002) 'UK Industrial Policy: Old Tunes on New Instruments?', *Oxford Review of Economic Policy*, 18 (2), 221–39.

Beetham, R. (ed.) (2001) *The Euro Debate: Persuading the People*, London: The Federal Trust.

Bender, B. (1991) 'Governmental Processes: Whitehall, Central Government and 1992', *Public Policy and Administration*, 6 (1), 13–20.

Benington, J. and Harvey, J. (1998) 'Transnational Local Authority Networking within the European Union: Passing Fashion or New Paradigm?', in D. Marsh (ed.), *Comparing Policy Networks*, Buckingham: Open University Press.

——(1999) 'Networking in Europe', in G. Stoker (ed.), *The New Management of British Local Governance*, London: Macmillan.

Bevir, M. and Rhodes, R. (2003) *Interpreting British Governance*, London: Routledge.

Bieler, A. (2003) 'Labour, Neo-liberalism and the Conflict over Monetary Union', *German Politics*, 12 (2), 24–44.

Blair, A. (1998) 'UK Policy Coordination during the 1990–91 Intergovernmental Conference', *Diplomacy and Statecraft*, 9 (2), 159–82.

——(2001) 'Permanent Representations to the European Union', *Diplomacy and Statecraft*, 12 (3), 173–93.

——(2002) *Saving the Pound? Britain's Road to Monetary Union*, London: Prentice Hall.

——(2004) 'Britain and the European Union: The Impact of Membership', *British Journal of Politics and International Relations*, 6, 584–90.

——(2004) 'Diplomacy: The Impact of the EU on its Member States', in Carlsnaes, W., Sjursen, H. and White, B. (eds), *Contemporary European Foreign Policy*, London: Sage.

Blair, T. (2000) Speech to the Polish Stock Exchange, 6 October, <http://www.number-10.gov.uk/output/Page3384.asp> (accessed 6 September 2005).

——(2002) 'A Clear Course for Europe', Speech in Cardiff, 2 December, <http://www.number-10.gov.uk/output/Page1739.asp> (accessed 6 September 2005).

Blyth, M. (1997) 'Any More Bright ideas? The Ideational Turn in Comparative Political Economy', *Comparative Politics*, 29 (2), 229–50.

Bogdanor, V. (2005) 'Footfalls Echoing in the Memory. Britain and Europe: The Historical Perspective', *International Affairs*, 81 (4), 689–701.

Bomberg, E. and Peterson, J. (2000) 'Policy Transfer and Europeanization', *Europeanisation Online Papers*, Queen's University Belfast, No. 2/2000.

Bonefeld, W., Brown, A. and Burnham, P. (1995) *A Major Crisis? The Politics of Economic Policy in Britain in the 1990s*, Aldershot: Dartmouth.

Börzel, T. (1999) 'Towards Convergence in Europe?', *Journal of Common Market Studies*, 39 (4), 573–96.

——(2002) 'Pace-Setting, Foot-Dragging, and Fence-Sitting: Member State Responses of Europeanization', *Journal of Common Market Studies*, 40, 193–214.

——(2005) 'Europeanization: How the EU Interacts with Its Member States', in S. Bulmer and C. Lesquesne (eds), *The Member States of the European Union*, Oxford: Oxford University Press.

Börzel, T. and Risse, T. (2000) 'When Europe Hits Home: Europeanization and Domestic Change', *EUI Working Papers*, No. RSC 2000/56.

——(2003) 'Conceptualising the domestic impact of Europe', in K. Featherstone and C. Radaelli (eds), *The Politics of Europeanization*, Oxford: Oxford University Press.

Bouget, D. and Prouteau, L. (2002) 'National and Supranational Government-NGO Relations: Anti-Discrimination Policy Formation in the European Union', *Public Administration and Development*, 22 (1), 31–37.

Bridges, T. (2002) 'The South West', in J. Tomaney and J. Mawson (eds), *England: The State of the Regions*, Bristol: Policy Press.

Brown, A. (1998) *Politics and Society in Scotland*, London: Macmillan.

Buller, J. (1995) 'Britain as an Awkward Partner', *Politics*, 15 (1), 33–42.

——(2000) *National Statecraft and European Integration: The Conservative Government and the European Union 1979–1997*, London: Pinter.

Buller, J. and Gamble, A. (2002) 'Conceptualising Europeanization', *Public Policy and Administration*, 17 (2), 4–24.

Buller, J. and Smith, M. (1998) 'Civil Service Attitudes Towards the European Union', in D. Baker and D. Seawright (eds), *Britain For and Against Europe – British Politics and the Question of European Integration*, Oxford: Clarendon Press.

Bulmer, S. (1983) 'Domestic Politics and European Community Policy-Making', *Journal of Common Market Studies*, 21, 349–63.
——(1992) 'Britain and European Integration: of Sovereignty, Slow Adaptation, and Semi-Detachment', in S. George (ed.), *Britain and the European Community: The Politics of Semi-Detachment*, Oxford: Clarendon Press.
——(1994) 'The Governance of the EU', *Journal of Public Policy*, 13 (4), 351–80.
——(2000) 'European Policy: Fresh Start or False Dawn?', in D. Coates and P. Lawler (eds), *New Labour in Power*, Manchester: Manchester University Press.
Bulmer, S. and Burch, M. (1998) 'Organising for Europe – Whitehall, the British State and the European Union', *Public Administration*, 76 (4), 601–28.
——(2000a) 'The Europeanization of British Central Government', in R. Rhodes (ed.), *Transforming British Government, Volume 1: Changing Institutions*, London: Macmillan/Palgrave.
——(2000b) 'Coming to Terms with Europe: Europeanization, Whitehall and the Challenge of Devolution', *Queen's Papers on Europeanization*, No. 9/2000, Belfast: Queen's University.
——(2001) 'The "Europeanization" of Central Government: The UK and Germany in Historical Institutionalist Perspective', in G. Schneider and M. Aspinwall (eds), *The Rules of Integration*, Manchester: Manchester University Press.
——(2002) 'British Devolution and European Policy Making: A Step Change Towards Multi-level Governance', *Politique Européenne*, 6, 114–36.
——(2005) 'The Europeanisation of UK Government: From Quiet Revolution to Explicit Step-Change', *Public Administration*, 83 (4), 861–90.
Bulmer, S., Burch, M., Carter, C., Hogwood, P. and Scott, A. (2002) *British Devolution and European Policy-Making: Transforming Britain into Multi-Level Governance*, London: Palgrave.
Bulmer, S., George, S. and Scott, A. (eds) (1992) *The UK and EC Membership Evaluated*, London: Pinter.
Bulmer, S. and Lesquesne C., (eds) (2005a) *The Member States of the European Union*, Oxford: Oxford University Press.
——(2005b) 'The EU and Its Member States: An Overview', in S. Bulmer and C. Lesquesne (eds), *The Member States of the European Union*, Oxford: Oxford University Press.
Bulmer, S. and Radaelli, C. (2004) 'The Europeanisation of National Policy?', *Europeanisation Online Papers*, No. 1/2004.
——(2005) 'The Europeanisation of National Policy', in S. Bulmer and C. Lesquesne (eds), *The Member States of the European Union*, Oxford: Oxford University Press.
Burch, M. and Gomez, R. (2002) 'The English Regions and the European Union', *Regional Studies*, 36 (7), 767–78.
——(2003) 'Europeanization and the English Regions', paper presented at ESRC/UACES Seminars on Europeanization of British Politics and Policy, University of Sheffield, May.
Burch, M., Gomez, R., Hogwood, P. and Scott, A. (2005) 'Devolution, Change and European Policy-making in the UK', *Regional Studies*, 39 (4), 465–75.
Burch, M. and Holliday, I. (1993) 'Institutional Emergence: The Case of the North West Region of England', *Regional Politics and Policy*, 3 (2), 29–50.
——(1996) *The British Cabinet System*, London: Prentice Hall.
——(2004) 'The Blair Government and the Core Executive', *Government and Opposition*, 39 (1), 1–21.
Burch, M. and Rhodes, M. (1993) 'The North West Region and Europe: Development of a Regional Strategy', *European Policy Research Unit Working Paper*, No. 3/93, Manchester University: Department of Government.

Butt Philip, A. and Baron, C. (1988) 'United Kingdom', in H. Siedentopf and J. Ziller (eds), *Making European Policies Work, Volume II: National Reports*, Brussels and London: Bruylant/Sage.

Callaghan, J. (2000) *The Retreat of Social Democracy*, Manchester: Manchester University Press.

Casey, J. (2004) 'Third Sector Participation in the Policy Process: A Framework for Comparative Analysis', *Policy and Politics*, 32 (2), 241–57.

Cawson, A. (1978) 'Pluralism, Corporatism and the Role of the State', *Government and Opposition*, 13, 178–98.

CEC (Commission of the European Communities) (1992) Communication from the Commission – An Open and Structured Dialogue Between the Commission and Special Interest Groups, SEC (92) 2272 final.

——(1996) 'Social and Economic Inclusion through Regional Development: The Community Economic Development Priority in European Structural Funds Programmes in Great Britain' (Lloyd Report), Luxembourg: Office for Official Publications of the European Communities.

——(1997a) Towards an Urban Agenda in the European Union, COM(97) 197 final.

——(1997b) Promoting the Role of Voluntary Organizations and Foundations in Europe, COM(97) 241 final, Brussels: European Commission.

——(1998) Sustainable Urban Development in the European Union: A Framework for Action, COM(1998) 605 final, Brussels: CEC.

——(2000) The Commission and NGOs: Building a Stronger Partnership, Discussion Paper, COM(2000) 11, Brussels: European Commission.

——(2001) European Governance: A White Paper, COM(2001) 428 final, Brussels: CEC.

——(2002) Towards a Reinforced Culture of Consultation and Dialogue: General Principles and Minimum Standards for Consultation of Interested Parties by the Commission, COM(2002) 704 final, Brussels: European Commission.

——(2004a) Review of the Framework for Relations between the European Union and the United States, commissioned by DG External Relations, Brussels: European Commission.

——(2004b) A New Partnership for Cohesion. Convergence – Competitiveness – Cooperation. Third Cohesion Report; COM(2004) 107, Brussels: European Commission.

——(2005) Inforegio Website on the European Regional Development Fund, <http://europa.eu.int/comm/regional_policy/funds/prord/prord_en.htm> (as of 27 July 2005).

Centre for Sustainable Urban and Regional Futures (2004) 'Releasing the National Economic Potential of Provincial City-regions: The Rationale for and Implications of a "Northern Way" Growth Strategy', Salford: SURF Centre.

Chapman, R. (2004) 'Europeanization and the Third Sector', paper presented at the ESRC/UACES conference 'Britain in Europe and Europe in Britain: The Europeanization of British Politics', Sheffield Town Hall, 16 July.

Christoph, J. (1993) 'The effects of Britons in Brussels', *Governance*, 6 (4), 518–37.

Cini, M. and McGowan, L. (1998) *Competition Policy in the European Union*, Basingstoke: Macmillan.

Clarke, M. (1992) *British External Policy Making in the 1990s*, London: Macmillan.

Clift, B. (2001) 'New Labour's Third Way and European Social Democracy', in M. Smith and S. Ludlam (eds), *New Labour in Power*, London: Macmillan.

Cochrane, A., Peck, J. and Tickell, A. (2002) 'Olympic Dreams: Visions of Partnership', in J. Peck and K. Ward (eds), *City of Revolution: Reconstructing Manchester*, Manchester: Manchester University Press.

Coen, D. (1997) 'The Evolution of the Large Firm as a Political Actor in the EU', *Journal of European Public Policy*, 4 (1), 91–108.

——(1998) 'The European Business Interest and the Nation State: Large Firm Lobbying in the European Union and Member States', *Journal of Public Policy*, 18 (1), 75–100.

Coen, D. and Dannreuther, C. (2003) 'Differentiated Europeanization: Large and Small Firms in the EU Policy Process', in K. Featherstone and C. Radaelli (eds), *The Politics of Europeanization*, Oxford: Oxford University Press.

Colwell, A. and McLaren, G. (1999) 'The Scottish Experience of Preparing and Implementing Structural Fund Programmes', *Scotland Europa Papers, No. 18*.

Commons, J. (1909) American Shoemakers, 1648–1895. Reprinted in S. Larson and B. Nissen (eds) (1987), *Theories of the Labor Movement*, Detroit: Wayne State University Press.

Conzelmann, T. (2002) *Große Räume, kleine Räume. Europäisierte Regionalpolitik in Deutschland und Großbritannien*, Baden-Baden: Nomos Verlagsgesellschaft.

——(2005a) Zwischen Baum und Borke – Regionale Wirtschaftsförderung unter Europäischen Vorzeichen, *Raumforschung und Raumordnung*, 63 (2), 99–108.

——(2005b) 'Contested Governance: Europeanized Regional Policy in Germany and Britain', paper presented at a conference 'Multilevel Governance in Europe', Athens, 5–7 May.

Cook, A. (2002) 'Listening to Civil Society: What Relationship Between the European Commission and NGOs?', in U. Rub (ed.), *European Governance: Views from the UK on Democracy, Participation and Policy-Making in the EU*, London: Federal Trust.

Cooper, R. (2003) *The Breaking of Nations: Order and Chaos in the Twenty-First Century*, London: Atlantic Books.

Corbett, R. (1998) *The European Parliament's Role in Closer EU Integration*, Basingstoke: Macmillan.

Cormack, J. (1998) Former Scottish Office Civil Servant: Secretary (DAFS) 1976–82, *Interview with author*, 30 March 1998.

Corry, D. and Stoker, G. (2002) *New Localism: Refashioning the Centre-Local Relationship*, London: New Local Government Network.

Cowles, M. (1995) 'Setting the Agenda for the New Europe: The ERT and the EC 1992', *Journal of Common Market Studies*, 33 (4), 501–26.

——(2001) 'The Transatlantic Business Dialogue and Domestic Business-Government Relations', in M. Cowles, J. Caporaso and T. Risse (eds), *Transforming Europe*, Ithaca, NY: Cornell University Press.

Cowles, M., Caporaso, J. and Risse, T. (eds) (2001) *Transforming Europe – Europeanization and Domestic Change*, Ithaca: Cornell University Press.

Cox, C., Lowe, P. and Winter, M. (1986) 'Agriculture and Conservation in Britain: A Policy Community Under Siege', in C. Cox, P. Lowe and M. Winter (eds), *Agriculture: People and Policies*, London: Allen and Unwin.

Craddock, P. (1997) *In Pursuit of British Interests: Reflections on Foreign Policy under Margaret Thatcher and John Major*, London: John Murray.

CRG (2003) *Mid-Term Evaluation of the Objective 1 Programme for West Wales and the Valleys – Final Report*: <http://www.wefo.cymru.gov.uk/resource/ Objective1Mid-TermEvaluation-MainReport.pdf> (accessed 18 September 2005).

Currie, D. (1997) *The Pros and Cons of EMU*, London: HM Treasury.

Daddow, O. (2004) *Britain and Europe Since 1945: Historiographical Perspectives on European Integration*, Manchester: Manchester University Press.

Dahl, R. (1961) *Who Governs?* New Haven: Yale University Press.

Dalton, R. (2000) 'The Decline of Party Identification', in R. Dalton and M. Wattenberg (eds), *Parties without Partisans: Political Change in Advanced Industrial Democracies*, Oxford: Oxford University Press.

Dalton, R., and Wattenberg, M. (eds) (2000) *Parties without Partisans: Political Change in Advanced Industrial Democracies*, Oxford: Oxford University Press.

Damesick, P. (1987) The Evolution of Spatial Economic Policy, in P. Damesick and P. Wood (eds), *Regional Problems, Problem Regions, and Public Policy in the United Kingdom*, Oxford: Clarendon Press, 42–63.

Daneshkhu, S. (2004) 'Putting a Better Shine on Brown's Golden Rule', *Financial Times*, 2 March.

Deas, I. and Ward, K. (1999) 'Switching Scales: From the "New Localism" to the "New Regionalism?"', in M. Gardner, S. Hardy and A. Pike (eds), *New Regional Strategies: Devolution, RDAs and Regional Chambers*, London: Regional Studies Association.

De Guistino, D. (1996) *A Reader in European Integration*, London: Longman.

De la Porte, C. (2002) 'Is the Open Method of Coordination Appropriate for Organising Activities at EU Level in Sensitive Policy Areas?', *European Law Review*, 8 (1), 38–58.

DETR (Department of the Environment, Transport and the Regions) (1997) *Building Partnerships for Prosperity: Sustainable Growth, Competitiveness and Employment in the English Regions*, London: HMSO.

——(1998) *A Mayor and Assembly for London: The Government's proposals for Modernising the Governance of London*, London: HMSO.

Dickie, J. (1992) *Inside the Foreign Office*, London: Chapmans.

——(2004) *The New Mandarins: How British Foreign Policy Works*, London: Tauris.

Dinan, D. (2004) *Europe Recast: A History of the European Union*, Basingstoke: Palgrave.

DoE (Department of the Environment) (1978) Pollution Control in Great Britain: How It Works, 2nd edn, Pollution Paper 9, London: HMSO.

——(1998) *A Mayor and Assembly for London: The Government's proposals for modernising the governance of London*, London: HMSO.

Dolowitz, D. and Marsh, D. (1996) 'Who Learns What From Whom? A Review of the Policy Transfer Literature', *Political Studies*, 44 (2), 343–57.

Dølvik, J. (1997) *Redrawing the Boundaries of Solidarity: ETUC, Social Dialogue and the Europeanization of Trade Unions in the 1990s*, Oslo: ARENA.

Dover, R. (2005) 'The Prime Minister and the Core Executive: A Liberal Intergovernmentalist Reading of UK Defence Policy Formulation 1997–2000', *The British Journal of Politics and International Relations*, 7 (4), 508–25.

DTI (Department of Trade and Industry) (1983) *Regional Industrial Development* (Cmnd. 9111), London: HMSO.

——(1984) *Relationship of Assisted Areas to the European Regional Development Fund ERDF*, in House of Commons (Public Accounts Committee), Regional Industrial Incentives, HC Paper 378-i, London: HMSO, 42–43.

——(1989) *Opening Markets: New Policy on Restrictive Trade Practices*, Cmnd 727, London: HMSO.

——(1995) *Competitiveness: Forging Ahead*, Cm. 2867, London: HMSO.

——(1996) *Tackling Cartels and Abuse of Market Position Green Paper (on monopoly control)*, London: HMSO.

——(2001a) *A World Class Competition Regime*, Cm. 5233 (White Paper), July, London: HMSO.

——(2001b) Peer Review of the UK Competition Policy Regime: A Report to the DTI (by PriceWaterhouseCoopers), London: HMSO.

Dunkerley, D. and Fudge, S. (2004) 'The Role of Civil Society in European Integration: A Framework for Analysis', *European Societies*, 6 (2), 237–54.

Dyson, K. (1994) *Elusive Union: The Process of Economic and Monetary Union*, London: Longman.

——(ed.) (2002) *European States and the Euro: Europeanization, Variation and Convergence*, Oxford: Oxford University Press.

Dyson, K. and Featherstone, K. (1999) *The Road to Maastricht: Negotiating Economic and Monetary Union*, Oxford: Oxford University Press.

Dyson, K. and Goetz, K. (2002) 'Germany and Europe: Beyond Congruence', paper given to the British Academy Conference, Germany and Europe: A Europeanised Germany? London, 11 March 2002.

——(eds) (2003) *Germany, Europe and the Politics of Constraint*, Oxford: Oxford University Press.

ECOTEC (2003) *Ex-Post Evaluation of Objective 1 1994–99: National Report UK*, Birmingham: ECOTEC.

Edwards, G. (1992) 'Central Government', in S. George (ed.), *Britain and the EC: The Politics of Semi-Detachment*, Oxford: Oxford University Press.

Eising, R. (2003) 'Interest Groups: Opportunity Structures and Governance Capacity', in K. Dyson and K. Goetz (eds), *Germany, Europe and the Politics of Constraint*, Oxford: Oxford University Press.

Etherington, S. (2002) 'The Role of NGOs in Implementing EU Policy: Opportunities, Constraints and Successes', in U. Rub (ed.), *European Governance: Views from the UK on Democracy, Participation and Policy-Making in the EU*, London: Federal Trust.

Eurobarometer (2004) *Standard Eurobarometer 62. Public Opinion in the European Union*, Brussels: European Commission.

Europa (2005) Regional Policy: *UK Structural Fund Programmes*, available at <europa.eu.int/comm./regional_policy/> (accessed 16 September 2005).

European Commission (2004) *A New Partnership for Cohesion. Convergence – Competitiveness – Cooperation. Third Cohesion Report*; COM(2004) 107, Brussels: European Commission.

European Council (2003) *A Secure Europe in a Better World: The European Security Strategy*, December.

Evans, D. (1973) *Britain in the EC*, London: Victor Gollancz.

Evers, A. and Laville, J. (eds) (2004) *The Third Sector in Europe*, Northampton: Edward Elgar.

Eyre, S. and Lodge, M. (2000) 'National Tunes and a European Melody? Competition Law Reform in the UK and Germany', *Journal of European Public Policy*, 7 (1), 63–79.

Fairbrass, J. (2002) 'The Europeanization of Interest Representation', paper presented at ESRC Seminar Series/UACES Study Group on the Europeanization of British Politics, University of Sheffield, 29 November.

——(2003) 'The Europeanization of Business Interest Representation: UK and French Firms Compared', *Comparative European Politics*, 1 (3), 313–34.

Fairbrass, J. and Jordan, A. (2001a) 'Making European Union Biodiversity Policy: National Barriers and European Opportunities', *Journal of European Public Policy*, 8 (4), 499–518.

——(2001b) 'European Union Environmental Policy and the Role of the UK Government: Passive Observer or Strategic Manager', *Environment Politics*, 10 (2), 1–21.

——(2002) 'Interest Representation and Europeanization', in A. Warleigh and J. Fairbrass (eds), *Integrating Interests in the European Union*, London: Europa.

——(2004) 'European Union Environmental Policy: A Case of Multi-level Governance?', in M. Flinders and I. Bache (eds), *Multi-Level Governance*, Oxford: Oxford University Press.

Featherstone, K. (2003) 'Introduction: In the Name of "Europe"', in K. Featherstone and C. Radaelli (eds), *The Politics of Europeanization*, Oxford: Oxford University Press.

Featherstone, K. and Radaelli, C. (eds) (2003) *The Politics of Europeanization*, Oxford: Oxford University Press.

Fielding, S. (2002) *The Labour Party: Continuity and Change in the Making of New Labour*, London: Palgrave Macmillan.

Finlayson, A. (2004) 'The Interpretive Approach in Political Science: A Symposium', *British Journal of Politics and International Relations*, 6 (2), 129–64.

Foreign and Commonwealth Office (1999) *Annual Departmental Report*, London: Stationery Office.

——(2000) *Annual Departmental Report*, London: Stationery Office.

——(2001) *Annual Departmental Report*, London: Stationery Office.

——(2003a) *Departmental Report*, London: Stationery Office.

——(2003b) *Strategy Document*, London: Stationery Office.

——(2004) *Annual Departmental Report*, London: Stationery Office.

Forster, A. (2000) 'Britain', in I. Manners and R. Whitman (eds), *The Foreign Policies of European Union Member States*, Manchester: Manchester University Press.

——(2002) *Euroscepticism in Contemporary British Politics: Opposition to Europe in the British Conservative and Labour Parties since 1945*, London: Routledge.

Forster, A. and Blair, A. (2002) *The Making of Britain's European Foreign Policy*, London: Longman.

Franchino, F. and Radaelli, C. (2004) 'Europeanization and the Italian Political System', *Journal of European Public Policy* (special issue), 11 (6), 941–1127.

Gaffney, J. (ed.) (1996) *Political Parties and the European Union*, London: Routledge.

Gamble, A. (1988) *The Free Economy and the Strong State: The Politics of Thatcherism*, London: Macmillan.

——(1993) 'The Entrails of Thatcherism', *New Left Review*, 198, 117–28.

——(2000) 'Policy Agendas in a Multi-level Polity', in A. Gamble *et al.* (eds), *Developments in British Politics*, 6, London: Macmillan.

——(2003) *Between Europe and America: The Future of British Politics*, Basingstoke: Palgrave Macmillan.

Gamble, A. and Kelly, G. (2000) 'The British Labour Party and Monetary Union', *West European Politics*, 23 (1), 1–25.

Geddes, A. (1997) 'Europe: Major's Nemesis', in A. Geddes and J. Tonge (eds), *Labour's Landslide: The 1997 British General Election*, Manchester: Manchester University Press.

——(2002) 'In Europe, not interested in Europe', in A. Geddes and J. Tonge (eds), *Labour's Second Landslide: The 2001 British General Election*, Manchester: Manchester University Press.

——(2004) *The European Union and British Politics*, London: Palgrave Macmillan.

——(2005a) 'The Politics of Nationalism: Immigration and European Integration in the 2005 Campaign', in A. Geddes and J. Tonge (eds), *Britain Decides: The 2005 General Election*, London: Palgrave Macmillan.

——(2005b) 'Europe', in K. Hickson (ed.), *The Political Thought of the Conservative Party since 1945*, London: Palgrave.

Geddes, M. (2001) 'Local Partnership and Social Exclusion in the United Kingdom', in M. Geddes and J. Benington (eds), *Local Partnerships and Social Exclusion in the European Union*, London: Routledge.

Geddes, M. and Benington, J. (eds) (2001) *Local Partnerships and Social Exclusion in the European Union: New Forms of Local Social Governance*, London: Routledge.

George, S. (1990) *An Awkward Partner: Britain in the European Community*, Oxford: Oxford University Press.

——(ed.) (1992) *Britain and the European Community: The Politics of Semi-Detachment*, Oxford: Clarendon Press.

——(1994) *An Awkward Partner: Britain in the European Community*, 2nd edn, Oxford: Oxford University Press.

——(1998) *An Awkward Partner: Britain in the European Community*, 3rd edn, Oxford: Oxford University Press.

Geyer, R. (1997) *The Uncertain Union: British and Norwegian Social Democrats in an Integrating Europe*, Aldershot: Avebury.

Giddings, P. and Drewry, T. (1996) *Westminster and Europe*, Basingstoke: Macmillan.

Giegerich, B. and Wallace, W. (2004) 'Not Such a Soft Power: The External Deployment of European Forces', *Survival*, 46 (2), 163–83.

Ginsberg, R. (2001) *The European Union in International Politics: Baptism by Fire*, Lanham MD: Rowman and Littlefield.

Giordano, B. (2002) 'England's North West', in J. Tomaney and J. Mawson (eds), *England: The State of the Regions*, Bristol: Policy Press.

GMB (1992a) *Winning Ways in Europe: A GMB Checklist for 1992*, London: GMB.

——(1992b) *General Secretary's Report*, London: GMB.

——(1993) *Jobs and Recovery: Report of Congress*, London: GMB.

——(2001) *European Union: CEC Statement to GMB Congress 2001*, London: GMB.

Goetz, K. (1996) 'Integration in a Europeanized State: Germany and the IGC', *Journal of European Public Policy*, 3 (1), 23–44.

——(2001) 'European Integration and National Executives: A Cause in Search of an Effect?', *West European Politics*, (special issue) 23 (4), 211–231.

——(2002) 'The four worlds of Europeanization', paper presented at the ECPR joint sessions of workshops, Turin, Italy, 22–27 March.

Goetz, K. and Hix, S. (eds) (2001) 'Europeanised Politics? European Integration and National Political Systems', *West European Politics* (special issue), 23 (4).

Goldsmith, M. and Sperling, E. (1997) 'Local Governments and the EU: The British Experience', in M. Goldsmith and K. Klausen (eds), *European Integration and Local Government*, Cheltenham: Edward Elgar.

Gomez, R. and Burch, M. (2002) 'The English Regions and European Initiatives', *Manchester Papers in Politics: Devolution and European Union Policy Making Series*, No. 4, European Policy Research Unit, Manchester: University of Manchester.

Gordan, C. (2001) *A Practical Guide to the United Kingdom Competition Act 1998*, London: European Legal Publishing.

Gourevitch, P. (1978) 'The Second Image Reversed: The International Sources of Domestic Politics', *International Organization*, 32 (4), 881–912.

Gowland, D. and Turner, A. (2000) *Reluctant Europeans: Britain and European Integration 1945–1998*, Harlow: Longman.

Grahl, J. (1997) *After Maastricht: A Guide to European Monetary Union*, London: Lawrence and Wishart.

Grant, W. (1989) *Pressure Groups, Politics and Democracy in Britain*, Hemel Hempstead: Phillip Allen.

——(1993) 'Pressure Groups and the European Community: An Overview', in S. Mazey and J. J. Richardson (eds), *Lobbying in the European Community*, Oxford: Oxford University Press.

——(2000) *Pressure Groups and British Politics*, Basingstoke: Macmillan.

Grant, W. and Marsh, D. (1977) *The Confederation of British Industry*, London: Hodder and Stoughton.

Grote, J. and Lang, A. (2003) 'Europeanization and Organizational Change in National Trade Associations: An Organizational Ecology Perspective', in K. Featherstone and C. Radaelli (eds), *The Politics of Europeanization*, Oxford: Oxford University Press.

Haas, E. (1958) *The Uniting of Europe: Political, Social and Economic Forces 1950–1957*, Stanford: Stanford University Press.

Hacking, I. (2000) *The Social Construction of What?* Cambridge, Mass: Harvard University Press.

Haigh, N. (1984) *EEC Environmental Policy and Britain*, London: ENDS.

——(1986) 'Devolved Responsibility and Centralization', *Public Administration*, 64, 197–207.

——(1989) *EEC Environmental Policy and Britain*, 2nd revised edn, Harlow: Longman.

Haigh, N. and Lanigan, C. (1995) 'Impact of the European Union on UK National Environmental Policy', in T. Gray (ed.), *UK Environmental Policy in the 1990s*, Basingstoke: Macmillan.

Hain, P. (2001) *The End of Foreign Policy? British Interests, Global Linkages and National Limits*, London: Fabian Society, Green Alliance and Royal Institute of International Affairs.

Hajer, M. (1995) *The Politics of Environmental Discourse*, Oxford: Oxford University Press.

Hall, P. (1993) 'Policy Paradigms, Social Learning and the State', *Comparative Politics*, 25 (3), 275–96.

Hanf, K. and Soetendorp, B. (eds) (1998) *Adapting to European Integration: Small States and the European Union*, Addison Wesly: Longman.

Harding, A. (1997) 'Urban Regimes in a Europe of the Cities?', *European Urban and Regional Studies*, 4 (4), 291–314.

Haseler, S. and Reland, J. (eds) (2000) *Britain and Euroland: A Collection of Essays*, London: Federal Trust.

Haverland, M. (2000) National Adaptation to European Integration: The Importance of Institutional Veto Points. *Journal of Public Policy*, 20 (1), 83–103.

——(2003) 'The Impact of the European Union on Environmental Policies', in K. Featherstone and C. Radaelli (eds), *The Politics of Europeanization*, Oxford: Oxford University Press.

Hay, C. (2002). *British Politics Today*, London: Polity.

Hay, C. and Rosamond, B. (2002) 'Globalization, European Integration and the Discursive Construction of Economic Imperatives', *Journal of European Public Policy*, 9 (2), 47–167.

Heath, A., McLean, I., Taylor, B. and Curtice, J. (1999) 'Between First and Second Order: A Comparison of Voting Behaviour in European and Local Elections in Britain', *European Journal of Political Research*, 35 (3), 389–414.

Heffernan, R. (2002) 'Beyond Euro-scepticism: Explaining the Europeanization of the Labour Party', *Political Quarterly*, 72 (2), 180–89.

Heinelt, H. (1996) 'Die Strukturfondsförderung – Politikprozesse im Mehrebenensystem der Europäischen Union', in H. Hubert (ed.), *Politiknetzwerke und europäische Strukturfondsförderung*, Opladen: Leske and Budrich.

Héritier, A. (2002) 'The Accomodation of Diversity in European Union Policy Making and Its Outcomes', in A. Jordan (ed.) (2002) *Environmental Policy in the European Union: Actors, Institutions and Processes*, Earthscan: London.

Héritier, A., Kerwer, D., Knill, C., Lehmkuhl, D., Teutsch, M. and Douillet, A.-C. (2001) *Differential Europe. The European Union Impact on National Policymaking*, Lanham, MD: Rowman and Littlefield.

Héritier, A., Knill, C. and Mingers, S. (1996) *Ringing the Changes*, Berlin: De Gruyter.

Heseltine, M. (1991) *The Challenge of Europe: Can Britain Win?* London: Pan.

Hildebrand, D. (1998) *The Role of Economic Analysis in the EC Competition Rules*, The Hague: Kluwer.

Hill, C. (1993) 'The Capability-Expectations Gap; or Conceptualising Europe's International Role', *Journal of Common Market Studies*, 31 (3), 305–08.

——(1996) 'United Kingdom: Sharpening contradictions', in Christopher Hill (ed.), *The Actors in Europe's Foreign Policy*, London: Routledge.

——(2003) *The Changing Politics of Foreign Policy*, Houndsmill: Palgrave.

Hill, D. (2000) *Urban Policy and Politics in Britain*, London: Macmillan.

Hix, S. (1999) 'Dimensions and alignments in European Union Politics: Cognitive Constraints and Partisan Responses', *European Journal of Political Research*, 35 (1), 69–106.

——(2005) *The Political System of the European Union*, 2nd edn, London: Palgrave Macmillan.

Hix, S. and Goetz, K. (2000) 'Introduction: European Integration and National Political Systems', *West European Politics*, 23 (4), 1–26.

Hix, S. and Lord, C. (1997) *Political Parties in the European Union*, London: Macmillan.

HM Treasury (2003) *Policy Frameworks in the UK and EMU*, London: HMSO.

——(2005) *Growth and Opportunity: Prioritising Economic Reform in Europe*, London: HM Treasury.

HM Treasury/DTI/ODPM (2003) *A Modern Regional Policy for the United Kingdom*, London: HMSO.

Hocking, B. (ed.) (1999) *Foreign Ministries. Change and Adaptation*, London: Macmillan.

Hocking, B. and Spence, D. (eds) (2005) *Foreign Ministries in the European Union*, Basingstoke: Palgrave Macmillan.

Home Office (2001) *European Funding: Sources of Information and Support for Voluntary and Community Organizations*, London: Home Office. <www.homeoffice.gov.uk/acu/european_funding_leaflet.htm> (accessed 4 February 2002).

Hooghe, L. (ed.) (1996) *Cohesion Policy and European Integration: Building Multi-Level Governance*, Oxford: Oxford University Press.

Hooghe, L. and Keating, M. (1994) 'The Politics of EC Regional Policy', *Journal of European Public Policy*, 3 (3), 367–93.

Hoppe, A. and Voelzkow, H. (2001) 'Angleichung und Differenzierung in der Europäischen Strukturpolitik: Deutschland und Großbritannien im Vergleich', in I. Tömmel and H. Ingeborg (eds), *Europäische Integration als Prozess von Angleichung und Differenzierung*, Opladen: Leske und Budrich.

House of Commons (2001) 'General Election Results, 7 June 2001', Research Paper 01/54, London: House of Commons Library.

House of Commons (Trade and Industry Committee) (1995) *Regional Policy*, Fourth Report by the Trade and Industry Committee, together with the proceedings of the Committee; Session 1994–95, London: HMSO.

House of Commons (Treasury and Civil Service Select Committee) (1983) *International Monetary Arrangements*, Fourth Report (4 vols), London: HMSO.

House of Lords (Select Committee on the European Communities) (1978) *Approximation of Laws Under A100 of the EEC Treaty*, 22nd Report, HL 131, London: HMSO.

House of Lords (Select Committee on the European Union) (2003) Forty-Seventh Report, London: House of Lords Paper HL 194.

Howard, M. (2002) 'Brown's Golden Rule Starts to Lose Its Lustre', *Financial Times*, 31 October.

Howell, K. (2003) 'The Europeanization of British Financial Services', paper presented to the ESRC Seminar Series/UACES Study Group on the Europeanisation of British Politics and Policy-Making, Sheffield, 2nd May, http://www.shef.ac.uk/ebpp/meetings.htm.

Howorth, J. (2005) 'From Security to Defence: the Evolution of the CFSP', in C. Hill and M. Smith (eds), *International Relations and the European Union*, Oxford: Oxford University Press.

Hyman, R. (1997) 'Trade Unions & Interest Representation in the Context of Globalisation', *Transfer*, 3 (3), 515–33. Brussels: ETUI.

——(2001) *Understanding European Trade Unionism: Between Market, Class and Society*, London: Sage.

John, P. (1994a) 'UK Sub-national Offices in Brussels: Diversification or Regionalization', *Regional Studies*, 28 (7), 739–46.

——(1994b) 'The Presence and Influence of United Kingdom Local Authorities in Brussels', *Contemporary Political Studies*, 2, 906–21.

——(1996) 'Europeanization in a Centralising State: Multi-Level Governance in the UK', *Regional and Federal Studies* 6 (2), 131–44.

John, P., Margetts, H. and Weir, S. (2005) 'One in Five Britons Could Vote Far Right', *New Statesman*, 24 January 2005.

Jones, M. and McLeod, G. (2002), 'Regional Tensions: Constructing Institutional Cohesion', in J. Peck and K. Ward (eds), *City of Revolution: Reconstructing Manchester*, Manchester: Manchester University Press.

Jordan, A. (1998) 'The Impact on UK Environmental Administration', in P. Lowe and S. Ward (eds), *British Environmental Policy and Europe*, London: Routledge.

——(1999) 'European Community Water Standards: Locked in or Watered Down?', *Journal of Common Market Studies*, 37 (1), 13–37.

——(2001a) 'The European Union: An Evolving System of Multi-Level Governance . . . or Government?', *Policy and Politics* (special issue), 29 (2), 193–208.

——(2001b) The Europeanization of National Government and Policy: A Departmental Perspective, paper presented at 7th ECSA Biennial Conference, Madison, June 2001.

——(2002) *The Europeanization of British Environmental Policy: A Departmental Perspective*, London: Palgrave.

——(2003) 'The Europeanisation of National Government and Policy: A Departmental Perspective', *British Journal of Political Science*, 33 (2), 261–82.

——(ed.) (2005) *Environmental Policy in the European Union: Actors, Institutions and Processes*, 2nd edn, London: Earthscan.

Jordan, A. and Greenaway, J. (1998) 'Shifting Agendas, Changing Regulatory Structures and the 'New' Politics of Environmental Pollution', *Public Administration*, 76 (3), 669–94.

Jordan, A. and Liefferink, D. (eds) (2004) *Environmental Policy in Europe: The Europeanization of National Environmental Policy*, London: Routledge.

Jordan, A. Wurzel, R. and Zito, A. (2005) 'The Rise of "New" Policy Instruments in Comparative Perspective: Has Governance Eclipsed Government?', *Political Studies*, 53 (3), 477–96.

Jordan, A., Wurzel, R., Zito, A. and Brückner, L. (2003) 'Policy Innovation or "Muddling Through"? "New" Environmental Policy Instruments in the UK', *Environmental Politics*, 12 (1), 179–98.

Jordan, G., Gustafsson, G. and Richardson, J. (1982) 'The Concept of Policy Style', in J. Richardson (ed.), *Policy Styles in Western Europe*, London: George Allen and Unwin.

Joshua, J. (2002) 'A Sherman Act Bridgehead in Europe, or a Ghost Ship in Mid-Atlantic? A Close Look at the United Kingdom Proposals to Criminalise Hardcore Cartel Conduct', *European Competition Law Review*, 23 (5), 231–45.

Kampfner, J. (2003) *Blair's Wars: A Liberal Imperialist in Action*, London: Free Press.

Kassim, H. (2000) 'Conclusion', in H. Kassim *et al.* (eds), *The National Coordination of EU Policy: The National Level*, Oxford: Oxford University Press.

——(2003) 'Meeting the Demands of EU Membership', in K. Featherstone and C. Radaelli (eds), *The Politics of Europeanization*, Oxford: Oxford University Press.

——(2005) 'The Europeanization of Member State Institutions', in S. Bulmer and C. Lesquesne (eds), *The Member States of the European Union*, Oxford: Oxford University Press.

Katz, R. S. and Mair, P. (1995) 'Changing Models of Party Organization and Party Democracy: The Emergence of the Cartel Party', *Party Politics*, 1 (1), 5–29.

Keating, M. (1997) 'The Invention of Regions: Political Restructuring and Territorial Government in Western Europe', *Environment and Planning C: Government and Policy* 15, 383–98.

Keegan, W. (2003) *The Prudence of Mr Gordon Brown*, Chichester: Wiley.

Kelleher, J., Batterbury, S. and Stern, E. (1999) *The Thematic Evaluation of the Partnership Principle: Final Synthesis Report*, London: Tavistock Institute.

Kendall, J. (2001) 'The Third Sector and the Development of the European Public Policy: Frameworks for Analysis?', *Civil Society Working Paper* 19, London: LSE.

——(2003) 'Third Sector European Policy: Organizations between Market and State, the Policy Process and the EU', *Third Sector European Policy Working Paper 1* London: LSE.

Kendall, J. and Anheier, H. (1999) 'The Third Sector and the European Union Policy Process: An Initial Evaluation', *Journal of European Public Policy*, 6 (2), 283–307.

Kerremans, B. and Beyers, J. (1998) 'Belgium: The Dilemma Between Cohesion and Autonomy', in K. Hanf. and B. Soetendorp (eds), *Adapting to European Integration*, London: Longman.

Kirchheimer, O. (1966) 'The Transformation of the Western European Party System', in J. LaPalombara and M. Weiner (eds), *Political Parties and Political Development*, Princeton, NJ: Princeton University Press.

Kissack, R. (2004) 'The European Security Strategy: A First Approach', *CFSP Forum*, 2 (1), 19–20.

Knill, C. (1998) 'European Policies: The Impact of National Administrative Traditions', *Journal of Public Policy*, 18, 1–28.

——(2001) *The Europeanization of National Administrations*, Cambridge: Cambridge University Press.

Knill, C. and Lehmkuhl, D. (1999) 'How Europe Matters: Different Mechanisms of Europeanization', *European Integration Online Papers*, 3 (7), 15 June 1999.

——(2002) 'The National Impact of EU Regulatory Policy: Three Mechanisms', *European Journal of Political Research*, 41 (2), 255–80.

Knill, C. and Lenschow, A. (1998) 'Coping With Europe', *Journal of European Public Policy*, 5 (4), 595–614.

Kohler-Koch, B. (1999) 'The Evolution and Transformation of European Governance', in B. Kohler-Koch and R. Eising (eds), *The Transformation of Governance in the European Union*, London: Routledge.

Kon, S. and Turnbull, S. (2003) 'Pricing and the Dominant Firm: Implications of the Competition Commission Appeal Tribunal's Judgement in the Napp Case', *European Competition Law Review*, 24 (3), 70–86.

Ladrech, R. (1994) 'Europeanization of Domestic Politics and Institutions: The Case of France', *Journal of Common Market Studies*, 32 (1), 69–88.

——(2002) 'Europeanization and Party Politics: Towards a Framework for Analysis', *Party Politics*, 8 (4), 389–403.

Laffan, B. and Stubb, A. (2003) 'Member States', in E. Bomberg and A. Stubb (eds), *The European Union: How Does it Work?* Oxford: Oxford University Press.

Lamont, N. (1999) *In Office*, London: Little Brown.

Lang, I. (1991) 'Agenda for Europe', *Secretary of State's Speech to Scottish Young Conservatives Business Group*, 25 February 1991.

Lawson, N. (1992) *The View From Number Eleven*, London: Bantam.

Layard, R., Buiter, W., Huhne, C., Hutton, W., Kenen, P. and Turner, A. (2002) *Why Britain Should Join the Euro*, London: Britain in Europe.

Le Galès, P. (2002) *European Cities: Social Conflicts and Governance*, Oxford: Oxford University Press.

Lehmkuhl, D. (2000) 'Under Stress: Europeanisation and Trade Associations in the Member States', *European Integration Online Papers*, 4 (14): http://eiop.or.at/eiop/texte/1999-007a.htm.

Lenschow, A. (2006) 'Europeanization', in J. Richardson (ed.), *European Union: Power and Policy Making*, 3rd edn, Routledge: London.

LGIB (Local Government International Bureau) (2005) <www.lgib.gov.uk> (accessed 12 September 2005).

Lipset, S. and Rokkan, S. (1967) *Party Systems and Voter Alignments*, New York: The Free Press.

Lodge, J. (1989) *The European Community and the Challenge of the Future*, London: Pinter.

Lowe, P. and Flynn, A. (1989) 'Environmental Policy and Politics in the 1980s', in J. Mohan (ed.), *The Political Geography of Contemporary Britain*, Basingstoke: Macmillan.

Lowe, P. and Goyder, J. (1983) *Environmental Groups in Politics*, London: Allen Unwin.

Lowe, P. and Ward, S. (eds) (1998) *British Environmental Policy and Europe: Politics and Policy in Transition*, London: Routledge.

Lowndes, V. (2004) 'Reformers or Recidivists? Has Local Government Really Changed?', in G. Stoker and D. Wilson (eds), *British Local Government into the 21st Century*, Basingstoke: Palgrave Macmillan.

Luddecke, R. (2004), 'Europeanization of National Foreign Policy Making: Comparing the Patterns of Impact in Britain and Germany', paper presented to Second Pan-European Conference, Bologna, 24–26 June.

Macintyre, D. (1999) 'Making Europe More Democratic Will Also Make It Too Powerful', *The Independent*, 19 March.

McAleavey, P. (1995) 'European Regional Development Fund Expenditure in the UK: From Additionality to "Subtractionality" ', *European Urban and Regional Studies*, 2 (3), 88–107.

McAteer, M. (1997) 'The End of the Regional Experiment? Some Implications of Scottish Local Government Reorganisation for English Regions', *Policy and Politics*, 25 (1), 61–9.

McCarthy, A. and Burch, M. (1994) 'European Regional Development Strategies: The Response of Two Northern Regions', *Local Government Policy Making*, 20 (5), 31–8.

McLaughlin, A. and Greenwood, J. (1995) 'The Management of Interest Representation in the European Union', *Journal of Common Market Studies*, 33 (1), 143–56.

McLaughlin, A. and Jordan, G. (1993) 'The Rationality of Lobbying in Europe: Why are Euro Groups so Numerous and so Weak?', in S. Mazey and J. J. Richardson (eds), *Lobbying in the European Community*, Oxford: Oxford University Press.

McLaughlin, A., Jordan, G. and Maloney, W. (1993) 'Corporate Lobbying in the European Community', *Journal of Common Market Studies*, 31 (2), 191–212.

Macrory, R. (1987) 'The United Kingdom', in G. Enyedi, J. Gijswijt and B. Rhode (eds), *Environmental Policies in East and West*, London: Taylor and Graham.

——(1991) 'Environmental Law: Shifting Discretions and the New Formalism', in O. Lomas (ed.), *Frontiers of Environmental Law*, London: Chancery Law.

Mahoney, C. (2004) 'The Power of Institutions: State and Interest Group Activity in the European Union', *European Union Politics*, 5 (4), 441–66.

Mair, P. (2000) 'The Limited Impact of Europe on National Party Systems', *West European Politics*, 23 (4), 27–51.

——(2004) 'The Europeanization Dimension', *Journal of European Public Policy*, 11 (2), 337–48.

Mair, P. and van Biezen, I. (2001) 'Party Membership in Twenty Democracies, 1980–2000', *Party Politics*, 7 (1), 5–21.

Maitland-Walker, J. (1999) 'Have English Courts Gone Too Far in Challenging the Effectiveness of E.C. Competition Law?', *European Competition Law Review*, 20 (1), 1–4.

Marks, G. and McAdam, D. (1996) 'Social Movements and the Changing Structure of Political Opportunity in the European Community', *West European Politics*, 19, 249–78.

Marks, G. and Wilson, C. (2000) 'The Past in the Present: A Cleavage Theory of Party Responses to European Integration', *British Journal of Political Science*, 30 (3), 433–59.

Marshall, A. (2003) 'European Regional Policy and Urban Governance: Assessing Reform and Renewal in Britain and Ireland', unpublished PhD thesis, University of Cambridge.

——(2005) 'Europeanization at the Urban Level: Local Actors, Institutions and the Dynamics of Multi-level Interaction', *Journal of European Public Policy*, 12 (4), 668–86.

Martin, S. and Pearce, G. (1992) 'The Internationalisation of Local Authority Economic Development Strategies: Birmingham in the 1980s', *Regional Studies*, 26 (5), 499–503.

——(1994) 'The Impact of "Europe" on Local Government: Regional Partnerships in Local Economic Development', *Contemporary Political Studies*, 2.

Mawson, J. and Spencer, K. (1995) 'Pillars of Strength? The Government Offices for the English Regions', in S. Hardy, M. Hebbert and B. Malbon (eds), *Region-Building, Proceedings of the Regional Studies Association Annual Conference*, London: Regional Studies Association.

Mayes, D. (2001) 'The European Monetary System', in A. M. El-Agraa (ed.), *The European Union: Economics and Policies*, 6th edn, London: Prentice Hall.

Mazey, S. and Richardson, J. (2001) 'Interest Groups and EU Policy-Making: Organizational Logic and Venue Shopping', in J. Richardson (ed.), *European Union, Power and Policy Making*, New York: Routledge.

Menon, A. (2004) *Britain and European Integration: Views from Within*, Oxford: Blackwell.

Meny, Y., Muller, P. and Quermonne, J. (1996) 'Introduction', in Y. Meny, P. Muller and J. Quermonne (eds), *Adjusting to Europe: The Impact of the European Union on National Institutions and Policies*, London: Routledge.

Michalowitz, I. (2001) 'EU Lobbying: Chaos or Functional Diversions?', paper presented at the European Consortium for Political Research, Canterbury: University of Kent, 6–8 September.

Michalowitz, M. (2002) 'Beyond Corporatism and Pluralism: Towards a New Theoretical Framework', in A. Warleigh and J. Fairbrass (eds), *Influence and Interests in the European Union*, London: Europa.

Miller, C. (2002) 'U.K. Competition Policy Reform: Impact of the Latest Proposals on Process and Influences', *European Competition Law Review*, 23 (2), 68–71.

Mitchell, J. (1996) *Strategies for Self-Government: The Campaigns for a Scottish Parliament*, Edinburgh: Polygon.

Mittag, J. and Wessels, W. (2003) 'The "One" and the "Fifteen"?', in W. Wessels, A. Maurer and J. Mittag (eds), *Fifteen Into One? – The European Union and its Member States*, Manchester: Manchester University Press.

Moravcsik, A. (1998) *The Choice for Europe*, Ithaca NY: Cornell University Press.

Morgan, K. (2002) 'The English Question: Regional Perspectives on a Fractured Nation', *Regional Studies*, 36 (7), 797–810.

Morphet, J. (1998) 'Local Authorities', in P. Lowe and S. Ward (eds), *British Environmental Policy and Europe: Politics and Policy in Transition*, London: Routledge.

Murphy, G. (2002) 'Two Powerful Resources for Competition Law Compliance Now in Place', *European Competition Law Review*, 23 (10), 479–81.

Nairn, T. (1972) *The Left Against Europe*, London, Penguin.

NCVO (National Council for Voluntary Organisations) (2001) *The EU: A Voluntary Sector Perspective*, London: National Council for Voluntary Organisations.

Nelsen, B. and Stubb, A. (eds) (1998) *The European Union: Readings on the Theory and Practice of European Integration*, Boulder: Lynne Rienner.

Nicol, D. (2001) *EC Membership and the Judicialization of British Politics*, Oxford: Oxford University Press.

Northcott, J. (1995) *The Future of Britain and Europe*, Policy Studies Institute: London.

Nuttall, S. (1992) *European Political Cooperation*, Oxford: Clarendon Press

Oatley, N. (ed.) (1998) *Cities, Economic Competition and Urban Policy*, London: Paul Chapman.

ODPM (Office of the Deputy Prime Minister) (2004) *Making it Happen: the Northern Way*, London: HMSO.

——(2005a) *Bidding Guidance for the SRB Rounds 1–6*, available at <http://www.odpm.gov.uk/stellent/groups/odpm_control/documents/contentservertemplate/odpm_index.hcst?n=3038&l=2> (as of 27 July 2005).

——(2005b) *Bidding Guidance for the SRB Round 6*, available at <http://www.odpm.gov.uk/stellent/groups/odpm_urbanpolicy/documents/page/odpm_urbpol_608010.hcsp> (accessed 27 July 2005).

OECD (Organisation for Economic Co-operation and Development) (2003) *Urban Renaissance – Glasgow: Lessons for Innovation and Implementation*, Paris: OECD.

OFT (Office of Fair Trading) (2002) First Fines for Cartel Activity, Press Release, PN 6/02, 30 January: <http://www.oft.gov.uk/News/Press+releases/2002/PN+06-02.htm> (accessed 16 September 2005).

Oliver, T. (2004) 'Blair's 10 Downing Street and British Foreign Policy Making', paper presented at the British International Studies Association Conference, University of Warwick, December.

Olsen, J. (2002) 'The Many Faces of Europeanization', *Journal of Common Market Studies*, 40 (5), 921–52.

——(2003) 'Towards a European Administrative Space?', *Journal of European Public Policy*, 10 (4), 506–31.

Owen, D. (2003) 'The Ever Growing Dominance of No 10 in British Diplomacy'. Lecture delivered at LSE, 8 October.

Page, E. and Wouters, L. (1995) 'The Europeanization of the National Bureaucracies?', in J. Pierre (ed.), *Bureaucracy in the Modern State*, London: Elgar.

Panebianco, A. (1988) *Political Parties: Organisation and Power*, Cambridge: Cambridge University Press.

Peel, Q. (1999) 'White Man's Burden Sharing', *Financial Times*, 11 March.

Pepper, G. (1998) *Inside Thatcher's Monetarist Revolution*, Basingstoke: Macmillan/IEA.

Peretz, G. (1998) 'Detection and Deterrence of Secret Cartels under the U.K. Competition Bill', *European Competition Law Review*, 19 (3), 145–50.

Peters, B. (1999) *Institutional Theory in Political Science*, London: Continuum.

Peterson, J. (1992) 'The European Technology Community: Policy Networks in a Supranational Setting', in D. Marsh and R. A. W. Rhodes (eds), *Policy Networks in British Government*, Oxford: Clarendon Press.

Pierre, J. (ed.) (1998) *Partnerships in Urban Governance: European and American Experience*, London: Macmillan.

Pierre, J. and Stoker, G. (2000) 'Towards Multi-level Governance', in P. Dunleavy, A. Gamble, I. Holliday and G. Peele (eds), *Developments in British Politics*, 6th edn, London: MacMillan.

Pimlott, B. and Rao, N. (2002) *Governing London*, Oxford: Oxford University Press.

Portillo, M. (2000) 'Rigorous Disciplines for Hard Times', *Financial Times*, 11 December.

Pratt, J. (1994) 'Changes in UK Competition Law: A Wasted Opportunity?', *European Competition Law Review*, 15 (2), 89–100.

Preston, R. and Parker, G. (1998) 'Cabinet Office to Keep Role as Independent Mediator', *Financial Times*, 21 April.

Radaelli, C. (2000) 'Whither Europeanization? Concept Stretching and Substantive Change', *European Integration Online Papers*, 4 (8).

——(2003), 'The Europeanization of Public Policy', in K. Featherstone and C. Radaelli (eds), *The Politics of Europeanization*, Oxford: Oxford University Press.

——(2004) 'Europeanisation: Solution or Problem?', paper presented to the ESRC/UACES conference on The Europeanization of British Politics, Sheffield, 16 July.

Radice, G. (1996) 'The Case for a Single Currency', *Political Quarterly*, 67 (3), 252–56.

——(2003) *How to Join the Euro*, London: Foreign Policy Centre.

Rae, D. and Taylor, M. (1970) *The Analysis of Political Cleavages*, New Haven, CT: Yale University Press.

Rasmussen, J. (2001) 'Britain: Aloof and Skeptical', in E. Zeff and E. Pirro (eds), *The EU and the Member States*, Boulder: Lynne Rienner.

Raunio, T. (2002) 'Why European Integration Increases Leadership Autonomy Within Political Parties', *Party Politics*, 8 (4), 405–22.

Rawcliffe, P. (1998) *Environmental Pressure Groups in Transition*, Manchester: Manchester University Press.

Redwood, J. (1997) *Our Currency, Our Country: The Dangers of European Monetary Union*, Harmondsworth: Penguin.

REGLEG (2003) 'A Constitution for Europe – Responsibility and New Opportunities for the Regions with Legislative Powers', Declaration of Salzburg adopted by the 4th Conference of Presidents of Legions with Legislative Powers 11th–12th November.

Reif, K. and Schmitt, H. (1980) 'Nine National Second Order Elections: A Systematic Framework for the Analysis of European Elections Results', *European Journal of Political Research*, 8 (1), 3–44.

Rhodes, R. (1997) *Understanding Governance: Policy Networks, Governance, Reflexivity and Accountability*, Buckingham: Open University Press.

Richardson, J. (ed.) (1982) *Policy Styles in Western Europe*, London: George Allen and Unwin.

——(ed.) (1993) *Pressure Groups*, Oxford: Oxford University Press.

Richardson, J. and Jordan, G. (1979) *Governing under Pressure*, Oxford: Martin Robertson.

Richards, D. and Smith, M. (2002) *Governance and Public Policy in the United Kingdom*, Oxford: Oxford University Press.

Riddell, P. (2003) *Hug Them Close: Blair, Clinton, Bush and the Special Relationship*, London: Politics.

Ridley, N. (1992) *My Style of Government*, London: Fontana.

Riordan, S. (2003) *The New Diplomacy*, London: Polity.

Risse, T. (2004) 'Social Constructivism and European Integration', in A. Wiener and T. Diez (eds), *European Integration Theory*, Oxford: Oxford University Press.

Risse, T., Cowles, M. and Caporaso, J. (2001) Europeanization and Domestic Change: Introduction, in M. Cowles, *et al.* (eds), *Transforming Europe. Europeanization and Domestic Change*, Ithaca: Cornell University Press.

Robertson, A. (1996) 'The Reform of UK Competition Law – Again?', *European Competition Law Review*, 17 (4), 210–18.

Rosamond, B. (1993) 'National Labour Organisations and European Integration: British Trade Unions and 1992', *Political Studies*, 41, 412–34.

——(1998) 'The integration of Labour? British trade union attitudes to European integration', in D. Baker and D. Seawright (eds), *Britain For and Against Europe: British Politics and the Question of European Integration*, Oxford: Clarendon Press.

——(2003) 'The Europeanisation of British Politics', in P. Dunleavy, A. Gamble, R. Haffernan and G. Peele (eds), *Developments in British Politics 7*, Palgrave: Basingstoke.

Rotherham Programme Directorate (2001) *Priority 4 Prospectus: Developing Economic Opportunities in Targeted Communities*, Rotherham: Objective 1 Programme Directorate.

RPC (Regional Policy Commission) (1996) *Renewing the Regions. Strategies for Regional Economic Development. Report of the Regional Policy Commission*, Sheffield: Sheffield Hallam University Press.

Russell, A. and Fieldhouse, E. (2005) *Neither Left nor Right: The Liberal Democrats and the Electorate*, Manchester: Manchester University Press.

Sartori, G. (1968) 'The Sociology of Parties: A Critical Review', in O. Stammer (ed.), *Party Systems, Organizations and the Politics of New Masses*, Berlin: Free University Press of Berlin.

Sbragia, A. (2000) 'Environmental Policy: Economic Constraints and External Pressures', in H. Wallace and W. Wallace (eds), *Policy Making in the European Union*, 4th edn, Oxford: Oxford University Press.

Scarrow, S. (2000) 'Parties Without Members? Party Organization in a Changing Electoral Environment', in R. Dalton and M. Wattenberg (eds), *Parties Without Partisans: Political Change in Advanced Industrial Democracies*, Oxford: Oxford University Press.

Scharpf, F. (1996) 'Negative and Positive Integration in the Political Economy of European Welfare States', in G. Marks, F. Scharpf, P. Schmitter and W. Streeck (eds), *Governance in the European Union*, London: Sage.

Schmidt, V. (1999) 'National Patterns under Siege: The Impact of European Integration', in B. Kohler-Kock and R. Eising (eds), *The Transforming of Governance in Europe*, London: Routledge.

Schimmelfennig, F. and Sedelmeier, U. (eds) (2005) *The Europeanization of Central and Eastern Europe*, Cornell University Press: Ithaca.

Schmitter, P. (1999) 'Reflections on the Impact of the EU Upon "Domestic Democracy"', in M. Egeberg and P. Laegreid (eds), *Organizing Political Institutions*, Oslo and Stockholm: Scandinavian University Press.

Schmitter, P. and Lehmbruch, G. (1979) *Trends Towards Corporatist Intermediation*, London: Sage.

Schneider, G. and Aspinwall, M. (2001) *The Rules of Integration: Institutionalist Approaches to the Study of Europe*, Manchester: Manchester University Press.

Scholes, J. (1998) 'The U.K. Draft Competition Bill: Comments Based on the Observations of the Competition Law Association', *European Competition Law Review*, 19 (1), 32–45.

Scottish Office (1991a) *The Scottish Office and the European Community – Implementation Plan for the Review Recommendations*, European Funds and Co-ordination Division, September 1991.
——(1991b) *Management Notice – The Scottish Office and the European Community*, No. 13/1991, 10 September 1991.
——(1995) *Conclusions and Working Papers of the 1995, Management Review of European Business in the Scottish Office.*
——(1997) *Summary and Working Papers of 1997, Survey of EC Posts in the Scottish Office.*
Scottish Executive (2004) *The Scottish Executive's European Strategy*, External Relations Division, January 2004.
Seldon, A. (1997) *Major: A Political Life*, London: Weidenfield & Nicolson.
——(2004) *Blair*, London: Free Press.
Seyfang, G. and Jordan A. (2002) ' "Mega" environmental conferences', in S. Stokke and O. Thommesen (eds), *Yearbook of International Co-operation on Environment and Development, 2002–2003*, London: Earthscan.
Skelcher, C. (1998) *The Appointed State: Quasi-Governmental Organisations and Democracy*, Buckingham: Open University Press.
Sloat, A. (2002) *Scotland in Europe: A Study of Multi-Level Governance*, Oxford: Peter Lang.
Smith, M. (1990) 'Pluralism, Reformed Pluralism and Neopluralism: The Role of Pressure Groups in Policy-Making', *Political Studies*, 38, 302–22.
——(1993) *Pressure, Power, and Policy*, Hemel Hempstead: Harvester Wheatsheaf.
——(1999) *The Core Executive in Britain*, Basingstoke: Palgrave.
Smith, M. P. (1996) 'Integration in Small Steps. The European Commission and Member-State Aid to Industry', *West European Politics*, 19 (3), 563–82.
Smith, R. (1999) 'European Union Policies and Funds – the Role of Urban Government in England', in B. Blanke and R. Smith (eds), *Cities in Transition: New Challenges, New Responsibilities*, Basingstoke: Macmillan.
Smith, J. (2001a) 'Cultural Aspects of Europeanization – The Case of the Scottish Office', *Public Administration*, 79 (1), 147–65.
——(2001b) 'Attitudes and Approaches to Europeanization', *Public Policy and Administration*, 16 (2), 63–76.
——(2003) 'An Incremental Odyssey – The Structural Europeanization of Government Bureaucracy,' *Scottish Affairs*, 44, 132–56.
Spence, D. (1993) 'The Role of the National Civil Service in European Lobbying: The British Case', in S. Mazey and J. Richardson (eds), *Lobbying in the European Community*, Oxford: Oxford University Press.
Stephens, P. (1996) *Politics and the Pound*, Basingstoke: Macmillan.
Stewart, A. (1998) Former Scottish Office Minister: Parliamentary Under-Secretary of State (with responsibility for Industry and Education) 1981–86 and 1990–95, *Interview with author*, 9 March 1998.
Stoker, G. (1996) 'Redefining Local Democracy', in L. Pratchett and D. Wilson (eds), *Local Democracy and Local Government*, London: Macmillan.
——(ed.) (1999) *The New Management of British Local Governance*, London: Macmillan.
Streeck, W. (1995) 'From Market Making to State Building? Reflections on the Political Economy of European Social Policy', in S. Leibfried and P. Pierson (eds), *European Social Policy*, Washington, DC: The Brookings Institute.
Streeck, W. and Schmitter, P. (1991) 'From National Corporatism to Transnational Pluralism: Organised Interests in the Single European Market', *Politics & Society*, 19, 133–64.
Suzuki, K. (2000) 'Reform of British Competition Policy: Is European Integration the Only Major Factor', *European Institute of Japanese Studies (EIJS) Working Paper No. 94*, Stockholm School of Economics.

Taggart, P. (1998) 'A Touchstone of Dissent: Euroscepticism in Contemporary Western European Party Systems', *European Journal of Political Research*, 33 (3), 363–88.

Taggart, P. and Szczerbiak, A. (eds) (2006) *Opposing Europe (Vol. 1)*. Cambridge: Cambridge University.

Taylor, J. and Wren, C. (1997) 'UK Regional Policy: An Evaluation', *Regional Studies*, 31 (9), 835–48.

Taylor, M., Craig, G., Monro, S., Parkes, T., Warbutton, D. and Wilkinson, M. (2004) 'A Sea Change or a Swamp? New Spaces for Voluntary Sector Engagement in Governance in the UK', *IDS Bulletin*, 35 (2), 67–75.

Teague, P. (1989) 'The British TUC and the European Community', *Millennium: Journal of International Studies*, 18 (1), 29–45.

Temple, M. (1994). *Regional Economics*, Houndmills etc: Macmillan Press.

Thatcher, M. (1993) *The Downing Street Years*, London: HarperCollins.

——(2004) 'Winners and Losers in Europeanisation: Reforming the national regulation of Telecommunications', *West European Politics*, 27 (2), 284–90.

Thompson, H. (1996) *The British Conservative Government and the European Exchange Rate Mechanism*, London: Pinter.

Tomaney, J. (2002) 'The Evolution of Regionalism in England', *Regional Studies*, 37 (7), 721–31.

Tömmel, I. (2002) Die Regionalpolitik der EU: Systementwicklung durch Politikgestaltung, in T. Conzelmann and M. Knodt (eds), *Regionales Europa: Europäisierte Regionen*, Frankfurt am Main: Campus Verlag.

Tonge, J. (2002) *Northern Ireland: Conflict and Change*, 2nd edn, London: Prentice Hall.

T&G (2001) Let's Make 2002 a Fight for Jobs, Not the Euro, Press Release PR02/001, 30 December.

——(2003a) Bill Morris Calls on Government to Lead the Euro Debate Not Divide the Country, Press release, PR03/167, 21 May 2003.

——(2003b) Morris on Euro: Time for Certainty Not Just Hope, Press release PR03/0180, 9 June 2003.

TUC (1975) *Report of Congress*, London: TUC Congress House.

——(1981) *Report of Congress*, London: TUC Congress House.

——(1983) *Report of Congress*, London: TUC Congress House.

——(1988) *Report of Congress*, London: TUC Congress House.

——(2000) *Report of Congress*, London: TUC Congress House.

TUFE (Trade Unionists For Europe) (2002) A Trade Union Agenda for Europe, London: TUFE.

Ugland, T. (2003) 'Adaptation and Integration through Policy Re-categorization', *Journal of Public Policy*, 23 (2), 157–70.

Undy, R., Ellis, V., McCarthy, W. and Halmos, A. (1981) *Change in Trade Unions. The Development of UK Unions since the 1960s*, London: Hutchinson.

van Waarden, F. and Drahos, M. (2002) 'Courts and (Epistemic) Communities in the Convergence of Competition Policies', *Journal of European Public Policy*, 9 (6), 913–34.

Vink, M. (2003) 'What is Europeanisation?', *European Political Science*, 3 (1), 63–74.

Visser J. (1998) 'Learning to Play: The Europeanization of Trade Unions', in P. Pasture and J. Verberckmoes (eds), *Working-Class Internationalism and the Appeal of National Identity: Historical Debates and Current Perspectives*, Oxford: Berg.

Waldegrave, W. (1985) 'The British approach', *Environmental Policy and Law*, 15 (3–4): 106–15.

Wallace, H. (1973) *National Governments and the European Communities. European Series No. 21*, London: Royal Institute of International Affairs.

——(1995) 'Britain Out on a Limb?', *Political Quarterly*, 66 (1), 46–58.
——(1996) 'Relations Between the European Union and the British Administration', in Y. Meny, P. Muller and J. Quermonne (eds), *Adjusting to Europe*, London: Routledge.
——(2000) 'Europeanisation and Globalisation: Complimentary or Contradictory Trends?', *New Political Economy*, 5 (3), 369–82.
——(2005), 'An Institutional Anatomy and Five Policy Modes', in H. Wallace, W. Wallace, and M. Pollack (eds), *Policy-Making in the European Union*, 5th edn, Oxford: Oxford University Press.
Wallace, H. and Wallace, W. (1973) 'The impact of Community Membership on the British Machinery of Government', *Journal of Common Market Studies*, 11, 243–62.
Wallace, W. (1975), *The Foreign Policy Process in Britain*, London: Royal Institute of International Affairs.
Wallace, W. and Oliver, T. (2005) 'A Bridge Too Far: Britain and the Trans-Atlantic Relationship', in D. Andrews (ed.), *Alliance Under Stress: Atlantic Relations After Iraq*, Cambridge: Cambridge University Press.
Walters, A. (1986) *Britain's Economic Renaissance: Margaret Thatcher's reforms, 1979–84*, Oxford: Oxford University Press.
——(1990) *Sterling in Danger*, London: Fontana.
Ward, S. (1995) 'The Politics of Mutual Attraction? UK Local Authorities and the Europeanization of Environmental Policy', in T. Gray (ed.), *UK Environmental Policy in the 1990s*, Basingstoke: Macmillan.
Ward, S. and Williams, R. (1997) 'From Hierarchy to Networks? Sub-Central Government and EU Urban Environmental Policy', *Journal of Common Market Studies*, 35 (3), 439–64.
Warleigh, A. (2000) 'The Hustle: Citizenship Practice, NGOs and "Policy Coalitions" in the European Union', *Journal of European Public Policy*, 7 (2), 229–43.
Warleigh, A. (2001) 'Europeanizing Civil Society: NGOs as Agents of Political Socialization', *Journal of Common Market Studies*, 39 (4), 619–39.
Watt, N. (2000) 'Labour Accused of Secrecy Over Special Envoys', *Guardian*, 29 March.
——(2001) 'Hain Seeks to End 'Nationalist Line on Foreign Policy', *Guardian*, 23 January.
Weale, A. (1992) *The New Politics of Pollution Control*, Manchester: Manchester University Press.
——(1997) 'United Kingdom', in M. Jänicke and H. Weidner (eds), *National Environmental Policies*, Berlin: Springer Verlag.
Weale, A., Pridham, G., Cini, M., Konstadakopulos, D., Porter, M. and Flynn, B. (2000) *Environmental Governance in Europe: An Ever Closer Ecological Union?* Oxford: Oxford University Press.
Webber, M. A., Smith, M. H., Allen, D. J. and Morgan, D. C. (2002) *Foreign Policy in a Transformed World*, Harlow: Prentice Hall.
Wells, P. (1995) 'Yorkshire and Humberside and the European Structural Funds', *Working Paper No. 3, Political Economy Research Centre*, Sheffield: University of Sheffield.
Wessels, W. and Rometsch, D. (1996a) 'Preface', in D. Rometsch and W. Wessels (eds), *The European Union and Member States: Towards Institutional Fusion?* Manchester: Manchester University Press.
——(1996b) 'Conclusion: European Union and National Institutions', in D. Rometsch and W. Wessels (eds), *The European Union and Member States*, Manchester: Manchester University Press.
White House (2002) 'The National Security Strategy of the United States of America', available at: http://www.whitehouse.gov/nsc/nss.html.

Wilks, S. (1996) 'The Prolonged Reform of United Kingdom Competition Policy', in G. B. Doern and S. Wilks (eds), *Comparative Competition Policy: National Institutions in a Global Market*, Oxford: Clarendon Press.

——(1999) *In the Public Interest: Competition Policy and the Monopoly and Mergers Commission*, Manchester: Manchester University Press.

Williams, A. (2003) 'Governance and Sustainability', *BRASS Working Paper No. 2*, Cardiff University, Cardiff: BRASS.

Williams, P. (2002) 'The Europeanization of British Foreign Policy and the Crisis in Zimbabwe', paper given to the FORNET workshop, LSE, 5 June.

Wilson, D. (2003) 'Unravelling Control Freakery: Redefining Central-local Government Relations', *British Journal of Politics and International Relations*, 5 (3), August 2003, 317–46.

Wilson, K. (1991) *Interest Groups*, Oxford: Basil Blackwell.

Wishlade, F. (2004) 'The Beginning of the End, or Just Another New Chapter?', *European Policies Research Paper 54*, Glasgow, University of Strathclyde: European Policy Research Centre.

Wishlade, F., Yuill, D. and Méndez, C. (2003) 'Regional Policy in the EU: A Passing Phase of Europeanisation or a Complex Case of Policy Transfer?', *Regional and Industrial Policy Research Paper Number 50*, University of Strathclyde, Glasgow: European Policy Research Centre.

WMIE (West Midlands in Europe) (2001) A Year in Europe: April 2000–March 2001. *Annual Report*, Brussels: WMIE.

Wong, R. (2005) 'The Europeanization of Foreign Policy', in C. Hill and M. Smith (eds), *International Relations and the European Union*, Oxford: Oxford University Press.

Wright, A. (2002) 'A Federalized Scotland – Alternatives to Independence: Scotland in Europe', in S. Henig (ed.), *Modernising Britain: Central, Devolved, Federal?* London: The Federal Trust.

Wurzel, R. (2002) *Environmental Policy Making in Britain, Germany and the European Union*, Manchester: Manchester University Press.

Young, H. (1998) *This Blessed Plot: Britain and Europe from Churchill to Blair*, Basingstoke and London: Macmillan.

Young, J. (2000) *Britain and European Unity 1945–1999*, 2nd edn, London: Macmillan.

Index

accommodation, 26–8, 70, 150, 274
  see also Europeanization
Afghanistan, 8, 194
Africa, 63, 189, 190, 194–6
Allen, D., 9, 12, 63, 187, 190,
  192, 274
Americanization, 227
Amsterdam Treaty, 192
Anderson, J., 14, 25, 30
Anglicization, 214
  of the EU, 237, 271
Anglo-American model, 8
Anglo-Saxon approach, 153
Anglo-social model, 8
Australia, 188, 227
Austria, 159
awkward partner, 4, 5, 7–10, 127, 238,
  265–6, 276–7

Bache, I., 4, 27, 85, 86, 87, 100, 103,
  146, 176, 180, 248, 255, 279
Bank of England, 49, 201, 203, 211–13
  see also monetary policy
Basle-Nybourg Agreement, 203
  see also monetary policy
Belgium, 47, 195
'Black Wednesday', 203, 207, 209, 210,
  212, 213
  see also monetary policy
Blair, A., 16, 46, 59, 60, 194, 199, 202
Blair, T., 5, 7, 8, 12, 275
  behaviour in the EU, 9, 42ff
  development of a more proactive
    approach to the EU, 51, 275
  election as Labour leader in 1994, 7
  election as prime minister, 8, 37, 42
  foreign policy objectives of, 192–3
  objectives in relation to competition
    policy, 219, 220
  'presidential style' of, 58
  'step-change' initiative of, 8, 44, 47,
    50, 276
  strategic goals in the EU, 42, 43–4,
    46, 48

third way philosophy of, 8
  see also awkward partner; Labour
    Party, the
Bogdanor, V., 5
Bomberg, E., 22
Börzel, T., 14, 18, 19, 20–2, 28, 100
Bosnia, 196, 199
Britain, 3
  1961 application to join the EEC,
    37, 39
  as an awkward member state, 4–5, 10,
    50, 265, 266, 276, 277
  behaviour in the EU, 4–5, 8–9
  entry into the EEC (1973), 3, 39,
    52, 271
  existing studies of the
    Europeanization of, 10–11
  expectations about EU
    membership, 10
  presidency of the EU (1998), 44
  referendum on membership
    (1975), 158
  relations with France, 47, 63
  relations with Germany, 47
  special relationship with the USA, 5
  traditional political studies approaches
    to understanding, 4, 265
  see also monetary policy
Britain in Europe (BiE) campaign,
  162, 210
British competition policy, 217–18
British Council, 57
British environmental policy, 101, 110,
  232–5, 269
British foreign policy, 187ff,
  197–200, 270
British monetary policy, 201ff
British National Party (BNP), 132
British political studies/science, 32
  approaches to understanding Britain,
    4, 10, 33, 279
  neglect of the EU dimension, 4,
    33, 279

Printed in the United States
97761LV00001B/11/A

9 781403 995193

DATE DUE
